The Family Tree of
Clois Miles Rainwater & Nancy Jane McIlhaney

One Texas Family's Origins
1706-2012

Genealogical research of Susan & R. Steven Rainwater
Irving, Texas

Copyright © 2013 Susan & R. Steven Rainwater
ISBN 978-1-304-71902-7
Creative Commons Attribution-NonCommercial-ShareAlike 3.0 Unported License

Printed by Lulu.com
Raleigh, North Carolina

Table of Contents

How we know..4

A Brief History of Rainwater Research..6

The Family Tree of Clois Miles Rainwater..8

Robert Rainwater...10

John Rainwater and Mary Fussell..13

James Rainwater..17

William Rainwater and Martha Hodges...19

Bartholomew Rainwater and Nancy McLaughlin......................................27

Josiah Wilson Rainwater and Elizabeth Jane Weddle.................................36

Roscoe Conklin Rainwater and Gertrude Alice Caughron.........................50

John Tarter and Catherine Logan..58

Jacob Tarter and his three wives..64

John Milton Weddle and Mary McDaniel..71

Solomon Weddle and Martha Tarter..78

Josiah W. Duck, Sr. and Sarah House...86

Josiah W. Duck, Jr. and Anna Cook...87

Banner Compton and Catherine Wilson..92

Micajah Compton and Margaret Rexroat...93

Erasmus D. Compton and Martha Jane Duck..98

William Trimble and Mary Fleming...104

Blatchley C. W. Caughron and Elizabeth E. Gossett................................106

Theophilous Walter Caughron and Arzona Belle Compton....................109

The Family Tree of Nancy Jane McIlhaney..114

James William McIlhaney and Mary Jane Gibson...................................116

The Problem of Jesse Gibson and Elizabeth Parmley...............................123

James Carter and Salina Roxanna Dean...130

William J. G. McIlhaney and Mary Charlesana Elizabeth Carter............135

John Richardson McIlhaney and Ollie Delilah Umberson......................140

John R. Goodrich and Sarah A. Richardson..148

James Calvin Kuykendall and Mary Frances Strawn................................153

Peter D. Kuykendall and Martha Conley	157
Fulton M. Goodrich and Callie Kuykendall	161
Richard Singleton and his two wives	163
Rev. Joseph T. Singleton and Delilah Robbins	168
Mary Jane Singleton and her three husbands	175
Jerome George Umberson and his two wives	189
Edward Kellum and Karenhappuch Tabor	196
William Tabor and Susannah Tubb	202
Joel Halbert and his two wives	208
William W. Halbert and his two wives	211
Levi Thompson Halbert, Sr. and Mary Ann Armstrong	219
Joe Singleton McIlhaney, Sr., and his two wives	223
How we became the world's leading experts on Dr. DeZita	233
Clois Miles Rainwater and Nancy Jane McIlhaney	240
They Served Their Country	252
Cause of Death	253
The Family Bible of William and Martha Rainwater	255
The Family Bible of Bartholomew and Nancy Rainwater	257
The Family Bible of Josiah and Elizabeth Jane Rainwater	264
The Family Bible of John P. and Lucy Rainwater Aderholt	268
Letter from Josiah W. Rainwater to Miles Rainwater, 1889	270
Letter from John Levi Elder to Josiah W. Rainwater, 1876	271
Register Report: Descendants of William Rainwater	275
Register Report: Descendants of James W. McIlhaney	332
About the Authors	347
Colophon	349
Acknowledgments	350
Creative Commons License	352

How We Know

Over the past twenty years of reading other people's genealogical documents, I have been repeatedly struck by this realization – *how we know* is just as important as *what we know*. So, how do we know?

Primary Documentary Evidence
For primary evidence, I am using state and federal census records, tax records, land records, tombstones, wills and probate, marriage licenses, legal documents, the Social Security death index and Social Security applications, state death indexes, newspaper articles, personal letters and memoirs, military service and pension records, selective service applications, birth certificates and birth indexes, obituaries, photographs, and so on. Naturally, all of these documents are subject to possible error.

The Research of Others
In some cases, I refer to information shared with us by other researchers. In each case, I have named the researcher and have double-checked the research where possible. These are all researchers whose work I respect, and with most, have had extensive correspondence.

Date Calculations
Marriage dates up through the mid-20th century are based on county courthouse records showing when the license was issued. A few include a minister's return that provides the actual marriage date; but most don't. This means that the marriage most likely took place within a week of the date I have given.

In some cases, I have a record such as a tombstone, showing the full date of birth and death. In an equal number of cases, I don't. Circa dates are based on something known, like a census record. Until 1900, the census simply showed a person's age, so if a child was listed as 9 in the 1850 census, I will say he was born c. 1841. There is a margin of error, based on the month of birth vs. the month in which the census was taken, so it's equally possible that he was born in 1840 or 1842. Some census records provide wildly different ages from one decade to the next, and in these cases, I will generally use an average of the two, or use the one that, in light of other evidence, appears to be more accurate.

For many of the death dates, all we know is that the person was, for example, listed in the 1870 census, but not in 1880 census, so he is said to have died between 1870 and 1880. This has a fair margin of error, because it's possible the person *was* living in 1880, but not recorded in the census. Therefore dates stated as "between," "before," "no later than," or "after" should be taken with a grain of salt.

In the case of calculated dates, I explain the basis of my calculation. For example, a man could not serve in a colonial-era militia until he was 16, so we assume that a person serving in a 1776 militia was born no later than 1750. It should go without saying that he could have been born earlier than 1750.

In the oldest records, we might know when the child was born, but not the parent. Here I am using a standard genealogical rule of thumb that, up to at least 1900, you can assume the parents were married between 16 and 18. So you subtract 16 from the birth year of the first known child to get the parents' approximate year of birth. This method has proved remarkably accurate in cases where I have later been able to determine the actual dates.

Names
Our ancestors were remarkably flexible with their names. It's not unusual to find an individual called by his first name in one census, by his middle name in the next, and by an entirely new name in his adult life. It's also a quirk of a world without birth certificates, that a child might be called Baby for several months while the family decided on a name.

Online Databases
I prefer to avoid using online databases because of the wildly variable quality of their information. I occasionally use WorldConnect and Ancestry.com for hints, but only when I can confirm the information independently. I have a higher opinion of FindaGrave.com, especially when photographs of the headstones are provided. I do cite a great many Rootsweb and USGenWeb transcriptions of cemeteries and original documents, to which I would otherwise not have had access. I use Ancestry.com primarily for the ability to perform complex searches on federal census records.

Knowability
In some cases, I am imputing an emotional state to an individual that I have no certain way of knowing. For example, I say that Micajah Compton was worried, but I might as well have said he was angry. I can't possibly know Micajah's state of mind with absolute certainty, but I had to impute some emotion to tell the story. This problem bedevils historians and genealogists, and I have used the same strategy they do – I have made my best guess based on the available evidence. I have tried to keep these cases to a minimum.

Probability and Certainty
It should go without saying that the more records you have for any statement, the more likely that statement is correct. If I have a birth index, obituary, and tombstone that all say an individual was born in 1900, I can feel pretty confident that he was. On the other hand, if I have only one record, I am far less certain. The worst possible situation is that all of the records conflict. Such is the case of Karenhappuch Tabor, who is called by a different name in nearly every record.

Accuracy
I have never read a genealogical document that did not turn out to contain unintentional mistakes. I'm sure this one does as well, despite my best efforts.

A Brief History of Rainwater Research

For centuries, genealogy was the preoccupation of royalty. Starting in the 20th century, Americans found themselves with enough leisure time to start asking questions like, "Where did I come from?" and "Who were my people?".

The resources necessary to answer these questions did not exist then as they exist today. There was no Internet, no email, no genealogical libraries containing thousands of books and rolls of microfilm. But there were city directories and postal mail, and the first intrepid Rainwater genealogists sent out letters to individuals with the same surname, looking for answers.

Then in the 1930s, the WPA put a great many young men and women to work microfilming old records – census, land, marriage, pension, military – and the tools that make genealogical research possible came into existence. Numerous genealogical clubs extended the information available with books of tombstone transcriptions, newspaper abstracts, and marriage records.

In the 1940s, a wealthy businessman, Robert H. Folmar, began researching the genealogy of his wife's Rainwater family. In the course of his research, he made contact with Walter Terrell Rainwater, Jr. As far as anyone knows, these two men were the first researchers to look at the Rainwater family as a whole – rather than simply researching a specific line. Their research was eventually organized into a large, unwieldy family tree, known today as the Folmar Chart.

Unfortunately, the Folmar Chart is as much speculation as fact. It has formed the basis for much Rainwater research, has been copied and passed around, added to, and passed around some more. Over time, the fiction and speculation have taken on the veneer of truth, and many of the ideas have taken such deep root that they are impossible to dislodge.

The second whole-family researcher began her work in the 1950s. Now in her 70s, Glidie Rainwater Mobley is widely acknowledged as the premier Rainwater researcher alive today. She is a rigorous researcher whose work is based primarily on documentary evidence. She has debunked numerous myths and half-truths in Rainwater research, and extended the family tree deeper and wider than any other researcher alive. We are indebted to her for her assistance in our own research.

In 1994, a Los Angeles-based researcher named Robert Albert, Jr. started a family newsletter called *The Rainwater Researcher*. Although he was personally interested in only the Moses Rainwater line, the newsletter printed information for all branches of the family, making him the third whole-family researcher. The newsletter ceased publication in 1998, because of the difficulty of getting other researchers to contribute articles.

Steve and I had begun researching his Rainwater line in 1992. Our research was based upon Roscoe Rainwater's 1972 work, *Here's the Plan of the Rainwater Clan*. I've always admired the snappy title, and Roscoe's efforts preserved a large amount of information and quite a few original documents that would otherwise have been lost.

With the emergence of the Internet, we felt a website had an advantage over a printed newsletter, because it did not rely on quarterly inputs of new information. The editor could simply add new information as it became available. Our idea was to create an archive for raw, uninterpreted data that could be used by researchers for their own work, making them independent of their limited local resources. So with the launch of *The Rainwater Collection (therainwatercollection.com)*, we became the fourth research team to view the Rainwater family as a single entity.

This book does not attempt to cover the entire American Rainwater family. Rather our intent is to present what we know about the many branches of both sides of Steve's personal family tree – from 1706 to the present day.

The Family Tree of Clois Miles Rainwater

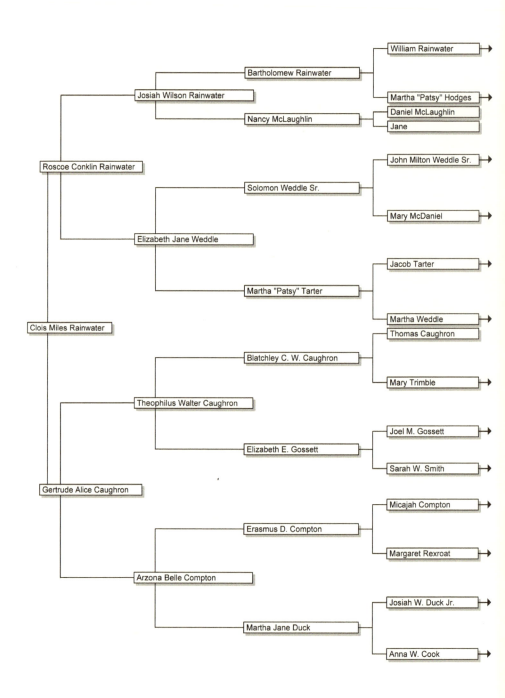

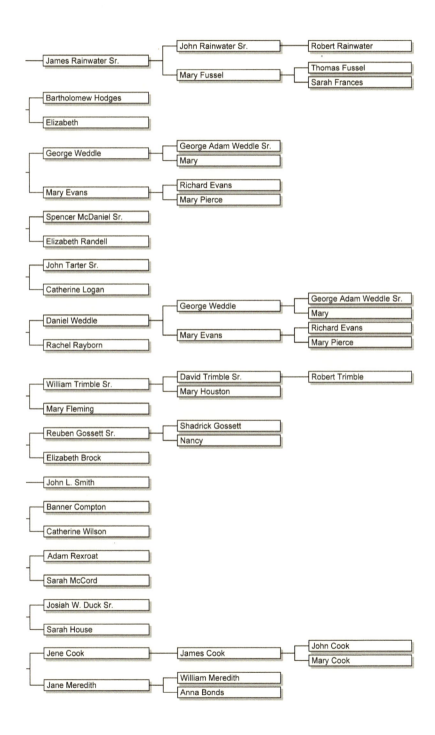

Robert Rainwater

Robert Rainwater
Born before 1690, England
Died after 1718, Virginia or North Carolina

Very little is known about Robert Rainwater. He was born in England, but we don't know exactly when. We don't know when or where he died, except that it was probably Virginia or North Carolina. We don't know who he married or the names of his children.

But we do know that in 1706, he signed an indenture to John Hurt to be transported to the Virginia Colony in America. Rainwater's name is affixed to a land patent (grant) issued to Hurt on 2 May 1706, that reads: [1]

> Land Patent issued to John Hurt, King William Co., VA
> Virginia Land Office Patent Book No. 9 1695-1706 Page 733, 734

To all ye whereas ye Now Know yee that the Edwd Nott Gov do with the advice and consent of the Councill of state accordingly give & grant unto John Hurt five hundred forty & six acres of Land in Pamunkey neck in [King Williams County formerly part of] King & Queen County being marked and bounded as follows the (viz) beginning at a Corner Hickory thirty six pole from the Ridge path running thence north two hundred & sixteen poles to a red oake Corner Tree by the mainskin path thence West half a point North forty one poles to a line of old markt trees of Benj. Arnold and John Hurts to a red oak in the vd Line thence south west sixty poles to a white oake on a hill side thence west by south twenty four poles to a great white oake on the brow of a hill thence north west forty pole to a gum thence north by west Eighty pole to a Corner white Oake by a branch side thence North fifty four pole to a corner white oake at the head of a branch thence South East by East of a branch to a main swamp at the fork thereof one hundred pole to a corner white oake just over the fork thence down the vd swamp the corner six hundred pole on a straight line to the mouth of the same emptying it self into the lower Herring Creek thence South South East half a point. East fifty pole to the mouth of the Herring Creek making into Mattopony River thence down the river South East by South one hundred pole to a Corner red oake on the bank of Mattopony River side being Hence Hendricks Corner trees by a pine shiny being formerly the old corner tree of Richard Yarborough by grant thence along Hendricks line north west by west a quarter point west eighty six pole to a hickory thence west half a point south thirty three pole to a corner red oake of Hance

---

[1] 402: Land patent issued to John Hurt, King William Co., VA, 2 May 1706, photocopy of original

Hendricks standing in the Bryory run thence west north west sixteen pole to an old corner Spanish oake thence the same corse continued west north west seventy six pole to a corner white oake standing by a branch side was Richard Yarboroughs Tobacco ground thence up the branch south west by south forty eight poles to a white oake thence south west fifty two poles to a saphired oake by a slash in a thicket being a corner of Mr. William Hurt Sen. thence west one hundred & four pole to a Spanish oake thence south west half a point west two hundred forty two pole and a half to the beginning place the [unreadable] land being due unto John Hurt by and for the transportation of eleven persons in to this Colony whose names are to be in the records mentioned under this Patent to have & to hold & to behold & yielding & paying & Provided & given under my hand & the seale of the colony this 2nd Day of May Anno Dom 1706.

John Hurt his Patent for 546 acres of Land Edw. Nott in Pamunkey Neck in King Wm. County

Tho. Solwell, Michaell Portugees, **Robert Rainwater,** Sarah Hoskins, Eliza. Bosford, Anne Gill, Wm. Skyles, Mary Parte, Susanna Good, Cha. Goodrich, Anne Hum

If this was a standard indenture, Robert Rainwater would work seven years for John Hurt, unpaid, in return for Hurt paying his transportation to the Colonies, and providing his food, clothing and lodging during the seven years. Robert would be free to sell his spare time to other colonists, allowing him to earn money that he could save for his eventual freedom. And he would be paid "freedom dues" on the date of his release from servitude. At least this was the theory.[2] In reality, indentures were often little more than seven years of miserable slavery and many indentured servants made their escape as soon as they were able.

It's unlikely that a landowner would have accepted a child as an indenture for transportation to the new world. To sign a contract, you had to officially be an adult, which means that Robert was at least 16 in 1706. This places his year of birth in 1690 or earlier.

There are only three new world records for Robert Rainwater.

In 1713, a Surry Co., Virginia court paid a bounty of 400 lbs of tobacco to Robert Rainwater for two wolves' heads.[3] Settlers blamed wolves for loss of their livestock, so counties often paid a bounty to anyone who could prove he had killed a wolf. Since the colonies were not permitted to strike their own coinage, these bounties were often paid in tobacco, which could be bartered with fellow colonists, or sold to ships bound for England.

---

[2] Wikipedia: Indentured Servant, http://en.wikipedia.org/wiki/Indentured_servant
[3] 46: Surry Co., VA Court Records, Vol. VII, 1712–1718, Weynette Parks Haun, publ. 1986, Durham, NC

The other two records are from 1718, also in Surry Co., Virginia. In these, the court makes a judgment for 300 lbs of tobacco plus court costs to be enforced by the local sheriff against Richard Pace on behalf of Robert Rainwater. No information about the nature of the suit is given, and the case was then postponed until the next session of the court.[4]

We don't know when Robert Rainwater died, and no other records have been found. Early colonists, if they were in good health and incredibly lucky, could expect to live to age 50. So Robert may have died as early as 1719 or as late as 1740.

Robert H. Folmar and a great many other researchers trace the Rainwater family's origins to Robert Rainwater. While we *believe* this to be correct, the evidence is entirely circumstantial.

A note on the Rainwater name

Many explanations have been put forth to explain the origins of the Rainwater name – that it's Native American (because it's a word from the natural world), Dutch (van Regenmorter), German or Jewish (Reggenwasser). But the most likely explanation is that it didn't start out as Rainwater.

We believe that the name originated in England. It's rendered in the very earliest English records as Rainmorter and Rainworter.[5] The difficulty of saying these names, particularly Rainworter, appears to have caused the name to become Rainwater through mispronunciation. The word *worter* meant bucket in Elizabethan English.

---

[4] ibid. Surry Co., VA court records after 1718 were destroyed in a fire.

[5] 987: Rainwater Surnames in England, original research of H. Ivan Rainwater, Bowie, MD, dated 7 Feb 1984

1005: Allegations for Marriage Licenses Issued By the Vicar General of the Archbishop of Canterbury, Vol. 34, 1669-1679, The Harleian Society, publ. 1892; 1006: A Register of All the Christninges, Burrialles & Weddings within the Parish of Saint Peeters upon Cornhill, 1667-1774, Part 2, Granville W. G. Leveson Gower F.S.A., publ. 1879; 1377: Boyd's Marriage Index, England, Vol. 16, microfilm #6026739; 1378: Boyd's Marriage Index, England, Vol. 25, 1676-1700, microfilm #6026747; 1379: Boyd's Marriage Index, England, Vol. 33, 1701-1725, microfilm #6026747; 1380: Boyd's Marriage Index, England, Vol. 68, 1676-1700, microfilm #6026791

174: The Rainwater Researcher, Vol 1 Issue 2 December 1994, page 5, which says "The following records were copied directly from the microfilms of original church records by Ellen Beth Robison (nee Rainwater) during 1982-1983 at the library in Norwich, England."

John Rainwater and Mary Fussell

John Rainwater
Presumed son of Robert Rainwater
Born between 1695 and 1705, probably Virginia[6]
Died after May 1777, Surry Co., North Carolina

Married between 1726 and 1735, probably North Carolina

Mary Fussell
Daughter of Thomas and Sarah Frances Fussell
Born between 1710 and 1719, St. Peter's Parish, New Kent Co., Virginia
Died c. 1782, Surry Co., North Carolina

In 1735, the will of Thomas Fussell of Bertie Co., North Carolina, went to probate. Written on 4 June and probated in August of the same year, it listed six of his children, including his married daughter, Mary Rainwater. On this single line hangs the identity of the second generation of American Rainwaters:

> Likewise to my daughter Mary the wife of John Rainwater, [I do give or bequeath] six hogs. [7]

We are not absolutely certain of the name of Thomas Fussell's wife. It has come down to us through tradition as Sarah Frances, maiden name unknown. Because she is not mentioned in the will, we assume that she died prior to her husband.

Many of the Fussell children were baptized in St. Peter's Parish, New Kent Co., Virginia, and Lynn Fussell, the lead researcher for the Fussell family, places Mary's birth in 1710, between her sisters Elizabeth and Sarah, for whom baptism records exist.[8] There is, however, no baptism record for Mary, but even if she was born as late as 1719, it's still pretty certain that she was born in St. Peter's Parish. Sometime after 1723, the year of the last daughter's baptism, the Fussell family moved to Bertie Co., North Carolina.

North Carolina was something of a wild frontier.[9] The western part of the state was occupied by tribes of Native Americans. The terrain was hilly and heavily wooded, and a great many runaway indentures vanished into the Great Dismal Swamp that sits on the northern border of the state. The North

---

[6] Traditionally he is said to have been born in Danbury, VA, but the US Geological Survey's historical database has no record of such a place. However, Danbury, NC may have been on the Virginia side of the border before the resurveying of the boundary line, or possibly Danville, VA may actually be intended.

[7] 303: Will of Thomas Fussell, 4 Jun 1735, Bertie Parish, NC, photocopy of original

[8] 180: Lynn E. Fussell, "*The Descendants of Nicholas Fussell (c. 1600 – c. 1660),*" publ. 1997, Richardson, TX

[9] William Byrd, "*The History of the Dividing Line betwixt Virginia and North Carolina,*" originally publ. 1728, reprinted in 1967 by Dover Publications, Mineola, NY

Carolina government took a minimal approach to record-keeping – recording land transactions and wills, but leaving marriages, births and deaths to local churches. As a result, North Carolina is something of a black hole when it comes to genealogy. If your ancestor didn't own land or write a will, there are frequently no records at all.

So we know from Thomas Fussell's will that John and Mary had wed prior to 1735, and we believe they could have married as early as 1726,[10] but there is no surviving marriage record. Naturally it is assumed that John Rainwater was the son of Robert Rainwater. While we feel this is likely, no documentary evidence ties the two men together with certainty.

In 1754, John Rainwater, his son James, and brother-in-law, Aaron Fussell, served in Captain Sugar Jones' colonial militia company in Granville Co., North Carolina.[11] The record does not indicate their duties, but we know they served from 8 Oct 1754 to 6 Dec 1754.[12]

Fortunately, John Rainwater owned a fair amount of land. Records for his land transactions can be found in the Granville, Surry, Edgecomb, and Bute Counties of North Carolina. This is, in part, because the county lines were still evolving – Granville County split off of Edgecomb; Bute split into Franklin and Warren, and so on. Rainwater seemed to favor parcels of 125 to 160 acres, and between 1739 and 1755, he bought and sold these parcels about every five years. He appears to have been something of a land speculator.

One transaction is particularly important to us because it names his wife.

12 Dec 1748 [13]

John Rainwater, a planter, and his wife Mary, sell 160 acres of land at Jenneto meadows Edgecombe Co, NC for 100 pounds sterling English money to Robert Williams. This land was previously owned by William Reeves. The land is said to be on Quonque swamp. Witnessed by William Green, Francis Williams, and Richard Bagly. A later deed for the same land in 1759 references this transaction.

Two records in 1777 inform us that John Rainwater has died. First, the May 1777 tax records for Surry County refer to Mary as "Widow Rainwater."[14] The second, John Rainwater's will, was recorded with the court in November 1777, and this document gives us the names of his children. Because he describes his

---

[10] If Mary was born in 1710, she could have been 16 in 1726, an age when girls were commonly married in those days.

[11] 996: The State Records of North Carolina, Vol. 22, Miscellaneous, Walter Clark, pgs 376-377, publ. 1907, Nash Brothers Book and Job Printers, Goldsboro, NC

[12] 211: Colonial Granville County and its people. Loose leaves from the lost tribes of North Carolina, Worth S. Ray, publ. 1965, Genealogical Publishing Company, Baltimore, MD

[13] 218: Abstracts of Deeds of Edgecombe Prescinct, Edgecombe Co., NC, 1732-1758, found in Halifax Co. Deed Books 1-6, pg 107, Margaret M. Hoffman, publ. 1969, Roanoke News Company, Weldon, NC

[14] 62: Surry Co., NC Court Minutes, Vol. 1, 1768-1785, pg 17, Mrs. W.O. Absher & Mrs. R.K. Harper, Sr., publ. 1985, Southern Historical Press, Easley, SC

land as a plantation rather than a farm, we can assume that he was growing tobacco or cotton.

4 November 1771 Surry Co., North Carolina

I, John Rainwater of Surry Co., North Carolina, being now in perfect sense and memory, thanks be to God, but yet considering that life and sense is uncertain, do make and ordain this my last will and testament. My soul I recommend unto the hands of God. My body I recommend to the earth to be buried in a Christian manner, and as to my worldly estate, I give, devise, bequest and dispose of the same in the following manner and form.

First, I give to my daughters, **Mary, Sarah, Betty, Winney, Milley and Molley,** to each Five Shillings Prov., money to them and raised out of my estate the same is in full and a bar from their obtaining any more. I give to my son, **John,** Five Shillings Prov., money to be raised aforesaid, the same is in full and a bar from his obtaining any more unless he should succeed his brother James as Trustee in the management of that part of the estate which I give for support of my wife and son **William.**[15] I give my plantation and all my land, my negro man Jack and all other of my estate of what kind soever to the whole and sole use, support and maintenance of my wife and son William during their lives, and do hereby will and subject the same into their hands, care and management of my son **James,** whom I hereby constitute and make Trustee to appropriate the said estate to their sole use, support and maintenance as aforesaid, to them either jointly or single in such way and manner as he the said James shall judge and think the most to their profit and best for their support and comfort. And if any part of the said estate should remain after their decease, my will and intent is that he, the said James, his heirs and assigns, enjoy the same forever. If my son, James, decease before my wife and son William, I will that my son John succeed my said son James in every point as Trustee.

Lastly, I appoint **my wife, Mary,** Executrix and my sons, John and James, Executors of this my last will to see that all things be performed according to their true intent and meaning thereof. And I hereby disannul and revoke every former will and ratify and confirm this and no othere one to be my last will and testament. In witness thereof I have hereunto set my hand and seal, this 4th day of November 1771.

---

[15] 212: Bute Co., NC Minutes of the Court of Pleas and Quarter Sessions, 1769-1779, Brent Howard Holcomb. Court records indicate that John had William exempted from the duties expected of an adult male on the grounds that he was "an idiot" or mentally handicapped. The language of the will makes clear that John is arranging for his son's financial maintenance.

North Carolina, Surry County Court, May 1777

Jesse Brimp, one of the subscribing witnesses to the last will and testament of John Rainwater made oath that he saw the said John Rainwater publish and declare the same to be his last will and testament; that he was of sound and disposing mind and memory and that at the same time, he saw John Pain sign the same as a witness and on motion it was ordered to be recorded.

Recorded accordingly, Jo Williams, County Clerk[16]

The last official record of Mary Fussell Rainwater is the Surry County tax list of 1782.[17] Since she is not included in the 1783 tax records, we assume she passed away in the interval.

---

[16] 302: Will of John Rainwater, 4 Nov 1771, Surry Co., NC, photocopy of original

[17] 121: North Carolina Taxpayers, 1679-1790, pg 164, Clarence E. Ratcliff, publ. 1984, Genealogical Publishing Co., Baltimore, MD

JAMES RAINWATER

James Rainwater
Son of John Rainwater and Mary Fussell
Born between 1735 and 1738 in North Carolina
Died before 1790 in North Carolina

Married between 1762 and 1765 in North Carolina

Wife, unknown

From his will, we know that John Rainwater had a son named James, but James' lack of records has vexed genealogical researchers for nearly a century. He left no will and no marriage record, though he did leave census, tax, and land records. We know where he was, in one case we know the composition of his household, but we don't have any names.[18]

James Rainwater's wife is also the source of no end of trouble to genealogists. She is traditionally identified as Catherine Ann Regan, but, along with many other researchers, we believe this to be utterly incorrect.

A letter written by Judge Clive Pettijohn to Jessie Rainwater Thompson in the mid-20th century gave the name Catherine Regan as the wife James Rainwater of *Sevier Co., Tennessee*.[19] When it was later proven that the wife of James Rainwater of *Sevier Co., Tennessee*, was Charity Fowler, Catherine was shifted in time about 80 years and grafted onto James Rainwater of *Surry Co., North Carolina*.[20] Frankly, it's not clear if Catherine Ann Regan even existed.

All that can be said with any certainty is that, based on the ages of his presumed children, James Rainwater of *Surry County* and his wife were married before 1765.[21]

In 1754, James Rainwater served with the local militia in Granville Co., North Carolina.[22] Since one would normally not serve until the age of 16, we can assume that he was born no later than 1738. James' brother John also served in the Granville County militia, making him roughly the same age. That their

---

[18] Early census records provide only the name of the head of household and some demographic data. The first census to record the names of all household members was taken in 1850.

[19] 485: The family record of James Rainwater & Charity Fowler, originally printed in The Rainwater Researcher, Vol. 2, Issue 3, April 1996, from a letter of Judge Clive Pettijohn to Jessie Rainwater Thompson, mid-20th century. There are several theories as to how the name Catherine Ann Regan became attached to James Rainwater of Surry County. After a long email discussion with the late Ray Rainwater, who was descended from the James Rainwater/Charity Fowler branch, I am in agreement with him that the Pettijohn theory is the most plausible.

[20] The Folmar Chart is almost certainly responsible for the time shift.

[21] 246: Eloise Groover Lovell, "*Richard Phillips Family History, 1791-1983*," publ. 1983, Hermitage, TN. We are assuming that Solomon, whose date of birth Lovell gives as 1765, is James' eldest child.

[22] 211: Colonial Granville County and its people. Loose leaves from The lost tribes of North Carolina, pg 294. Worth S. Ray, publ. 1965, Genealogical Publishing Company, Baltimore, MD

father designated James as the executor of his estate suggests that James was the elder brother.[23]

He is listed as James Rainwater son of John in the 1755 Granville Co., North Carolina tax list.[24] In 1762, he is listed simply as James Rainwater in a household of one person in the Bear Swamp District of Granville County which means that he had not married by that date.[25]

James Rainwater was recorded in one of the early state censuses of North Carolina. He is listed as the head of household in the Willeses district of Surry Co., North Carolina, in Feb 1786. The household contains one white male between 21-60, one white male under age 21 or over age 60, five white females, and one slave age 12-50.[26]

Census records suggest that James died before 1790.[27] A James Rainwater is listed in the 1790 and 1800 Federal Census records, but the households contain very young children, and a husband and wife both under age 45. Since our James Rainwater would have been close to 60 by 1790, these census households might belong to his son, but could not be his.

Which brings us to his children.

This problem we can lay squarely at the feet of the Folmar chart. With no will giving the names of James' children, a tradition grew up of attaching to James any spare Rainwaters found lying around North Carolina. Folmar listed seven children, and subsequent lists went as high as eleven. So we took a statistical approach, averaging the lists together to eliminate unlikely offspring. Any name that fell below 60% we considered to be too unlikely, and we were able to prove that all of the names below 30% were actually the offspring of James Rainwater of *Sevier Co., Tennessee*. Finally, the existence of the individual had to be independently verifiable by other evidence.

Our final list includes eight children. Four we feel confident belong to James: William, Abraham and Elizabeth who went to Kentucky, and Solomon who went to South Carolina. The remaining four we feel confident existed but may belong to another branch of the family: John, Miles, James, and Moses.

---

[23] 302: Will of John Rainwater, 4 Nov 1771, Surry Co., NC, photocopy of original

[24] 122: North Carolina Taxpayers, 1701-1786, pg 167, Clarence E. Ratcliff, publ. 1984, Genealogical Publishing Co., Baltimore, MD

[25] 1072: List of Taxables for 1762 in Granville Co., NC, North Carolina Genealogical Society Journal, Part 1 Aug 1986 and Part 2 Feb 1987, Ransom McBride

[26] 1081: State Census of North Carolina, 1784–1787, 2nd Edition Revised, Alvaretta Kenan Register, publ. 1973, Genealogical Publishing Co., Baltimore, MD

[27] Federal Census: 1790, North Carolina

WILLIAM RAINWATER AND MARTHA HODGES

William Rainwater
Son of James Rainwater
Born between 1765 and 1775 in North Carolina
Died 1825 in Faubush, Pulaski Co., Kentucky
Buried Rainwater Cemetery, Pulaski Co., Kentucky

Married c. 1800, probably Surry Co., NC

Martha "Patsy" Hodges
Daughter of Elizabeth and Bartholomew Hodges
Born c. 1785 in North Carolina
Died 1841 in Faubush, Pulaski Co., Kentucky
Buried Rainwater Cemetery, Pulaski Co., Kentucky

Based on census records, William Rainwater was born between 1765 and 1775.[28] Many researchers give 3 Jun 1774 as his birth date, but this appears to be a different William Rainwater in a different county.[29] Our William was probably born in Surry or Granville County. Two of his children indicated in the 1880 census that both of their parents were born in North Carolina.[30]

Based on the birth of his first child, William married his wife in or before 1802. Her given name was Martha, but she appears to have gone by a variety of nicknames. Daughter Patsy's marriage record calls her Martha.[31] The family Bible calls her Patty.[32] Son James' marriage record calls her Marty.[33] Her husband's will calls her Patsy, which was a common nickname for Martha in this era.[34]

Martha's parents are traditionally said to be Elizabeth and Bartholomew Hodges of Surry Co., North Carolina. Though no documentary data supports this, circumstantial evidence points in this direction. First, the 1790 census shows Bartholomew Hodges and James Rainwater, William's father, living in the same precinct of the Salisbury District of Surry County. Second, it's clear

---

[28] Federal Census: 1810, Surry Co., NC, pg 163

[29] 423: Johnson Co., NC County Court Minutes, 1787-1792, Book 4, Weynette Parks Haun, publ. 1974, Durham, NC. Court records from May 1787 mention the indenture of a William Rainwater, noting that he will be 13 on "the third day of June next." Since all of William's father's records are from Surry and Granville Counties, and Johnson is quite a distance from either, we feel that this cannot be the same person.

[30] Federal Census: 1880, Pulaski Co., KY, Miles Rainwater, pg 61A; Faribault Co., MN, pg 21, Elizabeth Rainwater Loveall. The 1880 census is the first census to ask for the parents' birthplaces.

[31] 49: Pulaski Co., Kentucky Marriage Records, Vol 1, 1797–1850, 2nd edition, Mary Weddle Kaurish, publ. 1984, Pulaski County Historical Society, Somerset, KY

[32] 178: William & Patsy Rainwater family Bible, photocopy of original. We are indebted to Frances Aderholt Smith who provided our copy of the family Bible.

[33] 49: Pulaski Co., Kentucky Marriage Records, Vol 1, 1797–1850, 2nd edition, Mary Weddle Kaurish, publ. 1984, Pulaski County Historical Society, Somerset, KY

[34] 304: Will of William Rainwater, 6 Jan 1825, Pulaski Co., Kentucky, Book 2 page 192

from the numerous Surry County land transactions between Rainwaters and Hodges that the two families were well acquainted. Third, Martha named one of her sons Bartholomew and one of her daughters Elizabeth – her parents' names. Moreover, the name Bartholomew shows up *only* in the Kentucky branch of the Rainwater family.[35] So we accept this parental tradition as plausible.

There are a number of legal records in Surry Co., North Carolina, for William Rainwater. On 15 May 1806, a deed from James Rainwater Sr. to Abraham Rainwater was proved in court by William Rainwater. William was also drafted by the county to assist with the laying out of several roads – one from Rockford to Dry Branch in 1806, another from Hogan's Creek to Fisher's Gap in 1807. Finally, he served jury duty on 14 Aug 1811.[36]

William's family was recorded in the 1810 Federal Census of Surry Co., North Carolina, and contained two adults and six children.[37] This corresponds exactly to the family Bible, and to the later census records that say the first six children were born in North Carolina.

The family moved from North Carolina to Kentucky sometime after William's 1811 jury duty date, arriving at least by 1813, when he purchased 200 acres on Wolf Creek in Pulaski County.[38]

It is likely that William chose Pulaski County because his brother Abraham was already there. Abraham is recorded in the 1810 Federal Census of Pulaski County with a family of three children and two adults.[39] Their spinster sister, Elizabeth, seems to have arrived in Pulaski County after 1810 and lived with William's family.[40] She survived both William and Martha, and in 1850, was living with her spinster niece, Susannah Rainwater.[41] She died prior to 1860. Their brother, Abraham moved his family to Russell Co., Kentucky, between 1820 and 1830[42].

We know the names of William and Martha's children from the family Bible. It has come to us as a many-times photocopied document, and we have no idea

---

[35] There are three Bartholomew Rainwaters among William and Martha's descendants; none in any other branch.

[36] 343: Surry Co., NC Court Minutes, County Court of Pleas & Quarter Sessions, Vol. 4, 1805–1809, Iris M. Harvey, 1990, Mount Airy, NC
344: Surry Co., NC Court Minutes, County Court of Pleas & Quarter Sessions, Vol. 5, 1810–1814, Iris M. Harvey, 1990, Mount Airy, NC

[37] Federal Census: 1810, Surry Co., NC, pg 163

[38] 90: Kentucky Land Grants, Parts 1 & 2, 1782–1924, Willard Rouse Jillson, ScD, publ. 1971, Genealogical Publishing Co., Baltimore, MD
1080: In a letter written by Josiah Rainwater to Julius Rainwater (his first cousin twice removed) in 1909, Josiah states that his grandfather William had come from Stokes Co., North Carolina in 1816. The county may be right, but the year is clearly wrong.

[39] Federal Census: 1810, Pulaski Co., KY, pg 141

[40] Federal Census: Pulaski Co., KY, 1820, pg 66, and 1840, pg 332

[41] Federal Census: 1850, Pulaski Co., KY, pg 131B

[42] Federal Census: 1820, Pulaski Co., KY, pg 58, and 1830, Russell Co., KY, pg 118B

who owns the original Bible or if it still exists. But the information conveyed by the copy is priceless.

> Lydda Rainwaters daughter of Wm. Rainwaters and Patty his wife was borned May the 8" 1802
> Bartholomew Rainwater son of ditto was borned the 20" of Jan. 1804
> James Rainwater son of ditto was borned the 8" of February 1806
> Abraham Rainwater son of ditto was borned the 3" of April 1808
> John R. Rainwater and Nancy Rainwater son and daughter of ditto was borned March the 5" 1810
> William Howard Rainwater son of ditto was borned June the 17" 1813
> Susannah Rainwater daughter [page damaged] borned September the 28" 1815
> Miles[43] Rainwater son of ditto [page damaged] May the 15 day 1818
> Elizabeth Rainwater was born October the [page damaged]
> Patsy Rainwater daughter *and son* of ditto was born March 15th 1823

Patsy's twin, remarked in the Bible with the words "*and son,*" died at birth. According to Frances Aderholt Smith, family tradition in her branch says the infant boy was dropped at birth by the midwife and died. A number of spurious children have been grafted onto this family over the years, including a son named Anson, which is a misreading of the words "*and son*"; a daughter named Sukey, which is a nickname for Susannah; and Joicie, who, based on the census record, appears to be a granddaughter.

William Rainwater was probably a farmer. He might have grown tobacco like his North Carolina ancestors, but it's likely he grew corn, Kentucky's primary crop. Corn was prized on the frontier because no part of the plant went to waste. The corncobs and stalks could be recycled as fuel or feed for pigs, the husks as toilet paper.[44] Moreover, it was a crop that could be grown without slaves, especially if you had a large family of free farm workers, which William did.

We know that both John and James Rainwater were slave owners. John mentions a slave named Jack in his 1771 will, and James' 1786 census record indicates that he owned one slave.[45] William, as far as we can tell, never did. According to Hodges researcher, Diana Flynn, this was due to Martha Rainwater, who refused to own slaves for religious reasons. This belief was passed down, putting her descendants firmly on the side of the North at the outbreak of the Civil War.

---

[43] The name Miles persists to present day in every branch of the Rainwater family. The most persuasive theory is that the name was originally given in honor of Rev. Miles Rainwater (1787-1826) who pastored Cedar Shoals Baptist Church, Spartanburg Co., South Carolina.

[44] Michael Pollan, "*The Omnivore's Dilemma*", pgs 100–101, published 2006, The Penguin Press, New York

[45] 1081: State Census of North Carolina, 1784-1787, 2nd Edition Revised, Alvaretta Kenan Register, publ. 1973, Genealogical Publishing Co., Baltimore, MD

Two myths have attached themselves to William – both involving his supposed service in the War of 1812. The first myth says that he was a captain of the local militia in Pulaski Co., but there's no record to support that claim. The second, more persistent myth is that he was one of three Rainwaters who served in the Battle of New Orleans. In fact, one of the Rainwaters who served in this conflict was named William, but he was from the Georgia branch of the family.[46]

William Rainwater died in 1825. According to Diana Flynn, William was suffering from gangrene of the foot. Local physician William Roy told him that the foot needed to be amputated, but William refused, and died of blood poisoning. He would have been between 50 and 60 years old.

He died intestate. His neighbor, Thomas Whitely, and Abraham Rainwater (son or brother, it isn't clear) went to court and delivered a nuncupative (oral) will, which the court accepted.

> 6 January 1825 Somerset, Pulaski Co., Kentucky
> Book 2 Page 192
>
> We, the undersigned, being called upon by William Rainwater, do in his last sickness to hear what disposition he wished made of all his goods and chattels, do declare that the said Decedent wished and desired all his goods and chattels, both real and personal, remain in the possession of his wife, Patsy, during her life or widowhood, to support herself and raise and educate his infant children. He made no further distribution.
>
> Attested to by Thomas Whitely and Abraham Rainwater[47]

Martha Hodges Rainwater lived to at least December 1841, when she consented to the marriage of her youngest daughter and namesake, Patsy.[48] She had died by 1850, according to the census.

Both Martha and William were buried in a graveyard on the family farm, the ownership of which passed to their son Miles. According to Rainwater researcher Don Webber, their graves were originally indicated by fieldstone markers into which the initials W.S.R. and M.S.R. had been scratched.[49] These homemade markers were not found in the most recent survey of the graveyard[50], made by Darren Waters and Scott Burton in 2008.

---

[46] 1069, 1070, 1071: Twelve Rainwaters served in the War of 1812, four from Kentucky. The military record of the real William Rainwater who served in this conflict says that he was born c. 1800 in Jackson Co., GA and served as a regimental musician. He served with his brothers, Edward and Newsom. This is Glidie Rainwater Mobley's branch of the family.

[47] 304: Nuncupative Will of William Rainwater, 6 Jan 1825, Pulaski Co., Kentucky, Book 2 page 192

[48] 49: Pulaski Co., Kentucky Marriage Records, Vol 1, 1797–1850, 2nd edition, Mary Weddle Kaurish, Pulaski County Historical Society

[49] 247: Donald S. Webber, *Genealogy of the Rainwater Family*, Dec 1981, copy of original

[50] 2315: Rainwater tombstones in Rainwater Cemetery, off the intersection of Wolf Creek and Roberts Roads, Faubush, Pulaski Co., KY, longitude 37.07420 latitude -84.84295, on private land,

The children of William and Martha Rainwater:

Lydia Rainwater

Born 8 May 1802, North Carolina, and died after 1880, Minnesota
Lydia never married. She moved with the family of her younger sister, Elizabeth, first to Indiana[51] and then to Minnesota.[52] She is believed to have died in Faribault Co., Minnesota.

Bartholomew Rainwater

Born 20 Jan 1804, North Carolina, and died 28 Jun 1889, Kentucky
See profile of Bartholomew Rainwater and Nancy McLaughlin

James Rainwater

Born 8 Feb 1806, North Carolina, and died c. 1862, Kentucky
James married Mary McDaniel on 19 Apr 1826 in Pulaski County.[53] They were the parents of ten children, nine of whom survived to adulthood. Census records and his will indicate that he was a farmer and moneylender.[54]

Abraham Rainwater

Born 3 Apr 1808, North Carolina, and died c. 1875, Indiana
Abraham Rainwater married Anna McLaughlin on 16 Apr 1828 in Russell County.[55] They were the parents of eight children, seven of whom survived to adulthood. Abraham was a farmer. The family moved to Indiana after 1850.[56] He and his wife were members of the White River Association of the Primitive Baptist Church in Brown Co., Indiana, in whose records their deaths are recorded.[57]

---

research by Darren Waters and photos by Scott Burton. Recorded in 1977 by volunteers of the Pulaski County Historical Society, knowledge of the cemetery's location was lost in the intervening years. Darren Waters and Scott Burton ran down every clue, searching for three years, before rediscovering and resurveying the location in 2008.

[51] Federal Census: 1860, Fayetteville, Lawrence Co., IN, pg 781, household of Zachariah Loveall

[52] Federal Census: 1880, Clark Twp., Faribault Co., MN, pg 11A, household of Zachariah Loveall

[53] 49: Pulaski Co., Kentucky Marriage Records, Vol 1, 1797–1850, 2nd edition, Mary Weddle Kaurish, publ. 1984, Pulaski County Historical Society, Somerset, KY

[54] 404: Will of James Rainwater, 1862, Pulaski Co., Kentucky, Book 6 pg 115
Federal Census: 1850, Pulaski Co., KY, pg 134; 1860, Pulaski Co., KY, pg 406.

[55] 321: Russell Co., Kentucky Marriage Certificates, Book 1, 1826–1954, Kentucky Ancestors (periodical), Vol 2, Mrs. Donald E. Jordan

[56] Federal Census: 1850, Pulaski Co., KY, pg 131B; 1860, Lawrence Co., IN, pg 812; 1870, Orange Co., IN, pg 70B

[57] 194: Indiana Source Book, Vol. 3, Willard Heiss, publ. 1997, Indiana Historical Society, Indianapolis, IN

John R. Rainwater (twin)

Born 5 Mar 1810, North Carolina, and died 1889, Kentucky
John married Elizabeth Lawless on 2 Dec 1837 in Pulaski County.[58] They were the parents of six children, four of whom survived to adulthood. John was a farmer. His tombstone in Grave Hill Cemetery, one of the few from this generation that survives, indicates that he was born in North Carolina.[59]

Nancy Rainwater Roy (twin)

Born 5 Mar 1810, North Carolina, and died 10 Aug 1891, Illinois
Nancy married William Merritt Roy on 22 Feb 1834 in Pulaski County.[60] They were a farm family and the parents of eleven children, including a pair of twins. They moved to Indiana around 1835, and to Illinois before 1860.[61]

William Howard Rainwater

Born 17 Jun 1813, Kentucky, and died c. 1889, Indiana
William married Nancy Ann Hodge on 2 Oct 1831 in Casey County.[62] They were divorced on 13 Jan 1837.[63] The marriage produced one son, James, who died in his twenties. William married his second wife, Minerva Ann Rayborn, on 4 May 1838 in Pulaski County.[64] They were the parents of ten children, nine of whom survived to adulthood. The couple died in Brown Co., Indiana.[65]

Susannah Rainwater

Born 28 Sep 1815, Kentucky, and died 14 Apr 1858, Kentucky
Susannah never married. She lived for many years with her Aunt Elizabeth Rainwater.[66] At the age of 40, she and J. J. Luster took out a marriage bond, witnessed by her brother Daniel, but it was never

---

[58] 49: Pulaski Co., Kentucky Marriage Records, Vol 1, 1797–1850, 2nd edition, Mary Weddle Kaurish, publ. 1984, Pulaski County Historical Society, Somerset, KY

[59] 48: Pulaski Co., Kentucky Cemetery Records, Vol. 2, Pulaski County Historical Society, published June 1977, Somerset, KY

[60] 49: Pulaski Co., Kentucky Marriage Records, Vol 1, 1797–1850, 2nd edition, Mary Weddle Kaurish, publ. 1984, Pulaski County Historical Society, Somerset, KY

[61] 1850 & 1860 Federal Census, Lawrence Co., IN; 1870 & 1880 Federal Census, Fulton Co., IL

[62] 197: Early Marriages of Casey Co., KY, 1807-1915, in two volumes compiled from official records in the Casey County Courthouse, Liberty, Kentucky, Phillip A. Rice, Kathleen Goff, Charlotte Mason and Edward Mason, publ. 1977, Polyanthos, New Orleans, LA

[63] Kentucky Footsteps, Vol. D, 1999

[64] 49: Pulaski Co., Kentucky Marriage Records, Vol 1, 1797–1850, 2nd edition, Mary Weddle Kaurish, publ. 1984, Pulaski County Historical Society, Somerset, KY

[65] Federal Census: 1850, Pulaski Co., KY, pg 242; 1860, pg 310; 1870, Brown Co., IN, pg 307; 1880, pg 293A

[66] Federal Census: 1850, Pulaski Co., KY, pg 131B

executed. She died of dropsy at the age of 43.[67] A persistent myth holds that Susannah married a man named Bucky Vaughan. There is no marriage or census record in Pulaski County or any of the nearby counties for an individual of this name. Moreover, she is listed as a single female in the Pulaski County death records.

Miles Rainwater

Born 15 May 1818, Kentucky, and died 9 Jan 1884, Kentucky
Miles married Frances Chaney on 29 Jul 1843 in Pulaski County.[68] They were the parents of eleven children, ten of whom survived to adulthood. Among their children are Silas Rainwater, who died at the Civil War Battle of Chickamauga Creek, Tennessee, in 1863[69]; Erasmus Rainwater, who became a saloon keeper in South Dakota during the Black Hills Gold Rush[70]; and Reverend Fountain Rainwater, a Baptist minister[71]. Miles inherited his father's farm upon his mother's death and is buried there.[72]

Elizabeth Rainwater Roberts Loveall

Born 1 Oct 1819/1822, Kentucky, and died after 1880, Minnesota
Elizabeth married Isaac Roberts on 24 Nov 1843 in Pulaski County.[73] The couple had three children, all born in Indiana. Isaac died c. 1854, and Betsy remarried to Zachariah Loveall on 15 Oct 1854.[74] The Lovealls had four children, three of whom survived to adulthood.[75] According to descendant, John D. Roberts, Elizabeth and Zachariah were buried on the family farm.[76]

---

[67] 263: Pulaski Co., Kentucky Vital Records, Birth & Death, 1852–1859, 1861, 1874–1878, Pulaski County Historical Society, Somerset, KY

[68] 49: Pulaski Co., Kentucky Marriage Records, Vol 1, 1797–1850, 2nd edition, Mary Weddle Kaurish, publ. 1984, Pulaski County Historical Society, Somerset, KY

[69] 45: Report of the Adjutant General of the State of Kentucky, Civil War, 1861-1866, Vol. I, Union, publ. 1889, reprinted by the Southern Historical Press, 1992, Greenville, SC

[70] Federal Census: 1880, Golden Gate Twp., Dakota Territory, pg 215B.
The 1878 Business Directory of Golden Gate, South Dakota contains a listing for Cox & Rainwater's Saloon. In December 2003, a stereogram showing the downtown of Deadwood City that included a sign for Cox & Rainwater's Cash Store was sold on Ebay. Not, unfortunately, to us.

[71] 52: Pulaski Co., KY Marriage Records, Vol 4, 1887-1900, Pulaski County Historical Society, publ. 1988, Somerset, KY

[72] 48: Pulaski Co., Kentucky Cemetery Records, Vol. 2, Pulaski County Historical Society, published June 1977, Somerset, KY

[73] 49: Pulaski Co., Kentucky Marriage Records, Vol 1, 1797–1850, 2nd edition, Mary Weddle Kaurish, publ. 1984, Pulaski County Historical Society, Somerset, KY

[74] 2682: Lawrence Co., IN Early Marriage Records, 1835-1843, Charles M. Franklin, publ. 1987, Ye Old Genealogie Shoppe, Indianapolis, IN

[75] Federal Census: 1860, Lawrence Co., IN, pg 781; 1880 Federal Census, Faribault Co., MN, pg 11AS

[76] 154: John D. Roberts (Rainwater-Roberts family), handwritten letter dated 17 Jul 1997

Martha "Patsy" Rainwater Devenport[77] (twin)

Born 15 Mar 1823, Kentucky, and died between 1858 and 1859 in Greene Co., Illinois

Patsy married Tilman Devenport on 14 Dec 1841 in Pulaski Co., Kentucky.[78] They were the parents of six children. Patsy died between 1858 and 1859.[79] Devenport remarried twice, both times in Greene Co., Illinois.

---

[77] The marriage record transcription says Davenport. The 1850 Federal Census, Russell Co., KY, pg 266, says Debenport. The 1860 Greene Co., IL census, pg 604, says Devenport, which seems to be the middle ground in terms of pronunciation. I am grateful to Richard Hollis for his post on the now defunct KYPulaski-L mailing list mentioning the alternate spellings of the family surname.

[78] 49: Pulaski Co., Kentucky Marriage Records, Vol 1, 1797–1850, 2nd edition, Mary Weddle Kaurish, publ. 1984, Pulaski County Historical Society, Somerset, KY

[79] After the birth of her sixth child in 1858, but before her husband's remarriage on 9 Jan 1859.

BARTHOLOMEW RAINWATER AND NANCY MCLAUGHLIN

Bartholomew Rainwater
Son of William Rainwater and Martha Hodges
Born 20 Jan 1804, Danbury, Stokes Co., North Carolina
Died 28 Jun 1889, Waterloo, Pulaski Co., Kentucky
Buried Rainwater Cemetery, Pulaski Co., Kentucky

Married 24 Feb 1825, Adair Co., Kentucky

Nancy McLaughlin
Daughter of Daniel and Jane McLaughlin
Born 20 Aug 1807, Russell Co., Kentucky
Died 20 Jan 1883, Pulaski Co., Kentucky
Buried Rainwater Cemetery, Pulaski Co.,Kentucky

Bartholomew Rainwater was born in North Carolina on 20 Jan 1804[80]. He is traditionally said to have been born in Danbury, Stokes Co., North Carolina.[81] His parents had moved to Surry Co., North Carolina by the time he was six, and to Pulaski Co., Kentucky by the time he was nine.

On 25 Feb 1825, he married Nancy McLaughlin in Adair Co., Kentucky[82]. Nancy was the daughter of Daniel and Jane McLaughlin[83], about whom we know almost nothing. Nancy's sister Anna married Bartholomew's brother Abraham in 1828.[84] The descendants of both lines believe that Daniel McLaughlin was an emigrant from Ireland or England, born around 1775. He appears to have died between 1825 and 1828 – he gave permission for Nancy to marry in 1825[85], but Jane gave permission for Anna in 1828, suggesting that Daniel was no longer living.

There are quite a few myths about Bartholomew and Nancy. Nancy is said to be related to Teddy Roosevelt, which simply isn't true. Bartholomew is said to have been a childhood friend of Abraham Lincoln, but in reality, they merely lived in the same state for a few years.[86] It's also claimed that Bartholomew

---

[80] 56: Bartholomew Rainwater family Bible, photocopy of original

[81] 544: Obituary of Josiah W. Rainwater, 17 Mar 1934, Vernon Daily Record

[82] 621: Bond for marriage for Bartholomew Rainwater & Nancy McLaughlin, Feb 1823, Adair Co., KY, photocopy of original

[83] 475: Loose marriage bonds reviewed in person in the Russell Co., Kentucky courthouse by James D. Garner in 1987

[84] 321: Russell Co., Kentucky Marriage Certificates, Book 1, 1826-1954, Kentucky Ancestors, Vol 2, Mrs. Donald E. Jordan

[85] 622: Permission for marriage of daughter Nancy by Daniel McLaughlin, Feb 1825, Adair Co., KY, photocopy of original

[86] Lincoln lived in Hodgenville, Kentucky, about 125 miles from Bartholomew's childhood home. In an era when most people never traveled more than 20 miles from their homes, it's highly unlikely that the two ever met.

was Cherokee, but it should be clear from the preceding pages, that this claim also is not true.[87]

What can be said truthfully about Bartholomew is that he was a farmer and a schoolteacher.[88] In 1834, he purchased 50 acres on Wolf Creek.[89] Like his father, he probably raised pigs and chickens, grew corn as a cash crop, and other vegetables for the family table. As a Baptist, Bartholomew probably abstained from distilling corn into whiskey, though plenty of his neighbors did.[90]

Bartholomew and Nancy's first child was born the year after they married. In all, they had 13 children, three of whom died at birth, including a pair of twins. They are recorded in the family Bible, a photocopy of which Roscoe Rainwater included in his genealogical research. We do not know who presently owns the original.

> Bartholomew Rainwater was born January the 20th day 1804 and died June 28, 1889
> Nancy McLaughlin was born August the 2nd day 1807 and died January 20 1883
> Anne Rainwater was born April the 15th day 1826 Saturday
> Emily Rainwater was born May the 17th day 1827 Thursday
> Daniel M. Rainwater was born November the 10th day 1828 on Monday
> Samantha Jane Rainwater was born January the 19th 1830 Tuesday
> Sally Rainwater was born February the 16th day 1832 on Thursday
> Susannah Rainwater was born February the 12th day 1834 on Tuesday
> Two girls born and deceased March the 13th day 1835
> Miles Rainwater was born April the 7th day 1836 on Friday
> Polly Rainwater was born December the 28th day 1837 on Wednesday
> Ciota Rainwater was born December the 26th day 1839 on Thursday
> Sarelda Ann Rainwater was born December 9th day 1841 on Thursday
> Josiah Wilson Rainwater was born October 10th day 1843 on Wednesday

---

[87] Indeed, this claim is made in nearly every Rainwater line but appears to be a romantic fantasy of relatively recent construction.

[88] Federal Census: 1850, Pulaski Co., KY, pg 245
544: Obituary of Josiah W. Rainwater, 17 Mar 1934, Vernon Daily Record

[89] 90: Kentucky Land Grants, Parts 1 & 2, 1782-1924, Willard Rouse Jillson, ScD, publ. 1971, Genealogical Publishing Co., Baltimore, MD

[90] Michael Pollan, "*The Omnivore's Dilemma*", published 2006, The Penguin Press, New York. Pollan points out that the overproduction of corn in states like Kentucky led to widespread alcohol production. Distilling corn into alcohol turned it into "a compact and portable, and less perishable, value-added commodity." The epidemic of alcoholic overindulgence that broke out in the United States in the middle of the 19th century and led directly to Prohibition, was the result of the need of farmers to turn their corn into something they could sell.

Bartholomew and Nancy Rainwater are recorded in the federal census records of Pulaski Co., Kentucky, starting in 1830 and ending in 1880. By the time they died, only half of their children remained in the county.

Nancy McLaughlin Rainwater died on 20 Jan 1883, of flux (severe diarrhea).[91] Treatable today, this was often a fatal illness in centuries past. She was buried on the Rainwater family farm. Six years later, Bartholomew Rainwater had a stroke and died after ten days[92] on 28 Jun 1889, and was buried with his wife.[93]

The children of Bartholomew and Nancy Rainwater:

Anne Rainwater Weddle

Born 15 Apr 1826, Kentucky and died between 1890 and 1900, Kentucky
See profile of Daniel S. Weddle, son of John Milton Weddle

Emily Rainwater Eastham

Born 17 May 1827, Kentucky and died 1914, Kentucky
Emily married Alexander Eastham on 1 Sep 1844.[94] In the 15 years that followed, nine children were born to this couple. Alexander died of tuberculosis on 4 Dec 1859[95], leaving Emily to raise the children on the income provided by his considerable land investment. On 17 Jul 1877, Emily married her late husband's widowed brother, Zachariah Eastham.[96] According to Eastham researcher Joanna Eads, this proved to be a terrible mistake. Zachariah sold the land and spent the money, eventually divorcing a poverty-stricken Emily. Only one of her children, Elizabeth Eastham Harris, was willing to take her in, suggesting that the family had opposed the marriage to Zachariah. Emily was institutionalized in the Boyle Co., Kentucky, poor house in 1913 and died there the following year.[97]

---

[91] 151: Frances Aderholt Smith (Rainwater–Aderholt families)

[92] 1880: Letter from Josiah W. Rainwater to Miles Rainwater regarding the death of their father, dated 9 Jul 1889, scan of photocopy of original, from Mark Sanborn

[93] On Roberts Road, just off of Wolf Creek Road, longitude 37.07420 latitude -84.84295, on private land

[94] 49: Pulaski Co., Kentucky Marriage Records, Vol 1, 1797–1850, 2nd edition, Mary Weddle Kaurish, publ. 1984, Pulaski County Historical Society, Somerset, KY

[95] 263: Pulaski Co., Kentucky Vital Records, Birth & Death, 1852–1859, 1861, 1874–1878, Pulaski County Historical Society, Somerset, KY

[96] 51: Pulaski Co., Kentucky Marriage Records, Vol 3, 1864–1886, publ. 1984, Pulaski County Historical Society, Somerset, KY

[97] 298: Joanna Eads (Rainwater-Eastham family)

Daniel McDaniel Rainwater

Daniel McDaniel Rainwater

Born 10 Nov 1828, Kentucky and died between June 1899 and 1900, Kentucky

On 14 Dec 1848, Daniel married Ann Whitaker, an orphan under the guardianship of Anderson Compton.[98] The couple had eleven children, ten of whom lived to adulthood, including a pair of twins.[99] Both Daniel and his wife died shortly before the turn of the century and are buried in New Hope Cemetery, Pulaski County.[100]

Samantha Jane Rainwater

Born 19 Jan 1830, Kentucky and died between 1860 and 1870, Kentucky

Samantha never married and almost nothing is known of her.[101]

---

[98] 49: Pulaski Co., KY Marriage Records, Vol 1, 1797-1850, 2nd edition, Mary Weddle Kaurish, publ. 1984, Pulaski County Historical Society, Somerset, KY

[99] Federal Census, Pulaski Co., KY: 1850, pg 244; 1860, pg 292; 1870, pg 162; 1880, pg 364

[100] 48: Pulaski Co., KY Cemetery Records, Vol. 2, Pulaski County Historical Society, published June 1977, Somerset, KY

[101] Federal Census: 1850, Pulaski Co., KY, pg 245; 1860, Pulaski Co., KY, pg 308; living with parents

Sarah "Sally" Rainwater Weddle

Born 16 Feb 1832, Kentucky and died 3 Apr 1906, Indiana
On 6 Jul 1847, Sally married Galen Edward Weddle, the brother of Daniel S. Weddle, her sister Anne's husband.[102] Like her sister, Sally had Justice of the Peace Josiah W. Duck perform the service. The couple remained in Pulaski County until after the Civil War, moving to Indiana between 1871 and 1874. They were the parents of fourteen children, thirteen of whom reached adulthood.[103] The couple is buried in Pleasant View Cemetery, Monroe Co., Indiana.[104]

Susannah Rainwater Hainey Pitman

Born 12 Feb 1834, Kentucky and died 29 Apr 1912, Kentucky
Susannah married Thomas Hainey, the son of a Methodist minister,[105] on 16 Jan 1856 in Pulaski County.[106] The family moved to Linn Co., Kansas c. 1857 and remained until c. 1862, when they moved back to Kentucky. During the Civil War, the family relocated to Indiana, where Thomas enlisted in Jan 1864, in either the 6th or 44th Indiana Infantry, and served for about nine months.[107] Thomas died before 1870, leaving Susannah with three small children to support.

She returned to Pulaski County and she took a position as a housekeeper for William Pitman. Pitman's first wife, Kissiah Norfleet, had borne him nine children and was now suffering a lingering illness. His relationship with Susannah took an illicit romantic turn, and in 1868, she gave birth to their first child, Silas Green Pitman, who is listed in the 1870 census as Silas G. Hainey.[108] Shortly after Kissiah died, William and Susannah were married on 23 Feb 1871.[109] Their union produced three more children. Susannah is buried in Cedar Point Cemetery, Pulaski County.[110]

---

[102] 49: Pulaski Co., Kentucky Marriage Records, Vol 1, 1797–1850, 2nd edition, Mary Weddle Kaurish, publ. 1984, Pulaski County Historical Society, Somerset, KY

[103] Federal Census: 1850, Pulaski Co., KY, pg 252; 1860, Pulaski Co., KY, pg 294; 1870, Casey Co., KY, pg 278; 1880, Morgan Co., IN, pg 199.

[104] 2312: Findagrave.com #32648340 and #32648362

[105] Federal Census: 1850, Wayne Co., KY, pg 255B

[106] 50: Pulaski Co., KY Marriage Records, Vol 2, 1851-1863, Pulaski County Historical Society, publ. 1970, Somerset, KY

[107] U. S. Civil War Soldiers and Profiles Index, Ancestry.com, paywalled. There two conflicting records for Thomas D. Hainey, which cannot be resolved on the basis of the index alone.

[108] 346: Two letters from Lola Pitman Snyder to Roscoe Rainwater, dated 22 Mar 1972 & 28 Apr 1972, originals
257: Joice Buis (Rainwater–Pitman families)
Federal Census: 1870, Pulaski Co., KY, pg 162

[109] 51: Pulaski Co., KY Marriage Records, Vol 3, 1864-1886, Pulaski County Historical Society, publ. 1984, Somerset, KY

[110] 48: Pulaski Co., KY Cemetery Records, Vol. 2, Pulaski County Historical Society, published June 1977, Somerset, KY

Cornelia and Miles Rainwater, c. 1865

Miles Rainwater

Born 7 Apr 1836, Kentucky and died 22 Dec 1914, California
At the outbreak of the Civil War, Miles and Josiah both joined the 3rd Kentucky Volunteer Infantry, Union. Miles served from 7 Aug 1861 to 5 Jan 1863, and was discharged as a result of chronic bronchitis and pleuritic adhesions of the lungs.[111] After recovering his health, he moved to Kansas and enlisted in the Kansas State Militia, where he led Company E (colored) as a 1st Lieutenant and later a Captain.[112]

On 13 Aug 1865, he married Cornelia Sawyer.[113] They had two daughters, both of whom died in their twenties. Miles' Civil War service had a deleterious effect on his health. By 1892, the list of his afflictions included kidney and bladder problems, bronchitis, chronic diarrhea, poor eyesight, neuralgia on the right side of his head and an enlarged prostate.[114] He died in 1914 and is buried with his wife in Bellview Cemetery, San Bernardino Co., California.[115]

---

[111] 490: Certified copy of Surgeon's Certificate of Discharge, dated 8 Dec 1862, Civil War pension papers of Cornelia E. Sawyer and Miles Rainwater, 1883–1914, photocopy of originals

[112] 1269: Muster roll of Company E (colored), 1st Battalion, Irregular Kansas State Militia, Mound City, KS, dated 15 Oct 1864 and 5 Nov 1864, photocopy from the files of the Linn Co., KS Historical Society

[113] 490: Civil War pension papers of Cornelia E. Sawyer and Miles Rainwater, 1883–1914, photocopy of originals

[114] 490: Civil War pension papers of Cornelia E. Sawyer and Miles Rainwater, 1883–1914, photocopy of originals

[115] 865: Death certificate #22–013887–1256, Cornelia E. Rainwater, San Bernardino Co., CA, 1922

866: Death certificate #14–037651–570547, Miles Rainwater, San Bernardino Co., CA, 1914

Polly and Alfred Holbrook, c. 1860

Mary "Polly" Rainwater Holbrook

Born 20 Dec 1837, Kentucky and died 20 Jan 1865, Kansas
Polly Rainwater moved to Linn Co., Kansas in the mid-1850s with her sister Susannah and brother-in-law, Thomas Hainey. In Kansas, she met Alfred Joseph Holbrook and they were married on 31 May 1859.[116] The couple had three children.[117]

Alfred served in Company K, 12th Regiment, Kansas Infantry, from Sep 1862 to Jun 1865.[118] Polly died in his absence in 1865, and was buried in Wesley Chapel Cemetery.[119] Her children were temporarily put in the care of James Osborn, a leader in the local abolitionist movement.[120] Alfred remarried and moved with his children and second wife to Oregon, where he died in 1908.[121]

Sciota Bethene Rainwater Elder

Born 26 Dec 1839, Kentucky and died 7 Jun 1908, Missouri
Sciota married John Levi Elder on 24 Feb 1859 in Pulaski County.[122] They were the parents of eleven children, ten of whom lived to adulthood.[123] In 1871, the couple moved their family to Holt Co., Missouri and purchased land on the "*Big Blew River in the Black Bob*

---

[116] 1263: Marriage record of Polly Rainwater and Alfred Holbrook, Linn Co., KS, 1859, photocopy of original
[117] Federal Census: 1860, Linn Co., KS, pg 98; 1870, Linn Co., KS, pg 14B
[118] 1270: 1865 state census of Kansas
[119] 1268: Sexton's map of Wesley Chapel Cemetery, Bradley, Linn Co., KS, photocopy of original
[120] 1865 census of Kansas and researcher Mark Sanborn (Rainwater–Holbrook families)
[121] 250: J. C. Halbrooks (Halbrook–Holbrook families)
[122] 50: Pulaski Co., KY Marriage Records, Vol 2, 1851-1863, Pulaski County Historical Society, publ. 1970, Somerset, KY

Reserve" near the town of Oregon.[124] Elder's mother moved with them, and her death is mentioned in Levi's letter to Josiah Rainwater, written in 1876.[125] Sciota was attacked by bees while attempting to hive a swarm, and died as a result in 1908.[126] She is thought to be buried in Maple Grove Cemetery, Holt Co., Missouri, with her husband.[127]

Sarelda Chumbley

Sarelda Ann Rainwater Chumbley

Born 9 Dec 1841, Kentucky and died 16 Oct 1927, Texas
Sarelda married Alexander Chumbley on 6 Feb 1859 in Pulaski County.[128] They were the parents of eleven children, all of whom lived to adulthood.[129] In 1893, the family moved to Sweat Box, Texas, in Fannin County. This was not a propitious move for Alexander, who died two years later and is buried in the now abandoned Hope Cemetery[130]. Sarelda took residence with her son James, and later with

---

[123] Federal Census: Pulaski Co., KY, 1860, pg 301 and 1870, pg 150; Holt Co., MO, 1880, pg 166B.

1303: The family Bible of John L. and Sciota Rainwater Elder, photocopies of originals, from Marjorie Thomas

[124] 347: Letter from John Levi Elder to Josiah Rainwater, 6 Aug 1876, 4 handwritten pages, original. Other than the fact that it is near the town of Oregon, MO, we have been unable to locate the Black Bob Reserve. The Blue River forms the border between Kansas and Missouri.

[125] See document appendix

[126] 108: Roscoe Rainwater, genealogical notes and files

[127] Holt Co., MO Death Notices from Area Newspapers, 1904-1906, Northwest Missouri Genealogical Society, St. Joseph, MO

[128] 50: Pulaski Co., KY Marriage Records, Vol 2, 1851-1863, Pulaski County Historical Society, publ. 1970, Somerset, KY

[129] Federal Census: Pulaski Co., KY, 1860, pg 254; 1870, pg 83; 1880, pg 4; Grayson Co., TX, 1910 pg 291

[130] 1409: Tombstone of Alexander Chumbley, Hope Cemetery (formerly Sweat Box Cemetery), CR 4805, Hunt Co., TX, original photographs taken by R. Steven Rainwater, 25 Aug 2001. This cemetery was, at the time of our visit, afflicted with a nearly Biblical plague of grasshoppers and

her son Robert, in Whitewright, Texas.[131] She died in 1927 of senility and old age.[132] Sarelda is buried in Vittitoe Cemetery, Grayson County.[133]

Josiah Wilson Rainwater

Born 10 Oct 1843, Kentucky and died 16 Mar 1934, Texas
See profile of Josiah Wilson Rainwater and Elizabeth Jane Weddle

---

contained the largest golden orb spiders we have ever seen.

[131] Federal Census: 1900, Runnels Co., TX, pg 25B; 1910, Grayson Co., TX, pg 291; 1920, Kentuckytown, Grayson Co., TX, pg 52B.

[132] 2369: Death certificate #33675; Sarelda Ann (Rainwater) Chumbley, 16 Oct 1927, Grayson Co., TX, scan from microfilm

[133] 1413: Chumbley family tombstones in Vittitoe Cemetery, Andy Thomas Drive, Kentuckytown, Grayson Co., Texas, photos by R. Steven Rainwater and Susan Rainwater, 25 Aug 2001

Josiah Wilson Rainwater
and Elizabeth Jane Weddle

Josiah and Elizabeth Jane Rainwater, c.1866[134]

Josiah Wilson Rainwater
Son of Bartholomew Rainwater and Nancy McLaughlin
Born 10 Oct 1843, Waterloo, Pulaski Co., Kentucky
Died 16 Mar 1934, Vernon, Wilbarger Co., Texas

Married 11 Jan 1866 in Pulaski Co., Kentucky

Elizabeth Jane Weddle
Daughter of Solomon Weddle and Martha "Patsy" Tarter
Born 7 Sep 1847, Pulaski Co., Kentucky
Died 25 Jun 1943, Vernon, Wilbarger Co., Texas

---

[134] From the collection of Betty Jo Rainwater Parker

Josiah Rainwater was the youngest son born to Bartholomew Rainwater and Nancy McLaughlin. Born in 1843 in Waterloo, Pulaski Co., Kentucky, he was one of eleven surviving children.[135] He was named for Rev. Josiah Wilson, a minister and Revolutionary War veteran with ties to both North Carolina and Kentucky.

Josiah was 17 when the Civil War erupted. With his brother, Miles, he joined the 3rd Regiment of the Kentucky Volunteer Infantry of the Union Army. He enlisted on 5 Nov 1861 at Camp Wolford, about eight miles south of Somerset, and was mustered into Company D at Camp Boyle on 1 Jan 1862. He started his service as a Private, but in Jan 1863, was promoted to Corporal, and then to Sergeant in July 1863. He was appointed Ordnance Sergeant on 23 Apr 1864.

Josiah was shot in the hand at the Battle of Stone River (Murfreesboro, Tennessee) on 31 Dec 1862, while serving under the command of General William S. Rosecrans. This was not a serious enough injury to warrant a discharge, so after recuperating, he returned to duty in time to join General William Tecumseh Sherman's march on Atlanta. He was shot in the hip and thorax at Marietta, Georgia, on Jun 27 1864. This injury put him in the hospital for two months He was finally discharged from service on 10 Jan 1865. In 1883, he applied for the pension due him for his service and was awarded $1.00 per month as compensation for his wounds.[136]

When his obituary was printed in the newspaper many years later, the article reported that he had been a *"Captain under General Grant"*.[137] However, Josiah's service records report that he had been promoted only to Ordnance Sergeant.[138] His pension application indicates that he was a Sergeant.[139] He also gave this answer in the 1890 Federal Census.[140] If he had been a Captain, he would have said so.

Two of Josiah's grandsons, Clois Rainwater and Eugene W. Rainwater, recalled that an ornate certificate hung over their grandfather's bed that older relatives said was Josiah's commission as a Captain in the Army of the Cumberland.

---

[135] 56: Bartholomew Rainwater family Bible, photocopy of original

[136] 45: Report of the Adjutant General of the State of Kentucky, Civil War, 1861-1866, Vol. I, Union, publ. 1889, reprinted by the Southern Historical Press, 1992, Greenville, SC

137: Abstracts from the List of United States Pensioners on the Roll, 1 Jan 1883, Government Printing Office, publ. 1883, reprinted 1983, The Gregath Company, Cullman, AL

327: Civil War service papers of Josiah W. Rainwater, 5 Nov 1861–10 Jan 1865, copies of the originals

[137] 544: Obituary of Josiah W. Rainwater, 17 Mar 1934, Vernon Daily Record, transcription. When we requested a copy of the original from the newspaper, they could not locate the issue.

[138] 327: Civil War service papers of Josiah W. Rainwater, 5 Nov 1861–10 Jan 1865, copies of the originals

[139] 328: Civil War pension papers of Josiah W. Rainwater and Elizabeth Jane Weddle Rainwater, 10 May 1879–2 Apr 1934, copies of the originals

[140] 1890 Federal Census (Civil War survivors & widows schedule), Pulaski Co., KY, pg 181

This, of course, is the source of the story in the obituary. So how to resolve the contradiction?

My first thought was that Josiah had been temporarily brevetted to Captain in a battlefield emergency. In the mid-1990s, I was having an unrelated email conversation with J. R. "Randy" McIlhaney, when he happened to mention that he was taking a class from an expert in the Civil War. I asked him to pose a question for me to his instructor regarding the possibility of a brevet commission. The answer that I received was that a brevet commission in the Union Army[141] might or might not be noted in Josiah's records, but would not have resulted in piece of paper reflecting the temporary increase in rank. I would later pose this same question to Lloyd de Witt Bockstruck, at the time the Supervisor of the Genealogy Section of the Dallas Public Library, and a nationally recognized genealogical scholar and military records expert. He agreed that a brevet commission was out of the question.

In September 2012, I took a class in military records for genealogists, sponsored by the Dallas Genealogical Society. The instructor, military records expert Craig R. Scott, suggested that Josiah might have served in the Kentucky militia, the historic equivalent of the National Guard.[142]

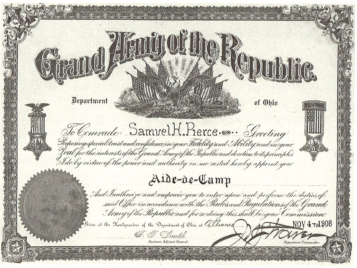

Example of a GAR certificate

On 9 Nov 2012, I called and spoke at length with Brandon Slone, a military historian in the Military Records and Research Branch of the Kentucky Department of Military Affairs. He gave me an overview of the Kentucky National Legion, the post-Civil War militia that lasted about 10 years before being reorganized as the Kentucky State Guard. He stated emphatically that

---

[141] The Confederacy did not confer brevet commissions.

[142] Craig R. Scott, CG, 29 Sep 2012, Military Records seminar at the Dallas Public Library, sponsored by the Dallas Genealogical Society

the Kentucky National Legion did not issue commissions of the sort that could be framed as Josiah's was. Officers were issued small paperboard ID cards that they could carry in a jacket pocket. Slone said that in his experience, this type of certificate was nearly always something issued by the GAR – the Grand Army of the Republic.

The GAR was a fraternal organization founded in 1866 at the close of the Civil War, with membership open to Union veterans from various branches of the service.[143] The GAR used military ranks instead of civil titles for its organizational chart. Instead of saying that a man was the president of a particular post, the GAR would say he was the Captain of a post. In Slone's experience, the type of certificate I described was consistent with a Captain's commission in the GAR. He also said that he had seen quite a few cases of obituaries in which relatives had confused GAR ranks with Union Army ranks. Unfortunately, the Grand Army of the Republic Museum and Library in Philadelphia does not have the GAR files from Kentucky in their collection, making it unlikely that these records survive.

Josiah Rainwater had nine children and fifty-two grandchildren. We have no idea which of them inherited the certificate and no way of knowing if it still exists. So I cannot say with absolute certainty that the document over Josiah's bed was a GAR Captain's Commission, but I think the available evidence suggests that it was.

A year after returning home from the war, Josiah married Elizabeth Jane Weddle, on 11 Jan 1866.[144] She was the daughter of Solomon Weddle and Martha "Patsy" Tarter. She was a timid, quiet woman, remembered by her granddaughter, Betty Jo Parker, as a tireless quilter and knitter. "*Everyone,*" Betty Jo told us "*eventually received a pair of Elizabeth Jane's knitted fingerless gloves.*" She had one vice, though she denied it – she chewed tobacco.[145]

The couple had nine children – seven daughters and two sons – all of whom lived to adulthood and married.

Josiah took up farming, and by 1890 he had acquired about 200 acres of farm land, valued at close to $3000.[146] In the off-season, he ran a small general store. His descendants would recall that Josiah had rigged up some kind of primitive telephone – a string and can affair – that ran from the house, which was up on a rise, down to the store next to the road.[147]

---

[143] WikiPedia: Grand Army of the Republic, http://en.wikipedia.org/wiki/GAR
[144] 349: Marriage license of Josiah W. Rainwater & Elizabeth Jane Weddle, 1866, Pulaski Co., Kentucky, certified copy
[145] Conversation with Betty Jo Rainwater Parker, Colorado Springs, Colorado, 18 Sept 1997
[146] 1890 Federal Census (Civil War survivors & widows schedule), Pulaski Co., KY, pg 181
[147] Both Clois Rainwater and Eugene W. Rainwater have told us this story.

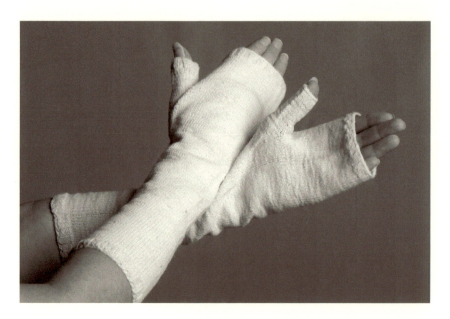

A pair of Elizabeth Rainwater's fingerless gloves, from Betty Jo Rainwater Parker

Josiah joined the Masons and became a Master Mason in 1867.[148] He also served as postmaster for the tiny town of Waterloo, Kentucky, and was for several years Tax Assessor and Collector for Pulaski County.[149] He was also a deputy sheriff for the county and Betty Jo Parker showed us his badge – the words "Deputy Sheriff of Pulaski County" struck over a half dime.[150] He and his wife were founding members of Somerset Missionary Baptist Church, the minutes of which were also in the possession of Betty Jo Parker.[151]

In 1880, Josiah was a census enumerator for his district in Pulaski County. In those days, the census was conducted by personal interview and the enumerator had to walk or ride from house to house, asking the questions and filling out the form with pen and ink. The entire district's census is in Josiah's handwriting. He would repeat this service as one of the enumerators of the 1910 census of Wilbarger Co., Texas.

---

[148] 77: Josiah Wilson Rainwater, pg 245, Williamson Co., Texas: Its History and Its People, Williamson Co. Genealogical Society, publ. 1985, Nortex Press, Austin, TX

[149] 544: Obituary of Josiah W. Rainwater, 17 Mar 1934, Vernon Daily Record, transcription

[150] http://en.wikipedia.org/wiki/Half_dime. A half dime is not a nickle, but a 5¢ coin that went in and out of fashion between 1792 and 1873. This coin is a 13-star Seated Liberty half dime, from the 1837-1873 era.

[151] Conversation with Betty Jo Rainwater Parker, Colorado Springs, Colorado, 18 Sept 1997

Despite writing a genealogical memoir, Josiah's youngest son, Roscoe, left no narrative describing his childhood. The Rainwater family experiences were probably similar to those of their neighbors. One of their neighbors, John Logan Tarter, described his childhood this way to a WPA researcher in the 1930s:[152]

> We raised and sold a few cattle, mules, hogs, sheep, chickens, geese and geese feathers. We grew apples and sold a little of those both green and dried. Also, we raised and sold some wheat and oats.
>
> Our shoes were made from the hides of cattle raised on our farm and tanned by the neighborhood tanner. The neighborhood shoemaker made the shoes. Our hats were, likewise, made by the local hatter. All of them craftsmen were paid corn, wheat and other produce of the farm.
>
> Mother and sisters knitted woolen socks and mittens, from yarn grown and spun by them, and sold hundreds of pairs. We lived on the supply of food produced on the farm and the clothes we wore was made from cloth that was spun and weaved from material produced on the farm. Father and the oldest boys trapped and hunted, and we made winter caps from the animals hides, also, coon and other skins were sold. We didn't need much money, because what was bought did not cost much and about the only things money was spent for were sugar, coffee, thread and buttons, and bees furnished the major portion of the sweets.
>
> The amusements, for the most part, was husking-bees, log-rollings for the men and quilting for the women, and once a year regularly the revival meeting for all.

By 1870, Josiah's parents, now in their 60s, were living in his home.[153] Though many of his relations and siblings were moving away, Josiah remained in Kentucky, tethered by the care of his aging parents. His mother, Nancy, died in 1883, and on 9 Jul 1889, Josiah wrote to inform his brother, Miles, of their father's death.

> Miles Rainwater
> Mehanna, Oregon
>
> Dear brother –
>
> You have no doubt before this noticed in The Republican of the sickness and death of father. He was stricken down on the night of the 20th of June and continued to git worse until he died, he was unconscious almost all the time from the stroke and he made but very

---

[152] 331: Reminiscences of J. L. Tarter, Tarrant Co., Texas, District S7, Document SFC240, Rangelore, WPA Federal Writers Project, Sheldon F. Gauthier, 1937
[153] Federal Census: 1870, Pulaski Co., KY, pg 168

little complaint, the greater part of the time appeared to be entirely easy.

He went to sleep about 3 o'clock PM on Wednesday and could not be aroused anymore, he apparently slept natural and easy from the time mentioned up to Friday, June 28" at 10 o'clock AM when he breathed his last, without a struggle. Everything was done for him that could be done, but human power could not save him. [154]

Immediately following Bartholomew's death, Josiah began to settle his affairs in Kentucky. He had determined to follow the lead of friends and family, and move to Texas, where the Caughrons, Comptons, Tarters, and Gossetts, had settled a few years earlier.[155]

In December 1890,[156] Josiah's family boarded a train and left for Texas.[157] The family arrived in Taylor in the middle of the night. They were met at the station by Charlie Gossett, who trooped them up Main Street on foot to his parents' house.[158]

Josiah soon acquired 300 acres of blackland prairie in the Caleb W. Baker survey[159] of Williamson Co., Texas.[160]

The family moved to or built a modest frame foursquare farm house, still standing in 1997. The rectangle of land is cut across on one corner by railroad tracks.[161] Here, Josiah took up farming and ran a small grocery store.

---

[154] 1880: Letter from Josiah W. Rainwater to Miles Rainwater, dated 9 Jul 1889, scan of original, from Mark Sanborn

[155] 491: The Autobiography of C. V. Compton, May 1950, pages 1-45 (incomplete), photocopy of original, from Betty C. Baskett

[156] Unpublished autobiographical sketch of Roscoe Rainwater written on First Guaranty State Bank stationary, original.

[157] Based on a 1910 copy of The Official Guide of the Railways that I located online (http://cprr.org/Museum/Official_Rail_Guide_1910.html), it appears they would have arrived in Taylor on an MKT train, but I was unable to discern by which line they might have left Somerset. I estimate the trip would have taken 4-5 days, with several changes of trains.

[158] 454: "Old in Years, Young In Spirit," (Mollie Rainwater Aderholt's 102nd birthday), 24 Apr 1981, newspaper clipping, Taylor Press, Taylor, Williamson Co., Texas, copy of original

[159] Texas Historical Association Online, http://www.tshaonline.org/, General Land Office article. Texas does not use the Public Land Survey System. Rather it uses an older method derived from Spanish Land Grants. Each of these grants still carries the name of the original grantee, or the person for whom the original legal survey was made, and in the case of Waterloo, TX, this was Caleb W. Baker.

[160] 133: Direct, General and Reverse Indexes to Deeds of Williamson Co., Texas, various volumes, Williamson County Courthouse, Georgetown, Texas, reviewed in person on 27 May 1997. We had the unusual experience of being sent down to the basement by ourselves to rummage unsupervised through hundred year old deed books. After about an hour, the entire staff of the courthouse came down into the basement because the tornado siren had sounded. Twelve miles north, the town of Jarrell, Texas was struck by an F5 tornado, which obliterated the subdivision of Double Creek Estates. We emerged to find large branches down all over the courthouse square, but no other damage. At the local newspaper office, we met a man from Jarrell who had run out behind his gas station with a 35mm film camera, photographed the tornado at close range and had the presence of mind to reload his camera and shoot another roll. We had difficulty finding a hotel room that evening because so many people had been displaced by the tornado.

[161] This land can be viewed using Google maps – a long rectangular tract fronting on CR 414, missing one corner where the road turns southeast.

Clara Stearns Scarborough's 1973 history of Williamson County mentions three pioneers who settled in this same part of the Caleb W. Baker survey – Josiah Rainwater, Jacob T. Bernard (who may have been a cousin), and Christian Gottfried Wuthrich, whose descendants owned Josiah's land in May 1997 when we visited.[162] When the first post office opened in May 1893, these men and their neighbors got together to name the community. They had been calling it Somerset, after the county seat of Pulaski Co., Kentucky, but this name was already taken in Texas. So Josiah suggested Waterloo, after his Kentucky hometown. The first postmaster was Patrick Green Tarter, Josiah's second cousin three times removed. Josiah served as postmaster in 1897 and 1901. At its height, the community contained two churches, a cotton gin, a post office, a blacksmith's shop, and the eighth largest school district in the county. By 1904, Waterloo had lost its post office, and by 1990, had a population of fewer than 60 people.[163]

One edge of Josiah's land bordered on Pecan Creek. Across the creek was the property of Emanuel M. Aderholt. Aderholt was as devoted to the Southern Cause as Josiah was to the Union. While serving in the 63rd Alabama Infantry, Aderholt had been captured at Blakely, Alabama, near Mobile Bay on 9 Apr 1865, and paroled at Meridian, Mississippi, on 13 May 1865. His month as a prisoner of war left him bitter towards Union men.[164] After the war, Aderholt had run a cotton gin in Springfield, St. Clair Co., Alabama. Having heard of a growing cotton town in Texas with railroad access and no gin, he moved with his second wife[165] to Waterloo and had his gin up and running by the fall of 1891.[166] Indeed, an abandoned cotton gin building was still standing on the land when we visited in 1997.

Emanuel Aderholt had a large family. Five sons and four daughters came to Texas; two sons remained behind in Alabama. Both the Rainwater and Aderholt families were Baptist, and their offspring soon became acquainted. So despite their fathers' antipathy, two Aderholt sons married two Rainwater daughters – John Pinkney Aderholt married Lucy Rainwater, and Charles A.

---

[162] We corresponded in June 1997 with Doris Meiske, the niece of the then owner, Tillie Wuthrich, then age 101, who was the daughter of Christian Gottfried Wuthrich. She confirmed that C. G. Wuthrich had purchased the land from Josiah Rainwater, but could not recall if the current house had been standing at the time of purchase, though it's of that era in an architectural sense.

[163] 94: Waterloo, page 464, Land of Good Water: Takachue Pouetsu. A Williamson County, Texas History, Clara Stearns Scarbrough, publ. 1973, Williamson County Sun Publishers, Georgetown, TX

132: Profile of Waterloo, Texas, Mark Odintz, A New Handbook of Texas, Vol. 6 SP-Z, pg 843, Texas State Historical Association

[164] 77: Profile of Emanual M. Aderholt by Frances Aderholt Smith, pg 47, Williamson Co., Texas: Its History and Its People, Williamson Co. Genealogical Society, publ. 1985, Nortex Press, Austin, TX

[165] His first wife was Saphronia Elizabeth Stone, 1851–1885. His second wife was Amanda James Madison Jones, 1855–1940.

[166] 94: Land of Good Water: Takachue Pouetsu. A Williamson County, Texas History, Clara Stearns Scarbrough, publ. 1973, Williamson County Sun Publishers, Georgetown, TX

Aderholt married Mollie Rainwater.[167] According to family legend, the two patriarchs never spoke to each other.

We don't know all of the reasons that motivated Josiah and so many of his children to relocate to Wilbarger County around 1907. His daughter Doretta and her husband Ranzy Luttrell appear to have been the first to make this move in 1906.[168] Eventually seven of Josiah's children and their families would make the move, all before 1910. Josiah later grumbled that he had been tricked, that the land in Wilbarger County was no better than the land in Williamson Co., and certainly the climate is a bit harsher.

If Wilbarger County did not exactly suit Josiah, he seems to have made the best of it. He joined the First Baptist Church of Vernon and became a deacon. He joined the Scottish Rite Masons and achieved the rank of Worshipful Master. He served on the school board from 1914 to 1927, and became a Director of First Guaranty State Bank.[169] From 1907 to 1919, he lived on a farm five miles northeast of Oklaunion.[170] At the age of 76, he retired from farming, and moved into the city of Vernon, where he spent the rest of his life.

Josiah Rainwater died on 16 Mar 1934 of heart failure and was buried in East View Cemetery, Vernon.[171]

In the opinion of several of her grandchildren, it was after her husband's death that Elizabeth Jane Rainwater blossomed. Her grandson, Gene Rainwater, recalled that she bought an electric refrigerator, something Josiah would have spurned as unnecessary luxury, but Gene had to explain to her where the ice cubes came from. Because Elizabeth Jane was somewhat afraid of being alone at night, Miles Rainwater sent his youngest daughter to sleep at the house every evening, and Betty Jo came to know her grandmother better than any of the other grandchildren. Betty Jo recalled to us watching her grandmother make a patchwork quilt that contained the names of all of the grandchildren.[172]

Elizabeth Jane Weddle Rainwater died on 25 Jun 1943 of bronchitis and pneumonia, contracted after going out in a driving rain storm to put up the chickens.[173] She is buried with her husband in East View Cemetery, Vernon.[174]

---

[167] 57: Josiah Rainwater family Bible, photocopy of original

[168] 94: Land of Good Water: Takachue Pouetsu. A Williamson County, Texas History, Clara Stearns Scarbrough, publ. 1973, Williamson County Sun Publishers, Georgetown, TX

[169] 77: Williamson Co., Texas: Its History and Its People, Williamson Co., Genealogical Society, publ. 1985, Nortex Press, Austin, TX

[170] 328: Civil War pension papers of Josiah W. Rainwater and Elizabeth Jane Weddle Rainwater, 10 May 1879–2 Apr 1934

[171] 1418: Rainwater & related tombstones in East View Cemetery, Vernon, Wilbarger Co., Texas, photos by R. Steven Rainwater and Susan Rainwater, April 1997. Additional photos by Randy Rainwater, 29 Jan 2006.

[172] Conversation with Betty Jo Rainwater Parker, Colorado Springs, Colorado, 18 Sept 1997

[173] Eugene Walter Rainwater, grandson of Josiah Rainwater

[174] 1418: Rainwater & related tombstones in East View Cemetery, Vernon, Wilbarger Co., Texas, photos by R. Steven Rainwater and Susan Rainwater, April 1997. Additional photos by Randy

The children of Josiah and Elizabeth Jane Rainwater:

Rainwater reunion, 1916, Wilbarger Co., Texas

Martha Jane Rainwater Rainwater

Born 24 Oct 1866, Pulaski Co., Kentucky and died 2 Aug 1961, Wilbarger Co., Texas

On 28 Jun 1893, Martha Rainwater married her second cousin, Peter C. Rainwater in Williamson Co., Texas.[175] They were the parents of five children, four of whom lived to adulthood. The couple is buried in East View Cemetery, Vernon.[176]

Nancy Frances Rainwater Gossett

Born 28 Aug 1869, Pulaski Co., Kentucky and died 3 Aug 1942, Williamson Co., Texas

Nannie, as she was called, married Charles Gossett on 15 Nov 1893 in Williamson Co., Texas.[177] They were the parents of five children, four of whom lived to adulthood. In his youth, Charles was a transfer driver. He owned several teams of mules and horses and with his wagons hauled (or transferred) baled cotton from the cotton yards to the cotton presses. Gossett Feed & Produce grew out of the original business. Founded in 1898, it was still growing in 1956, but had gone into decline by 1990 when the building was torn down.[178] The Gossetts are

---

Rainwater, 29 Jan 2006.

[175] Their common ancestors were William and Martha Hodges Rainwater. William and Martha's son Bartholomew was the grandfather of Martha Jane; Bartholomew's brother Abraham was the grandfather of Peter C.

[176] 1418: Rainwater & related tombstones in East View Cemetery, Vernon, Wilbarger Co., Texas, photos by R. Steven Rainwater and Susan Rainwater, April 1997. Additional photos by Randy Rainwater, 29 Jan 2006.

[177] 82: Williamson Co., TX Marriage Records, Vol 2, Books 2-3-4-5,1860-1884, and Books 6-7-8, 1885-1900, Frances T. Ingmire, from original records compiled by J. Stoddard, publ. 1985, St. Louis, MO

buried in Taylor City Cemetery, Williamson County.[179] Frances Aderholt Smith, who has provided us with much valuable information on the Rainwater line, is a granddaughter of this couple.

Lucy Isadore Rainwater Aderholt

Born 7 Jan 1872, Pulaski Co., Kentucky and died 12 Jan 1963, Wilbarger Co., Texas

Lucy was named for her Aunt Lucy Weddle Cooper. On 14 Dec 1892, she and her sister Doretta had a double wedding – Doretta married Ranzy Luttrell, and Lucy married John Pinkney Aderholt.[180] Pink, as he was known, was a farmer, a cotton gin engineer during the season and a carpenter out of season.[181] Lucy and Pink joined Taylor Baptist Church the year after they were married.[182] They were the parents of five children all of whom lived to adulthood. The family moved to Wilbarger County in 1907, and many of the family members are buried in East View Cemetery, Vernon.[183]

Doretta Rainwater Luttrell

Born 18 Mar 1874, Pulaski Co., Kentucky and died 6 Apr 1966, Wichita Co., Texas

Doretta was named for her Aunt Doretta Weddle Gosser. She married fellow Kentuckian Ranza Lee Luttrell, known as Ranzy, in a double wedding with her sister.[184] Ranzy was primarily a farmer, though he served as postmaster of the post office in Waterloo, Texas, in 1895.[185] They were the parents of six children, one of whom died at birth. The family moved to Wilbarger County in 1906 and purchased 200 acres in

---

[178] 450: "Gossett Feed In Business Since 1898," 23 Nov 1956, Taylor Press, Taylor, Williamson Co., Texas, photocopy

[179] 496: Taylor City Cemetery Sexton's Records, Taylor, Williamson Co., Texas, seen in person
   1423: Taylor City Cemetery, Taylor, Williamson Co., Texas, Compton, Caughron, Aderholt & Gossett tombstones, photos by R. Steven Rainwater and Susan Rainwater, Feb 1997 and May 1997

[180] 82: Williamson Co., TX Marriage Records, Vol 2, Books 2-3-4-5,1860-1884, and Books 6-7-8, 1885-1900, Frances T. Ingmire, from original records compiled by J. Stoddard, publ. 1985, St. Louis, MO

[181] 77: Williamson Co., Texas: Its History and Its People, Williamson Co., Genealogical Society, publ. 1985, Nortex Press, Austin, TX

[182] 77: Williamson Co., Texas: Its History and Its People, Williamson Co., Genealogical Society, publ. 1985, Nortex Press, Austin, TX

[183] 1418: Rainwater & related tombstones in East View Cemetery, Vernon, Wilbarger Co., Texas, photos by R. Steven Rainwater and Susan Rainwater, April 1997. Additional photos by Randy Rainwater, 29 Jan 2006.

[184] 82: Williamson Co., TX Marriage Records, Vol 2, Books 2-3-4-5,1860-1884, and Books 6-7-8, 1885-1900, Frances T. Ingmire, from original records compiled by J. Stoddard, publ. 1985, St. Louis, MO

[185] 94: Land of Good Water: Takachue Pouetsu. A Williamson Co., Texas History, pg 464, Clara Stearns Scarbrough, publ. 1973, Williamson County Sun Publishers, Georgetown, TX

the Elliott community[186]. Many of the family members are buried in East View Cemetery, Vernon.[187]

Miles Rainwater

Miles Rainwater

Born 15 Jun 1876, Pulaski Co., Kentucky and died 20 May 1956, Wilbarger Co., Texas
On 16 Mar 1898, Miles married fellow Kentuckian Ollie Frances Cooper.[188] Her family was from Pulaski Co., and she was descended from the same Gossett line as Charles Gossett, Miles' sister Nannie's husband.[189] In 1904, he sold his land in Williamson County to his father and moved his family by covered wagon to Temple, Cotton Co., Oklahoma.[190] One can only assume that things did not work out, because by 1907, he had moved to Wilbarger Co., Texas. Miles and

---
[186] 83: Luttrell Profile, pg 243, Wilbarger Co., Texas History, Sylvia Jones, editor, Wilbarger Co. Historical Comsn., publ. 1986, Vernon, TX

[187] 1418: Rainwater & related tombstones in East View Cemetery, Vernon, Wilbarger Co., Texas, photos by R. Steven Rainwater and Susan Rainwater, April 1997. Additional photos by Randy Rainwater, 29 Jan 2006.

[188] 57: Josiah Rainwater family Bible, photocopy of original

[189] Federal Census: 1880, Pulaski Co., Kentucky, pg 383, household of William T. and Mattie Cooper

[190] 83: Rainwater–Koontz Profile, pg 224, Wilbarger Co., Texas History, Sylvia Jones, editor, Wilbarger Co. Historical Commission, publ. 1986, Vernon, TX

Ollie were the parents of eight children, including Betty Jo Parker, to whom we are indebted for much of our information on Elizabeth Jane Weddle Rainwater. The couple is buried in East View Cemetery, Vernon.[191]

Mary "Mollie" Rainwater Aderholt

Born 28 Apr 1879, Pulaski Co., Kentucky and died 4 Nov 1984, Williamson Co., Texas

Mollie Rainwater Aderholt was the longest-lived Rainwater in the entire Rainwater clan, nationwide. She lived to 106, outliving her husband and at least two of her children. A plaque honoring her 100th birthday hangs in the lobby of the First Baptist Church of Taylor.[192] Mollie married Charles Aderholt on 22 Dec 1898,[193] and they were the parents of six daughters, one of whom died at birth. The Aderholts are buried in Taylor City Cemetery, Taylor.[194]

Cornelia Rainwater Gaston

Born 17 Apr 1881, Pulaski Co., Kentucky and died 17 Oct 1967, Los Angeles Co., California

On 29 Oct 1902, Neely, as she was called, married Alva Fenton Gaston.[195] The couple moved from Williamson County to Wilbarger County in 1907. They were a farm family, the parents of seven children, and members of the Bethel Baptist Church.[196] Following Alva's death in 1949, Neely moved to Los Angeles to live with her eldest daughter, Louise. She died there in 1967. Alva and Cornelia are buried in East View Cemetery, Vernon.[197]

---

[191] 1418: Rainwater & related tombstones in East View Cemetery, Vernon, Wilbarger Co., Texas, photos by R. Steven Rainwater and Susan Rainwater, April 1997. Additional photos by Randy Rainwater, 29 Jan 2006.

[192] 1885: Plaque presented to Molly Rainwater Aderholt (Mrs. Charles) on her 100th birthday by the congregation of 1st Baptist Church of Taylor, Texas, photographed May 1997

[193] 57: Josiah Rainwater family Bible, photocopy of original

[194] 496: Taylor City Cemetery Sexton's Records, Taylor, Williamson Co., TX, seen in person (no copies)

1423: Taylor City Cemetery, Taylor, Williamson Co., TX, Compton, Caughron, Aderholt & Gossett tombstones, photos by Susan & R. Steven Rainwater, Feb 1997 and May 1997

[195] 57: Josiah Rainwater family Bible, photocopy of original

[196] 83: Wilbarger Co., Texas History, Sylvia Jones, editor, Wilbarger Co. Historical Commission, publ. 1986, Vernon, TX

[197] 1418: Rainwater & related tombstones in East View Cemetery, Vernon, Wilbarger Co., Texas, photos by R. Steven Rainwater and Susan Rainwater, April 1997. Additional photos by Randy Rainwater, 29 Jan 2006.

Roscoe Conklin Rainwater

Born 4 Jul 1883, Pulaski Co., Kentucky and died 8 Nov 1972, Wilbarger Co., Texas
See profile of Roscoe C. Rainwater and Gertrude Alice Caughron

Minnie Rainwater Brownlee

Born 15 Jul 1885, Pulaski Co., Kentucky and died 15 Jul 1971, Wichita Co., Texas
On 27 Feb 1908, Minnie married John H. Brownlee.[198] He was a banker, rancher and oil man.[199] Their first two children died shortly after birth.[200] The couple then adopted two children, Wilma and Robert Maurice. A third biological son, Jack, was born in 1925. The census indicates that Minnie worked as a life insurance agent. John Brownlee died in 1938.[201] Around 1955, Minnie married Thomas Powers, who died in 1960.[202] Minnie's death certificate was issued under the surname Powers, but she is buried under the name Brownlee.[203] Minnie and John Brownlee are buried in East View Cemetery, Vernon.[204]

---

[198] 57: Josiah Rainwater family Bible, photocopy of original
[199] Federal Census: 1910, Wilbarger Co., TX, pg 97; 1920, Deaf Smith Co., TX, pg 117B; 1930, Wichita Co., TX, pg 184
[200] 2312 Findagrave.com #23252732 and #23252863, East View Cemetery, Wilbarger Co., TX
[201] 2568: Death certificate #26351; John Brownlee, 19 Jun 1939, Temple, Bell Co., TX, scan from microfilm
[202] 108: Roscoe Rainwater, genealogical notes and files
[203] 1592: Texas Death Index online database, Rootsweb, 1964-1998, and Ancestry.com (paywalled), 1903-2000
[204] 1418: Rainwater & related tombstones in East View Cemetery, Vernon, Wilbarger Co., Texas, photos by R. Steven Rainwater and Susan Rainwater, April 1997. Additional photos by Randy Rainwater, 29 Jan 2006.

Roscoe Conklin Rainwater and Gertrude Alice Caughron

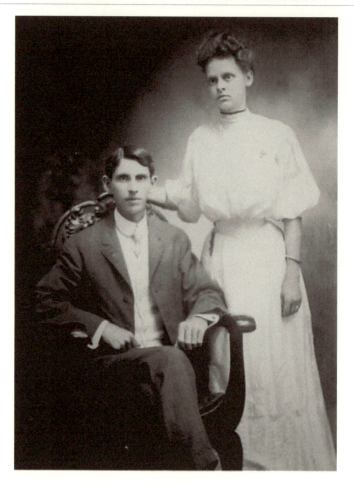

Roscoe and Gertrude Rainwater, c. 1906

Roscoe Conklin Rainwater
Son of Josiah Wilson Rainwater and Elizabeth Jane Weddle
Born 4 Jul 1883, Pulaski Co., Kentucky
Died 8 Nov 1972, Vernon, Wilbarger Co., Texas

Married 23 May 1906, Taylor, Williamson Co., Texas

Gertrude Alice Caughron
Daughter of Theophilus Walter Caughron and Arzona Belle Compton
Born 19 Oct 1884, Taylor, Williamson Co., Texas
Died 17 Aug 1969, Vernon, Wilbarger Co., Texas

Our genealogical research began in 1991 with a flimsy department store box containing the research notes, drafts, and writings of Roscoe Rainwater.[205] Among the yellowing newspaper clippings and letters were two drafts of an autobiography that never made it into the final version of *Here's the Plan of the Rainwater Clan*. In these sketches, Roscoe said of himself:

> Born in a log house at Waterloo, Kentucky, July 4th 1883. In December 1890, moved with family to Williamson Co., Texas.[206]

Between these two sentences, seven years vanish. Roscoe took a trip back to Kentucky in 1966, with his wife, daughter Cristine, and her husband, Lee. He clearly remembered Kentucky fondly enough to return, yet he never wrote a word about the first seven years of his childhood, and very little about his early years in Texas.

Roscoe Rainwater was born into a generation of men who left the farm. They left in droves – to become teachers, store clerks, bookkeepers, railroad agents, newspaper writers; in short, they were the first generation of the white collar middle class. And it affected the women as well as the men. Scores of young women attended one or two-year Normal Schools (teacher's colleges) and got their teaching certificates. I have seen this phenomenon in every family I have researched.

In Roscoe's writing , it's clear that he thought of his life starting when he earned his teaching certificate in August 1901. He received Second Grade certification, which allowed him to teach high school students at Sandavol, Texas, the following year.[207] Apparently this occupation did not suit, because in the summer of 1903 he attended Hill's Business College in Waco to study accounting, stenography (shorthand) and banking.[208] He taught at Lawson Springs for the 1903-04 school year, then returned that summer to complete his studies at Hill's.

Following graduation, Roscoe accepted a position with J. E. Stevens & Sons in Coleman, Texas, as a bookkeeper and stenographer. He was paid $65 per month. The following February he took a position in Laredo, which lasted about two months. He then found employment in Houston with the Southern Pacific Railroad, quitting in July of the same year to sign on with the Isthmian Canal Commission. He was initially employed as a stenographer in

---

[205] Like the hundreds of other Roscoe Conklins, he was named for Senator Roscoe Conkling (1829-1888), a popular Republican politician from New York. I have 31 Roscoes in my database, all of this generation, all related.

[206] 108: Two draft copies of Roscoe Rainwater's autobiograpy. The undated sketch covers 1890-1925. The sketch dated 1965 covers 1890-1929, plus some minor present day information. These two documents and the Greenbelt Profile from the Vernon Daily Record are our primary sources for Roscoe.

[207] 108: The 1965 draft says he earned a First Grade Teaching Certificate (Elementary School). The undated draft says he earned a Second Grade Teaching Certificate (High School).

[208] 461: "Roscoe Rainwater: Panama Duty Career Highlight," Greenbelt Profile, Vernon Daily Record, Vernon, Wilbarger Co., Texas, Jan 1963, original clipping

the Auditor's Office for a salary of $125 per month. In less than a year, he had doubled his income.

Roscoe left for Panama on 19 Jul 1905 from the port of New Orleans on the S.S. Ellis, and arrived in Colón, Panama on the 24th. He was sent by rail roughly 50 miles to Panama City on the Pacific side of the narrow country, only to discover that no quarters had been prepared for the employees. This city of 45,000 inhabitants had no water system, no sewers, and unpaved streets. It took the Commission over 18 months to remedy the situation. So if typhoid and cholera failed to kill the residents, then there were always the regular outbreaks of yellow fever, malaria, and bubonic plague to look forward to.[209]

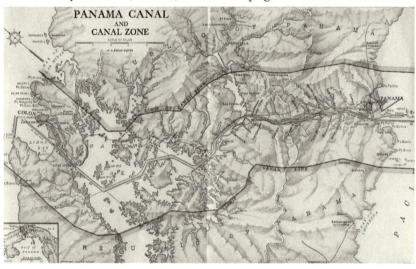

*Map of the Panama Canal Zone from "Panama and The Canal in Pictures and Prose" by Willis J. Abbot
publ. 1913 by the Syndicate Publishing Company, New York*

After nine months on the job, Roscoe returned to Taylor, Texas, to get married. He arrived at Ellis Island, New York, on the S.S. Advance out of Colón on 29 Apr 1906 and headed home to Taylor on the train.[210]

On 23 May 1906, at the close of the Sunday evening service, Rev. J. A. Arbuckle invited the congregation to remain for the wedding of Roscoe Rainwater and Gertrude Alice Caughron. Gertrude was the daughter of T. W. Caughron and Arzona Belle Compton, both Pulaski Countians.

The bride wore white organdy and the groom a business suit. Friends returned with them to the Caughron home for punch and cookies, and a couple of talented locals played the piano and sang sentimental Victorian songs. The

---

[209] "*The Panama Canal*," The American Experience, WGBH, Boston, MA

[210] 2072: The Statue of Liberty and Ellis Island Foundation, American Family Immigration History Center, ships passenger list archives online

following day, the couple boarded the "Katy" (Missouri-Kansas-Texas Railroad). Their honeymoon took them to Dallas, St. Louis, Washington D.C., and eventually New York, where they boarded a ship for Colón.[211]

Roscoe and his new bride returned to Panama City for six months, and then moved to the newly completed administration center at Empire, which included 300 staff housing units.

In June 1906, he was promoted to Private Secretary to the Auditor and Disbursing Officer, with another pay raise to $150 per month plus quarterly bonuses of $150. In November 1906, he became a Receiving Teller. He was promoted again in May 1907, to Pay Clerk, a position he held until his resignation in August 1909. Roscoe's 1963 interview with the Vernon Daily News described his work as a Pay Clerk in detail:

> He became one of five paymasters who rode in a railway pay car along the canal route, meeting a very close schedule in which they were met by groups of workers who filed through the pay car past special teller windows.
>
> Four of the paymasters, including Mr. Rainwater, paid the workmen in silver, issued to the paymasters in bags of $1,000 each which weighed 55 pounds per bag. A fifth teller paid in gold coin. The paymasters averaged disbursing $100,000 each per day during a four-day trip across the Isthmus, then spent the fifth day balancing up. They made up any shortages out of their own pocket, including possible losses for forged time cards.
>
> Although one paymaster lost several hundred dollars to forgeries on a single trip - all later recovered - Mr. Rainwater luckily never had to make up any such losses.[212]

Roscoe and Gertrude returned to Texas for a vacation in August 1909, and upon reflection, decided not to return to the Canal. During their time in Panama, they had brought their first child into the world, Roscoe Compton Rainwater, called Comp, born at Empire on 1 Oct 1908. The other children were born in Oklaunion, Wilbarger Co., Texas – Cristine Minnie, born in 1910, Johnie Wayne, born in 1913, Walter Eugene, born in 1915, and Clois Miles, born in 1923.[213]

Gertrude would later recall that, when she visited her relations in Taylor, she would take up the hems on Christine's dresses to please her fashion-conscious sisters, and then let them down on the train trip back to Vernon to please her

---

[211] 462: "Happily Wed," 23 May 1906, Taylor, Williamson Co., Texas, Rainwater-Caughron wedding, original newspaper clipping
463: "Orange Blossoms," 23 May 1906, Taylor, Williamson Co., Texas, Rainwater-Caughron wedding, original newspaper clipping
[212] 461: "Roscoe Rainwater: Panama Duty Career Highlight," Greenbelt Profile, Vernon Daily Record, Vernon, Wilbarger Co., Texas, Jan 1963, original clipping
[213] 17: Roscoe Rainwater, "Here's the Plan of the Rainwater Clan," genealogical document, 1972

conservative husband.[214] Though her granddaughter, Linda Rainwater Davis, recalls Gertrude being a happy person, she was apparently quite camera-shy – no photo shows her smiling.

In July 1909, Roscoe took a job with the King Bank and Mercantile Company in Elliott and remained there for three years. In 1913, he bought out the King brothers and ran the mercantile business until 1920. At the same time, he became involved in organizing First Guaranty State Bank, where he became Chief Cashier and President. He also took an interest in local activities, becoming a deacon in the Baptist Church, Sunday school teacher, choir director, 32° Mason and Shriner, as well as a member of numerous civic service clubs.

In 1920, Roscoe sold out of the mercantile business, though he continued to own a hardware store in Elliott. He purchased 3,500 acres of farmland, which he planted in cotton and grain. After First Guaranty State Bank failed in 1929,[215] he moved from Oklaunion to Vernon and focused his business acumen on the Rainwater Insurance Agency, which he had started in 1909. This became his primary business interest, from which he retired in 1961, when his son Johnie took over. In retirement, Roscoe's income derived from a number of rental houses that he owned. Despite all of his accomplishments, his years with the Isthmian Canal Commission remained his defining moment and his business cards identified him as "*The Big Ditch Digger*," even though he had never turned a shovelful of dirt in Panama.

Roscoe's genealogical interests had started in the 1930s or 1940s[216], but it was in 1966 when inspiration struck to visit his "*old Kentucky home*." With several family members, he packed up the car for an extended visit. He found Waterloo all but gone, only the old schoolhouse remained. Bartholomew Rainwater's home was gone, and the road to Josiah's homestead, on which he had lived as a child, so thicketed over that it was impassable by car. He visited the courthouse, living cousins, and dead relatives in cemeteries. Whether he found what he was looking for he never makes clear, despite a long letter written in May 1966 describing the trip.

In August 1969, Gertrude Rainwater fell, and, as is often the case, the fall was a prelude to death. She had broken her jaw and was taken into surgery; but she never came out. Gertrude died on the operating table on 17 Aug 1969[217] and is buried in Wilbarger Memorial Park, Lockett.[218]

---

[214] 19: Conversations with Nancy McIlhaney Rainwater, between 1991 and 1997

[215] Roscoe's autobiography says that he retired in 1929, but Randy Rainwater recalls being told that his grandfather's bank had failed during the Depression, which given the coincidence of the year seems right.

[216] His earliest notes are so dated.

[217] 350: Death certificate #68705, Gertrude Alice Rainwater, Wilbarger Co., TX, 1969, certified copy

[218] 2234: Rainwaters in Wilbarger Memorial Park, US 70 S, Lockett, Wilbarger Co., TX, photos by Randy Rainwater, 28 Jan 2006

All of Roscoe's descendants say that part of Roscoe died that day, that he was never the same. In May 1972, possibly sensing the end, he sent to his children, grandchildren, and fellow researchers his genealogical opus, "*Here's the Plan of the Rainwater Clan.*" Like every genealogical document ever written (including the one you are now reading), it contains mistakes, but they are minor ones and unintentional.

Roscoe checked into the hospital in November of that year for exploratory surgery, under the belief that he was suffering a recurrence of colon cancer. He wasn't. But he contracted hepatitis from a transfusion he was given during surgery, and died on 17 Nov 1972.[219] He is buried with Gertrude and other family members in Wilbarger Memorial Park, Lockett. The Vernon Blue Lodge of Scottish Rite Masons rendered full Masonic honors at his funeral.[220]

The children of Roscoe and Gertrude Rainwater:

Roscoe Compton Rainwater

> Born 1 Oct 1908, Empire, Panama, and died 13 Dec 1993, Arlington, Tarrant Co., Texas
> Comp, as he was called, married Daisy Jane Rutland in 1934 in Fort Worth, Texas. He was a rural mail carrier, and she had been a teacher prior to their marriage. They were the parents of three children. Comp and Daisy are buried in Moore Memorial Gardens, Arlington.[221]

Cristine Minnie Rainwater Fletcher Lee

> Born 5 Dec 1910, Oklaunion, Wilbarger Co., Texas, and died 9 Sep 1989, Orange Co., California
> Cristine was married to and divorced from Earl Fletcher, between 1931 and 1939.[222] She served in the US Navy as a Chief Petty Officer in the Waves[223] during World War II. She remained in the Navy as a director of Wave recruiting in Texas until 1953, when she was assigned the job of Assistant to Secretary of the Navy, R. B. Anderson.[224]

> In 1956, she was stationed at Pearl Harbor in Hawaii, where she met her second husband, Leonard Lee, whom everyone called Lee. Lee's loudness and neediness simply wore out everyone he met. The Rainwater family thought him a fast talker and didn't trust him.

---

[219] 351: Death certificate #87001, Roscoe Rainwater, Wilbarger Co., TX, 1972, certified copy
[220] 494: Obituary; Roscoe Rainwater, Nov 1972, Vernon Daily Record, Vernon, TX, original newspaper article
[221] 1426: Rainwater tombstones in Moore Memorial Gardens, Randol Mill at Davis Road, Arlington, Tarrant Co., TX, photos by Susan & R. Steven Rainwater, 3 Sept 2001
[222] Federal Census: 1940, Beaumont, Jefferson Co., TX, pg 270B, divorced, surnamed Fletcher
[223] Wikipedia: WAVES, http://en.wikipedia.org/wiki/WAVES. WAVES stood for Women Accepted for Volunteer Emergency Service
[224] 2531: "Wave Secretary Helps Anderson," 9 Jan 1953, Wichita Falls Record News, Wichita Falls, Texas

Cristine's inheritance was structured to prevent Lee from having access to her money.²²⁵ She retired from the Navy in 1963, becoming an insurance agent, and later an insurance adjuster with her husband. She died on 9 Sep 1989, and is buried in Wilbarger Memorial Park, Lockett.²²⁶ Lee remarried in 1990. His second wife, Mary Louise Jensen Phillips, died in 2011, and Lee died in 2012, both in McKinney, Texas.

Johnie Wayne Rainwater

Born 29 Jun 1913, Wilbarger Co., Texas and died 19 Jun 1996, Vernon, Wilbarger Co., Texas

Johnie joined the Navy on 1 Jan 1942, and was married on 11 Jul 1942, to his high school sweetheart, Mary Katherine "Kay" Barnett. He served in the Atlantic theater of operations until 1944, when he was transferred to the Pacific. He was a Chief Yeoman on the U.S.S. Oahu. After the war, he worked for Bentz Printing Company, the Vernon Daily Record, and Montgomery Ward, before taking over his father's insurance business. He was elected mayor of Vernon in 1958, and served a 2-year term.²²⁷ Johnie and Kay were the parents of two children. He died on 19 Jun 1996, and is buried in Wilbarger Memorial Park, Lockett.²²⁸

Walter Eugene Rainwater

Born 18 Jul 1915, Oklaunion, Wilbarger Co., Texas, and is still living in 2013

Gene volunteered for the Army Air Corps in March 1941, trained as a navigator, and achieved the rank of Captain during his service. He earned a degree from Texas Tech and married Georgia Isbell in 1946. They are the parents of two children. Gene worked for the IRS until retirement. He and Georgia are active in the Baptist Church, the Optimists Club and used their military retiree privileges to travel the world.

Clois Miles Rainwater

Born 12 Mar 1923, Wilbarger Co., Texas, and died 9 Jan 2010, Bonham, Fannin Co., Texas

See profile of Clois Miles Rainwater and Nancy Jane McIlhaney

---

²²⁵ 330: Will of Roscoe Rainwater, 14 Nov 1972, Wilbarger Co., TX

²²⁶ 2234: Rainwaters in Wilbarger Memorial Park, US 70 S, Lockett, Wilbarger Co., TX, photos by Randy Rainwater, 28 Jan 2006

²²⁷ History of Elected Officials, Vernon, Texas official city website, http://www.vernontx.gov

²²⁸ 2536: Obituary, Johnie W. Rainwater, 20 June 1996, Vernon Daily Record, Vernon, Wilbarger Co., TX, photocopy of original

Back L>R: Roscoe, Gertrude, Compton, Johnie
Front L>R: Clois, Cristine, Gene
Roscoe and Gertrude's 50th anniversary, 1956, with children

John Tarter and Catherine Logan

John Tarter
Born between 1760 and 1770, Virginia
Died c. 1849, Pulaski Co., Kentucky

Married in or before 1779

Catherine Logan
Born before 1769
Died before 1850, Pulaski Co., Kentucky

There are two commonly-used references for the Tarter family: Oscar H. Darter's "*The Darter-Tarter Family*," published in 1965, and Elmerlee Tarter Oakley's "*The Kentucky Tarters*," published in 1981. Both books are flawed and contain numerous unsupported assertions.[229]

Oscar Darter traces the family to the arrival in 1750 of Johann Anton Doerter at the port of Philadelphia. Born in Laubach, Germany, Doerter had sailed on the Patience, and is recorded as having taken an oath of allegiance upon his arrival.[230]

Whether Doerter is the progenitor of the Tarter family is unclear. His son, Balzer Darter, made his home in Wythe Co., Virginia, and left a will naming some, but not all of his children. Elmerlee Tarter Oakley makes a leap of faith to connect Balzer Darter to John Tarter supported only by the phrase in his will, "*my three younger sons*." Oakley conveniently assumes that John Tarter is one of the unnamed sons. Oscar Darter, on the other hand, believes that John Tarter was the son of Balzer's brother Jacob, but his date evidence makes little sense.

Pulaski County historian, Alma Owens Tibbals, says John is the son of [Peter] Christian Tarter, a Revolutionary War veteran originally from Germany, who settled in Pennsylvania.[231] There actually was a Peter C. Tarter who was born in Pennsylvania, served in the Revolutionary War, and moved to Pulaski County.[232] He had a son named John, who married Nancy Lawrence in

---

[229] 229: Elmerlee Tarter Oakley, "*The Kentucky Tarters*," 1981, Jet Press reprint, Hopkinsville, KY
238: Oscar H. Darter, "*The Darter-Tarter Family*," publ. 1965, Garrett and Massie Inc., Richmond, VA

[230] 275: New World Imigrants, Vol. 2, Michael Tepper, editor, publ. 1980, Genealogical Publishing Company, Baltimore, MD. Passenger list of The Patience, 1750, port of Philadelphia.

[231] 58: A History of Pulaski Co., Kentucky, pg 54, Alma Owens Tibbals, publ. 1952, Moore Publishers, Bagdad, KY

[232] 74: Genealogical Abstracts of Revolutionary War Pension Files, Vol 3, N-Z, pg 3411, Virgil D. White, publ. 1992, National Historical Publishing Co., Waynesboro, TN

1826.²³³ But "our" John, died in 1849 and Peter's John is still living in the 1860 census.²³⁴ So Tibbals has confused the two John Tarters, as so many people do.

Then there are the popular 19th century biography books containing florid profiles of notable men. The biography of John Tarter's great-grandson, Judge Jerome T. Tarter, says John Tarter was born in Germany.²³⁵ The profile of James Ballinger Tarter, M.D., another great-grandson, says John Tarter was born in Virginia, and, in the same volume, the biography of Professor Add Tarter indicates that John Tarter was born in Ireland.²³⁶ So it should be clear at this point that it's practically impossible to say for certain. I lean to Virginia, because his first three children were born there.

John Tarter was born between 1760 and 1770.²³⁷ In or before 1779, he married. Most sources name his wife Catherine Logan. A few sources call her Nancy Logan, apparently conflating her with Nancy Lawrence. The name Catherine appears on an 1842 deed along with her husband's name,²³⁸ so I lean to Catherine. The only support for her surname, Logan, is that it was her eldest son's middle name.

John and Catherine had eleven, possibly twelve children, whose birthplaces describe the couple's migration. Christiana and Jacob were born in Virginia. Nancy was born in North Carolina. The rest – Jesse, Millie, Alfred, William, Eliza, Celia, Sally, and Ephriam – were born in Kentucky between 1800 and 1819.²³⁹

John Tarter arrived in Pulaski County after the 1800 census. In 1806, he purchased 150 acres on King's Creek and, over the years, added at least another 120 acres to his holdings.²⁴⁰ He is recorded in the Federal Census records of Pulaski County in 1810, 1820 and 1840, but not in 1850.

So we assume John Tarter died in 1849 or very early 1850, based on the flurry of probate filings with the county court. He left no will, so the estate was inventoried by a representative of the court, assessed for taxes, and a settlement

---

[233] 49: Pulaski Co., KY Marriage Records, Vol 1, 1797-1850, 2nd edition, Mary Weddle Kaurish, publ. 1984, Pulaski County Historical Society, Somerset, KY

[234] Federal Census: 1860, Pulaski Co., KY, pg 272

[235] 239, Profile of Hon. J. T. Tarter, pg 988, Kentucky: A History of the State, W. H. Perrin, G. C. Kniffin, and J. H. Battle, publ. 1888, F. A. Battey and Co., Louisville, KY

[236] 59: pgs 434-435 and 481-482

[237] Federal Census: 1840, Pulaski Co., KY, pg 332, lists John Tarter as a man between 70 and 80 years of age.

[238] 58: A History of Pulaski Co., KY, Alma Owens Tibbals, publ. 1952, Moore Publishers, Bagdad, KY

[239] Alfred's only census record, 1850, says he was born in Virginia, but, datewise, this is very unlikely

[240] 90: Kentucky Land Grants, Parts 1 & 2, 1782-1924, Willard Rouse Jillson, ScD, publ. 1971, Genealogical Publ. Co., Baltimore, MD

was made among the heirs.[241] The final settlement of his estate, filed with the courts in 1854, totaled over $1600, a considerable sum in those days.[242]

Because no Catherine Tarter of the right age is found in the 1850 census, and because she is not mentioned in the settlement of the estate, we assume she also died before 1850.

The children of John Tarter and Catherine Logan:

Christian Logan Tarter

> Born 1788, Wythe Co., Virginia[243], and died c. 1863, Pulaski Co., Kentucky[244]
> Chrisley, as he is called in most records, married Elizabeth Rayburn Trimble on 23 Nov 1817, in Pulaski Co., Kentucky.[245] They were the parents of six children. Chrisley was a blacksmith and owned a considerable amount of land on King's Creek, White Oak Creek, and Wolf Creek.[246] Family legend says that during the Civil War a gang of Confederate deserters broke into his home and tortured him in an attempt to locate the money he was said to have hidden on the property. He died of his injuries and is buried in Coffey Chapel Cemetery in Russell Co., Kentucky.[247]

Jacob Tarter

> Born 21 Nov 1795, Wythe Co., Virginia, and died 19 Nov 1874, Russell Co., Kentucky
> *See profile of Jacob Tarter and his three wives*

---

[241] 53: Pulaski Co., KY Index to Wills, 1800-1935, Pulaski County Historical Society, publ. 1977, Somerset, KY

[242] 1404: Final administrator's report on the estate of John Tarter, 29 May 1854, Pulaski Co., Kentucky, Will Book 4, pg 328-329. This is the last of seven documents that constitute the probate of John Tarter's estate.

[243] 1860 Federal Census, Russell Co., KY, pg 761

[244] 53: Pulaski Co., KY Index to Wills, 1800-1935, pg 70, Pulaski County Historical Society, publ. 1977, Somerset, KY. Inventory and Administration, Book 6 pg 161, & Sale Bill, Book 6 pg 163.

[245] 49: Pulaski Co., KY Marriage Records, Vol 1, 1797-1850, 2nd edition, pg 140, Mary Weddle Kaurish, publ. 1984, Pulaski County Historical Society, Somerset, KY

[246] 90: Kentucky Land Grants, Parts 1 & 2, 1782-1924, Willard Rouse Jillson, ScD, publ. 1971, Genealogical Publ. Co., Baltimore, MD

[247] 58: A History of Pulaski Co., Kentucky, page 54, Alma Owens Tibbals, publ. 1952, Moore Publishers, Bagdad, KY, and 239: Kentucky: A History of the State, W. H. Perrin, G. C. Kniffin, and J. H. Battle, publ. 1888, F. A. Battey and Co., Louisville, KY

Nancy Tarter Trimble

Born c. 1799, North Carolina, and died 13 Mar 1862, Kentucky[248]
Nancy married David Franklin Trimble on 15 Nov 1821, in Pulaski Co., Kentucky.[249] They were the parents of ten children. David was the son of William Trimble and Mary Fleming, mentioned in a later chapter. He died in 1856; Nancy died in 1862.[250]

Jesse Tarter

Born c. 1801, Pulaski Co., Kentucky, and died after 1880, Pulaski Co., Kentucky[251]
n Nov 1819, Jesse married Sally Weddle, the daughter of Daniel Weddle and Rachel Rayborn.[252] They were the parents of sixteen children, including a pair of twins. They were members of the Separate Baptist church. Jesse and Sally are buried on the family farm off of Route 761.[253]

Millie Tarter Trimble

Born c. 1806, Pulaski Co., Kentucky, and died after 1880, Pulaski Co., Kentucky[254]
Millie married John Trimble on 4 Oct 1822 in Pulaski Co., Kentucky.[255] Millie was the daughter of William Trimble and Mary Fleming, mentioned in a later chapter. They were the parents of seven children. John died in 1880; Millie died before 1900.

---

[248] 982: Bank Book and Day Book of James F. Trimble, transcription and scans of original by Charles Turpin, charles@turpin.net

[249] 49: Pulaski Co., KY Marriage Records, Vol 1, 1797-1850, 2nd edition, pg 145, Mary Weddle Kaurish, publ. 1984, Pulaski County Historical Society, Somerset, KY

[250] 263: Pulaski Co., KY Vital Records, Birth & Death, 1852-1859, 1861, 1874-1878, Pulaski County Historical Society, Somerset, KY
982: Bank Book and Day Book of James F. Trimble, transcription and scans of original by Charles Turpin

[251] Federal Census: 1880, Pulaski Co., KY, pg 9

[252] 49: Pulaski Co., KY Marriage Records, Vol 1, 1797-1850, 2nd edition, pg 141, Mary Weddle Kaurish, publ. 1984, Pulaski County Historical Society, Somerset, KY

[253] 47: Pulaski Co., KY Cemetery Records, Vol. 1, Pulaski County Historical Society, published Jan 1976, Somerset, KY

[254] 1880 Federal Census, Pulaski Co., KY, pg 36

[255] 49: Pulaski Co., KY Marriage Records, Vol 1, 1797-1850, 2nd edition, pg 145, Mary Weddle Kaurish, publ. 1984, Pulaski County Historical Society, Somerset, KY

Alfred Tarter

Born c. 1807, Pulaski Co., Kentucky, and died May 1860, Adair Co., Kentucky

Alfred married Eliza Todd on 25 Oct 1827 in Pulaski Co., Kentucky.[256] They were the parents of at least eleven children. Alfred died in May 1860 of a throat infection,[257] and Eliza carried on running the farm. In 1863, she filed a mother's pension on the basis of the Civil War service of her deceased son, Henry.[258] She does not appear in the census after that date.

William Tarter

Born c. 1808, Pulaski Co., Kentucky, and died after 1880, Pulaski Co., Kentucky[259]

William married his sister-in-law Elizabeth Weddle on 19 Apr 1830 in Pulaski Co., Kentucky. They were the parents of at least two children. Elizabeth died prior to 1835. He married Nancy "Patsy" Roberts on 24 Feb 1835, also in Pulaski County,[260] and they were the parents of at least ten children. They appear in only two census records, and appear to have died after 1880.[261]

Eliza Tarter Roberts

Born c. 1812, Pulaski Co., Kentucky, and died after 1880, Pulaski Co., Kentucky[262]

Eliza was the second wife of James Roberts, married on 18 Mar 1841 in Pulaski Co., Kentucky.[263] He had five children from his first marriage to Nancy Dove, and the second marriage produced seven more. The couple died after 1880.[264]

---

[256] 49: Pulaski Co., KY Marriage Records, Vol 1, 1797-1850, 2nd edition, pg 140, Mary Weddle Kaurish, publ. 1984, Pulaski County Historical Society, Somerset, KY. The records give an alternate date of 25 Oct 1839, but, based on the ages of their children, the 1827 date is more likely.

[257] 1860 Federal Mortality Schedule, Adair Co., KY

[258] 950: Ancestry.com, Civil War Pension Index, General Index to Pension Files, 1861-1934, paywalled

[259] Federal Census: 1880, Pulaski Co., KY, pg 388

[260] 49: Pulaski Co., KY Marriage Records, Vol 1, 1797-1850, 2nd edition, pg 151, Mary Weddle Kaurish, publ. 1984, Pulaski County Historical Society, Somerset, KY

[261] Federal Census: 1850, Casey Co., KY, pg 330A; 1880, Pulaski Co., KY, pg 388.

[262] Federal Census: 1880, Pulaski Co., KY, pg 5

[263] 49: Pulaski Co., KY Marriage Records, Vol 1, 1797-1850, 2nd edition, pg 122, Mary Weddle Kaurish, publ. 1984, Pulaski County Historical Society, Somerset, KY

[264] Federal Census: Pulaski Co., KY, 1850, pg 256; 1860, pg 274; 1870, pg 69; 1880, pg 5

Celia Tarter Weddle

Born c. 1814, Pulaski Co., Kentucky, and died after 1880, Pulaski Co., Kentucky[265]
Celia married William Harrison Weddle on 13 Jan 1835 in Pulaski Co., Kentucky.[266] They were the parents of nine children.[267] William died on 23 Oct 1874.[268] Celia died before 1880.

Sally Tarter Wilson

Born c. 1818, Pulaski Co., Kentucky
Sally married Isaac Wilson on 9 Mar 1836 in Pulaski Co., Kentucky.[269] I have not been able to learn any more about this couple.

Ephriam Tarter

Born c. 1819, Pulaski Co., Kentucky
Ephriam married Jane Roberts on 25 Jun 1835 in Pulaski Co., Kentucky.[270] They were the parents of at least seven children. Jane died prior to 1860 in Green Co., Missouri.[271]

---

[265] Federal Census: 1880, Pulaski Co., KY, pg 14, in the household of Samuel G. Muse, her nephew-in-law

[266] 49: Pulaski Co., KY Marriage Records, Vol 1, 1797-1850, 2nd edition, pg 153, Mary Weddle Kaurish, publ. 1984, Pulaski County Historical Society, Somerset, KY

[267] Federal Census: Pulaski Co., KY, 1850, pg 29; 1860, pg 252; 1870, pg 355

[268] 248: UKCC Kentucky Death Index or Rootsweb Kentucky Death Index

[269] 49: Pulaski Co., KY Marriage Records, Vol 1, 1797-1850, 2nd edition, pg 158, Mary Weddle Kaurish, publ. 1984, Pulaski County Historical Society, Somerset, KY

[270] 49: Pulaski Co., KY Marriage Records, Vol 1, 1797-1850, 2nd edition, pg 141, Mary Weddle Kaurish, publ. 1984, Pulaski County Historical Society, Somerset, KY

[271] Federal Census: Phelps & Spring River PO, Green Twp, Lawrence Co., MO, pg 805A

Jacob Tarter and his three wives

Jacob "Jake" Tarter
Son of John Tarter and Catherine Logan
Born 21 Nov 1795 Virginia
Died 19 Nov 1874 Kentucky

Married 1st, August 1818, Pulaski Co., Kentucky

Martha "Polly" Weddle
Daughter of Daniel Weddle and Rachel Rayborn
Born c. 1802 Virginia
Died between 1850 and 1858 Kentucky

Married 2nd, 28 Oct 1858, Pulaski Co., Kentucky

Mariah Warner
Daughter of Joseph Warner and Mary Cain
Born 18 Jul 1835, Kentucky
Died 20 Mar 1888, Kentucky

Married 3rd, 11 Dec 1879, Russell Co., Kentucky

Mary Ann "Polly" Cooper Bird
Born c. 1830, Kentucky
Died after 1880, Kentucky

John and Catherine Tarter's second son, Jacob Tarter, was born in Virginia, and came to Kentucky with his parents c. 1800.[272] In August 1818, Jake married Martha "Polly" Weddle, the daughter of Daniel Weddle and Rachel Rayborn.[273] Jake and Polly were the parents of twelve children, all of whom lived to adulthood.

Jake owned a large amount of acreage in Russell County[274] and made his living as a farmer, landlord, and money lender.[275] He owned several horses, considered quite fine specimens by his neighbors, as well as hogs, mules, and cattle. He also owned two slaves: a housekeeper named Luce and a farmhand

---

[272] Federal Census: 1850, Pulaski Co., KY, pg 248

[273] 49: Pulaski Co., Kentucky Marriage Records, Vol 1, 1797-1850, 2nd edition, Mary Weddle Kaurish, Pulaski County Historical Society. Daniel Weddle was the brother of John Milton Weddle, and provided surety for his daughter's marriage.

[274] 90: Kentucky Land Grants, Parts 1 & 2, 1782-1924, Willard Rouse Jillson, ScD, publ. 1971, Genealogical Publ. Co., Baltimore, MD

[275] 567: Tarter v. Tarter, the divorce proceedings of Jacob Tarter v. Mariah Warner Tarter, 16 May 1859 through Sept 1869, transcribed by James Garner for kykinfolk.com, including cast of characters and chronology of events. The transcription of the original handwritten document is 42 pages. I am indebted to Carole Frederick Marcum for calling these court documents to my attention, and to James D. Garner for his excellent transcription and analysis. My page numbers throughout refer to the transcription, not the original documents.

named Henry.[276] Jack M. Weddle, a Pulaski County sheriff, estimated his cousin's[277] worth at almost $10,000.

Between 1850 and 1858, Jake's first wife, Martha Weddle Tarter, died. What followed is unlike anything I have ever read in twenty years of genealogical research.

On 28 Oct 1858, Jake married Mariah Warner.[278] She was the daughter of Joseph Warner, a local blacksmith, and his wife, Mary Cain. Warner was not a wealthy man, and his daughter, Mariah, was a 23-year-old spinster with no prospects when the prosperous Jacob Tarter proposed.[279]

Jacob was 40 years older, set in his ways, and the marriage went wrong almost immediately. He constantly criticized Mariah's household management,[280] and the couple soon began fighting. Fighting turned to physical abuse, which was not surprising, since Jacob had also abused his first wife.[281] Mariah would tell Jacob's son, Daniel, that *"when she saw other women of her age with young men their equals in age, it almost broke her heart."*[282] Jacob's daughter, Rachel, recalled that Mariah had admitted she was in love with young Greenberry Buchanan, though apparently her affections were not returned.[283] Then, in November 1858, she became pregnant.

All of this sank Mariah into a deep depression. She attempted to cause a miscarriage by drinking cedar bud tea.[284] She took to her bed, refusing to leave, and was described by various witnesses as *deranged, flighty, having a wild look in her eyes, distracted,* and *bewitched*. Both Joshua Taylor, a local physician, and Helen Compton, a neighbor, suggested that Jacob hire a *witch doctor*, though in context, it appears that they were recommending he hire an exorcist.[285]

By February 1859, Mariah had separated from her husband, returning home to live with her parents. A few months later, she returned to Jacob's home, where she lived *"for upwards of a month."* Then, in May 1859, Jacob and Mariah agreed in writing to a separation, and Jacob paid her $100 to stay out of his

---

[276] Federal Census: 1860, Slave Schedule, Pulaski Co., KY, pg 36B, shows him owning 2 slaves. They are mentioned several times in the depositions. The Pulaski County death records show that he at one time owned a third slave, named Eliza.

[277] 567: pgs 38-40, deposition of Sheriff Jack M. Weddle. Jack was a cousin by marriage, through Jacob's first wife.

[278] 50: Pulaski Co., Kentucky Marriage Records, Vol 2, 1851-1863, pg 105, Pulaski County Historical Society, publ. 1970, Somerset, KY

[279] Federal Census: 1860, Pulaski Co., KY, pg 278, assesses the total value of his property at $200.

[280] 567: pg 21, deposition of Nancy Warner, Mariah's sister

[281] 567: pg 26, deposition of John Tarter, unknown relationship

[282] 567: pg 14, deposition of Daniel Tarter, Jacob's son from his first marriage

[283] 567: pg 33, deposition of Rachel Tarter Norfleet, Jacob's daughter from his first marriage

[284] 567: pg 32, deposition of Henrietta Gose Weddle, daughter-in-law of Sheriff Jack M. Weddle
567: pg 35, deposition of Wyatt Norfleet, Mariah's brother-in-law

[285] 567: pg 17, deposition of Joshua Taylor, and pg 25, deposition of Helen Compton

life.[286] A petition for divorce was filed the following year, and on 9 Aug 1859, Mariah gave birth to a daughter whom she named Queen Victoria.[287]

The divorce should have run through the courts fairly smoothly. Jacob represented himself as the innocent victim whose wife had abandoned him *"without cause or provocation."* But someone, and because of his own unusual family circumstances, I suspect it was her brother-in-law, Jack Weddle, persuaded Mariah that the $100 settlement was insufficient to support herself and her child.[288] In June 1860, Mariah filed a cross petition, asking for more money.[289] The case would drag on for ten years, with Jacob and Mariah's lawyers taking depositions from twenty of their neighbors and relations. Quite of few of Jacob's children from his first marriage would be deposed, and their testimony, often less than supportive of their father's position, would have consequences when his will was read.

In Mariah's own deposition, she described her husband as *"a cross, crabbed and disagreeable old man [who] forgot his God and worshiped the almighty dollar."* She charged him with physical abuse, but perhaps the most shocking charge was that Jacob *"kept a set of prostitutes about him for the basest purpose."*[290]

There were on Jacob's land a number of tenant farms with their own houses, which was common in those days. Remember, one of Jacob's occupations was landlord. Around the date of his marriage, Jacob had leased a house, two or three hundred yards from his own, to Thomas and Polly Bird. Franklin Weddle described Thomas as a poor man who worked for Ivey Tarter as a farm hand, and occasionally worked for Jacob himself, operating an apple brandy still.[291] Polly, on the other hand, is described by every witness as *unchaste, of base character, of poor moral character, of doubtful reputation,* and by two witnesses as *"a clever woman,"* which in context, appears to be a euphemism for a prostitute. Franklin Weddle also described observing a tryst between Jacob and Polly in the apple orchard.

Jacob's tryst eventually bore fruit, and I don't mean apples. In 1861, Polly Bird gave birth to a son named William Thomas, and in 1865, to a son named Elias Jefferies. Both of these children carried the expedient surname Bird, but it was an open secret that Jacob Tarter was their father. It's not clear exactly when Thomas Bird died, but on 11 Dec 1870, Jake married Polly Cooper Bird.[292]

---

[286] 567: pg 12, deposition of Theophilus Pennington, one of the witnesses to the separation agreement

[287] 263: Pulaski Co., Kentucky Vital Records, Birth & Death, 1852-1859, 1861, 1874-1878, Pulaski County Historical Society, Somerset, KY

475 A transcription of her death certificate provided me by James D. Garner gives her married name as Queen Victoria Tarter Tarter.

[288] Jack Weddle's role in these events is fascinating when you consider his own extra-marital relationship with Elizabeth Huffman Kissee, described in a later section.

[289] 567: pg 8, petition in equity and answer & cross petition

[290] 567: pg 9, deposition of Mariah Warner Tarter, plaintiff

[291] 567: pg 36-37, deposition of Franklin Weddle, grandson-in-law of Jacob Tarter

Polly had three daughters from her first marriage and two sons born "on the wrong side of the blanket." The marriage lasted four years.

In January 1863, the Court of Appeals found in favor of Mariah, ruling that she was clearly unable to support herself and her daughter, and stating that *"the child should not be left to suffering and want in consequence of the misconduct of its parents, especially as the father is shown to be amply able to support it."* Support was set at $10 every three months, and Mariah had to go back to court at least twice to collect.[293] Mariah died in 1888 and was buried in Tarter-Hudson Cemetery in Pulaski County.[294]

On 18 Dec 1874, Jacob Tarter died, succumbing to injuries he received falling off a wagon.[295] His will, written in 1872, left one third of his land on the Cumberland River to *"my beloved wife Polly"*, and nearly everything else to his sons, William Thomas Tarter and Elias Jefferies Tarter. One hundred acres on Faubush Creek was left to *"the orphan children of my deceased son, Wesley Tarter"*.

Queen Victoria Tarter is not mentioned at all, and of the five living children from his first marriage, he says:

> "Having heretofore given lands to all my other children by my first wife and as I do not think they have for some years back treated me as they should have done, I will or give them nothing out of my estate." [296]

A nominal Baptist, Jacob Tarter's notorious behavior probably precluded his being buried in a church cemetery. He is believed to have been buried on his farm in Russell Co., Kentucky, the location of which has since been lost.

The children of Jacob and Martha Tarter:

Martha Tarter Weddle

> Born 18 Jul 1822, Kentucky, and died 17 Dec 1896, Kentucky
> *See profile of Solomon Weddle and Martha Tarter*

---

[292] 277 Newly Discovered Russell Co., KY Marriage Records, 1826-1869, pg 7, Carol L. Sanders, publ. 1988, Blue Ash, OH

263: Pulaski Co., KY Vital Records, Birth & Death, 1852-1859, 1861, 1874-1878, Pulaski County Historical Society, Somerset, KY, transcription

Elmerlee Tarter Oakley call her Polly *Seaton*, but I can find no evidence to support this surname. Her 1856 marriage record to Thomas Bird calls her Polly Ann Cooper. Her daughter's birth record gives Cooper as her surname, and is one of two records that calls her Mary Ann instead of Polly Ann. The second is the 1880 Federal Census, Russell Co., KY, pg 548B-549A.

[293] 567: pgs 4 & 6

[294] 48: Pulaski Co., KY Cemetery Records, Vol. 2, Pulaski County Historical Society, publ. Jun 1977, Somerset, KY

[295] 475 Russell Co., Kentucky Vital Statistics, James D. Garner transcription

[296] 481 Will of Jacob Tarter, 21 Dec 1872, Russell Co., Kentucky, Book 3 Page 293-294, transcribed by James D. Garner

Rachel Tarter Norfleet

Born c. 1819, Kentucky, and died between 1860 and 1864, Kentucky
Rachel married Henry Norfleet on 2 Jun 1835, in Pulaski County.[297]
They were the parents of seven children. Following his wife's death, Henry remarried twice – first to Hulda Crutchfield on 18 Aug 1864, and second to Rachel's cousin Martha Jane Tarter on 8 Sep 1869.[298]

Catherine Tarter Molen

Born 4 Nov 1820, Kentucky, and died 22 Jul 1911, Kentucky
Katie married Wesley Molen on 10 Jun 1841, in Pulaski County.[299] They were the parents of fourteen children. Wesley is buried in Old Dibrell-Molen Cemetery, Wayne County.[300] Catherine is buried in Tarter Hudson Cemetery, Pulaski County.[301]

Elizabeth Tarter Hudson

Born 25 Apr 1824, Kentucky, and died 21 Oct 1879, Kentucky
Betsy was the first wife of Richard S. Hudson. They were married on 27 Sep 1841, in Pulaski County.[302] Their union produced ten children. Elizabeth is buried with her husband in Hudson Cemetery, Pulaski County.[303]

Daniel Tarter

Born 16 Sep 1826, Kentucky, and died 28 Apr 1894, Kentucky
Daniel married Sarah Jane Molen on 13 Sep 1847, in Wayne County.[304] She was the niece of Wesley Molen, husband of Daniel's sister Katie. The couple had nine children, one of whom died in childhood. They are buried in Tarter Hudson Cemetery, Pulaski County.[305]

---

[297] 49: Pulaski Co., KY Marriage Records, Vol 1, 1797-1850, 2nd edition, Mary Weddle Kaurish, publ. 1984, Pulaski County Historical Society, Somerset, KY

[298] 51: Pulaski Co., KY Marriage Records, Vol 3, 1864-1886, Pulaski County Historical Society, publ. 1984, Somerset, KY

[299] 49: Pulaski Co., KY Marriage Records, Vol 1, 1797-1850, 2nd edition, Mary Weddle Kaurish, publ. 1984, Pulaski County Historical Society, Somerset, KY

[300] 323: Wayne Co., KY Pioneers, Biographical Sketches and Civil Court Records, Vol. 4, June Baldwin Bork

[301] 48: Pulaski Co., KY Cemetery Records, Vol. 2, Pulaski County Historical Society, published June 1977, Somerset, KY

[302] 49: Pulaski Co., KY Marriage Records, Vol 1, 1797-1850, 2nd edition, Mary Weddle Kaurish, publ. 1984, Pulaski County Historical Society, Somerset, KY

[303] 47: Pulaski Co., KY Cemetery Records, Vol. 1, Pulaski County Historical Society, publ. Jan 1976, Somerset, KY

[304] 320: Wayne Co., KY Marriage & Vital Records, Vol. 2, K-Z, June Baldwin Bork, publ. 1971, Huntington Beach, CA

[305] 48: Pulaski Co., KY Cemetery Records, Vol. 2, Pulaski County Historical Society, published June 1977, Somerset, KY

Wyatt Tarter

Born c. 1834 Kentucky, and died 18 Mar 1855 Kentucky
On 5 Apr 1851, Wyatt married Emily Kissee (Weddle), the eldest of the illegitimate children of John Milton Weddle, Jr. and Elizabeth Huffman Kissee. She was the only child that her father did not formally adopt, because she was already married when her nominal father died. Wyatt and Emily were the parents of two children.

Iva "Ivey" Tarter

Born c. 1838 Kentucky, and died 17 Jul 1920, Pottawatomie Co., Oklahoma
Ivey served in Company D of the 3rd Kentucky Volunteer Infantry as a 2nd Sergeant. He was discharged in June 1865.[306] This is unusual in that he was a married man with children, having married Emily Dunbar on 13 Jul 1856, in Russell County.[307] A gap in the birth years between the second and third children testifies to his absence. All eight of the children were born in Kentucky. In 1881, he moved the family to Collin Co., Texas, and ten years later, to Chickasaw Nation territory, and then to Pottawatomie Co., Oklahoma.[308] Ivey and Emily are buried in Sacred Heart Cemetery, Pottawatomie County.[309]

Mary Ann Tarter Gadberry

Born c. 1839 Kentucky, and died between 1860 and 1863, Kentucky
Mary Ann became the first wife of Andrew Gadberry on 7 Sep 1854.[310] They were the parents of three children. After the birth of her third child, Mary Ann died, and Andrew married her second cousin once removed, Martha Ann Tarter.[311]

Wesley Tarter

Born c. 1843 Kentucky, and died between 1865 and 1872
Wesley married Pharaba E. Hammonds on 10 Feb 1861, in Pulaski County.[312] They were the parents of two children. Wesley's father's will

---

[306] 238: Oscar H. Darter, "*The Darter-Tarter Family*," publ. 1965, Garrett & Massie Inc., Richmond, VA

[307] 277: Newly Discovered Russell Co., KY Marriage Records, 1826-1869, Carol L. Sanders, publ. 1988, Blue Ash, OH

[308] 238: Oscar H. Darter, "*The Darter-Tarter Family*," publ. 1965, Garrett & Massie Inc., Richmond, VA

[309] 229: Elmerlee Tarter Oakley, "*The Kentucky Tarters*," 1981, Jet Press reprint, Hopkinsville, KY

[310] 50: Pulaski Co., Kentucky Marriage Records, Vol 2, 1851-1863, Pulaski County Historical Society, Somerset, KY

[311] 50: Pulaski Co., Kentucky Marriage Records, Vol 2, 1851-1863, Pulaski County Historical Society, Somerset, KY

calls him *my deceased son*, so we know he died between the birth of his son Daniel and the writing of his father's will.

The children of Jacob and Mariah Tarter:

Queen Victoria Tarter Tarter

Born 9 Aug 1859 Kentucky, and died 30 Oct 1913 Kentucky
On 21 Sep 1884, Victoria Tarter married her half-nephew, Frederick Tarter.[313] Frederick's father, Daniel Tarter, was Victoria's half-brother. They were the parents of seven children. The couple moved to Pottawatomie Co., Oklahoma, for at least a decade, but returned to Pulaski County between 1910 and 1913.[314] Victoria died of tuberculosis of the larynx.[315] Fred married his 3rd cousin, the widowed Selecta Weddle Wilson, between 1913 and 1919. They were the parents on one son who died in childhood. Fred died of enteritis and diabetes.[316] He and Victoria are buried in Weddle Cemetery in Pulaski Co., Kentucky.[317]

The children of Jacob and Mary Ann "Polly" Tarter:

William Thomas Tarter

Born c. 1861 Kentucky[318]
William married Sarah Jane Dixon on 8 Jan 1878, in Russell County, and they were the parents of twin daughters.[319] I have not been unable to learn anything more about this couple.

Elias Jefferies Tarter

Born c. 1865 Kentucky[320]
Elias moved to Missouri and c. 1888, married his wife, Ada. They were the parents of three sons, two born in Missouri and one in Arkansas.[321] Both Elias and his wife appear to have died between 1900 and 1910.

---

[312] 50: Pulaski Co., Kentucky Marriage Records, Vol 2, 1851-1863, Pulaski County Historical Society, Somerset, KY

[313] 51: Pulaski Co., Kentucky Marriage Records, Vol 3, 1864-1886, Pulaski County Historical Society, Somerset, KY

[314] Federal Census: 1910, Maud, Moore Twp, Pottawatomie Co., OK, pg 16B

[315] 475 Transcription of her death certificate provided by James D. Garner

[316] 950: Ancestry.com, scan of death certificate #20850, Pulaski Co., KY

[317] 48: Pulaski Co., KY Cemetery Records, Vol. 2, Pulaski County Historical Society, publ. Jun 1977, Somerset, KY

[318] Federal Census: 1880, Russell Co., KY, pg 548B

[319] 475: James D. Garner (Laton B. Weddle family)

[320] Federal Census: 1880, Russell Co., KY, pg 548B

[321] Federal Census: 1900, Ouachita, Polk Co., AR, pg 310A

John Milton Weddle and Mary McDaniel

John Milton Weddle
Son of George Weddle and Mary Evans
Born 3 Sep 1776, Wyethville, Wyeth Co., Virginia
Died 3 Jul 1842, Pulaski Co., Kentucky

Married 29 Aug 1803, Pulaski Co., Kentucky

Mary "Polly" McDaniel
Daughter of Spencer McDaniel, Sr. and Elizabeth Randall
Born 5 Oct 1783, Virginia
Died 26 Jul 1852, Pulaski Co., Kentucky

John Milton Weddle was born in Wyethville, Wyeth Co., Virginia.[322] Named for the British author of *Paradise Lost*, he was born two months after the signing of the Declaration of Independence.

Of his parents, Thomas Kintigh writes, "*His father, George Weddle was an Ensign in the Virginia Militia during the Revolution and later served in the Pennsylvania Militia. He owned 290 acres in Washington Co., Pennsylvania in 1783 before migrating to Clark Co., Kentucky with his father-in-law Richard Evans. George was born c. 1745 and died in 1800. His will, written 7 Feb 1800, is on file in Clark County, Book 1, page 183.*" However, I am unconvinced by claims that this George Weddle was the son of George Adam Weddle of Rostraver Township, Westmoreland Co., Pennsylvania. The numerous applications to the Sons of the American Revolution filed on George Adam Weddle make no mention of a son named George.[323]

When John was age 7, his family moved to Clark Co., Kentucky. He arrived in Pulaski County after the 1800 census.[324] Later county histories would say he was *the first white man in the county*, but this is clearly incorrect.[325] The county was chartered in 1798 and numerous records show settlers prior to that date. At best, Weddle was an early settler in the county.

Another early couple to settle in the county was Elizabeth Randall and Spencer McDaniel, Sr..[326] McDaniel was a substantial land owner, holding

---

[322] Occasionally, the claim is made that he was born in Pennsylvania. The fact that he owned land in the Grants South of Green River, reserved for Virginia veterans of the Revolution, should put paid to this claim.

[323] 2680: Sons of the American Revolution membership application database, 1889-1970, Ancestry.com, paywalled

[324] 58: Alma Owens Tibbals disagrees, saying he had come to the county by 1788 directly from Wythe Co., Virginia. The 1790 Federal Census does not support this assertion.

[325] 58: ibid. Many of the early county histories are obsessed with "the first white man" statistics that modern readers may find both off-putting and irrelevant.

[326] 263: Pulaski Co., KY Vital Records, Birth & Death, 1852-1859, 1861, 1874-1878, Pulaski County Historical Society, Somerset, KY

about 450 acres near the confluence of Kings and Wolf Creeks.[327] They had five children who survived to adulthood: Mary, Elizabeth, Spencer, Jr., John, and William.

Two of their sons, Spencer, Jr. and William, served in the War of 1812.[328] Spencer, Jr.'s regiment, commanded by Col. Thomas Deye Owings, was responsible for guarding the ironworks that produced much of the shot and cannonballs for Gen. Andrew Jackson's forces at the Battle of New Orleans.[329]

On 29 Aug 1803, John Milton Weddle married Mary "Polly" McDaniel.[330] A year later, Mary gave birth to their first child, Spencer Weddle, born in 1804. Ten children would follow. The eighth was Solomon Weddle, born 9 May 1822.[331]

On 10 Nov 1814, John Milton Weddle signed up as a Private in the Detached Kentucky Militia, Slaughter's Regiment, serving for six months under Capt. John Evans.[332]

In a typical case of an unfunded mandate, the United States government requested militia troops from Kentucky to come to the aid of New Orleans' battle against the British, but furnished no money to support the effort. In Nov 1814, several regiments, nearly 2,500 men, were assembled on the banks of the Ohio River for transport to New Orleans. Most of the men had no guns of their own, and had arrived only with the clothes they wore and maybe a blanket.

The officers raised enough money to buy some old barges, many badly patched up. Some of the barges were rowed the 1,500 miles to New Orleans with axes, because paddles were unavailable. Upon their arrival on 4 Jan 1815, General Andrew Jackson noted in his official report that *"Not one man in ten was well armed, and only one man in three had any arms at all."* The citizens of New Orleans provided enough firearms and ammunition to equip most of the men, and furnished clothes and bedding.

267: Profile of Harvey McDaniel, Counties of Morgan, Monroe & Brown, IN, Historical & Biographical, Charles Blanchard, editor, publ. 1884, F. A. Battey & Co., Publishers, Chicago, IL

[327] 90: Kentucky Land Grants, Parts 1 & 2, 1782-1924, Willard Rouse Jillson, ScD, publ. 1971, Genealogical Publishing Co., Baltimore, MD

[328] 267: Profile of Harvey McDaniel, Counties of Morgan, Monroe & Brown, IN, Historical & Biographical, Charles Blanchard, editor, publ. 1884, F. A. Battey & Co., Publishers, Chicago, IL

[329] "Thomas Deye Owings of Maryland, Kentucky, and Texas: Frontier Iron-Smelterer and Military Hero," by W. T. Block, http://www.wtblock.com/wtblockjr/thomas_deye_owings.htm

[330] 49: Pulaski Co., Kentucky Marriage Records, Vol 1, 1797-1850, 2nd edition, Mary Weddle Kaurish, Pulaski County Historical Society.

58: History of Pulaski Co., KY, Alma Owens Tibbals, publ. 1952, Moore Publishers, Bagdad, KY

[331] 47: Pulaski Co., Kentucky Cemetery Records, Vol. 1, Pulaski County Historical Society, published Jan 1976

[332] 173: Roster of the Volunteer Officers and Soldiers from KY in the War of 1812-1815, Adjutant General's Office, 1891, printed by authority of the legislature of Kentucky by E. Polk Johnson, public printer in Frankfort, KY

Slaughter's Regiment was assigned to hold the left bank of the Mississippi. By all accounts, this small band of raw recruits handled themselves well, holding their position against the best trained and armed navy on the face of the earth. The men still unarmed stood by, ready to take up the weapons of their fallen comrades. The troops under the command of Col. Thornton, positioned on the right bank of the river, were less successful, having "*ingloriously fled*" when they came under fire, resulting in the court martial of the regiment's officers. This led to the claim that all of the Kentucky troops had fled, a charge eventually set straight by an 1828 letter from General Jackson.[333]

Slaughter's Regiment was discharged on 18 Mar 1815, the men left to find their own way home, unpaid. They reached Kentucky in early May.[334] Though they would eventually receive payment for their service, the United States Congress did not make available pensions for War of 1812 veterans until 1871, by which time most of them had died. Pensions for their widows were made available in 1878. Weddle received neither pension not bounty lands for his service.

John Milton Weddle is said to have founded the village of Old Harrison, which, like many villages of that era, no longer exists.[335] He purchased a truly impressive quantity of land – 1,788 acres in 11 separate parcels.[336] Historian Alma Owens Tibbals says he purchased enough land so that he could leave each of his living children a workable holding.

On 23 Jun 1842, John Milton Weddle wrote his will. The document leaves the entire estate to his wife Polly during her lifetime, and then calls for it to be divided among his children. The two daughters, Polly and Margaret, also received $50 in cash.[337] Weddle died on 3 Jul 1842,[338] and the will was registered with the court on 19 Sep 1842.[339]

---

[333] Quisenberry's account does not make clear to whom General Jackson's letter was addressed, but I assume it was the Kentucky Adjutant General's Office.

[334] Anderson Chenault Quisenberry, *Kentucky in the War of 1812*, Chapter 10: The Battle of New Orleans, pgs 134-149, publ. 1915, The Kentucky Historical Society, Frankfort, KY, reprinted 1969, Genealogical Pub. Co., Baltimore, MD

[335] 58: A History of Pulaski Co., KY, Alma Owens Tibbals, publ. 1952, Moore Publishers, Bagdad, KY. The community was said to be near the villages of Faubush and Nancy.

[336] 90: Kentucky Land Grants, Parts 1 & 2, 1782-1924, Willard Rouse Jillson, ScD, publ. 1971, Genealogical Publishing Co., Baltimore, MD

[337] 305: Will of John Milton Weddle, 23 Jun 1842, Pulaski Co., Kentucky, Book 3 pg 556

[338] 48: Pulaski Co., Kentucky Cemetery Records, Vol. 2, Pulaski County Historical Society, published June 1977

[339] 305: Will of John Milton Weddle, 23 Jun 1842, Pulaski Co., Kentucky, Book 3 pg 556

His wife, Mary, died ten years later on 26 Jul 1852.[340] Her cause of death is listed in the county death records as flux (severe diarrhea).[341] She is buried with her husband in Weddle Cemetery, Pulaski County.[342]

The children of John Milton and Mary Weddle:

Spencer Weddle

> Born c. 1804, Kentucky, and died between 1855 and 1860, Kentucky
> Spencer Weddle married Nancy Cooper, the daughter of Levi Cooper and Drewsilla Green, on 17 Jun 1834 in Pulaski County.[343] They were the parents of nine children.[344] Following her husband's death, Nancy moved with her son Levi to Piatt Co., Illinois, and then to Kansas.[345] She died in 1895 and is buried in Walnut Cemetery, Crawford Co., Kansas.[346]

Margaret Weddle Connell

> Born c. 1807, Kentucky, and died unknown in Missouri
> Margaret married James Connell on 28 Jul 1830 in Pulaski County.[347] She and her husband settled in Missouri between 1833 and 1836. They were the parents of nine children.

John Milton "Jack" Weddle, Jr.

> Born 12 Dec 1807, Kentucky, and died 10 Apr 1891, Kentucky
> Like his father, Jack Weddle owned a large amount of land, primarily on Wolf Creek. The land records show 17 purchases between 1843 and 1875, totaling just over 3,000 acres.[348] He was a slave owner and probably grew tobacco.[349] He also served as a county sheriff.

---

[340] 48: Pulaski Co., Kentucky Cemetery Records, Vol. 2, Pulaski County Historical Society, published June 1977

[341] 263: Pulaski Co., Kentucky Vital Records, Birth & Death, 1852-1859, 1861, 1874-1878, Pulaski County Historical Society

[342] 48: Pulaski Co., Kentucky Cemetery Records, Vol. 2, Pulaski County Historical Society, published June 1977

[343] 49: Pulaski Co., Kentucky Marriage Records, Vol 1, 1797-1850, 2nd edition, Mary Weddle Kaurish, Pulaski County Historical Society

[344] Federal Census: Pulaski Co., KY, 1850, pg 251; 1860, pg 281

[345] 1870, Piatt Co., IL, pg 342B; 1880, Bourbon Co., KS, pg 359C; 1885 state census, Walnut Twp, Bourbon Co., KS, pg 48

[346] 2312: Findagrave.com #13998623

[347] 49: Pulaski Co., KY Marriage Records, Vol 1, 1797-1850, 2nd edition, Mary Weddle Kaurish, publ. 1984, Pulaski County Historical Society, Somerset, KY

[348] 90: Kentucky Land Grants, Parts 1 & 2, 1782-1924, Willard Rouse Jillson, ScD, publ. 1971, Genealogical Publishing Co., Baltimore, MD

[349] Federal Census: 1860, Slave Schedule, Pulaski Co., KY, pg 202A

Jack's personal life is truly intriguing. In 1834, his neighbor[350], Elizabeth Huffman Kissee, gave birth to a daughter. In the succeeding 16 years, she would give birth to eight additional children, all nominally fathered by her husband, Jesse Kissee. Except they weren't. All nine children were the offspring of Jack Weddle, and following Jesse Kissee's death, Jack adopted them.[351]

Elizabeth Huffman Kissee died in 1856 and is buried in a nearly unmarked grave in Weddle Cemetery that researcher James D. Garner believes reflects the family's disapproval of her unorthodox lifestyle. Buried with her brother, Jeremiah, the tombstone reads *J. Huffman, 1803-1873, Sister of J. 1808-1856*.[352]

On 4 Feb 1858, Jack married Julia Warner, daughter of Joseph Warner and Mary Cain, which made him the brother-in-law of Mariah Warner Tarter.[353] Together they had five children. Jack died in 1891, leaving a large estate to his wife and children. Most wills of this era open with formulaic religious sentiments. Jack's contains an unusually heartfelt message to his wife at the end:

"I want you to counsel with Julia and direct her how to manage and all counsel together for the best and all do right and live in peace, and the God of peace will bless you and your children and posterity. I exhort you all to seek and serve the Lord while you live on earth, that we may all meet again in the bright mansions in heaven there to live throughout eternity never to part no more."[354]

Julia Warner Weddle died in 1929. Both are buried in Weddle Cemetery, Pulaski County.[355]

George Weddle

Born c. 1812, Kentucky, and died after 1880, Kentucky
On 14 Jul 1827, George married Mabel Lockett, the daughter of Josiah Lockett, in Pulaski County.[356] The couple settled in Missouri until Mabel's death and seems to have had no children. By 1880, George

---

[350] Federal Census: 1850, Pulaski Co., KY, pg 251
[351] 1984 letter from Mary Weddle Karusih to James D. Garner describing court records of the adoption
[352] 48: Pulaski Co., Kentucky Cemetery Records, Vol. 2, Pulaski County Historical Society, published June 1977
[353] 50: Pulaski Co., Kentucky Marriage Records, Vol 2, 1851-1863, Pulaski County Historical Society
[354] 507: Will of John M. Weddle, Jr., Pulaski Co., KY, Will Book 7, pages 195-197, transcription by James D. Garner
[355] 48: Pulaski Co., Kentucky Cemetery Records, Vol. 2, Pulaski County Historical Society, published June 1977
[356] 49: Pulaski Co., KY Marriage Records, Vol 1, 1797-1850, 2nd edition, Mary Weddle Kaurish, publ. 1984, Pulaski County Historical Society, Somerset, KY

was resident in his brother Daniel's household, remarked as insane, which could mean any of a number of conditions including old-age senility.[357]

William Harrison Weddle

Born c. 1814 Kentucky, and died 23 Oct 1874, Kentucky
William married Celia Tarter, the daughter of John Tarter and Catherine Logan on 13 Jan 1835, in Pulaski County.[358] They were the parents of nine children.[359] In 1850, William Harrison Weddle was appointed the administrator of his deceased father-in-law's estate.[360]

Daniel S. Weddle

Born 14 Mar 1817, Kentucky, and died 17 Sep 1885, Kentucky
On 5 Jul 1829, Daniel married Elizabeth Cooper, the sister of his brother Spencer's wife.[361] The couple had three children. Between 1844 and 1846, Elizabeth died, and Daniel married again. His second wife was Anne Rainwater, the daughter of Bartholomew and Nancy Rainwater. They were married on 26 Jul 1846, by Justice of the Peace Josiah W. Duck.[362] The couple had twelve children, all of whom lived to adulthood.[363] Daniel is buried in Cedar Point Cemetery, Pulaski County.[364] Anne may be buried with him, but her grave is not marked.

James Weddle

Born c. 1819, Kentucky, and died between 1860 and 1870, Kansas
Jimmy married Minerva Fox prior to 1843. The couple had at least four children and moved to Kansas prior to the 1860 census. Jimmy died in Wilson, Linn Co., Kansas after 1860.[365] According to Weddle researcher, Victoria Day-Cook, he was buried at night on the family

---

[357] Federal Census: 1880, Pulaski Co., KY, pg 373, household of Daniel S. Weddle

[358] 49: Pulaski Co., KY Marriage Records, Vol 1, 1797-1850, 2nd edition, Mary Weddle Kaurish, publ. 1984, Pulaski County Historical Society, Somerset, KY

[359] Federal Census: Pulaski Co., KY, 1850, pg 250; 1860, pg 250; 1870, pg 355

[360] 1403: Administrator's report on the estate of John Tarter, 6 Jun 1853, Pulaski Co., Kentucky, Will Book 4, pg 195-197

1404: Final administrator's report on the estate of John Tarter, 29 May 1854, Pulaski Co., Kentucky, Will Book 4, pg 328-329

[361] 49: Pulaski Co., KY Marriage Records, Vol 1, 1797-1850, 2nd edition, Mary Weddle Kaurish, publ. 1984, Pulaski County Historical Society, Somerset, KY

[362] 49: Pulaski Co., KY Marriage Records, Vol 1, 1797-1850, 2nd edition, Mary Weddle Kaurish, publ. 1984, Pulaski County Historical Society, Somerset, KY

[363] Federal Census: Pulaski Co., KY, 1850, pg 251; 1860, pg 293; 1870, pg 162; 1880, pg 373

[364] 48: Pulaski Co., Kentucky Cemetery Records, Vol. 2, Pulaski County Historical Society, published June 1977

[365] Federal Census: Pulaski Co., KY, 1850, pg 252; Linn Co., KS, 1860, pg 98

farm, out of fear of the neighboring Indians knowing that the man of the house had died.

Solomon Weddle

Born 9 May 1822, Kentucky, and died 21 Mar 1890, Kentucky
See profile of Solomon Weddle and Martha "Patsy" Tarter

Mary Weddle Eastham

Born c. 1824, Kentucky, and died after 1860, Illinois
Polly married Obediah Eastham on 3 Feb 1841 in Pulaski County.[366]
The couple had eight children, seven of whom lived to adulthood.[367] Obediah was the brother of Alexander and Zachariah Eastham, the husbands of Emily Rainwater.

Galen Edward Weddle

Born 10 May 1829, Kentucky, and died 25 Feb 1914, Indiana
On 6 Jul 1847, Galen married Sally Rainwater, the daughter of Bartholomew and Nancy Rainwater.[368] The couple had fourteen children, thirteen of whom lived to adulthood.[369] Based on the children's birth places, between 1871 and 1874, the family relocated to Monroe Co., Indiana. Sally died in 1906, Galen in 1914. They are buried in Pleasant View Baptist Cemetery, Morgan County.[370]

---

[366] 49: Pulaski Co., KY Marriage Records, Vol 1, 1797-1850, 2nd edition, Mary Weddle Kaurish, publ. 1984, Pulaski County Historical Society, Somerset, KY

[367] Federal Census: Pulaski Co., KY, 1850, pg 252; 1860 pg 107

[368] 49 Pulaski Co., KY Marriage Records, Vol 1, 1797-1850, 2nd edition, Mary Weddle Kaurish, publ. 1984, Pulaski County Historical Society, Somerset, KY

[369] Federal Census: Pulaski Co., KY, 1850, pg 252; 1860 pg 294; Casey Co., KY, 1870, pg 278; Morgan Co., IN, 1880, pg 199

[370] 2312 Findagrave.com #32648340 and #32648362

Solomon Weddle and Martha Tarter

Solomon and Martha Weddle, c. 1870

Solomon Weddle
Son of John Milton Weddle, Sr. and Mary McDaniel
Born 9 May 1822, Pulaski Co., Kentucky
Died 21 Mar 1890, Pulaski Co., Kentucky

Married 6 May 1841, Pulaski Co., Kentucky

Martha "Patsy" Tarter
Daughter of Jacob Tarter and Martha Weddle
Granddaughter of Daniel Weddle and Rachel Rayborn
Born 18 Jul 1822, Pulaski Co., Kentucky
Died 17 Dec 1896, Pulaski Co., Kentucky

On 6 May 1841, Solomon Weddle married his first cousin once removed, Martha "Patsy" Tarter.[371] He was the son of John Milton Weddle, Sr. She was the daughter of the notorious Jacob Tarter, and granddaughter of Daniel Weddle, John Milton Weddle's younger brother. Considering that most

---

[371] 49: Pulaski Co., Kentucky Marriage Records, Vol 1, 1797-1850, 2nd edition, Mary Weddle Kaurish, Pulaski County Historical Society

people in this era married someone who lived within walking distance, it was not all that unusual for cousins to marry.

Solomon and Patsy were the parents of thirteen children, all of whom lived to adulthood. Their names and dates of birth are recorded in the family Bible of Abraham Lincoln Weddle, which was transcribed by the Mississippi Genealogical Society in 1978.[372]

County land records show Solomon owning a 50-acre farm about a mile south of Waterloo, Kentucky.[373] He would also have inherited land from his father, and his wife may have received a small amount of land from her father before family relations deteriorated.

Solomon served as a magistrate for Waterloo for twenty-five years, and also served several terms as a deputy sheriff. He was an active Republican, as the names of two of his sons reflect.[374]

Solomon died on 21 Mar 1890.[375] His will, which has faded to near illegibility, leaves his entire estate to his wife for the remainder of her life, and then divides the estate in equal shares among his living children.[376] Patsy died six years later on 17 Dec 1896.[377] They are buried in Chesterview Cemetery, Pulaski County.[378]

The children of Solomon and Martha Weddle:

Jenetta Weddle Warner

> Born 3 Apr 1842, Pulaski Co., Kentucky, and died 25 Jul 1908, Kentucky
> Jenetta married Jacob Warner, the son of Joseph Warner and Mary Cain, on 30 Oct 1876, in Pulaski County.[379] Jacob was a blacksmith, like his father, a tanner, and a farmer.[380] They were the parents of eight

---

[372] 593: Bible of Abraham Lincoln Weddle, Pulaski Co., Kentucky, printed in Mississippi Cemetery and Bible Records, Vol. 17, 1978, pgs. 74-77, Mississippi Genealogical Society, original owned by Mrs. J. P. Wilkerson, transcription of original

[373] 90: Kentucky Land Grants, Parts 1 & 2, 1782-1924, Willard Rouse Jillson, ScD, publ. 1971, Genealogical Publishing Co., Baltimore, MD

[374] 59: History of Kentucky, Vol 5, by William Elsey Connelley and E. M. Coulter, edited by Judge Charles Kerr, publ. 1922, The American Historical Society, Chicago, IL

[375] 593: Bible of Abraham Lincoln Weddle, Pulaski Co., Kentucky, printed in Mississippi Cemetery and Bible Records, Vol. 17, 1978, pgs. 74-77, Mississippi Genealogical Society, original owned by Mrs. J. P. Wilkerson, transcription of original

[376] 310: Will of Solomon Weddle, 6 May 1890, Pulaski Co., Kentucky, Book 7 pg 182

[377] 57: Josiah Rainwater family Bible, photocopy of original

[378] 47: Pulaski Co., Kentucky Cemetery Records, Vol. 1, Pulaski County Historical Society, published Jan 1976

[379] 50: Pulaski Co., Kentucky Marriage Records, Vol 2, 1851-1863, Pulaski County Historical Society

[380] 58: A History of Pulaski Co., KY, Alma Owens Tibbals, publ. 1952, Moore Publishers, Bagdad, KY

59: History of Kentucky, Vol 5, by William Elsey Connelley and E. M. Coulter, edited by Judge Charles Kerr, publ. 1922 The American Historical Society, Chicago

children, all of whom lived to adulthood.[381] The Warners are buried in Weddle Cemetery.[382]

Galen E. Weddle

Born 6 Sep 1843, Pulaski Co., Kentucky, and died 10 Jan 1905, Kentucky
Galen E. Weddle answered his country's call in 1861 and enlisted in the 3rd Kentucky Volunteer Infantry, Company D of the Union Army. He was promoted to Sergeant on 31 Aug 1862, reduced back to Private in March 1863, and then promoted to Corporal in June 1863.[383] He was discharged on 10 Jan 1865 and in civilian life, joined the Laubon Tarter Post No. 92 of the GAR. He married Kissiah F. Jasper on 3 Apr 1867, at the home of her parents William Jasper and Nancy Ida Ford.[384] Galen and Kissiah were the parents of nine children who lived to adulthood.[385] They are buried in Chesterview Cemetery, Pulaski County.[386]

Elizabeth Jane Weddle Rainwater

Born 7 Sep 1847, Pulaski Co., Kentucky, and died 25 Jun 1943, Wilbarger Co., Texas
See profile of Josiah W. Rainwater and Elizabeth Jane Weddle

Mary Weddle Jasper

Born 2 Aug 1845, Pulaski Co., Kentucky, and died 25 Jan 1931, Pulaski Co., Kentucky
According to Frances Aderholt Smith, Mary married Union Army veteran John A. Jasper on 28 Feb 1864. They were the parents of twelve children, six of whom lived to adulthood.[387] In the 1900 census, John Jasper's occupation is recorded as U.S. Guager, which means he was a federal agent charged with closing down illegal stills. John died in

---

[381] Federal Census: Pulaski Co., KY, 1860, pg 297; 1870, pg 174; 1880, pg 12
[382] 48: Pulaski Co., Kentucky Cemetery Records, Vol. 2, Pulaski County Historical Society, published June 1977
[383] 45: Report of the Adjutant General of the State of Kentucky, Civil War 1861-1866, Vol. I, Union, publ. 1889
420: Pulaski Co., Kentucky 1890 Federal Census of Surviving Soldiers, Sailors, Marines and Widows and the 1890 County Taxpayers List, transcription, Pulaski County Historical Society
[384] 51: Pulaski Co., Kentucky Marriage Records, Vol 3, 1864-1886, Pulaski County Historical Society
[385] 324: Civil War (Union) pension papers of Galen E. Weddle and Kissiah Jasper Weddle, 9 Apr 1888-21 Apr 1931, photocopies of microfilmed originals, contributed by Christy Campbell
[386] 47: Pulaski Co., Kentucky Cemetery Records, Vol. 1, Pulaski County Historical Society, published Jan 1976
[387] Federal Census: Pulaski Co., KY, 1870, pg 250B; 1880, pg 73B; 1900, pg 119B

1929, and Polly followed in 1931. The couple is buried in Somerset City Cemetery, Pulaski Co., Kentucky.[388]

Jacob Tarter Weddle

Born 23 Mar 1850, Pulaski Co., Kentucky, and died 1933, Kentucky
Named for his maternal grandfather, Jake was a merchant, farmer, and school teacher.[389] He married Christina Dye on 12 Jul 1876.[390] Christina passed away before 1880 and on 3 Jul 1883, he married Sarah Elizabeth Ware.[391] The couple had three children, four of whom lived to adulthood.[392] Jake is buried with his second wife in Somerset City Cemetery, Pulaski County.[393]

Jerome and Margaret Tarter

Margaret Weddle Tarter

Born 20 Feb 1852, Pulaski Co., Kentucky, and died 22 Feb 1944, Kentucky
Maggie married Jerome Terrell Tarter on 4 Jan 1872 in Pulaski County.[394] Jerome was a great-grandson of John Tarter and Catherine Logan, which meant that he and his wife were second cousins. Jerome was a Baptist, a Royal Arch Mason, a lawyer, and eventually a county

---

[388] 2312: Findagrave.com #34580584 and #34580413

[389] 59: History of Kentucky, Vol 5, by William Elsey Connelley and E. M. Coulter, edited by Judge Charles Kerr, publ. 1922, The American Historical Society, Chicago
Federal Census: 1880, Pulaski Co., pg 97A, household of James Dick

[390] 51: Pulaski Co., Kentucky Marriage Records, Vol 3, 1864-1886, Pulaski County Historical Society

[391] 51: Pulaski Co., Kentucky Marriage Records, Vol 3, 1864-1886, Pulaski County Historical Society

[392] Federal Census: 1900, Somerset, Pulaski Co., KY, pg 7B

[393] 47: Pulaski Co., Kentucky Cemetery Records, Vol. 1, Pulaski County Historical Society, published Jan 1976

[394] 51: Pulaski Co., Kentucky Marriage Records, Vol 3, 1864-1886, Pulaski County Historical Society

judge. In 1888, while on a speaking tour for Republican congressional candidate Frank Finley, Judge Tarter drowned attempting to cross Pitman Creek, which had flooded after a heavy rainstorm. His widow was appointed postmistress of Somerset in 1889, and held the post until 1894.[395] Maggie died in 1944. She and her husband are buried in Somerset City Cemetery, Pulaski County.[396] Among Jerome and Maggie's children are Judge Roscoe Conklin Tarter, whom Roscoe Rainwater mentions in his five-page letter entitled *My Old Kentucky Home*, and Helen Gertrude Tarter Cooper, the mother of Senator John Sherman Cooper (1901-1991).

Emily Evelyn Weddle Eastham

Born 26 Feb 1854, Pulaski Co., Kentucky, and died 25 Mar 1937, Pulaski Co., Kentucky
Emily married James T. Eastham on 2 Sep 1875, in Pulaski County.[397] He was a farmer and school teacher.[398] They were the parents of at least eight children.[399] Emily and James are buried in Grave Hill Cemetery, Casey County.[400]

Lucy Ann Weddle Cooper

Born 18 Jan 1856, Pulaski Co., Kentucky, and died 28 Oct 1939, Kentucky
On 22 Dec 1872, Lucy married David Milton Cooper, a merchant.[401] They were the parents of at least fourteen children, four of whom had died by 1910.[402] David died in 1896, and is buried in Hopeful Baptist Cemetery, Pulaski County.[403] Lucy is buried in Salem Baptist Cemetery, Russell County.[404]

---

[395] 58: A History of Pulaski Co., KY, Alma Owens Tibbals, pgs 54-55, publ. 1952, Moore Publishers, Bagdad, KY

[396] 47: Pulaski Co., Kentucky Cemetery Records, Vol. 1, Pulaski County Historical Society, published Jan 1976

[397] 51: Pulaski Co., Kentucky Marriage Records, Vol 3, 1864-1886, Pulaski County Historical Society

[398] 59: History of Kentucky, Vol 5, by William Elsey Connelley and E. M. Coulter, edited by Judge Charles Kerr, publ. 1922, The American Historical Society, Chicago

[399] Federal Census: 1880, Pulaski Co., KY, pg 85A; 1900, Pulaski Co., KY, pg 143A

[400] 196: Casey Co., KY, 1806-1983, A Folk History Including Communities and Cemeteries, compiled and edited by Gladys Cotham Thomas, publ. 1983, Bicentennial Heritage Corp., Casey Co., KY

[401] 51: Pulaski Co., Kentucky Marriage Records, Vol 3, 1864-1886, Pulaski County Historical Society

[402] Federal Census: 1880, Pulaski Co., KY, pg 387, 1990, Russell Co., KY, pg 84B; 1910, Russell Co., KY, pg 64B

[403] 48: Pulaski Co., Kentucky Cemetery Records, Vol. 2, Pulaski County Historical Society, published June 1977

[404] 2312 Findagrave.com #70917504

John Milton Weddle III, campaign poster, 1917

John Milton Weddle III

Born 30 Mar 1859, Pulaski Co., Kentucky, and died 21 Mar 1948, Kentucky
On 14 Nov 1878, John married Elvira Brown.[405] He was a farmer, owning a 90-acre farm south of Somerset. He also served several terms as county sheriff. He was Republican and a member of the Crescent City Lodge No. 60 Knights of Pythias.[406] John and Elvira were the parents of four children, including a pair of twins.[407] The couple divorced between 1920 and 1930, and John married a younger widow, Mattie (surname unknown). They are found in the 1930 census, living in the county jail, supervising a roster of nineteen prisoners.[408] John is buried in Somerset City Cemetery[409] and Elvira is buried in Sardis Church Cemetery[410], both Pulaski County.

---

[405] 51: Pulaski Co., Kentucky Marriage Records, Vol 3, 1864-1886, Pulaski County Historical Society

[406] 59: History of Kentucky, Vol 5, by William Elsey Connelley and E. M. Coulter, edited by Judge Charles Kerr, publ. 1922, The American Historical Society, Chicago

[407] Federal Census: 1880, Pulaski Co., KY, pg 385

[408] Federal Census: 1930, Somerset, Pulaski Co., KY, pg 32A

[409] 47: Pulaski Co., Kentucky Cemetery Records, Vol. 1, Pulaski County Historical Society, published Jan 1976

[410] 48: Pulaski Co., Kentucky Cemetery Records, Vol. 2, Pulaski County Historical Society, published June 1977

Martha Helen Weddle Compton

Born 29 Nov 1861, Pulaski Co., Kentucky, and died 27 Jun 1961, Casey Co., Kentucky

On 22 Mar 1887, Martha married Christopher Columbus Compton.[411] They were a farm family and lived in Casey County. Four children were born to this couple.[412] They are buried in Middleburg Cemetery, Casey Co., Kentucky.[413]

Abraham Lincoln Weddle

Born 21 Mar 1864, Pulaski Co., Kentucky, and died 2 Sep 1929, Clay Co., Mississippi

Abe married Emily Elizabeth Cain on 15 Feb 1885.[414] She was a granddaughter of Daniel S. Weddle and Elizabeth Cooper, making the couple first cousins once removed. Five children are named in the family Bible.[415] Prior to 1920, the family moved to Clay Co., Mississippi.[416] Abe died there in 1929, and Emily relocated first to Illinois, and then back to Pulaski County. The couple is buried in Somerset City Cemetery, Pulaski County.[417]

Andrew Johnson Weddle

Born 14 Nov 1865, Pulaski Co., Kentucky, and died 27 Nov 1954, North Carolina

On 6 Sep 1891, Andrew Johnson Weddle married Martha J. Cain, the sister of Emily Elizabeth Cain.[418] Like his brother, Andrew and his wife were first cousins once removed. The couple were the parents of seven children, two of whom died in childhood. Andrew was a dry goods merchant in Lincoln Co., Kentucky, but retired to Ashville, North Carolina, between 1920 and 1930.[419] They are buried in Green Hills Cemetery, Ashville, Buncombe Co., North Carolina.[420]

---

[411] 52: Pulaski Co., Kentucky Marriage Records, Vol 4, 1887-1900, Pulaski County Historical Society

[412] Federal Census: 1900, Pulaski Co., KY, pg 229

[413] 2312: Findagrave.com #18193333 and #18193329

[414] 51: Pulaski Co., KY Marriage Records, Vol 3, 1864-1886, Pulaski County Historical Society, publ. 1984, Somerset, KY

[415] 593: Bible of Abraham Lincoln Weddle, Pulaski Co., KY, printed in Mississippi Cemetery and Bible Records, Vol. 17, 1978, pgs. 74-77, publ. 1978, Mississippi Genealogical Sociery, original owned by Mrs. J. P. Wilkerson, transcription of original

[416] Federal Census: 1920, Clay Co., MS, pg 113A

[417] 47: Pulaski Co., KY Cemetery Records, Vol. 1, Pulaski County Historical Society, published Jan 1976, Somerset, KY

[418] 52: Pulaski Co., Kentucky Marriage Records, Vol 4, 1887-1900, Pulaski County Historical Society

[419] Federal Census: 1930, Asheville, Buncombe Co., NC, pg 16B; 1940, Asheville, Buncombe Co., NC, pg 259B

[420] 2312: Findagrave.com #43829892 and #43830014

Doretta Weddle Gosser

Born 24 Feb 1872, Pulaski Co., Kentucky, and died 1940 Doretta married Hannibal Gosser on 31 May 1896, in Pulaski County.[421] They were a farm family, and raised seven children, at least one of whom died in childhood.[422] The couple is buried in Union Baptist Cemetery, Fonthill, Russell Co., Kentucky.[423]

---

[421] 52: Pulaski Co., Kentucky Marriage Records, Vol 4, 1887-1900, Pulaski County Historical Society

[422] Federal Census: 1910, Wolf Creek, Russell Co., KY, pg 102B; 1920, Pulaski Co., KY, pg 86A; 1930, Casey Co., KY, pg 57B

[423] 2312: Findagrave.com #10171417 and #10171414

Josiah W. Duck, Sr. and Sarah House

Josiah W. Duck, Sr.
Born between 1750 and 1760, Nansemond Co., Virginia
Died between 1830 and 1840, Pulaski Co., Kentucky

Married 2 Jan 1792, Isle of Wight Co., Virginia

Sarah House
Born between 1770 and 1780, Virginia
Died between 1840 and 1850, Pulaski Co., Kentucky

In 1807, Josiah W. Duck, Sr., acquired 200 acres on White Oak Creek in Pulaski County.[424] He had come to Kentucky from Virginia, from Nansemond County. Many years later, one of his descendants would fancifully recall that he was born in *Nancy Moon*, Virginia.

Josiah was married to Sarah House on 2 Jan 1792, at Mill Swamp Baptist Church in Isle of Wight Co., Virginia.[425] They were the parents of at least six children: Rebecca, James, Lucy, Sally, Eliza, and Josiah W., Jr. Except for Lucy, they were all married in Pulaski County.[426]

The tiny number of records that exist for Josiah Sr., give us few clues to his life. But we do know that when, along with 300 of his fellow citizens, he signed a petition on 20 Nov 1784 asking the government to establish a ferry route between Isle of Wight and Nansemond counties, he was one of five individuals surnamed Duck to sign.[427]

He is last listed in the 1830 census of Pulaski Co., in a household containing one white male, aged 70-80 and one white female, aged 50-60. Josiah Duck, Sr. died prior to the 1840 census. His widow Sarah took up residence with her son Josiah Jr., in whose 1840 census household she is found.[428] She died prior to the 1850 census.

---

[424] 90: Kentucky Land Grants, Parts 1 & 2, 1782-1924, Willard Rouse Jillson, ScD, publ. 1971, Genealogical Publishing Co., Baltimore, MD

[425] 142: Marriages of Some Virginia Residents, 1607-1800, Dorothy Ford Wulfeck, publ. 1986, Genealogical Publishing Co., Baltimore, MD. The marriage record gives her maiden name as Duck, which may mean her marriage to Josiah Sr. was her second to someone named Duck, or may just be a mistake. Terry and Pat Chesney, researchers in this line, give her maiden name as House, but it's not clear on what basis.

[426] 49: Pulaski Co., Kentucky Marriage Records, Vol 1, 1797-1850, 2nd edition, Mary Weddle Kaurish, Pulaski County Historical Society

[427] 123: Virginia Genealogist, Vol 5-6, pgs 106-109, John Frederick Dorman editor

[428] Federal Census: 1840, Pulaski Co., KY, pg 328

JOSIAH W. DUCK, JR. AND ANNA COOK

Josiah W. Duck, Jr
Son of Josiah Duck, Sr. and Sarah House
Born c. 1801 in Isle of Wight Co., Virginia
Died 13 Dec 1855 in Pulaski Co., Kentucky

Married 12 Oct 1817 in Pulaski Co., Kentucky

Anna W. Cook
Daughter of Jene Cook and Jane Meredith
Born c. 1799 in Virginia or North Carolina
Died between 1870 and 1880 in Pulaski Co., Kentucky

On 12 Oct 1817, 16-year-old Josiah Duck, Jr., married 18-year-old Anna Cook.[429] She was the daughter of Phillip Jene Cook, who is named on her marriage license and whose lineage, according to Cook researchers, Terry and Pat Chesney, stretched back to Mordecai Cook, who arrived in Virginia in 1660.

Josiah probably started his married life on his parents' farm, but by 1826 he had begun buying land on White Oak Creek, about 375 acres in all.[430] In 1839, he served a one-year term as the Postmaster for Waterloo, Kentucky.[431] In the 1840s, he was appointed one of Pulaski County's Justices of the Peace. In this capacity, he issued marriage licenses, performed the marriage ceremonies for a great many couples in his district, witnessed wills, and testified to their validity at probate.

Individuals under the age of 18 who wanted to marry required their parents' permission, and parents who for lack of education could not write these permissions themselves would go to the local Justice of the Peace who wrote out the necessary paperwork for the clerk of the court. These JP permission slips occasionally crossed county lines. In 1972, June Baldwin Bork, in her book of Wayne County records, noted that only three of the authors of these notes had outstandingly beautiful and graceful handwriting – and one of the three was JP Josiah W. Duck. His spelling, though, was amusingly phonetic – directing the clerk of the court to "*ishue a lisons*" for the marriage of his son, George and future daughter-in-law, Evalina White.[432]

---

[429] 49: Pulaski Co., Kentucky Marriage Records, Vol 1, 1797-1850, 2nd edition, Mary Weddle Kaurish, Pulaski County Historical Society

[430] 90: Kentucky Land Grants, Parts 1 & 2, 1782-1924, Willard Rouse Jillson, ScD, 971, Genealogical Publishing Co., Baltimore, MD

[431] 58: A History of Pulaski Co., Kentucky, Alma Owens Tibbals, 1952, Moore Publishers, Bagdad, Kentucky

[432] 102: Wayne Co., Kentucky Marriage & Vital Records, Vol 1, 1801-1860, pg 89, June Baldwin Bork, 1972, Huntington Beach, CA

In the 1850s, Pulaski County kept detailed cause of death records, and for that reason we know that Josiah died on 13 Dec 1855, of enteritis, or swelling of the small intestine, resulting in lethal dehydration.[433]

Anna Cook Duck first moved in with her daughter Helen Duck Compton and son-in-law John R. Compton, where she is found in the 1860 census. A decade later, she was residing with her daughter Martha Duck Compton and son-in-law Erasmus Compton, where she is found in the 1870 census.[434] She died prior to 1880.

The couple's final resting place is not known, which means it was probably on the family farm and is now lost.

A domed sterling silver butter server owned by this couple and engraved with the Duck name was left to their daughter Martha Jane Duck Compton, and eventually came into the possession of Clois and Nancy Rainwater.

The children of Josiah and Anna Duck:

Polly A. Duck Jeffreys

>Born c. 1819, Pulaski Co., Kentucky, and died between 1860 and 1865, Camden Co., Missouri
>Polly married James Madison Jeffreys on 18 Aug 1835.[435] Their first child was born in Kentucky, the six that followed, in Camden Co., Missouri. Polly died between 1860 and 1865.[436]

Elizabeth Duck Lay

>Born 1825, Pulaski Co., Kentucky, and died 1887, San Antonio, Bexar Co., Texas
>Elizabeth married Daniel Lay on 1 May 1848.[437] They were the parents of at least nine children. They moved to Texas in the 1850s, settling first in San Antonio, then moving to Wilson County, and then returning to San Antonio in the 1880s.[438] The couple is buried in Alamo Masonic Cemetery, San Antonio, Bexar Co., Texas.[439]

---

[433] 263: Pulaski Co., KY Vital Records, Birth & Death, 1852-1859, 1861, 1874-1878, Pulaski County Historical Society, Somerset, KY

[434] Federal Census: 1870, Pulaski Co., KY, pg 172

[435] 49: Pulaski Co., KY Marriage Records, Vol 1, 1797-1850, 2nd edition, Mary Weddle Kaurish, publ. 1984, Pulaski County Historical Society, Somerset, KY

[436] Federal Census: 1850, Camden Co., MO, pg 314A; 1860, Camden Co., MO, pg 6; 1870, Camden Co., MO, pg 513B

[437] 49: Pulaski Co., KY Marriage Records, Vol 1, 1797-1850, 2nd edition, Mary Weddle Kaurish, publ. 1984, Pulaski County Historical Society, Somerset, KY

[438] Federal Census: 1860, San Antonio, Bexar Co., TX, pg 491B; 1870, Wilson Co., TX, pg 459A; 1880, Wilson Co., TX, pg 53A; 1900, San Antonio, Bexar Co., TX, pg 162A

[439] 2312: Findagrave.com #15779247 and #15779246

George W. M. Duck and second wife, Rachel Martin, c. 1899

George Washington Marion Duck

Born 4 Oct 1828, Pulaski Co., Kentucky, and died 22 May 1899, Atascosa Co., Texas

On 4 Feb 1849, George Washington Marion Duck married Evalina M. White in neighboring Wayne Co., Kentucky.[440] Their first two children were born in Kentucky, but the next seven were born in Texas. The couple settled in Atascosa Co., southwest of San Antonio, and G. W. M. served as a county sheriff for twenty-five years. Legend has it that he never carried a gun.[441] Evalina died in 1891 and G.W.M. married Rachel Martin in 1892.[442] He died in 1899 and is buried in Pleasanton City Cemetery.[443]

Helen M. Duck Compton

Born c. 1831, Pulaski Co., Kentucky, and died 12 Oct 1897, Pulaski Co., Kentucky

On 19 Aug 1846, Helen married John R. Compton.[444] The couple produced twelve children, ten of whom lived to adulthood. Compton

---

[440] 102: Wayne Co., KY Marriage & Vital Records, Vol 1, 1801-1860, June Baldwin Bork, publ. 1972, Huntington Beach, CA

[441] 1129: George W. M. Duck biography, Atascosa County History, Atascosa History Committee, article submitted by William D. Morris, great-grandson, transcription. Some minor errors.

[442] 99: Atascosa Co., TX Marriage Records, 1856-1899, Registers 1-4, Lisa Lodholz & Frances T. Ingmire, publ. 1985, St. Louis, MO

[443] 1501: Will and probate records of G. W. M. Duck, Atascosa Co., TX, 1898, photocopies of originals

was a slave holder,[445] but joined the Union cause, serving four years as a 1st Sergeant in the 3rd Kentucky Volunteer Infantry, Company D.[446] He later drew a disability pension, describing what sounds to modern ears like post traumatic stress syndrome. He died in 1896, worn out by the *"nervous disease and general debility"* that had plagued him since the end of the war.[447] Helen and John were buried on their farm, but their gravestones have since been plowed under, according to Beth Walker, a descendant.

Bernetta Duck Gossett

Born 3 Mar 1834, Pulaski Co., Kentucky, and died 26 Jun 1916, Pulaski Co., Kentucky

Bernetta married Christopher C. Gossett on 19 Dec 1853.[448] They were the parents of six children, five of whom survived to adulthood. Christopher served with Company D, 3rd Kentucky Volunteer Infantry, as a 1st Sergeant, eventually being promoted to 1st Lieutenant.[449] Christopher died in 1905, and Bernetta moved in with her daughter, Lula, for the remaining years of her life.[450] The couple is buried in Weddle Family Cemetery in Pulaski County.[451]

Selina F. Duck Gossett

Born 16 Apr 1837, Pulaski Co., Kentucky, and 14 Dec 1904, Williamson Co., Texas

On 20 Jan 1858, Selina wed Joel Thomas Gossett at the Duck family home.[452] They were the parents of nine children, eight of whom survived to adulthood. Joel served as a sergeant in Company D, 3rd Kentucky Volunteer Infantry.[453] Like many of his neighbors, Joel returned from the war uneasy about raising his children in still-infested Kentucky. The family moved first to Palestine, Texas, and eventually to

---

[444] 49: Pulaski Co., KY Marriage Records, Vol 1, 1797-1850, 2nd edition, Mary Weddle Kaurish, publ. 1984, Pulaski County Historical Society, Somerset, KY

[445] Federal Census: 1860, Slave Schedule, pg 201B

[446] 45: Report of the Adjutant General of the State of Kentucky, Civil War, 1861-1866, Vol. I, Union, publ. 1889, reprinted by the Southern Historical Press, 1992, Greenville, SC

[447] 1890 Federal Census (Civil War survivors & widows schedule), Pulaski Co., KY, pg 160

[448] 50: Pulaski Co., KY Marriage Records, Vol 2, 1851-1863, Pulaski County Historical Society, publ. 1970, Somerset, KY

[449] 45: Report of the Adjutant General of the State of Kentucky, Civil War, 1861-1866, Vol. I, Union, publ. 1889, reprinted by the Southern Historical Press, 1992, Greenville, SC

[450] Federal Census: 1910, Science Hill, Pulaski Co., KY, pg 20B

[451] 48: Pulaski Co., KY Cemetery Records, Vol. 2, Pulaski County Historical Society, published June 1977, Somerset, KY

[452] 50: Pulaski Co., KY Marriage Records, Vol 2, 1851-1863, Pulaski County Historical Society, publ. 1970, Somerset, KY

[453] 261: Kentucky Online Civil War Roster Index, http://www.rootsweb.ancestry.com/~kymercer/CivilWar/Union/

Taylor. Joel died in 1896, and Selina died in 1904.[454] They are buried in Taylor City Cemetery, Williamson Co., Texas.[455]

Martha Jane Duck Compton

Born 7 May 1841, Pulaski Co., Kentucky, and died 22 Sep 1912, Taylor, Williamson Co., Texas
See profile of Erasmus D. Compton and Martha Jane Duck

Clayton Duck and Mason Duck

Died in childhood, before 1860[456]

---

[454] Federal Census: 1900, Taylor, Williamson Co., TX, pg 20B
[455] 2312 Findagrave.com #18620527 and #18620491
[456] Federal Census: 1850, Pulaski Co., KY, pg 253

Banner Compton and Catherine Wilson

Banner Compton
Born before 1774, Virginia
Died Sep 1818, Adair Co., Kentucky

Married before 1790

Catherine Wilson
Born between 1760 and 1770
Died between 1830 and 1840, Adair Co., Kentucky

Nearly everything we know about Banner Compton comes from his will and county property records.[457] He was a farmer, surveyor, blacksmith, and carpenter. He owned a considerable amount of land on Wolf and Goose Creeks in Adair County and served as a surveyor of roads in 1807.[458]

Banner died in 1818, leaving real estate to his sons William, Burrell, John, and Micajah, along with personal property. Micajah received his blacksmith's and carpenter's tools, but Burrell and John both got stills. His wife Catherine received property and money to support her in her widowhood, and daughters Charlotte, Sally, Sukey, Rachel, Polly, and Catherine all received cash. The land was left to their husbands, since married women were generally not able to independently own property.

Banner named as his executors several of his sons-in-law. His final request was for executors *"to have an eye over my son, John Compton, as guardian that he may not mismanage the property bequeathed to him."* This sense of mistrust expressed in a will would be repeated in the will of Banner's son Micajah.

---

[457] 306: Will of Banner Compton, 3 Aug 1818, Adair Co., KY, photocopy of original

[458] 90: Kentucky Land Grants, Parts 1 & 2, 1782-1924, Willard Rouse Jillson, ScD, publ. 1971, Genealogical Publishing Co., Baltimore, MD

146: Adair Co., KY Court Orders, 1802-1808, Marilyn P. Laird, Vivian P. Jackson, Judith Krause Reid, publ. 1978, Poe Publishers, Calumet Park, IL

Micajah Compton and Margaret Rexroat

Micajah Compton
Son of Banner Compton and Catherine Wilson
Born c. 1798 in Virginia or North Carolina
Died between February and June 1853, Pulaski Co., Kentucky

Married 22 Feb 1820, Adair Co., Kentucky

Margaret Rexroat
Daughter of Hans Adam Rexroat and Sarah McCord
Born c. 1800, Pennsylvania or North Carolina
Died after 1880, Pulaski Co., Kentucky

The tale of Micajah Compton and Margaret Rexroat is something out of Charles Dickens or Jane Austin. It is a story of purloined wills, scheming servants, foolish wives, faithful friends, and lots of money.

Micajah Compton was a farmer, miller, and moneylender. Based on the many misspellings of his name, his first name was pronounced Meh-kay'-ger, and his last name more Cumpton than Compton. He owned the equipment to mill both corn and wheat. While he called himself a farmer, today we would probably call him a rancher because of the considerable quantity of horses, cattle, and sheep that he owned. By the standards of the day, Micajah Compton was a prosperous man.[459]

He married Margaret Rexroat, the daughter of a German emigrant, Adam Rexroat.[460] Rexroat was a surveyor for Russell County,[461] and may have been acquainted with Banner Compton, Micajah's father. Rexroat was also the guardian for a pair of orphans, Samuel and Dorcus Whitaker, who had been in his care since the 1840s. There were two other Whitaker orphans – Polly, who was the charge of Samuel Combest, and later married Anderson Compton, and Ann, whose guardian was Anderson Compton, and later married Daniel McDaniel Rainwater.[462] Anderson Compton's close relations with the Whitakers would have repercussions later.

By the 1850 census, the roles had been reversed – the orphans, Dorcas and Samuel, were caring for the elderly Adam Rexroat.[463] In December 1850,

---

[459] 307: Will of Micajah Compton, Feb 1853, Pulaski Co., KY, Book 4 pgs 233-236, photocopy of original. This document, along with census records, provides most of the evidence for this section.

[460] Federal Census: 1820, Adair Co., KY, pg 44; 1830, Russell Co., KY, pg 119; 1840, Russell Co., KY, pg 28B; 1850, Pulaski Co., KY, pg 249

[461] 279: Russell Co., KY First Order Book, 1826-1827, pgs 9 & 38, Carol L. Sanders, publ. 1991, Blue Ash, OH

[462] 49: Pulaski Co., KY Marriage Records, Vol 1, 1797-1850, 2nd edition, pgs 41 & 116, Mary Weddle Kaurish, publ. 1984, Pulaski County Historical Society, Somerset, KY. Samuel Combest provided surety for Polly's marriage. Anderson provided permission for Ann's marriage saying, "*Her parents are dead and she lives with us.*"

[463] Federal Census: 1850, Pulaski Co., KY, pg 249

Micajah Compton graciously paid Dorcas' marriage bond.[464] Micajah also took on Samuel Whitaker as a hired hand. This would turn out to be a mistake, because Samuel Whitaker was the cowbird in the nest, the spanner in the works.

Micajah Compton's February 1853 will is the work of a worried man. He knew he was dying, and he knew that behind his back, his young hireling had been flirting with his middle-aged wife. So he wrote an entailed will.

An entailment, as every Jane Austin fan knows, is a way of reaching beyond the grave to set specific terms on how your money or property are used. Its frequent purpose was to prevent one's widow (or widow's second husband) from spending down the inheritance before it could be passed to the children.[465] The practice has been abolished in all but four states today, but was common in previous centuries. It has been the McGuffin in numerous works of fiction – *Sense and Sensibility*, *Pride and Prejudice*, and *Downton Abbey*, just to name a few.

In Micajah's case, he left his farm, livestock, tools, and household furnishings to Margaret, provided that "*she remains my widow.*" The phrase is repeated three times in the course of the will. After her death, the estate in her tenancy would be divided between their daughters, Mary and Martha, with the household property going to the sons.

Micajah's intent was clear. He was attempting to both preserve his estate for his children and protect his wife from the predatory attentions of Samuel Whitaker. Under the terms of the will, if Margaret remarried, she would be left penniless.

But his plan didn't work. Between February and June 1853, Micajah Compton died. On 14 Jul 1853, Margaret Rexroat Compton married Samuel Whitaker.[466] In October of that year, Margaret and Samuel went to court and stated that Micajah's will had been *purloined* and asked, since the will couldn't be found, would the court kindly just hand over the entire estate to her and her second husband?

At that moment, Justice of the Peace Josiah W. Duck arose to inform the court that he had been one of the witnesses to Compton's will and could produce a copy for the court, not the official copy, but apparently the only surviving copy. The Whitakers protested, as did Margaret's eldest son, Anderson, but the court accepted the will and forced Margaret to relinquish her claim on the estate.

Rexroat appears to have died in Russell Co., KY in Nov 1859 according to the 1860 Federal Mortality Schedule.

[464] 49: Pulaski Co., KY Marriage Records, Vol 1, 1797-1850, 2nd edition, pg 73, Mary Weddle Kaurish, publ. 1984, Pulaski County Historical Society, Somerset, KY

[465] Wikipedia: Fee Tail (Entail), http://en.wikipedia.org/wiki/Fee_tail

[466] 50: Pulaski Co., KY Marriage Records, Vol 2, 1851-1863, pg 119, Pulaski County Historical Society, publ. 1970, Somerset, KY

Though she continued to live with Samuel Whitaker through 1860, by 1870, he had died or abandoned her. She lived alone for at least the next ten years, under the name Margaret Compton, an admission, apparently, of her mistake. She died after 1880.[467]

The children of Micajah and Margaret Compton:

Sarah Ann Compton Bernard

Born c. 1820, Kentucky, and died 1890, Casey Co., Kentucky
Sally married Thornton Bernard on 5 Jun 1842, in Russell Co., Kentucky.[468] They were the parents of fifteen children, including a set of triplets.[469] In the 1880s, they operated one of the county poor farms. Sally died in 1890, Thornton in 1896. They are buried in Thomas Ridge Cemetery, Casey Co., Kentucky.[470]

Anderson W. Compton

Born 20 Jan 1822, Kentucky, and died 12 Jan 1883, Pulaski Co., Kentucky
Anderson married Mary "Polly" Whitaker on 14 Nov 1841.[471] Samuel Combest, her guardian, provided the marriage bond. The couple had six children.[472] They were also briefly the guardians of Mary's youngest sister, Ann, until her marriage to Daniel McDaniel Rainwater. During the Civil War, Anderson served four years in Company D, 3rd Kentucky Volunteer Infantry as a Private.[473] In civilian life, he was a farmer and a miller. The couple is buried in the Compton family farm cemetery.[474]

John Riley Compton

Born c. 1825 Kentucky, and died 2 Nov 1896, Pulaski Co., Kentucky
See profile of Helen M. Duck Compton, daughter of Josiah W. Duck, Jr.

---

[467] Federal Census: Pulaski Co., KY, 1850, pg 249; 1860, pg 309; 1870, pg 171; 1880, pg 376
[468] 348: Russell Co., KY Marriages, 1826-1865, Bailey through Butler, Gary L. Flanagan, rootsweb transcription
[469] Federal Census: Pulaski Co., KY, 1850, pg 250; 1860, pg 296; Casey Co., KY, 1880, pg 686C
[470] 2312: Findagrave.com #18266530 and #69873334
[471] 49: Pulaski Co., KY Marriage Records, Vol 1, 1797-1850, 2nd edition, Mary Weddle Kaurish, publ. 1984, Pulaski County Historical Society, Somerset, KY
[472] Federal Census: Waterloo, Harrison Dist., Pulaski Co., KY, 1850, pg 250; 1860, pg 309; 1870, pg 168
[473] 45: Report of the Adjutant General of the State of Kentucky, Civil War, 1861-1866, Vol. I, Union, publ. 1889, reprinted by the Southern Historical Press, 1992, Greenville, SC
[474] 47: Pulaski Co., KY Cemetery Records, Vol. 1, Pulaski County Historical Society, published Jan 1976, Somerset, KY

Samuel B. Compton

Born c. 1829, Kentucky, and died after 1900
Samuel served with Company G, 19th Kentucky Infantry as a Private from 1 Nov 1861 - 9 Aug 1862.[475] He was discharged at Cumberland Gap for unspecified reasons, probably illness. He never married, and is believed to be buried with his brother Anderson on the Compton farm.

William A. Compton

Born c. 1832, Kentucky, and died c. 1875, Kentucky
William married Mary Jane Hines around 1854.[476] They were the parents of four children, all born before the Civil War. William volunteered for a year with Company C, 3rd Kentucky Volunteer Infantry, serving as a Private.[477] Mary Jane died between 1860 and 1870, and William died around 1875, leaving two minor children in the care of Solomon Weddle and Claiborn Collins.[478]

Mary Compton

Born c. 1834, Kentucky, and died after 1853.

Martha E. Compton Rainwater

Born 7 Jun 1836, Pulaski Co., Kentucky, and died 16 Aug 1898 Pulaski Co., Kentucky
On 22 Dec 1852, Martha married Enoch Rainwater, the son of James Rainwater and Polly McDaniel, grandson of William Rainwater and Martha Hodges.[479] The couple brought twelve children into the world, one of whom died in infancy. Enoch was a farmer and a Justice of the Peace. Martha died in 1898, after which Enoch married Mary E. Roy.[480] He died in 1906. Martha and Enoch are buried in New Hope

---

[475] 45: Report of the Adjutant General of the State of Kentucky, Civil War, 1861-1866, Vol. I, Union, publ. 1889, reprinted by the Southern Historical Press, 1992, Greenville, SC

[476] 263: Pulaski Co., KY Vital Records, Birth & Death, 1852-1859, 1861, 1874-1878, Pulaski County Historical Society, Somerset, KY. Based on the birth of their first child – I have never found a marriage record.

[477] 45: Report of the Adjutant General of the State of Kentucky, Civil War, 1861-1866, Vol. I, Union, publ. 1889, reprinted by the Southern Historical Press, 1992, Greenville, SC

[478] 2521: Index to Order Books, County Court, Pulaski Co., KY, page 4213; and pages 36, 46, 48, 54 from those Order Books related to the Guardianship of Erasmus L. and Permelia I. Compton, 1875. Photocopies of original copied by Mark Stone, Archivist, 8 Aug 1997

[479] 50: Pulaski Co., KY Marriage Records, Vol 2, 1851-1863, Pulaski County Historical Society, publ. 1970, Somerset, KY

[480] 236: Pulaski Co., KY Marriage Records, Vol 5, 1901-1910, Pulaski County Historical Society, Somerset, KY

Cemetery in Pulaski County.[481]

Enoch and Martha Rainwater

Harrison A. Compton

Born 16 Feb 1839, Pulaski Co., Kentucky, and died 30 May 1909, Kentucky
On 1 Sep 1860, Harrison married Enoch Rainwater's sister, Sarah.[482] They were the parents of seven children. She died in 1883; Harrison died in 1909. They are buried in the Compton family farm cemetery.[483]

Erasmus A. Compton

Born 17 Jul 1841, Russell Co., Kentucky, and died 11 Apr 1924, Taylor, Williamson Co., Texas
See profile of Erasmus A. Compton and Martha Jane Duck

Jacob Compton

Other than being mentioned in his father's will, there is no evidence for this individual. He appears to have died prior to 1850.

---

[481] 48: Pulaski Co., KY Cemetery Records, Vol. 2, Pulaski County Historical Society, published June 1977, Somerset, KY

[482] 50: Pulaski Co., KY Marriage Records, Vol 2, 1851-1863, Pulaski County Historical Society, publ. 1970, Somerset, KY

[483] 47: Pulaski Co., KY Cemetery Records, Vol. 1, Pulaski County Historical Society, published Jan 1976, Somerset, KY

Erasmus D. Compton and Martha Jane Duck

Erasmus D. Compton
Son of Micajah Compton and Margaret Rexroat
Born 17 Jul 1841, Russell Co., Kentucky
Died 11 Apr 1924, Taylor, Williamson Co., Texas

Married 31 Jul 1831, Pulaski Co., Kentucky

Martha Jane Duck
Daughter of Josiah W. Duck, Jr. and Anna Cook
Born 7 May 1841, Pulaski Co., Kentucky
Died 22 Sep 1912, Taylor, Williamson Co., Texas

Erasmus Compton was 12 when his father died. History does not record what he thought of the legal turmoil that followed, or how he felt about his new step-father. We do know that by 1860, he had moved out of his mother's house.[484]

His father had left him half of the value of *"the home tract of land, also all the stock which may be on the farm, wagons, tools, etc."* and one quarter of *"all my cash notes."*[485] Whether he received the value of his inheritance as cash or land we don't know because the Kentucky State Archives was unable to locate the guardianship reports.

At the age of 20, Erasmus went to Camp Dick Robinson in Garrard County to enlist in the Union Army. It was probably the farthest he had been from home in his lifetime. He was officially enlisted on 7 Aug 1861, as a Private in Company D of the 3rd Kentucky Volunteer Infantry. He was promoted to Corporal on 9 Dec 1861.[486] The 3rd Kentucky Volunteer Infantry was attached to the Army of the Ohio through the end of 1862, and then folded into the Army of the Cumberland at the start of 1863. Most of the unit's early battles were fought in Kentucky and Tennessee.

According to his service papers, Erasmus was seriously wounded in the left thigh at the Battle of Stone's River (Murphreesboro, TN, 31 Dec 1862 to 2 Jan 1863). By his own description in his pension application, Erasmus was carried to the rear after being shot and when the battle moved close to his position, managed to get himself into a ditch, but sustained injuries to his right arm in the process. While in the regimental hospital, doctors discovered that he was

---

[484] Federal Census: 1860, Pulaski Co., KY, pg 309

[485] 307: Will of Micajah Compton, Feb 1853, Pulaski Co., KY, Book 4 pgs 233-236, photocopy of original

[486] 325: Civil War (Union) service papers of Erasmus D. Compton, 7 Aug 1861-9 May 1863, photocopies of microfilmed originals

326: Civil War (Union) pension papers of Erasmus D. Compton and Martha Jane Duck Compton, 7 Sep 1871-10 May 1924

suffering from hypertrophy of the heart[487], and discharged him with a surgeon's certificate of disability in May 1863. His discharge papers describe him as 6'1" tall, 175 lbs., with light hair and blue eyes.

Erasmus returned to Pulaski County to take up farming, and on 31 Jul 1863, married Martha Jane Duck. One of his mother's relations, Rev. William Rexroat, performed the ceremony.[488] The couple had three children, Arzona Belle, William Taylor and Charles Volantus.

In the years following the Civil War, Erasmus and his neighbors grew increasingly uneasy over the moral character of their old Kentucky home. At issue was the perception that the quiet Christian life they had known as children was vanishing. While this is easy to dismiss as nostalgia, they may have had a point.

John Logan Tarter

John Logan Tarter, a neighbor and relation by marriage, moved with his parents to Texas in 1875. He was interviewed in 1938 by WPA writer, Sheldon F. Gauthier, about his life experiences. Tarter's honest assessment of the whiskey problem in his natal state makes for some pretty funny reading:

---

[487] Enlargement of the heart, indicating high blood pressure
[488] 50: Pulaski Co., KY Marriage Records, Vol 2, 1851-1863, Pulaski County Historical Society, publ. 1970, Somerset, KY

In our section of Kentucky, the folks drank a great many gallons of liquor. The only disadvantage a still operator had to contend with was his inability to be accepted into the church. All other folks were saved regularly each year. Occasionally a still operator would decide to quit making whiskey and join the church. Then great rejoicing would take place among the brethren and sisters.

Well, the still operator would have all his wealth in whiskey and the still and he could not be expected to destroy the produce and leave himself destitute. Therefore the brethren would gather at the convert's house to arrange for distiller's livelihood after the liquor was destroyed, until the party could rearrange his affairs.

I accompanied father to a couple of the meetings when the brethren were supposed to destroy the whiskey and provided the distiller with goods in the place of the produce. The brethren would discuss the convert's change of heart and express their pleasure over the happy event and then take up the matter of disposing of the whiskey.

Some of the brethren would state that their wife needed some good whiskey to make bitters used for stomach disorders, some needed whiskey to make rock-and-roy which was used for coughs and there [were] various their remedies mentioned for which whiskey was needed. The act of tasting the whiskey stored in the various kegs was the next procedure. The brethren would take a sample drink of the whiskey in each keg and repeat the act several time to be sure which keg's whiskey was the best. By the time the brethren had been at the sampling process, everyone was in the mood for a good revival. The brethren would [settle on the amount of] the distiller's whiskey to be used for medicinal purpose only, but the amount bought for making bitters and other medicine, indicated that there was a great amount of sickness in the country. Some distillers had to be saved each year, but the brethren did not seem to object.[489]

In *The Omnivore's Dilemma*, Michael Pollan notes that by 1820, the average American was drinking half a pint of corn liquor a day, frequently abstaining only on Sunday morning. "*Americans simply did not gather – whether for a barn raising or quilting bee, corn husking or political rally – without passing the whiskey jug. The results were entirely predictable: a rising tide of public drunkenness, violence and family abandonment, and a spike in alcohol-related diseases.*"[490]

This makes the story told by C. V. Compton all the more poignant. Compton, writing in 1950, set down the story of his family's move from Kentucky to Texas. Later related to the Rainwaters by the marriage of Roscoe Rainwater to

---

[489] 331: Reminiscences of J. L. Tarter, Tarrant Co., TX, District S7, Document SFC240, Rangelore, WPA Federal Writers Project, Sheldon F. Gauthier, http://memory.loc.gov/ammem/index.html

[490] Michael Pollan, "*The Omnivore's Dilemma*," pgs 100-101, published 2006, The Penguin Press, New York

Gertrude Caughron, they were among the first to move to Texas on the advice of George Washington Marion Duck, who had moved to Texas in the 1850s. This excerpt confirms Pollan's observation of the pervasive problems caused by corn alcohol.

> One of my earliest recollections is of a conversation between my father and Uncle Tom (Gossett) – they were standing in our yard talking earnestly, paying no heed to me, when father said:
>
> "Yes, Tom, you are right, that is the only way out – we must break up, sell out, and move away to some new place where our children can be brought up free from the influences and temptations that face them here."
>
> Uncle Tom replied: "Yes, Raz, Saline and I have stayed awake several nights recently, discussing this, and have reached the same conclusion. What can we look forward to? What can we hope for or expect? We have stills, operated by moonshiners, in the knobs, hills and hollows near us, which are the meeting place day and night of the boys in this neighborhood. We both know that so much drinking and drunkenness can be charged to this condition."
>
> Then they decided that the families should get together and agree on what should be done. Accordingly, Uncle Tom and Aunt Saline and some of their families came over to our home, bringing along a geography. Mother and Aunt Saline seemed to lead in the conversation. Mother said: "Yes, we should move from this still-infested community."
>
> The geography was placed on the table, and the map of Texas was studied. Their eyes fell on the name of Palestine; finally all agreed that as soon as arrangements could be made, we would leave for Palestine, Texas.[491]

Among those related families who moved to Texas were Joel Thomas Gossett and his wife Salina Duck, and their children; Erasmus D. Compton and his wife Martha Jane Duck, Salina's sister, and their children; Joel's widowed sister, Elizabeth Gossett Caughron Gossett, her son T. W. Caughron and his future wife Arzona Belle Compton, who was the daughter of Erasmus Compton; William Thomas Cooper and his wife Martha Jane Floyd, whose daughter would later marry into the Rainwater family; Silas Tarter, his son John Logan Tarter and daughter Leora with her husband Joel Thomas Caughron, the brother of T. W. Caughron, and their children; and eventually Josiah Rainwater and his family. While the names may not be immediately familiar, they

---

[491] 491: From an incomplete draft of a memoir written by Charles Volantus Compton in May 1950, pages 1-45

represent a real exodus of a related community from Kentucky to Texas, between 1880 and 1890.[492]

C. V. Compton would later recall that the family visited the quaint log cabin of his grandmother, Margaret Rexroat Compton shortly before they left Kentucky in 1879. His father, Erasmus, had $80 stolen from him by a pickpocket during the train trip. Martha's money remained safe – she had sewn a money belt into the waistband of her dress.[493]

Erasmus purchased a considerable amount of land in the countryside near Waterloo, Texas,[494] and later, a home on 10th Street in Taylor that no longer exists. He made his living farming and breaking mustangs, and later in the feed business and as a carpenter.[495] He was called by the nickname, Uncle Raz, by which he is remembered in the county history.[496] He was also a member of the local chapter of Masons, and of the First Baptist Church of Taylor.

In 1912, Martha Duck Compton died following a stroke.[497] Nine years later, on 15 Apr 1921, Erasmus Compton suffered a heart attack and a stroke, the result of many years of high blood pressure that his youthful enlarged heart had presaged. He was confined to bed for the next few years, dying in 1924.[498]

The couple is buried in Taylor City Cemetery on 4th Street with their Caughron relations.[499]

The children of Erasmus and Martha Compton:

Arzona Belle Compton Caughron

Born 1 Oct 1865, Pulaski Co., Kentucky, and died 5 Feb 1949, Vernon, Wilbarger Co., Texas
See profile of Arzona Belle Compton and Theophilus Walter Caughron

William Taylor Compton, "Uncle Billy"

Born 10 Mar 1871, Pulaski Co., Kentucky, and died 30 Nov 1949, Williamson Co., Texas
Known universally as "Uncle Billy", William T. Compton was one of Taylor's most beloved characters. He started his working life as a

---

[492] All of these individuals are related by marriage to the Rainwaters

[493] 491: From an incomplete draft of a memoir written by Charles Volantus Compton in May 1950, pages 1-45

[494] 133: Direct, General and Reverse Indexes to Deeds of Williamson Co., TX, various volumes, Williamson County Courthouse, Georgetown, TX, reviewed and photographed 27 May 1997

[495] 452: "Comptons Early Kentucky Family," 23 Nov 1956, Taylor Press, Taylor, Williamson Co., TX, photocopy

[496] 94: Land of Good Water: Takachue Pouetsu. A Williamson Co., Texas History, pg 464, Clara Stearns Scarbrough, publ. 1973, Williamson County Sun Publishers, Georgetown, TX

[497] 359: Death certificate #22594, Martha J. Compton, Williamson Co., TX, 1912, certified copy

[498] 358: Death certificate #14684, Erasmus D. Compton, Williamson Co., TX, 1924, certified copy

[499] 1423: Taylor City Cemetery, Taylor, Williamson Co., TX, Compton, Caughron, Aderholt & Gossett tombstones, photos by Susan & R. Steven Rainwater, Feb 1997 and May 1997

bookkeeper for a local grocery store, and continued this work even after he took employment with the post office as a rural mail carrier.

When he retired from the post office, he occupied himself visiting the sick on behalf of First Baptist Church of Taylor, and was eventually recognized for having visited more sick people than anyone else in Taylor.[500] William married Martha Ann Luttrell c. 1896, and the union produced two sons, Louis and Clare. The couple also raised their granddaughter, Marjorie. He died in 1949 – both his tombstone and death certificate call him "Uncle Billy."[501]

Charles Volantus Compton

Born 7 Jan 1873, Pulaski Co., Kentucky, and died 12 Jan 1960, Dallas, Dallas Co., Texas[502]
Born Volantus Green Compton, C. V. changed his name to the more distinguished Charles Volantus Compton as an adult. He was admitted to the state bar in 1896, and made a name for himself as a prison reformer. He was a vocal opponent of the use of "the bat" on prisoners – the practice of administering beatings as a form of discipline – and his efforts were successful in 1941 when the Texas legislature outlawed this punishment.[503]

C. V. was an active member of the Salvation Army and gave a considerable amount of money for the building of the Compton Citadel and Gymnasium at Corinth & Browder Streets in Dallas.[504] His long support was recognized with the Distinguished Auxiliary Service Award, the Salvation Army's highest honor. He was also an active real estate investor and developer. C. V. married Jessie Sallie Shapard around 1900, and they were the parents of three daughters. He died in 1960, memorialized by lengthy obituaries in both the Dallas Morning News and Dallas Times Herald.[505]

---

[500] 453: "Meet the People: W.T. Compton," 2 Jul 1948, Taylor Press, Taylor, Williamson Co., TX, photocopy

[501] 362: Death certificate #56009, W.T. "Uncle Billy" Compton, Williamson Co., TX, 1949, certified copy

[502] 1461: Compton tombstones in Hillcrest Memorial Park (Sparkman-Hillcrest), Northwest Highway, Dallas, Dallas Co., TX, photos by Susan & R. Steven Rainwater, 29 Sept 2001

[503] 2582: "House, Prison Board Vote to Abolish Bat" and "Compton is Happy", page 6, 12 Feb 1941, Dallas Morning News, Dallas, TX, scan from microfilm

[504] Part of the building still exists, but is owned by a private company.

[505] 429 & 430: Obituaries, Dallas Times Herald, 13 Jul 1960, section A, page 12, and Dallas Morning News, 13 Jun 1960, section 4, pg 13

William Trimble and Mary Fleming

William Trimble
Son of David Trimble and Mary Houston
Born c. 1760, Augusta Co., Virginia
Died 6 Jun 1840, Pulaski Co., Kentucky

Married 19 Aug 1787 in Greenbriar Co., Virginia

Mary Fleming
Born 14 Apr 1772, Virginia
Died between 1842 and 1850

The Trimble family has a long pedigree. The original emigrant, David, was born in Scotland in 1720. His family moved to Armagh Co., Ireland in the early 1730s, and came to the American colonies a few years later. He and his wife, Mary Houston, settled in Augusta Co., Virginia, and had ten children.[506] Some years later, the family moved to the frontier lands of Kentucky for cheap land, and David died in Bourbon County in 1799, leaving his son, William, six silver shillings.[507]

William Trimble volunteered for service in the Virginia Militia in Sep 1777.[508] He served in the brigade of General Hann in Augusta Co., Virginia, under Captain Joseph Patterson and Colonel Dickinson. Trimble would later recall being marched from Staunton, Virginia, through Greenbriar County to The Point on the Ohio River (probably Point Pleasant), a journey of about 260 miles if you were to drive it today. His unit remained there for three months on guard against Indian hostilities, after which, he was discharged.

In 1779, William served as a substitute for his brother, James, who had been drafted to serve in an action against an Indian tribe he recalled as the "*Tuschaway.*"[509] He served under Captain William Henderson and Colonel William Boyer, in the brigade of General Lachlan McIntosh. He saw no action during his tour of duty, because General McIntosh succeeded in making a treaty with the Indians.[510]

---

[506] 286: Don Raney, "*Caughron Family History: Including Associated Families (West, Comption, Jones, Newell, Strong, Shook, Duck, Gossett, Cook & Trimble),*" draney@nutshell.org, publ. 1999, Dallas, TX

[507] 311: Will of David Cooper, 6 Sep 1798 Bourbon Co., KY, transcribed by Delene Dee Robinson

[508] The information for this profile comes from the following sources, unless otherwise noted:
74: Genealogical Abstracts of Revolutionary War Pension Files, Vol 3, N-Z, Virgil D. White
984: Revolutionary War pension application of William Trimble, dated 12 Oct 1833, Pulaski Co., KY, transcription provided by Don Raney
985: Revolutionary War pension application of Mary Fleming Trimble, widow of William, dated 14 Apr 1842, Pulaski Co., KY, transcription provided by Don Raney

[509] This name does not correspond to any known tribe. My best guess is that he meant the Tuscaroras.

[510] Historical evidence suggests that these events took place in 1776, not 1779. According to Joseph Addison Waddell's "*Annals of Augusta County, Virginia, from 1726 to 1871,*" Captain

In December 1780, William was drafted to serve in a rifle company commanded by his brother, Captain James Trimble. Their purpose was to defend the coastline from British attack, and they did a great deal of marching in support of this goal, but never fired a shot. Finally in 1781, he served for another three months, again under the command of James Trimble, during which time they marched 200 miles north with the intention of reaching New York, but could not have gotten farther than Baltimore. Again, the unit never engaged in battle.

William later recalled that he had been discharged *"about two months before the surrender of Cornwallis"*, which would

have been about August 1781, since Cornwallis surrendered at Yorktown on 19 Oct 1781.[511]

On 19 Aug 1787, in Greenbriar Co., Virginia, William married Mary Fleming. Their first two children were born in Virginia; nine were born in Kentucky.

The family moved to Bourbon Co., Kentucky, in October 1792, and Harrison Co., Kentucky three years later. By 1810, they had moved to Pulaski County.[512] Three of his offspring would marry into the Tarter family. One daughter, Mary "Polly" Trimble, would marry Thomas Caughron.

William filed for a pension on his Revolutionary War service on 12 Oct 1833, in Pulaski County Court. He was awarded $32.77 annually, a fairly typical amount for an enlisted soldier.[513] He died in 1840, and on 19 Sep 1842, Mary filed for a widow's pension. She appears to have died prior to the 1850 census.

William Bowyer was sent to reinforce General McIntosh on the Ohio River, in August, 1776. The McIntosh Wikipedia article (http://en.wikipedia.org/wiki/Lachlan_McIntosh), says that in 1779, General McIntosh had been ordered to South Carolina and Georgia by General George Washington, where he served for over a year. This would make unlikely the 1779 time frame for the events Trimble describes. Since he was describing the events 50+ years after they happened, small errors are not surprising.

[511] Wikipedia: Siege of Yorktown, http://en.wikipedia.org/wiki/Siege_of_Yorktown

[512] Federal Census: 1810, Pulaski Co., KY, pg 10

[513] 2558: Kentucky Pension Roll of 1835, United States War Department, publ. 1959, Southern Book Company, Baltimore, MD

BLATCHLEY C. W. CAUGHRON AND ELIZABETH E. GOSSETT

Blatchley C. W. Caughron
Son of Thomas Caughron and Mary Trimble
Born c. 1823, Pulaski Co., Kentucky
Died Aug 1873, Pulaski Co., Kentucky

Married 15 Oct 1849, Pulaski Co., Kentucky

Elizabeth E. Gossett
Daughter of Joel M. Gossett and Sarah M. Gordon
Born Jun 1828, Kentucky
Died between 1900 and 1903, Texas

In 1849, Mary "Polly" Trimble, the daughter of Revolutionary War veteran William Trimble, married Thomas Caughron. Born in Virginia, the census places Caughron in Wythe County in 1810. He arrived in Pulaski County by 1814, where he married Polly on 8 Nov 1814.[514] Thomas made his living as a haymaker and a farmer.[515] The couple had four children – two boys and two girls. They named their eldest son Blatchley, which was probably a family name. This name was mangled in a number of official records as Bladely and Blackley, and the middle initials appear as both H.W. and G.W. But his will says B. C. W., and we assume he knew his own name. He seems to always have referred to himself as B. C.

On 15 Oct 1849, B. C. married Elizabeth "Bessie" Gossett.[516] The Gossetts had also come to Kentucky from Virginia. Elizabeth was one of six children, two of whom married into the Duck family.

B. C. took over the operation of his father's farm. He and Bessie brought eight children into the world; four of whom died in childhood. The two surviving daughters remained in Kentucky, while their two surviving sons would eventually move to Texas.

B. C. was 38 at the outbreak of the Civil War, and was a married man with a family. So his joining up was rather unusual, but not unheard of. On 1 Jan 1862, he enlisted as a Private in Company D of the 3rd Kentucky Volunteer Infantry of the Union Army, and was mustered out 10 Jan 1865, at the end of the war.[517] Since he never filed for a pension, there is no indication that he suffered unduly during his service, and no indication from his service papers

---

[514] 49: Pulaski Co., KY Marriage Records, Vol 1, 1797-1850, 2nd edition, Mary Weddle Kaurish, publ. 1984, Pulaski County Historical Society, Somerset, KY
[515] Federal Census: Pulaski Co., KY, 1850, pg 247; 1860, pg 307
[516] 49: Pulaski Co., KY Marriage Records, Vol 1, 1797-1850, 2nd edition, Mary Weddle Kaurish, publ. 1984, Pulaski County Historical Society, Somerset, KY
[517] 45: Report of the Adjutant General of the State of Kentucky, Civil War, 1861-1866, Vol. I, Union, publ. 1889, reprinted by the Southern Historical Press, 1992, Greenville, SC

that he was ever wounded. In the course of his service, he would have been part of the Chattanooga and Atlanta campaigns.

In August 1873, B. C. wrote his will, stating that he was *"sick and weak of body."* He left his personal property to his wife and $115 to each of his children. Bessie received life tenancy of the family farm, which was to be sold after her death and the proceeds split among the surviving children.[518] We do not know exactly when B. C. died, but it must have been shortly thereafter. He was buried in a cemetery on the family farm which was surveyed in the 1970s.[519]

Bessie remarried six years later. On 5 Nov 1879, she married William B. Gossett, her first cousin once removed.[520] All that can be said for certain is that he died prior to 1888, since she was a widow living in Texas by that year. Williamson County land records indicates that Elizabeth E. Gossett donated land in the Caleb W. Baker survey to County Judge D. S. Chissum for the location of a school.[521] The deed shows land was purchased 1 Mar 1888.

Bessie is recorded living in the household of her son T. W. in Taylor, Texas, in the 1890 census of Civil War Veterans and Widows. She is recorded again in 1900. After that, it's not clear. There is no death record, which suggests that she died before 1903, but might have died as late as 1910.[522] She is not listed in the sexton's records of Taylor City Cemetery.[523]

The children of B.C.W. and Elizabeth Caughron:

John P., William J., Mary M. and James Caughron

Died in childhood. Probably buried on the family farm.

Theophilous Walter Caughron

Born 12 Jun 1859, Pulaski Co., Kentucky, and died 14 May 1947, Williamson Co., Texas
See profile of Theophilous Walter Caughron and Arzona Belle Compton

---

[518] 309: Will of Blatchley C. W. Caughron, 18 Aug 1873, Pulaski Co., KY, Book 7 pg 28, photocopy of original

[519] 48: Pulaski Co., KY Cemetery Records, Vol. 2, Pulaski County Historical Society, published June 1977, Somerset, KY

[520] 51: Pulaski Co., KY Marriage Records, Vol 3, 1864-1886, Pulaski County Historical Society, publ. 1984, Somerset, KY

[521] 133: Direct, General and Reverse Indexes to Deeds of Williamson Co., TX, Book 54 page 299, Williamson County Courthouse, Georgetown, TX, reviewed and photographed 27 May 1997 in the basement of the Williamson County Courthouse

[522] Texas officially began issuing death certificates in 1903, but it took some counties more than a decade to comply, so lack of a death certificate is not certain proof that she died prior to 1903.

[523] 496: Taylor City Cemetery Sexton's Records, Taylor, Williamson Co., TX, seen in person (no copies)

Joel Thomas Caughron

Born Jul 1852, Pulaski Co., Kentucky, and died 21 Mar 1940, Irion Co., Texas

On 29 Mar 1877, Joel married Leora Frances D. Tarter, the daughter of Silas Tarter and America Logan.[524] They were the parents of seven children, most of whom were born in Texas. Joel originally settled in Williamson Co., then moved to neighboring Travis County.[525] By 1910 he had moved to Runnels County and remained there until at least 1930.[526] He died in Irion County in 1940 and is buried with his wife in Evergreen Cemetery, Ballinger, Runnels Co, Texas.[527]

Caroline Ellen Caughron Hudson

Born 22 May 1856, Pulaski Co., Kentucky and died 29 Jan 1939, Pulaski Co., Kentucky

On 10 Sep 1873, Caroline married Daniel Hudson.[528] They were the parents of eleven children, one of whom died at birth. They lived in Pulaski County all of their lives and are buried in Somerset City Cemetery.[529]

Sarah C. Caughron

Born c. 1867, Pulaski Co., Kentucky and died after 1880

Sarah lived to at least 1880, and appears never to have married. She is probably buried on the family farm.

---

[524] 51: Pulaski Co., KY Marriage Records, Vol 3, 1864-1886, Pulaski County Historical Society, publ. 1984, Somerset, KY

[525] Federal Census: 1910, Travis Co., TX, pg 19B

[526] Federal Census: Runnels Co., TX, 1910, pg 14; 1920, pg 124; 1930, pg 51B in son Augustus' home

[527] 314: Texas Death Record Index, 1903-1940, A-F, Microfilm Roll #1
2312: Findagrave.com #61822610 and #55610143

[528] 51: Pulaski Co., KY Marriage Records, Vol 3, 1864-1886, Pulaski County Historical Society, publ. 1984, Somerset, KY

[529] 47: Pulaski Co., KY Cemetery Records, Vol. 1, Pulaski County Historical Society, published Jan 1976, Somerset, KY

Theophilous Walter Caughron
and Arzona Belle Compton

Drawing from wedding photo of T.W. and Arzona Caughron, c.1881

Theophilous Walter Caughron
Son of B.C.W. Caughron and Elizabeth Gossett
Born 12 Jun 1859, Pulaski Co., Kentucky
Died 14 May 1947, Taylor, Williamson Co., Texas

Married 22 Dec 1881, Taylor, Williamson Co., Texas

Arzona Belle Compton
Daughter of Erasmus Compton and Martha Jane Duck
Born 1 Oct 1865, Pulaski Co., Kentucky
Died 5 Feb 1949, Taylor, Williamson Co., Texas

Theophilous Walter Caughron was born in Pulaski Co., the eldest surviving son of his parents. In 1880, he, his mother, his brother Joel, Joel's wife Leora Tarter, Leora's father Silas and her brother John Logan, joined the Compton family and moved to Texas. They settled in Williamson County, and shortly thereafter, T.W. married Arzona Belle Compton on 22 Dec 1881.[530] T. W. and Arzona brought seven children into the world.

---

[530] 82: Williamson Co., TX Marriage Records, Vol 2, Books 2-3-4-5, 1860-1884, and Books 6-7-8, 1885-1900, Frances T. Ingmire, from original records compiled by J. Stoddard, publ. 1985, St. Louis, MO

Her name was pronounced Arr-zona. It appears in some official documents as Arizona, and indeed state names were very popular girls' names in the mid-19th century.[531] However, her enormous tombstone clearly says Arzona, and her descendants are insistent upon this pronunciation.

In the years following the marriage, T.W. acquired large amounts of land in the vicinity of Waterloo, Texas. He registered brands for horses and cattle at the county courthouse.[532] By 1900, the family had moved into Taylor, and T.W. had taken a job as a railroad baggage handler. In 1910, he listed his occupation as carpenter, and in 1930, as truck farmer.[533] T.W. was also regarded as an expert ox handler.[534]

On 23 Dec 1913, the Dallas Morning News reported that Walter Caughron of Taylor, Texas, had been stabbed twice by a man he did not know. The assailant, Mose Richardson, attacked him for no apparent reason, and then ran, evading capture for several hours. A posse led by constables cornered Richardson in a barn loft near Circleville, killing him in a brief shootout. Though Caughron's physicians believed he would die of the wounds, he survived.[535]

T.W. and Arzona Caughron, c. 1946

In December 1946, the Caughrons received a second mention in the Dallas Morning News; this time under happier circumstances. The couple celebrated

---

[531] Alabama, Missouri, Mississippi, and Arizona were particularly popular girls' names, based on their frequent appearance in the census records

[532] 144: Index of Livestock Brands, Williamson County Court House, Georgetown, TX, reviewed and photographed 27 May 1997

[533] Federal Census, Williamson Co., TX: 1900, pg 136-137; 1910, pg 255A; 1920, pg 271A; 1930, pg 77

[534] 491: C. V. Compton, "*The Autobiography of C. V. Compton*", May 1950, pages 1-45 (incomplete), photocopy of original, from Betty C. Baskett

[535] 2675: "Shot Resisting Arrest," pg 13, Dallas Morning News, 23 Dec 1913, scan of original

their 64th wedding anniversary, surrounded by their seven children, eighteen grandchildren, and nine great-grandchildren.[536]

Late in life, T. W. began exhibiting symptoms that one would now associate with Alzheimer's Disease.[537] He died in his sleep, officially of heart failure.[538] Arzona was by this time so unwell that she moved to Vernon at the insistence of her son-in-law and daughter, Roscoe and Gertrude Rainwater. There, the doctor told the Rainwaters that owing to diabetes, Arzona needed to have one of her feet amputated, but she had so little time left, that there was no point in putting her through the trauma.[539] She died in 1949 of thrombosis of the femoral artery and arteriosclerosis.[540]

The Caughrons are buried in Taylor City Cemetery in a plot shared with the Comptons.[541] The large central tombstone is engraved with the Compton information on one side and the Caughron information on the other; a testament to decades of close friendship.

The children of T.W. and Arzona Caughron:

Pearl Caughron Arbuckle

Born 15 Sep 1882, Williamson Co., Texas, and died 29 May 1969, Austin Co., Texas

According to Nancy Rainwater, Pearl was named and raised by one of her grandmothers, though it's not clear which one. On 11 Sep 1902, she married William Arbuckle, a local contractor.[542] They were the parents of two children.[543] The Arbuckles are buried in Taylor City Cemetery with William's brother Matthew.[544]

Gertrude Alice Caughron Rainwater

Born 19 Oct 1884, Williamson Co., Texas, and died 17 Aug 1969, Wilbarger Co., Texas

See profile of Roscoe Rainwater and Gertrude Alice Caughron

---

[536] 2656: "Wed 64 Years," pg 12, Dallas Morning News, 22 Dec 1946, scan of original

[537] 19: Nancy McIlhaney Rainwater, deceased, (McIlhaney Family), conversations between 1991 and 1997

[538] 352: Death certificate #23533, T.W. Caughron, Williamson Co., TX, 1947, certified copy

[539] 19: Nancy McIlhaney Rainwater, deceased, (McIlhaney Family), conversations between 1991 and 1997

[540] 353: Death certificate #20161, Arizona Belle Caughron, Wilbarger Co., TX, 1949, certified copy

[541] 1423: Taylor City Cemetery, Taylor, Williamson Co., TX, Compton, Caughron, Aderholt & Gossett tombstones, photos by Susan & R. Steven Rainwater, Feb 1997 and May 1997

[542] 286: Don Raney, "*Caughron Family History: Including Associated Families (West, Comption, Jones, Newell, Strong, Shook, Duck, Gossett, Cook & Trimble)*",draney@nutshell.org, 1999, Dallas, TX

[543] 1920 Federal Census, Williamson Co., TX, pg 209.

[544] 1423: Taylor City Cemetery, Taylor, Williamson Co., TX, Compton, Caughron, Aderholt & Gossett tombstones, photos by Susan & R. Steven Rainwater, Feb 1997 and May 1997

Myrtle Caughron Heap

Born Aug 1886, Williamson Co., Texas, and died 6 Apr 1976, Williamson Co., Texas

Myrtle worked as a bookkeeper until at least 1930. She married Fred Heap, c. 1912, and they were the parents of one daughter.[545] The couple is buried in Taylor City Cemetery.[546]

Zena Caughron Taegel

Born 21 Dec 1890, Williamson Co., Texas, and died 16 Feb 1978, Pulaski Co., Arkansas

Zeze, as she was called by her family, worked as a department store bookkeeper as a young woman. She married William Taegel on 26 May 1914.[547] They were the parents of four children.[548] The couple had separated by 1940.[549] Zeze is buried in the family plot with her parents in Taylor City Cemetery.[550]

Bert Alvie Caughron

Born 12 Feb 1894, Williamson Co., Texas, and died 26 Sep 1967, Rapides Parish, Louisiana

Bert's first job was as a messenger for the weather bureau in Taylor, but he would later operate a confectionary in Hereford and work as a cotton buyer in Galveston.[551] During the depression, he worked for the Federal Housing Administration, based in the Cotton Exchange Building in Dallas and later as a bank loan officer.[552] After World War II, he worked for the Veteran's Administration.[553] On 5 Oct 1918, he married Cassie Maurine West in Post, Garza Co., Texas.[554] They were

---

[545] Federal Census: Williamson Co., TX, 1910, pg 255A; 1920, pg 158B, 1930, pg 104B

[546] 1423: Taylor City Cemetery, Taylor, Williamson Co., TX, Compton, Caughron, Aderholt & Gossett tombstones, photos by Susan & R. Steven Rainwater, Feb 1997 and May 1997

[547] 469: McLennan Co., TX Marriage Records, Vol 4, Jan 1901-Jul 1916, Betty Ross Crook, published 2009, Central Texas Genealogical Society, Waco, TX

[548] Federal Census: 1910, Williamson Co., TX, pg 255A; 1920, Milam Co., TX, pg 169B; 1930, Bell Co., TX, pg 41A

[549] Federal Census: 1940, 616 W 5th St, Taylor, Williamson Co., TX

[550] 1423: Taylor City Cemetery, Taylor, Williamson Co., TX, Compton, Caughron, Aderholt & Gossett tombstones, photos by Susan & R. Steven Rainwater, Feb 1997 and May 1997

[551] Federal Census: 1910, Williamson Co., TX, pg 136-137; 1920, Galveston, Galveston Co., TX, pg 73B

2564: World War I Selective Service Registration Card #1793, Bert Alvie Caughron, photocopy

[552] Federal Census: 1930 Dallas Co., TX, pg 148A; 1940, Dallas Co., TX, pg 37A

[553] 2581: Obituary; Bert A. Caughron, page 28A, 24 Sep 1967, Dallas Morning News, Dallas, TX, scan from microfilm

[554] 286: Don Raney, "*Caughron Family History: Including Associated Families (West, Comption, Jones, Newell, Strong, Shook, Duck, Gossett, Cook & Trimble),*" draney@nutshell.org, 1999, Dallas, TX

the parents of two children. He and his wife are buried in Grove Hill Memorial Park off of I-30 in east Dallas.[555]

Walter Eugene Caughron

Born 17 Nov 1901, Williamson Co., Texas, and died 2 Dec 1988, Thorndale, Milam Co., Texas

His obituary says of him, "*He lived in Thorndale as a young man working as a salesman. Lived in Austin for 39 years, retiring in 1968 after 42 years with Higginbotham-Bailey Co. of Dallas, in whose employ he served as General Manager of the Central Texas Division. Member of First Baptist Church of Austin, serving as president of the J.N. Marshall Bible class.*" He married Ruth Summerlin c. 1925, and they were the parents of two children. He is buried in Thorndale City Cemetery, Milam Co., Texas.[556]

Martha C. "Bess" Caughron Nance

Born 11 Dec 1905, Williamson Co., Texas, and died 18 Feb 2004, Nueces Co., Texas

Bess, as she was called, attended Mary Hardin Baylor College and took a position as a schoolteacher in San Saba, Texas. There she met Worth Nance, and they were married in 1939. They were the parents of three daughters. Bess was a lifelong Baptist and her love of baking was noted in her obituary. She died at the age of 98, and is buried with her husband in Seaside Memorial Park, Corpus Christi, Nueces Co., Texas.[557]

---

[555] 286: Don Raney, "*Caughron Family History: Including Associated Families (West, Comption, Jones, Newell, Strong, Shook, Duck, Gossett, Cook & Trimble),*" draney@nutshell.org, 1999, Dallas, TX
[556] 2312: Obituary transcription, Findagrave.com #21129437
[557] 19: Nancy McIlhaney Rainwater, deceased, (McIlhaney Family), conversations between 1991 and 1997
Worth Nance is found as a single man in the 1930 Federal Census in San Saba Co., TX, pg 110A. Bess is not found in the 1930 census at all. They are found as a married couple with their first child in the 1940 Federal Census, San Saba Co., TX, pg 30B.
2312: Obituary, Austin American Statesman, 19 Feb 2004, transcription, Findagrave.com #100515034 and #89225701

The Family Tree of Nancy Jane McIlhaney

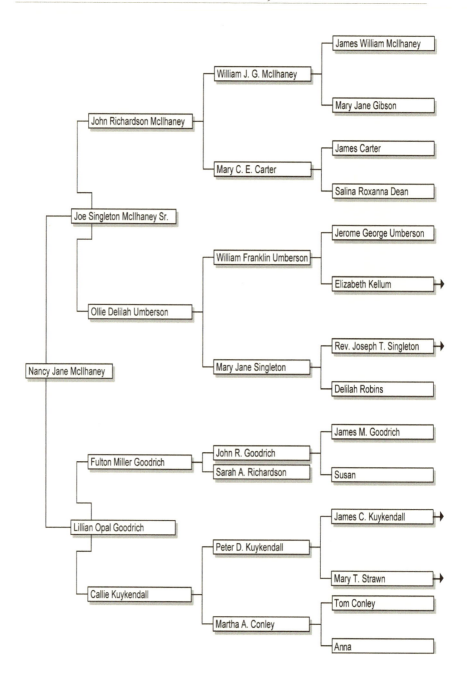

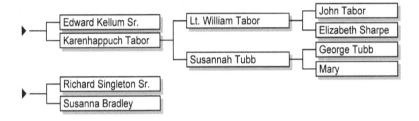

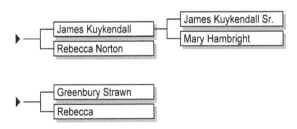

JAMES WILLIAM MCILHANEY AND MARY JANE GIBSON

L>R: Mary Jane Gibson McIlhaney in chair; Frank B McIlhaney; Oliver Lee McIlhaney; William Arthur McIlhaney; John Richardson McIlhaney; Lula Belle McIlhaney; William J. G. McIlhaney and wife Mary C. E. Carter McIlhaney; Ethel Elizabeth McIlhaney.
In front of McIlhaney homestead, Waldo, Coryell Co., TX, c. 1890

James William McIlhaney
Born c. 1795, Ireland
Died 3 Dec 1869, Coryell Co., Texas

Married before 1828, Tennessee

Mary Jane Gibson
Born 10 Mar 1803, Kentucky or Tennessee
Died 18 Dec 1891, Coryell Co., Texas

In 1801, William McElhinay died in Grainger Co., Tennessee, leaving a will naming his wife Mary and his children Robert, John, Moses, Peggy, Martha, Nan, Rebecca, Rachel, Jennet, Ann, and James.[558]

It is said that this same McIlhaney family came to America from Ireland in the 1730s with the Buchanan family, settling in Augusta Co., Virginia, and eventually moving to Grainger Co., Tennessee.[559] Jeannette Tileotson Acklen,

---

[558] 379: The Will of William McElhinay, Loose Wills, Grainger Co., TN, copied under the Works Progress Administration by Mrs. John Trotwood Moore, 1938, publ. 1995

[559] 381: Tennessee Records, Tombstone Inscriptions and Manuscripts, "Buchanan Historical Facts," pgs 126-127, Jeannette Tileotson Acklen, publ. 1967, Genealogical Publishing Co., Baltimore, MD

the author of the book in which this comment appears, uses the contemporary spelling of McIlhaney, which is why her claim has drawn so much attention. However, this spelling doesn't appear in the verifiable older records of this family – the contemporary spelling appears only after the family has arrived in Texas. So Acklen's spelling is a red herring and the James mentioned in William McElhinay's will is probably unrelated to ours.[560]

Moreover, whenever he was asked, James William McIlhaney said that he was born in 1795 *in Ireland*.[561] A profile of his son, W. J. G. McIhaney, published in 1893, says of James, "*a native of Ireland, [he] emigrated to American when a young man, and after landing in the United States, came to Tennessee.*"[562] So if James was born in Ireland in 1795, his parents could not have arrived in America in 1730.

The first record that appears to be clearly James occurs in the 1830 census of Henderson Co., Tennessee, where he is the head of a household of five persons – himself, a wife, two daughters, and another woman over twenty, who might have been any female relative.

James William McIlhaney married Mary Jane Gibson in or before 1828, in Tennessee.[563]

Mary Jane Gibson comes with her own set of genealogical problems.[564] A mistake regarding her parentage printed in the McIlhaney-Gibson-Warren newsletter, *Country Ties*, has influenced a generation of researchers to believe she is the daughter of Jesse Gibson and Elizabeth Parmley. This assertion is incorrect, but it so complicated that it requires a chapter of its own to disprove.

Between 1833 and 1835, James McIlhaney, his wife, their children, and other relations, left Henderson Co., Tennessee, for Tippah Co., Mississippi. James purchased three parcels of land, approximately 160 acres,[565] and was living in District #2 in the 1850 census, with his Gibson relations in nearby households.[566]

---

[560] It does appear that the Gibson family was intermarried with the Buchanan family of Augusta Co., VA. Post on genforum.com/gibson, "Randolph Gibson, South Carolina Will," Carolyn Sparks, 18 Feb 2003 and Mary Sue Austin, 4 Sep 2004

[561] 1897: Light on the Prairie: The History of the Organization of Coryell Baptist Church in 1855 and the Story of the Endeavors and Influences Wielded in 100 Years, pg 22, Mary Boyd, publ. 1955, bound photocopied edition held by the Dallas Public Library

1850 Federal Census, Tippah Co., MS, pg 410B; 1860 Federal Census, Coryell Co., TX, og 267B

[562] 54: A Memorial & Biographical History of McLennan, Falls, Bell & Coryell Counties, TX, pg 327, publ. 1893, The Lewis Publishing Co., Chicago, IL

[563] 54: A Memorial & Biographical History of McLennan, Falls, Bell & Coryell Counties, TX, pg 327, publ. 1893, The Lewis Publishing Co., Chicago, IL. We base the year of their marriage on the birth of their first child in 1829. According to census records, the first three children were born in Tennessee. I have personally checked the following Tennessee Counties for a marriage record: Anderson, Blount, Campbell, Carter, Claiborne, Davidson, Grainger, Greene, Hardeman, Henry, Jefferson, Knox, McMinn, and Roane.

[564] I would be remiss if I failed to mention that one of these issues is the unsupported claim that she was ¼ Cherokee.

[565] 1087: Bureau of Land Management online database, http://www.glorecords.blm.gov

The McIlhaneys sold out in the fall of 1853, receiving $2,100 for their land and surplus personal property.[567] They moved to Dallas Co., Texas, in the fall of 1853, and then to Coryell Co., Texas, in 1854.

James W. and Jane McIlhaney were the parents of seven children – four girls and three boys.[568] All three of their sons fought for the Confederacy in the Civil War, and two lost their lives as a result.

In 1854, Coryell Baptist Church was founded by sixteen individuals, including James and Jane McIlhaney and their four daughters. Four years later, on 24 Sep 1858, the church sent three "messengers" to the Leon River Baptist Association, to assist in the forming of a new church. James McIlhaney was one of those messengers.[569]

In 1869, James W. McIlhaney drowned in Coryell Creek. T. Hugh McIlhaney writing in *Country Ties* related the following story:

> James W. and Jane were allowed to preempt 320 acres of land out of the Isaac Franks survey. The custom was to purchase the land without the customary survey, agree to build and settle on the land, then pay the price that the other land around yours sold for. James had purchased his 320 acres because it had Coryell Creek [on it] with wood and pasture. James had some scrub brush in one area and would often go cut wood and bring it home. It is believed that he drowned while crossing the creek fetchin' home some wood. His heavy woolen clothing prevented his saving himself, that and the cold. His body was not found for three days and some three miles downstream near Mound, Texas.[570]

James was buried in the graveyard of the church he helped found.[571]

The widowed Jane McIhaney lived on the family farm in the now vanished Waldo[572] with her surviving son, W. J. G. McIlhaney, and his family until her death in 1891. She is also buried in Coryell Baptist Church Cemetery.

---

[566] T. Hugh McIlhaney's article says that Elizabeth Parmley Gibson was living in Tippah Co., MS in the 1850 census. This is incorrect. Elizabeth Parmley Gibson was living in the household of her son George Stewart Gibson in Hardeman Co., TN. The woman living in Tippah Co., MS was Margaret Gibson.

[567] 105: Country Ties, Winter 1990, Vol 1 No 1, pgs 7-8, article by T. Hugh McIlhaney

[568] Federal Census: 1850, District #2, Tippah Co., MS, pg 410B

[569] 1897: Light on the Prairie: The History of the Organization of Coryell Baptist Church in 1855 and the Story of the Endeavors and Influences Wielded in 100 Years, pgs 8 & 13, Mary Boyd, publ. 1955, bound photocopied edition held by the Dallas Public Library

[570] 635: T. Hugh McIlhaney, Country Ties (Gibson, McIlhaney & Warren newsletter). Vol 1 No 1 Winter 1990, pgs 8-9, slightly abridged.
Ancestry.com's Texas Land Title database confirms 320 acres in Isaac Franks survey, Vol 15, patent 1090, file 1398, 12 Dec 1857

[571] 1478: McIlhaney and Gibson tombstones in Coryell Missionary Baptist Church Cemetery, Coryell Co., TX, photos by Susan & R. Steven Rainwater, 28 Nov 1997

[572] Waldo was about nine miles northwest of McGregor, putting it about halfway between Crawford and Valley Mills on Highway 317. The Handbook of Texas Online, http://www.tshaonline.org

The children of James William and Mary Jane McIlhaney:

Margaret McIlhaney Wiggens

Born 17 Jan 1829, Tennessee, and died 15 May 1879, McLennan Co, Texas[573]

Margaret married widower John William Wiggins, a school teacher from Tennessee, between 1855 and 1860. They were the parents of three, possibly four children. Margaret and William were among the founders of Coryell Baptist Church.[574] The couple lived to at least 1869, but are not listed in the 1870 census. A household containing five Wiggins children is listed in the 1880 census along with their uncle, Patrick Doyle, widower of Margaret's sister Manervia.[575] Margaret and her husband were originally buried in Speegleville Cemetery, but their graves were moved to Chapel Hill Cemetery when Lake Waco was created.[576]

Catherine McIlhaney James

Born c. 1830, Tennessee[577]

The historical marker at Coryell Baptist Church indicates that Catherine and Jesse James (not the outlaw) were founders of the church.[578] But for the marker and one census record, one would never know she had existed.

In 1850, Catherine McIlhaney is listed in the household of her parents in Tippah Co., Mississippi. Two pages prior, Jesse James is listed with his parents, Isaac and Rachel James.[579] Apparently Catherine and Jesse married between 1850 and 1853, though the Tippah County marriage records of that era were lost in a courthouse fire. They were the parents of four daughters – Minerva (married Jesse Givins), Rachel (married Henry Polson),[580] Maggie (married William Fowler) and Sallie – born

---

[573] 105: Country Ties (Gibson, McIlhaney & Warren newsletter). Vol 1 No 1 Winter 1990

[574] 411: Texas Historical Commission Marker at Coryell Baptist Church Cemetery, FM185, Coryell Co., TX, photograph

[575] Federal Census: 1880, McLennan Co., TX, pg 216B

[576] 214: McLennan Co., TX Cemetery Records, Vol 4, Central Texas Genealogical Society, publ. 1982, Waco, TX. Country Ties says she is buried in the now abandoned McLennan Cemetery on Lake Waco, confusing this cemetery with Speegleville. It is still not clear whether the couple is buried in the old Chapel Hill Cemetery on Old Southland Road or the modern Chapel Hill Memorial Park on I-35.

[577] Federal Census: 1850, District #2, Tippah Co., MS, pg 410B

[578] 411: Texas Historical Commission Marker at Coryell Baptist Church Cemetery, FM185, Coryell Co., TX, photograph

[579] Federal Census: 1850, District #2, Tippah Co., MS, pg 409B

2624: Death Notices of Tippah Co., MS, Vol. 1, 1837-1914, Don Martini, publ 1976, Old Timer Press, Ripley, MS

[580] 2622: Death certificate #42501; Rachel James Polson, Grandview, Johnson Co., TX, 11 Sep 1941, transcription from microfilm

between 1854 and 1861, all in Texas. However, I can find no census record after 1850 for either Catherine or Jesse.

Rachel and Henry Poulson are found in the 1880 census in Waco. Sharing their household are Rachel's sisters, Maggie and Sallie James, which confirms their existence.[581] The fact that these two girls are living in their sister's household, suggests to me that Catherine had died by that date. A. E. Phillips' research says she died on 28 Jul 1912 in Hamilton Co., Texas, but he has confused Catherine with her sister, Rebecca (*see next entry*).[582]

Rebecca Jane McIlhaney Gibson

Born 26 Apr 1833, Tennessee, and died 28 Jul 1912, Hamilton Co., Texas[583]
On 19 Oct 1851, Rebecca married Ephriam Parmley Gibson, the son of Jesse Gibson and Elizabeth Parmley. She and her husband were among the founders of Coryell Baptist Church, and their son Randolph Hunter Gibson was the pastor from 1903 to 1905, and again in 1916 to 1919.[584] They were the parents of twelve children, three of whom died in childhood. Ephriam is buried at Coryell Baptist Church;[585] Rebecca in Carlton Cemetery in Hamilton County.[586] Rebecca is traditionally said to have died from injuries sustained when her buggy overturned on a return trip from a visit to relatives.[587]

Manervia Ann McIlhaney Johnson Doyle

Born c. 1837, Tippah Co., Mississippi, and died 18 Nov 1873, Coryell Co., Texas[588]
Manervia married Isham F. Johnson on 16 Jan 1861, in Coryell County.[589] They were the parents of two sons, William C. and Cicero Judson Johnson.

---

[581] Federal Census: 1880, Waco, McLennan Co., TX, pg 213A

[582] 22: A. E. "Phil" & Marion Phillips, *"The Descendants of James William McIlhaney"*, introduction by Sam McIlhaney, 1987

[583] 105: Country Ties (Gibson, McIlhaney & Warren newsletter). Vol 1 No 1 Winter 1990

[584] 1897: Light on the Prairie: The History of the Organization of Coryell Baptist Church in 1855 and the Story of the Endeavors and Influences Wielded in 100 Years, pgs 8, 26, 27, Mary Boyd, publ. 1955, bound photocopied edition held by the Dallas Public Library

[585] 89: Cemetery Records, Coryell Co., TX, Fern Maxwell & Bobbie F. Thornton, Mary Shirley McGuire Chapter NSDAR

[586] 503: Hamilton Co., TX Cemetery Records, pg 30, Mrs. Brent Witty, publ. 1983, Hamilton County Historical Society, Hico, TX

[587] 635: Packet of genealogical information from T. Hugh McIlhaney to Joe S. McIlhaney Sr., 10 Aug 1984, photocopies of originals

[588] 89: Cemetery Records, Coryell Co., TX, Fern Maxwell & Bobbie F. Thornton, Mary Shirley McGuire Chapter NSDAR

[589] 1444: Coryell Co., TX Marriage Records, Books A & B, 1854-1870, Lisa Ludholz and Frances T. Ingmire, publ. 1985, St. Louis, MO

Isham F. Johnson died shortly after the 1870 census,[590] and Manervia married a second husband, Patrick Doyle, but the marriage lasted a mere four years.[591] In 1874, stating to the court that both (biological) parents were dead, W. J. G. McIlhaney, applied to be the boys' guardian.[592] Presumably Doyle did not want custody of step-children he had known such a short time. He died in 1902 and is buried beside his wife Manervia in Coryell Baptist Church Cemetery.[593]

Ephriam P. and Rebecca Jane Gibson

---

[590] Federal Census: 1870, Coryell Co., TX, pg 314A. I. F. is found with his two children in the household of Henry Johnson. Manervia is not listed in any household in 1870.

[591] There is no marriage record in either Coryell or McLennan counties.

[592] 127: Coryell Kin, Bulletin of the Coryell Co. Genealogical Society, 1995 Spring, Volume IXX, Issue 1

[593] 89: Cemetery Records, Coryell Co., TX, Fern Maxwell & Bobbie F. Thornton, Mary Shirley McGuire Chapter NSDAR

William James Gibson McIlhaney

> Born 8 May 1839, Tippah Co., Mississippi, and died 30 Jul 1904, Waldo, Coryell Co., Texas
> *See profile of William James Gibson McIlhaney and Mary Charlesana Elizabeth Carter*

Randall H. McIlhaney

> Born 1842, Tippah Co., Mississippi, and died 4 Apr 1863, Camp Douglas, Illinois[594]
> At the outbreak of the Civil War, Randall enlisted in the Texas 10th Infantry, Company H, CSA, and served as a 1st Corporal.[595] He was captured and interned at Camp Douglas, Illinois, a Union prisoner of war camp for Confederate soldiers, where he died of malaria.[596]

Henry Clay McIlhaney

> Born 1844, Tippah Co., Mississippi, and died 4 Jul 1862, Little Rock, Arkansas[597]
> Following the lead of his brother Randall, Henry enlisted in the Texas 10th Infantry, Company H, CSA as a private. He enlisted on 12 May 1862 and died of pneumonia in July of the same year.[598]

---

[594] 91: Confederate POWs: Soldiers and Sailors Who Died in Federal Prisons and Military Hospitals in the North, Frances Ingmire and Carolyn Ericson, publ. 1984, Ingmire Publications, St. Louis, MO

[595] 125: Roster of Confederate Soldiers, 1861-1865, all volumes, Janet B. Hewett, publ. 1995, Broadfoot Publishing Co., Wilmington, NC

[596] 264: Texas 10th Infantry website (CSA Civil War) http://members.aol.com/SMckay1234/index2.htm, now offline

[597] 125: Roster of Confederate Soldiers, 1861-1865, all volumes, Janet B. Hewett, publ. 1995, Broadfoot Publishing Co., Wilmington, NC

[598] 264: Texas 10th Infantry website (CSA Civil War) http://members.aol.com/SMckay1234/index2.htm, now offline

The Problem of Jesse Gibson and Elizabeth Parmley

Jesse Gibson
Son of Randolph Gibson and Mary Crowley
Born between 1765 and 1770, Virginia
Died Oct 1838, Livingston Co., Kentucky

Married ca 1800, probably Grainger Co., Tennessee

Elizabeth Parmley
Daughter of Ephriam Parmley and Mary Hines
Born ca 1783, South Carolina
Died 7 Feb 1854, Hardeman Co., Tennessee

The inaugural edition of the McIlhaney-Gibson newsletter, *Country Ties*, contained the following statement: "*Mary Jane Gibson McIlhaney, the wife of James W. McIlhaney. Father: Jesse Gibson; Mother: Elizabeth Parmley.*"[599] Thanks to the Internet, this incorrect theory of her parentage has been widely circulated and is widely believed. In July 2012, public family trees that represented this theory as true included twelve on World Connect, eighteen on Family Search.org, and forty on Ancestry.com. This idea just won't go away, so it needs to be addressed. While I cannot definitely prove who Mary Jane Gibson McIlhaney's parents were, I believe I can prove who they were not.

First, I need to establish exactly who Jesse Gibson and Elizabeth Parmley were.

In 1838, George Gibson, the son of Randolph Gibson and Mary Crowley, died in Wayne Co., Kentucky. He had written no will and had no wife or children, so his estate was divided among his siblings. The estate administration names the following individuals: John Gibson (wife Nancy Johnson), Millie Gibson Hatfield (husband Valentine Hatfield), Mary "Polly" Gibson Crowly (husband Littleberry Crowly), James Gibson (wife Mary Finley), Archibald Gibson (wife Priscilla Cecil), Travis Francis Gibson (wife Malinda Adkins), Catherine Gibson Parmley (husband John Parmley), and *Jesse Gibson (wife Elizabeth Parmley)*.[600]

On 11 Oct 1838, Jesse Gibson filed an indenture (meaning a binding contract) in Wayne Co., Kentucky court, witnessed by the estate's executors. In it, he states that he is the brother of the deceased George Gibson, that George Gibson had no wife or children, that Jesse is one of the lawful heirs of George

---

[599] 105: Country Ties, Winter 1990, Vol. 1, No. 1, pg 12 and repeated in Country Ties, Spring 1991, Vol. 2, No. 2, pg 3. The article is unsigned.
[600] 97: Biography of Randolph Gibson and Mary Crowley, June Baldwin Bork, US GenWeb online edition, Wilkes Co., GA section, http://files.usgwarchives.net/ga/wilkes/bios/gibsonra.txt. Bork was a professional genealogist, the author of over a dozen books.

Gibson's estate, and that he is selling his interest in the estate to his brother Travis.[601]

According to his tombstone, Jesse Gibson was born in Virginia in 1777, died in Kentucky in 1847, and was married in Knoxville, Tennessee, in 1800.[602] Some of this information is wrong, notably the date of death. The tombstone is in such pristine condition that it cannot date from 1838, Jesse's actual date of death.[603] It must have been placed quite some time after his death and the information carved in the stone based on faulty memories. In fact, while Jesse Gibson died in Livingston Co., Kentucky, the headstone is in Gibson Cemetery, Hardeman Co., Tennessee, suggesting that it was placed to complete a family grouping, not mark the location of Jesse's actual remains.

Regarding Jesse's marriage, researcher Elreeta Weathers writes, "*In the summer of 1997 we were in Knox Co., Tennessee. There was not a marriage record for Jesse Gibson and Elizabeth Parmley in Knox County or in any of its surrounding counties.*" So the marriage information appears to be partially incorrect, though the date is probably right.

Jesse Gibson's married life began in May 1800, when a Grainger Co., Tennessee court charged him with "*begatting a bastard child on the body of Elizabeth Parmley.*" He was ordered to pay $3 per month child support.[604] It is generally assumed that a marriage followed, though no one thus far has located a marriage record.[605] June Baldwin Bork's work on the Gibson family suggests that the child of this illicit union was William Gibson, born c. 1800, in Davidson Co., Tennessee.[606]

Elizabeth Parmley was the daughter of Ephriam Parmley, Sr. and Mary Hinds.[607] Bork says she was born in Wilkes Co., Georgia, though in the 1850 census, Elizabeth herself indicates that she was born in South Carolina.[608] The

---

[601] 2623: Wayne Co., KY Deed Book G, 1835-1839, pg 62, June Baldwin Bork, publ. 1995, Apple Valley, CA

[602] 2312: Findagrave.com #67087604, photograph of Jesse Gibson's tombstone in Gibson Cemetery, Toone, Hardeman Co., TN

[603] Having tramped through dozens of cemeteries recording tombstones, I feel I can say this with a fair degree of confidence.

[604] 88: Tennessee Tidbits, Vol 3, 1778-1914, Marjorie Hood Fischer & Ruth Blake Burns

[605] I have personally checked the following Tennessee Counties: Anderson, Blount, Campbell, Carter, Claiborne, Davidson, Grainger, Greene, Hardeman, Henry, Jefferson, Knox, McMinn, Roane. Records are available for Loudon, Sevier and Union Counties. I have also checked Livingston Co., KY. There is always the possibility that they were never officially married or that the records have been destroyed.

[606] 97: Biography of Randolph Gibson and Mary Crowley, June Baldwin Bork, US GenWeb online edition, Wilkes Co., GA section, http://files.usgwarchives.net/ga/wilkes/bios/gibsonra.txt, sampled 24 Jul 2012

[607] 97: Biography of Randolph Gibson and Mary Crowley, June Baldwin Bork, US GenWeb online edition, Wilkes Co., GA section, http://files.usgwarchives.net/ga/wilkes/bios/gibsonra.txt

[608] Federal Census: 1850, Hardeman Co., TN, pg 118B, living in her son George's household.

later census records of her children also say South Carolina.[609] All records agree that she was born c.1783.

The Gibson family moved several times before putting down roots. Their second son, George Stewart Gibson, was born in Davidson Co., Tennessee, but, the next seven children were born in Kentucky.[610] By 1808, the family had settled in Livingston Co., Kentucky, where Jesse is listed on the tax rolls of Deer Creek District from 1808 through 1830. His taxable assets varied, but in most tax years he owned one or two slaves, several mares and stud horses, and between three hundred and six hundred acres of land.[611]

Jesse Gibson died in 1838. His nuncupative (oral) will was delivered for probate by his witnesses, James Reed and Samuel Gibson, and was accepted by the Livingston Co., Kentucky court on 5 Nov 1838. He entailed the farm and farm house to his widow Elizabeth during her lifetime, left a filly to his son Heil, and a sorrel colt to his son Archibald. All of the property was to be sold, the proceeds shared among his surviving children, who are not named.[612] The estate administration is more forthcoming, naming George S. Gibson, Hardy Gibson, Johnson McGlothlin and wife Jane Gibson, Samuel Gibson, Ephriam Gibson, Heil Gibson, Frederick H. Croft and his wife Mary Gibson, Stephen Gibson, and Archibald Gibson.[613] Missing from this list is Jesse's firstborn, William Gibson, who had apparently died prior to his father.

Elizabeth Parmley Gibson remained in Livingston Co., Kentucky, through the 1840 census.[614] By 1850, she moved into the household of her eldest living son, George Stewart Gibson, in Hardeman Co., Tennessee.[615] She died on 4 Feb 1854, and is buried in Gibson Cemetery with dozens of Gibson relations.[616] Her confusing tombstone gives the name Parmley across the top curve of the stone, and Elizabeth Gibson below, suggesting that the stone was commissioned by her Parmley relations rather than her Gibson kin. A casual observer would conclude that her name had been Elizabeth Gibson Parmley, not Elizabeth Parmley Gibson.

---

[609] Federal Census: Ephriam Parmley Gibson, 1900, Osage, Coryell Co., TX, pg 185A; George Stewart Gibson and Heil B. Gibson, 1880, Hardeman Co., TN, pg 533A

[610] 2628: The History of Fayette and Hardeman Counties of Tennessee, page 915, Goodspeed Publishing Co., Chicago, IL, publ. 1887, transcribed except from the profile of George Stewart Gibson

[611] Transcriptions of tax records by Ruth Ann Godwin

[612] 318: Livingston Co., KY Wills, Books A-B, 1799-1873, pg 62, Brenda Joyce Jerome, publ. 1991, Newburgh, IN

[613] 476: Appraisal of the estate of Jesse Gibson, 16 Nov 1838, Livingston Co., KY, photocopy of original

477: Sale bill of the estate of Jesse Gibson, pg 211-212, 1 Apr 1839, Livingston Co., KY, photocopy of original

478: Settlement of the estate of Jesse Gibson, 4 Jan 1841, Livingston Co., KY, photocopy of original

[614] Federal Census: 1840, Smithland, Livingston, KY, pg 131

[615] Federal Census: 1850, Hardeman Co., TN, pg 118B

[616] 2312: Findagrave.com #52267336, Gibson Cemetery, Hardeman Co., TN

I now want to call out three of Jesse Gibson's proven children for special examination. First, I want to prove that neither Jane Gibson nor Mary Gibson can be Mary Jane Gibson McIlhaney. Second, I want to consider how Mary Jane Gibson McIlhaney actually does intersect with one of Jesse Gibson's sons. Finally, I want to propose an explanation for the origins of this confusion.

The first child is the Gibson's eldest daughter, Jane Gibson, who married Johnson McGlothlin in Livingston Co., Kentucky, on 26 Oct 1831.[617] The couple were the parents of eight children, all named in the family Bible.[618] Johnson McGlothlin is listed on the tax rolls of Livingston County from 1829 through 1841. According to his descendants, McGlothlin was stabbed to death in 1846 in Hardeman Co., TN. The widowed Jane and her children are found in that county in the 1850 census.[619] Jane Gibson McGlothlin died prior to the 1870 census.

It should now be obvious that Jane Gibson and Mary Jane Gibson McIlhaney have different husbands, different children, and lived in different locations. They cannot be the same person.

The second of Jesse Gibson and Elizabeth Parmley's children I want to consider is their daughter Mary. In Jesse's 1841 estate settlement, she and her husband are referred to as "*Frederick H. Croft and his wife Mary Gibson.*" The couple married on 3 Dec 1835, in Livingston Co., Kentucky.[620] F. Hulet Croft, as he is called in nearly every record, is found in the 1850 through 1880 census records of Crittenden Co., Kentucky.[621] The couple were the parents of five, possibly six children.[622] Some researchers believe that Mary Gibson Croft died in 1846, and that Hulet married a second Mary. In the absence of a second marriage record, I am reluctant to concur with this conclusion. As with the case of Jane Gibson McGlothlin, it should be clear that Mary Gibson Croft and Mary Jane Gibson McIlhaney are not the same person, and for the same reasons – they have different husbands, different children, and lived in different locations.

My point is this. All of Jesse Gibson's children are named in his estate administration, with the exception of the deceased William. And we know what happened to Jesse's daughters, Mary and Jane. To claim that Mary Jane

---

[617] 2625: Livingston Co., KY Marriage Records, Vol. 1, 1789-1839, pg 115, Joyce M. Woodyard, publ. 1992, Smithland, KY
Their surname is spelled McLaughlin on the marriage bond, and in every conceivable way in other records, including Mcglauphlin and Mclothlin. McGlothlin is the canonical spelling.
[618] A copy of the Bible's births page is included in the grave record of Johnson McGlothlin at Findagrave.com #52865669. I am deeply indebted to Michael Mason for preserving this record.
[619] Federal Census: 1850, Hardeman Co., TN, pg 180B
[620] 2625: Livingston Co., KY Marriage Records, Vol. 1, 1789-1839, pg 140, Joyce M. Woodyard, publ. 1992, Smithland, KY
[621] Federal Census, Crittenden Co., KY: 1850, pg 233B; 1860, pg 356B; pg 1870, pg 401A; 1880, pg 65A.
[622] According to the 1850 census, Margaret J. Croft was born in 1831, and thus belongs to a prior marriage.

Gibson McIlhaney is also Jesse's daughter strains credulity. Why would he have daughters named Mary and Jane, *and* Mary Jane? Why would Mary Jane be the only child not to receive an inheritance?

The only logical conclusion is that Mary Jane Gibson McIlhaney is not the daughter of Jesse Gibson and Elizabeth Parmley. So how did this notion arise?

This is where the third child of Jesse Gibson and Elizabeth Parmley comes into play. Ephriam Parmley Gibson was born on 25 Sep 1817, in Livingston Co., Kentucky. On 19 Oct 1851, he married Rebecca Jane McIlhaney, the daughter of James W. and Mary Jane Gibson McIlhaney. This makes Jesse Gibson and Elizabeth Parmley the in-laws of Mary Jane Gibson McIlhaney, not her parents.

This is an important distinction. What the promoters of the Gibson-Parmley parentage theory have overlooked is this: if Mary Jane Gibson and Ephriam Parmley Gibson were brother and sister, then the marriage of Ephriam Parmley Gibson to Rebecca Jane McIlhaney Gibson fell within a prohibited degree of kinship. Uncle-niece marriages had been prohibited in European society since the middle ages. Americans played fairly loose with first cousin marriages in the 18th and 19th centuries (now illegal), but, because of the cross-generational aspect, an uncle-niece marriage would have been legally defined as incest (and still is). I can't see these starchy Baptist folk condoning incest. So again, Mary Jane Gibson McIlhaney simply cannot be the daughter of Jesse Gibson and Elizabeth Parmley.

So who were Mary Jane Gibson McIlhaney's parents? I'm afraid the answer is unsatisfying. We simply don't know.

In antebellum census records, the proximity of one family to another is often indicative of relationship. In fact, the reason farm land in Texas is still zoned multi-family is the historic assumption that multiple related families will build homes on a single tract of farmland.[623] So when families are recorded sequentially in a census, you have to consider the possibility of relatedness.

The 1850 census of District No. 2, Tippah Co., Mississippi, page 410B contains one of these possible family groupings. Household 243 contains William C. Gibson, age 50, his wife and two daughters. Household 244 contains Margaret Gibson, a 70-year-old widow, and her son, John. Household 245 contains James W. McIlhaney and his wife Mary Jane Gibson, and their children. So are they somehow related?

First, we need to consider Margaret Gibson. She was born in Virginia c. 1780. By 1805, she had married and moved to Tennessee, based on the age and birthplace of her son John. She's not listed heading her own household in

---

[623] I know this because it's the excuse that the Irving City Council uses for allowing the over-development of apartment complexes in the city – that all of the open land is zoned multi-family and under Texas law, they can't preemptively rezone it.

1840 – there are only five households in the entire country headed by women named Margaret Gibson in 1840 – so her husband must have died between 1840 and 1850. She is clearly not one of the sisters of Jesse Gibson – Gibson is her married name – and her name doesn't match any of the wives of Jesse's brothers, though she could be a second wife, married after the 1838 will was probated. She is absent from later census records, leading to the conclusion that she died before 1860.

We also need to take a hard look at William C. Gibson. *Country Ties* concludes that he is Jesse Gibson's eldest son, and, to be fair, he was born in the right place and at the right time – c. 1800 in Tennessee.[624] But William was not mentioned in Jesse's will – Jesse's son William was deceased prior to 1838.

The other thing we know about William Culton Gibson is that he was a land speculator. It's from the land records that we know his middle name. Between January 1839 and November 1848, Tippah Co., Mississippi deed records detail fifteen separate land transactions – four purchases and eleven sales.[625] The Bureau of Land Management database contains scans of ten transactions in Tippah County and thirteen transactions in nearby counties.[626] Five of the Tippah County sales involve buyers also surnamed Gibson. On 9 Nov 1840, William Gibson bought land from his neighbors, James and Jane McIlhaney, spelled McIlhiney in this record.

So, are Margaret Gibson, William C. Gibson and Mary Jane Gibson McIlhaney related? There's a 50/50 chance, and it revolves around another Mary Gibson.

On 5 Feb 1844, William C. Gibson is recorded selling land to his sister, identified as Mary Curlock. This gives us another two-Mary problem. If Margaret Gibson is the mother of William Culton Gibson and Mary Gibson Curlock, she cannot be the mother of Mary Jane Gibson McIlhaney. If she is a second wife of one of Jesse's brothers married after 1838, she again cannot be Mary Jane Gibson McIlhaney's mother because Mary Jane Gibson McIlhaney was born in 1803. And, there is a quite reasonable possibility that William Culton Gibson is the son of Randolph Gibson and Jane Culton of Tennessee, which would very definitely mean that Margaret was not his mother.[627]

So if Margaret *is not* a second wife, and *is not* the mother of William Culton Gibson and Mary Gibson Curlock, she just might be the mother of Mary Jane Gibson McIlhaney. I think it's worth noting that Mary Jane Gibson McIlhaney named her eldest daughter Margaret. It's not proof, but it's interesting.

---

[624] Country Ties, Spring 1991, Vol. 2, No. 2, pg 3

[625] 93: Abstracts of Tippah Co., MS Land Deeds, 1836-1870, Don Martini and Bill Gurney, publ. 1983, Old Timer Press, Ripley, MS

[626] 1087: Bureau of Land Management online database, http://www.glorecords.blm.gov

[627] Post on genforum.com/gibson, "Randolph Gibson, South Carolina Will," Carolyn Sparks, 18 Feb 2003 and Mary Sue Austin, 4 Sep 2004

Sadly, we may never know. Mary Jane Gibson McIlhaney died in 1891, twenty-six years before Coryell County issued their first death certificate, so the knowledge of her true parentage may have been lost forever.

James Carter and Salina Roxanna Dean

James Carter
Born 22 Apr 1815, North Carolina
Died 15 Jul 1892, Coryell Co., Texas

Married 27 Apr 1836, Hardeman Co., Tennessee

Salina Roxanna Dean
Born 1 Jun 1819, Georgia
Died 10 Mar 1903, Coryell Co., Texas

By most accounts, James Carter was born in North Carolina, and, as a young man, moved to Tennessee, then Mississippi.[628] Carter married Salina Roxanna Dean on 27 Apr 1836, in Hardeman Co., Tennessee.[629] They were the parents of eight children, one of whom died in childhood.

In 1850, the Carters are found living in the same census district of Tippah County as the McIlhaneys and Gibsons. By 1860, they had moved to Webberville, in Travis County, where James Carter worked for the railroad as a waggoner and served as a deputy sheriff.[630] By 1870, the family had moved to Waco in McLennan County. Both James and Salina Carter died in Coryell Co. Texas, and are buried in Osage Cemetery.[631]

The children of Roxanna and James Carter

William Lafayette Carter

Born Apr 1837, Tennessee, and died 17 Mar 1906, McLennan Co., Texas
William appears to have been married three times, based on census data. His first wife was Mattie Barnhill, whom he married c. 1869.[632] They were the parents of one daughter. Mattie died before 1880. William next married Sarah A. Thomas prior to 1880.[633] She died c. 1882. He finally married Martha Allison on 9 Apr 1882, in Hill Co.,

---

[628] Carter gives as his birthplace North Carolina in the 1850 census, Alabama in the 1860 census, South Carolina in the 1870 census. However, both parents are present in the 1850 household, and they give North Carolina as their birthplace, lending some weight to this choice of state.

[629] 1438: Marriage license of Salina R. Dean and James Carter, 27 Apr 1836, Hardeman Co., TN, photocopy of original, gift of Sharon Hitt

[630] 54: A Memorial & Biographical History of McLennan, Falls, Bell & Coryell Counties, TX, profile of William Summers, published 1893, The Lewis Publishing Co., Chicago, IL

[631] 1420: Carter, Kellum & Kirkland tombstones in Osage Cemetery, Osage, Coryell Co., TX, 1 Jan 2000, photos by Susan and R. Steven Rainwater

[632] Federal Census: 1870, Waco, McLennan Co., TX, pg 41B

[633] Federal Census: 1880, Hill Co., TX, pg 371B

Texas.[634] This union produced five children.[635] William died in 1906.[636] His burial place has not been identified.

Robert M. Carter

Born 1841, Mississippi, and died 21 Aug 1897, McLennan Co., Texas Robert married Rebecca S. Karnes on 24 Oct 1866, in Coryell County.[637] The couple were the parents of five children, one of whom died in childhood. By 1880, the couple had separated, and Rebecca had returned to her parents' home, taking her four surviving daughters with her.[638] Shortly thereafter, she and three of her daughters joined a fascinating organization in Belton, Texas, called the Woman's Commonwealth.

This organization was made up entirely of women who had divorced or separated from abusive husbands. They lived communally, pooled their resources, and supported themselves running a number of successful business, notably a boarding house and a commercial laundry. Their book collection eventually became the basis of the Belton Public Library, and their substantial donation helped fund the building of the local opera house. Though the men of Belton initially opposed their efforts, the business successes of the Woman's Commonwealth eventually won them over.[639]

The Woman's Commonwealth moved to Washington, DC, in 1898, taking Rebecca and her daughters, Lota Bell, Lela Rebecca, and Susie Effie with them. Lota Bell died shortly after the move. Rebecca died in 1924.[640] Her daughter Lela became the organization's leader in the 1950s, dying in 1956 on the communal farm in Maryland.[641] Susie

---

[634] 499: Sharon Hitt (Carter family)

[635] Federal Census: 1900, East of the Brazos River, McLennan Co., TX, pg 13B

[636] 80: Index to Early McLennan Co., TX Deaths, John M. Usry, Central Texas Genealogical Society, Waco, TX

[637] 1444: Coryell Co., TX Marriage Records, Books A & B, 1854-1870, Lisa Ludholz and Frances T. Ingmire, publ. 1985, St. Louis, MO

[638] Federal Census: 1880, Coryell Co., TX, pg 485C

[639] 2639: Texas History 101: Belton Woman's Commonwealth, Lindsay Meeks, Texas Monthly, Dec 2005 edition

2640: Sally L. Kitch, *This Strange Society of Women*, publ. 1993, Ohio State University Press, Columbus, OH

2641: Texas State Historical Association, Belton Woman's Commonwealth, http://www.tshaonline.org/handbook/online/articles/vib01

The organization's archives are managed by The Briscoe Center for American History at the University of Texas, Austin.

[640] 2643: Burial permit; Rebecca Karnes Carter, 7 Jun 1924, Montgomery Co., MD, scan of original

2644: Death certificate #19334; Rebecca Karnes Carter, 6 Jun 1924, Montgomery Co., MD, scan of original

[641] 2642: Burial transit permit; Lela Rebecca Carter, 3 Aug 1956, Montgomery Co., MD, scan of original

Effie left the organization, but never married, supporting herself as a clerk at the Interior Department.⁶⁴² Rebecca and Lela are buried in Rock Creek Cemetery in Washington, DC, with other members of the Commonwealth.⁶⁴³

Robert M. Carter died in 1897, and is buried in Holy Cross Cemetery, Waco.⁶⁴⁴

Mary Charlesana Elizabeth Carter McIlhaney

Born Sep 1844, Tippah Co., Mississippi, and died Oct 1911, Coryell Co., Texas
See profile of W. J. G. McIlhaney and Mary Charlesana Elizabeth Carter

Sarah Etta Carter Summers

Born 7 Mar 1847, Mississippi, and died 15 Dec 1921, Fort Worth, Tarrant Co., Texas
On 1 Jan 1867, Sarah married William Summers.⁶⁴⁵ She wore a gown of dotted swiss, and an unexpected ice storm nearly caused the postponement of the ceremony.⁶⁴⁶ They were the parents of nine children, seven of whom survived to adulthood. Summers was a Confederate veteran, having served in Company B of the 18th Texas Cavalry. He was wounded at the Battle of Chickamauga, and was captured and exchanged at least three times. After the war, Summers worked as a saddler, ran a grocery store, and was the mayor of Crawford, Texas.⁶⁴⁷ He and his wife were members of the Methodist Episcopal Church.⁶⁴⁸ They are buried in Crawford Cemetery, McLennan County.⁶⁴⁹

Amanda Roxanna Carter Hunter

Born 1851, Mississippi, and died 23 Jun 1917, Kaufman Co., Texas
Amanda married Thomas Ephriam Hunter on 12 Sep 1877, in Coryell

---

⁶⁴² Federal Census: 1930, 1828 California St, Washington DC, pg 24A; 1940C HH, 1828 California St, Washington DC, pg 462B
⁶⁴³ 2312: Findagrave.com #34621233 and #96736813
⁶⁴⁴ 80: Index to Early McLennan Co., TX Deaths, John M. Usry, Central Texas Genealogical Society, Waco, TX
⁶⁴⁵ 149: Travis Co., Texas Marriage Records, 1840-1882, Lucie Clift Price, publ. 1973, Austin, TX
⁶⁴⁶ 499: Sharon Hitt (Carter family)
⁶⁴⁷ Federal Census: 1900, Crawford, McLennan Co., TX, pg 251B
⁶⁴⁸ 54: A Memorial & Biographical History of McLennan, Falls, Bell & Coryell Counties, TX, profile of William Summers, publ. 1893, The Lewis Publishing Co., Chicago, IL
⁶⁴⁹ 2207: Carter-Summers tombstones in Crawford Cemetery, Peaceful Lane, Crawford, McLennan Co., TX, 19 June 2005, photos by Susan & R. Steven Rainwater

Co., Texas.⁶⁵⁰ They were the parents of one daughter.⁶⁵¹ They farmed the Carter family farm until James Carter's death, then moved to Van Zandt County.⁶⁵² Sometime after 1910, Amanda was committed to the North Texas Hospital for the Insane in Terrell, Texas, where she died n 1917 of cancer of the uterus.⁶⁵³ Thomas moved to Collin County, where he died in 1928.⁶⁵⁴ The couple are buried in Wilson Chapel Cemetery in Collin County.⁶⁵⁵

Anna Belle Carter Cary

Born Oct 1854, Texas, and died 1925, Van Zandt Co., Texas
Belle married Francis Brook Cary on 23 Dec 1873, in McLennan Co., Texas.⁶⁵⁶ They were the parents of eight children, two of whom died in childhood.⁶⁵⁷ The couple moved to Bell County shortly after marrying, and then settled in Van Zandt County, where they spent the rest of their lives.⁶⁵⁸ They are buried in Old Bethel Cemetery in Canton.⁶⁵⁹

James Buchanan Carter

Born 23 Dec 1856, Texas, and died 23 Dec 1930, Wichita Co., Texas
James married Sarah Jane Kirby on 19 Jul 1876.⁶⁶⁰ They were the parents of nine children, two of whom died in childhood. Sarah died in 1901 and is buried in Osage Cemetery, Coryell County.⁶⁶¹ James moved his family to San Angelo by 1900, and married Martha Burleson c. 1903. By 1910, James and Martha had relocated to Garza County, and by 1920, to Wichita Falls.⁶⁶² In the 1930 census, the couple are listed as residents of the Wichita County Farm for the Dependent.⁶⁶³ James died in December of that year, and is buried in Lakeview Cemetery, Wichita Falls, Texas.⁶⁶⁴

---

⁶⁵⁰ 499: Sharon Hitt (Carter family)
⁶⁵¹ Federal Census: 1880, Waco, McLennan Co., TX, pg 214B
⁶⁵² Federal Census: 1900, Van Zandt Co., TX, pg 85B
⁶⁵³ 2650: Death certificate #16847; Amanda (Carter) Hunter, 23 June 1914, Terrell, Kaufman Co., TX, scan of original
⁶⁵⁴ Federal Census: 1920, Wylie, Collin Co., TX, pg 116A
⁶⁵⁵ 2312: Findagrave.com #11739715 and #11739712
⁶⁵⁶ 120: McLennan Co., TX Marriage Records, Vol. 2, 1871-1892, Central Texas Genealogical Society, publ. 1963, Waco, TX
⁶⁵⁷ Federal Census: 1900, Van Zandt Co., TX, pg 87B
⁶⁵⁸ Federal Census: 1880, Bell Co., TX, pg 421D; 1910, Van Zandt Co., TX, pg 81B; 1920, Van Zandt Co., TX, pg 102B
⁶⁵⁹ 2242: Cary tombstones in Old Bethel Cemetery, Van Zandt Co., TX, 1 Jul 2006, photos by Susan and R. Steven Rainwater
⁶⁶⁰ 499: Sharon Hitt (Carter family)
⁶⁶¹ 2312: Findagrave.com #8236440
⁶⁶² Federal Census: 1880, Coryell Co., TX, pg 470A; 1900, San Angelo, Tom Green Co., TX, pg 336B; 1910, Garza Co., TX, pg 21B; 1920, Wichita Falls, Wichita Co., TX, pg 59A
⁶⁶³ Federal Census: 1930, Wichita Co., TX, pg 245A
⁶⁶⁴ 2312: Findagrave.com #27443797

Missie Lena Carter Oliver

Born Nov 1859, Texas, and died 1907, Tom Green Co., Texas
Missie married James Stephen Oliver on 12 Feb 1880, in McLennan Co., Texas.[665] They were the parents of five children, one of whom died in childhood. James made his living as a carpenter and later, as an oil well driller. The family moved from McLennan County to San Angelo prior to the 1900 census.[666] Missie died in 1907, and is buried with her husband in Fairmount Cemetery, San Angelo, Tom Green Co., Texas.[667]

---

[665] 120: McLennan Co., TX Marriage Records, Vol. 2, 1871-1892, Central Texas Genealogical Society, publ. 1963, Waco, TX

[666] Federal Census: 1880, Waco, McLennan Co., TX, pg 214B; 1900, San Angelo, Tom Green Co., TX, pg 272B

[667] 2312: Findagrave.com #63765720 and #34260624

William J. G. McIlhaney and Mary Charlesana Elizabeth Carter

Mary Carter McIlhaney

William James Gibson McIlhaney

Son of James William McIlhaney and Mary Jane Gibson
Born 8 May 1839, Tippah Co., Mississippi
Died 30 Jul 1904, Waldo, Coryell Co., Texas

Married 7 Feb 1867, Austin, Travis Co., Texas

Mary Charlesana Elizabeth Carter

Daughter of James Carter and Salina Roxanna Dean
Born Sep 1844, Tippah Co., Mississippi
Died Oct 1911, Waldo, Coryell Co., Texas

In 1861, at the outbreak of the Civil War, W.J.G. McIlhaney enlisted in Company H, Texas 10th Infantry of the Confederate Army, known as Nelson's Regiment. He enlisted as a Private and was advanced to 1st Sergeant. Though he was not a slave owner, he was a loyal southerner, and fought in support of the southern cause. He was discharged in 1863 due to illness.[668]

In 1867, he married Mary Charlesana Elizabeth Carter, the daughter of James Carter and Salina Roxanna Dean. Most of the family stories call her Mollie, though in one census record, she is called Charlie. She is remembered as having "Black Welsh" ancestry. This phrase is used to support the claim of part Native American ancestry, but the term is so ambiguous and has gained so many meanings that it's impossible to say exactly what it meant 150 years ago.[669]

We don't know what took W.J.G. McIlhaney to Travis Co., but we feel certain that the couple met there. They were married on 7 Feb 1867, Austin, Travis County.[670] By 1870, the couple had moved to Gatesville, Coryell County, where they are recorded in the census under the name "Mclehany."[671] By 1880, W.J.G.'s widowed mother had moved in with the family, and would for live with them for the rest of her life.[672] In 1884, the county tax assessment shows the McIlhaneys being taxed for 300 acres, carriages, manufactured items, horses, cattle and hogs.[673] Prior to 1900, the family moved to the town of Osage.[674]

W.J.G. and Mollie McIlhaney were the parents of ten children. Three of their daughters died in childhood and are memorialized by now crumbling obelisks in Coryell Baptist Church cemetery.[675]

Light on the Prairie, a history of Coryell Baptist Church published in 1955, says this of W.J.G McIlhaney:

> W. J. G. McIlhaney was sent as a delegate to the Sunday School Convention in Dallas in June, 1893. He was the first delegate ever sent to the Sunday School Convention by this church. Bro. McIlhaney was born in Mississippi in 1839. His father James McIlhaney was born in Ireland, and he with his wife Jane Gibson McIlhaney, were charter

---

[668] 125: Roster of Confederate Soldiers, 1861-1865, all volumes, Janet B. Hewett, publ. 1995, Broadfoot Publ. Co., Wilmington, NC

2554: Texas Confederate Soldiers, 1861-1865, Janet B. Hewett and Joyce Lawrence, publ. 1997, Broadfoot Publ. Co., Wilmington, NC

[669] See Wikipedia's article on the term, Black Irish, http://en.wikipedia.org/wiki/Black_Irish

[670] 149: Travis Co., Texas Marriage Records, 1840-1882, Lucie Clift Price, publ. 1973, Austin, TX

[671] Federal Census: 1870, Gatesville PO, Coryell Co., TX, pg 310B

[672] Federal Census: 1880, JP #6 & 7, Coryell Co., TX, pg 470A

[673] 315: Coryell Co., TX 1884 Tax Roll (www.rootsweb.com/~txcoryel/1884tax.html), 19 Feb 1999, now offline

[674] Federal Census: 1900, Osage, Coryell Co., TX, pg 10A

[675] 1478: McIlhaney and Gibson tombstones in Coryell Missionary Baptist Church Cemetery, Coryell Co., TX, photos by Susan & R. Steven Rainwater, 28 Nov 1997

members of this church. In February of 1893, Brother McIlhaney resigned as Clerk of the Church after serving for several years.

In 1853, the McIlhaneys came to Texas, and in 1854, they came to Coryell County. He lived here until the Lord called him to his heavenly home. Uncle Billy, as he was lovingly called served his country as a soldier and his Lord as a servant. He married Miss Mollie Carter in 1867.[676]

The church gathered each Sunday on the ground floor of a nearby schoolhouse. One Sunday in 1885, the congregation assembled in the upstairs of the schoolhouse, where they could light the stove. The combined weight caused the second floor to fall through to the floor below, and took the parishioners with it. No one was seriously injured, but building and finance committees were soon organized, and W.J.G. served on both. Coryell Baptist Church completed their own one-story building in 1888.[677] In later years, W.J.G. served as Assistant Superintendent of the Sunday School.[678] In the civic realm, W.J.G. served as a Justice of the Peace for Coryell County.[679]

W.J.G. McIlhaney died on 30 Jul 1904.[680] Mollie died in October 1911. Because Coryell County was very late in complying with the state regulations regarding death certificates, and did not issue certificates for either of them, we do not know the circumstances of their deaths. They are buried in Coryell Baptist Church Cemetery.[681]

The children of W.J.G. and Mollie McIlhaney:

James M. McIlhaney

Born 24 Jan 1868, Coryell Co., Texas, and died 14 Feb 1916, Texas Jim married Bettie Hardin on 7 Jul 1886.[682] They were the parents of thirteen children, five of whom died in childhood.[683] The family farmed land in Coryell, McLennan, and Wilbarger Counties. Jim is buried at

---

[676] 1897: Light on the Prairie: The History of the Organization of Coryell Baptist Church in 1855 and the Story of the Endeavors and Influences Wielded in 100 Years, pg 22, Mary Boyd, publ. 1955, bound photocopied edition held by the Dallas Public Library

[677] 1897: Light on the Prairie: The History of the Organization of Coryell Baptist Church in 1855 and the Story of the Endeavors and Influences Wielded in 100 Years, pg 17, Mary Boyd, publ. 1955, bound photocopied edition held by the Dallas Public Library

[678] 1897: ibid, pg 20

[679] 84: Coryell Co., TX Families, Parts 1-3, 1854-1985, pg 40, Coryell Co. Genealogical Society, publ. 1986, Taylor Publishing, Dallas, TX.

[680] 414: Book 1, Coryell Co., TX Death Records, 1903-1917, pg 7, Gladys L. Treadway, publ. 1986, Gatesville, TX

[681] 1478: McIlhaney and Gibson tombstones in Coryell Missionary Baptist Church Cemetery, Coryell Co., TX, photos by Susan & R. Steven Rainwater, 28 Nov 1997

[682] 105: Country Ties (Gibson, McIlhaney & Warren newsletter), Vol 1 No 1 Winter 1990, Vol 2 No 2 Spring 1991, and Vol 2 No 1 Fall 1992

[683] Federal Census: 1900, McLennan Co., TX, pg 271B; 1910, Wilbarger Co., TX, pg 209B; 1920, McLennan Co., TX, pg 14A 1930, Waco, McLennan Co., TX, pg 273A

Coryell Baptist Church cemetery with three of their infant children,[684] and Bettie is buried at Harris Creek cemetery with her daughter Gladys McIlhaney Warren, and T. Hugh McIlhaney and his wife.[685]

Lula Belle McIlhaney Smith

Born 12 Sep 1870, Coryell Co., Texas, and died 25 Jul 1929, McLennan Co., Texas

Lula is one of those individuals with name issues. Called Fanny in the census taken twelve days after her birth, she is recorded as Sorda B. in 1880. The county history calls her Cordia.[686] In her adult life, she preferred Lula. She married James Monroe Smith, known as Uncle Doc, on 10 Mar 1892.[687] He was a cotton farmer. They were the parents of three children.[688] Both Lula and her husband are buried at Coryell Baptist cemetery.[689]

John Richardson McIlhaney

Born 5 Jul 1873, Coryell Co., Texas, and died 25 Sep 1949, Lubbock, Lubbock Co., Texas
See profile of John Richardson McIlhaney and Ollie Delilah Umberson

William Arthur McIlhaney

Born 5 Dec 1876, Coryell Co., Texas, and died Mar 1963, Temple, Bell Co., Texas[690]

On 27 Jun 1897, William married Addie May Davis in McLennan County.[691] They were the parents of seven children.[692] Addie died in 1938. She and William are buried in Temple Masonic Cemetery in Cotton Co., Oklahoma, along with their son Joe and his wife.[693]

---

[684] 1478: McIlhaney and Gibson tombstones in Coryell Missionary Baptist Church Cemetery, Coryell Co., TX, photos by Susan & R. Steven Rainwater, 28 Nov 1997

[685] 2208: McIlhaney-Warren in Harris Creek Cemetery, Harris Creek Lane, McGregor, McLennan Co., TX, 19 June 2005, Susan & R. Steven Rainwater

[686] 54: A Memorial & Biographical History of McLennan, Falls, Bell & Coryell Counties, TX, publ. 1893, The Lewis Pub. Co., Chicago, IL

[687] 105: Country Ties (Gibson, McIlhaney & Warren newsletter), Vol 1 No 1 Winter 1990, Vol 2 No 2 Spring 1991, and Vol 2 No 1 Fall 1992

[688] Federal Census: 1900, Osage, Coryell Co., TX, pg 10A; 1910, Taylor, Williamson Co., TX, pg 153B; 1920, McLennan Co., TX, pg 243B

[689] 1478: McIlhaney and Gibson tombstones in Coryell Missionary Baptist Church Cemetery, Coryell Co., TX, photos by Susan & R. Steven Rainwater, 28 Nov 1997

[690] 22: A. E. "Phil" & Marion Phillips, *"The Descendants of James William McIlhaney"*, introduction by Sam McIlhaney, 1987

[691] 210: McLennan Co., TX Marriage Records, Vol. 3, 15 Aug 1892-19 Jan 1901, publ. 1963, Central Texas Genealogical Society, Waco, Texas

[692] Federal Census: 1910, Dawson Co., TX, pg 6B; 1930, Doan's Village, Wilbarger Co., TX, pg 252A

[693] 2312: Findagrave.com #45070886 and #45070954

Oliver Lee McIlhaney

Born 7 Nov 1878, Coryell Co., Texas, and died 24 Sep 1956, Vernon, Wilbarger Co., Texas[694]

Ollie, as he was known, married Minnie Era Holcolm on 24 Feb 1901.[695] They were the parents of two daughters. In his early life, Ollie was employed as a farm hand, but in the 1930 census, he was listed as a butcher in a meat market.[696] He and his wife are buried in Eastview Memorial Park, Vernon, Wilbarger Co., Texas.[697]

Frank B. McIlhaney

Born 20 Oct 1882, Coryell Co., Texas, and died 14 Mar 1962, McCamey, Upton Co., Texas[698]

Frank married Bertha Ellen Hancock on 6 Oct 1918.[699] They were the parents of five children. Frank was a farmer and a cowboy on a stock ranch.[700] They are buried in Mertzon Cemetery, Irion Co., Texas.[701]

Ethel Elizabeth McIlhaney Davis

Born 4 Dec 1887, Coryell Co., Texas, and died 12 Oct 1960, Gatesville, Coryell Co., Texas[702]

Ethel married Mack McGruder Davis c. 1904. They were the parents of three children.[703] They farmed in McLennan and Coryell Counties.[704] Ethel and Mack are buried in Restland Cemetery, Gatesville, Coryell Co., Texas.[705]

Annie Ester, Selena Jane, and Ida May McIlhaney

Died in childhood and are buried with their parents in Coryell Baptist Church Cemetery.[706]

---

[694] 22: A. E. "Phil" & Marion Phillips, *"The Descendants of James William McIlhaney"*, introduction by Sam McIlhaney, 1987

[695] 499: Sharon Hitt (McIlhaney-Carter family)

[696] Federal Census: 1930, Vernon, Wilbarger Co., TX, pg 10A

[697] 2312: Findagrave.com #37706314 and #37706409

[698] 22: A. E. "Phil" & Marion Phillips, *"The Descendants of James William McIlhaney"*, introduction by Sam McIlhaney, 1987

[699] 499: Sharon Hitt (McIlhaney-Carter family)

[700] Federal Census: 1920, Irion Co., TX, pg 15; 1930, Upton Co., TX, pg236

[701] 2312: Findagrave.com #52504767 and #52505616

[702] 22: A. E. "Phil" & Marion Phillips, *"The Descendants of James William McIlhaney"*, introduction by Sam McIlhaney, 1987

[703] Federal Census: 1910, Crawford, McLennan Co., TX, pg 175

[704] Federal Census: 1910, McLennan Co., TX, pg 175A; 1920, McLennan Co., TX, pg 234A; 1930, Coryell Co., TX, pg 141B

[705] 2312: Findagrave.com #45838333 and #45838332

[706] 1478: McIlhaney and Gibson tombstones in Coryell Missionary Baptist Church Cemetery, Coryell Co., TX, photos by Susan & R. Steven Rainwater, 28 Nov 1997

John Richardson McIlhaney and Ollie Delilah Umberson

John Richardson McIlhaney, 1907
From "A Home in the Famous Wheatland Valley of Wilbarger Co., Texas"

John Richardson McIlhaney

Son of W.J.G. McIlhaney and Mary Charlesana Elizabeth Carter
Born 5 Jul 1873, Coryell Co., Texas
Died 25 Sep 1949, Lubbock, Lubbock Co., Texas

Married 16 Sep 1897, Gholson, McLennan Co., Texas

Ollie Delilah Umberson

Daughter of William Franklin Umberson and Mary Jane Singleton Presnall
Born 19 Mar 1877, Gholson, McLennan Co., Texas
Died 13 Jul 1966, Lubbock, Lubbock Co., Texas

John Richardson McIlhaney was part of the generation of men who couldn't get off the farm fast enough. Tired of the hard-scrabble existence of mucking around in the dirt, these men wanted professional careers and middle class lives in town. John R. McIlhaney had also been bitten by the "get rich quick" bug, and the infection would drive him for the rest of his life.

His occupations include instructor of Spencerian handwriting, dairyman, operator of a drug store, butcher in a meat market, tailor shop owner, cafe owner, real estate agent, and land promoter.[707] He was successful at none of them.

He moved relentlessly in search of his pot of gold – according to his daughter Louise McIlhaney Deering, the family moved over fifty times in the course of the marriage. Among the places they lived that Aunt Louise could remember were Oglesby (1898), Waldo (1900), Gholson (1902), La Mesa, Tolbert (1907), San Angelo (1910), Lubbock (1913), Fort Worth, and El Paso – all in Texas; and Mountainair (1918), Carrizozo (1920), and Las Vegas – all in New Mexico.[708]

We don't know how John met Ollie Delilah Umberson. She was the only surviving child of her parents marriage, though both had children from previous marriages. Her three siblings had died in early childhood. As a result, the golden-haired Ollie was doted on to an extent that probably wasn't healthy, and left her with a self-centered flaw in her personality. A number of her grandchildren and great-grandchildren have remarked on her selfish behavior, one commenting that she was the most deeply selfish person he had ever met. Others remarked that she was highly judgmental and seemed to look down her nose at others. But she was a talented painter and had attended Baylor University as an art student, attending in the first graduating class that included women, though Ollie herself did not graduate.[709] Her artistic gift was passed on to several of her descendants, particularly her daughter Louise. Her second cousin, Minnie Humberson Guyton noted that Ollie was very particular in her manner of dress.[710]

John and Ollie were married on 16 Sep 1897 in Gholson by Rev. Rufus Burleson, a local Baptist minister.[711] They made a movie-star handsome couple, two decades too early to put their looks to use in the silent pictures. I

---

[707] 22: A. E. "Phil" & Marion Phillips, *"The Descendants of James William McIlhaney"*, introduction by Sam McIlhaney, 1987
Federal Census, Tom Green Co., TX, 1910, pg 132, real estate agent; Carrizozo, Lincoln Co., NM, 1920, pg 183B, dairyman. He is not found in the 1900 or 1930 census under any spelling of McIlhaney.

[708] Son William was born 1898 in Oglesby; daughter Johnye was born 1900 in Waldo; son Jesse was born 1907 in Tolbert; son Joe was born 1902 in Gholson; son Jack was born 1910 in San Angelo; daughter Louise was born 1913 in Lubbock; 1918, son William's draft card says he works for his father in Mountainair; 1920 Federal Census, Carrizozo, Lincoln Co., NM, pg 163B.

[709] 22: A. E. "Phil" & Marion Phillips, *"The Descendants of James William McIlhaney"*, introduction by Sam McIlhaney, 1987. According to the Phillips' notes, pg 19, Ollie chose not to graduate, not uncommon in an era when an educated woman was seen as less marriageable.

[710] 1106: Minnie Humberson Guyton, *"Once Upon A Journey: The descendants of John H. Humberson and Sallie Presnall"*, written pre-1987

[711] 210: McLennan Co., TX Marriage Records, Vol. 3, 15 Aug 1892-19 Jan 1901, publ. 1963, Central Texas Genealogical Society, Waco, Texas

have often thought that it was ironic that they had missed the destiny for which their looks and temperaments had so obviously intended them.

Their first child was born in June 1898, and seven children followed, born between 1900 and 1916.

In 1907, John joined with Benjamin Carter Wood, his wife's half sister's husband, to promote the development of Tolbert, Texas, a few miles northwest of Vernon. Now utterly extinct, Tolbert was a classic railroad land scheme. The railroads needed stops at regular intervals along their lines for water, fuel, freight and paying passengers. So they would buy up the often worthless land on either side of the tracks and flog it at a loss in order to populate their railroad stops. Tolbert, like Vernon, is on the edge of the high plains desert – land that receives 10 to 20 inches of rain per year. It's arid, hot in the summer, subject to the blue northers that blow down off the Rockies in the winter. The soil is thin and not suited to most crops, though the shortgrass and scrub can be used to support livestock.

But Wood and McIlhaney promoted Tolbert as prime agricultural land with their sales brochure, *A Home in the Famous Wheatland Valley of Wilbarger Co., Texas*.[712] While you could probably grow wheat in Tolbert today with modern irrigation systems, it would have been darned difficult in 1907. The economy of the region in modern times revolves around oil, cattle, horses, and corn farming.[713] So the development of Tolbert failed too, but the couple was there long enough for their son Jesse to be born.

The endless moving took its toll on the marriage, and every move made their financial situation a little worse. Prior to 1930, the couple separated, and Ollie moved in with her son William, in Lubbock, Texas.[714] She and her husband remained separated for the next 19 years. They do not appear to have formally divorced.

Like her father, Ollie McIlhaney seems to have suffered panic attacks. One story related to us by Nancy McIlhaney Rainwater illustrates Ollie's tendency to panicked overreaction.

Joe Singleton McIlhaney was taking his mother, Ollie, to Coryell County to visit some of her relations. As Joe drove over a bridge that crossed Coryell Creek, he remarked that it was in this very stream that James William McIlhaney had drowned. Ollie became so frightened, that she pulled the door handle off of the inside of the car door. On a cemetery photographing trip in November 1997, we also crossed this bridge, and stopped to view the creek. It was apparent that except at flood stage, no one could possibly be in any danger.

---

[712] 633: A Home in the Famous Wheatland Valley of Wilbarger Co., TX, promotional pamphlet for Wilson-McIlhaney Land Co., 16 Aug 1907, original

[713] Wikipedia: Vernon, Texas, http://en.wikipedia.org/wiki/Vernon,_Texas

[714] Federal Census: 1930, Lubbock, Lubbock Co., TX, pg 227. Ollie is listed as married in this record.

Ollie McIlhaney's fear of it was entirely in her own imagination.

Ollie Umberson McIlhaney, 1951

John Richardson McIlhaney died in 1949 from hepatitis contracted during a gall bladder operation.[715] After John's death, Ollie married Thomas R. Bousman, but her descendants seem to barely remember him. Ollie died in 1966 of ateriosclerotic heart disease.[716] She and John McIlhaney are buried together at Resthaven Memorial Park in Lubbock, along with several of their children.[717]

---

[715] 356: Death certificate #44267, John R. McIlhaney, Lubbock Co., TX, 1949, certified copy

Nancy McIlhaney Rainwater believed that the hepatitis story was a cover-up, and claimed to have heard the doctors talking about the real cause, which was not stated on the death certificate. By the time she told us the story, she had forgotten the supposed cause.

[716] 361: Death certificate #47217, Ollie Delilah Bousman, Lubbock Co., TX, 1966, certified copy

[717] 1418: McIlhaney tombstones in Resthaven Memorial Park (formerly Texas Tech Memorial Park), Lubbock, Lubbock Co., TX, photos by Susan & R. Steven Rainwater, Apr 1997

The children of John and Ollie McIlhaney:

William Umberson McIlhaney

Born 25 Jun 1898, Coryell Co., Texas, and died 20 Jan 1976, Hamilton Co., Texas[718]
William McIlhaney made his living as rancher and dairy farmer. He married Deema Boyd Bradley in Mar 1923, and the union produced two daughters.[719] They were divorced between 1940 and 1943. He is buried with his second wife, Cladye Loraine Massengale, in Hico Cemetery.[720] Deema married Cleon B. Endsley on 24 May 1943.[721] He died in 1970. She married William L. Cato the same year. Deema died in 1978 and is buried in Resthaven Memorial Park, Lubbock with her second husband.[722]

Johnye Mae McIlhaney Green Gholson

Born 26 Dec 1900, Coryell Co., Texas, and died 3 Aug 1993, Valencis Co., New Mexico[723]
Originally named Johnye Mary, her name mutated to Johnye May in childhood. She married William "Billie" Marion Green on 8 May 1920, in Las Vegas, San Miguel Co., New Mexico. Billie Green was a firey Baptist revival preacher who was said to have "burned out" and left the ministry to run a tourist court motel. We were told by Nancy McIlhaney Rainwater that Billie was later discovered to have had an extra wife and family, and may have retired from the ministry to avoid exposure.

Following Billie Green's death, Johnye Mae married Clarence T. Gholson, owner of Gholson Brothers' Candy Company, on 18 Nov 1938, in Albuquerque, Bernalillo Co., New Mexico. The couple is buried in Sunset Memorial Park, Albuquerque.[724] The town of Gholson, Texas, was named for Clarence T. Gholson's cousin Samuel, a surveyor.

---

[718] 268: Social Security Administration Online Death Index, Ancestry.com paywalled database
[719] 22: A. E. "Phil" & Marion Phillips, *"The Descendants of James William McIlhaney"*, introduction by Sam McIlhaney, 1987
[720] 959: Hico Cemetery, Hamilton Co., TX, Hamilton County Genealogical Society, Horace Griffitts, publ. 1995, Hico, TX
[721] 950: Ancestry.com, Washington Marriage records, 1865-2004
[722] 2312: Findagrave.com #20395526
[723] 22: A. E. "Phil" & Marion Phillips, *"The Descendants of James William McIlhaney"*, introduction by Sam McIlhaney, 1987
[724] 2312: Findagrave.com #64041288 and #64041290

Joe Singleton McIlhaney

Born 18 Oct 1902, McLennan Co., Texas, and died 27 Nov 1999, Lubbock, Lubbock Co., Texas
See profile of Joe Singleton McIlhaney and his two wives

George Truett McIlhaney

Born 21 Sep 1904, Coryell Co., Texas, and died 15 Nov 1972, Bernalillo Co., New Mexico
George was named for George Washington Truett, whom Wikipedia calls, "*one of the most significant Southern Baptist preachers of his era.*"[725] George made his living as a dairyman, and moved to New Mexico between 1910 and 1920. He married Mary Elizabeth Walker Rich, a widow, on 22 Jun 1928, in Farmington, San Juan Co., New Mexico.[726] They were the parents of six children. The couple is buried in Sandia Memorial Cemetery, Albuquerque, New Mexico.[727]

Jesse Roland McIlhaney

Born 12 Apr 1907, Wilbarger Co., Texas, and died 4 Mar 1998, Lubbock Co., Texas[728]
Jesse worked as a milkman for the McIlhaney Creamery in Lubbock while in high school and college. He attended Baylor University and Texas Tech, with a stint at Southwest Theological Seminary. He spent some part of his life as a Baptist minister, but his obituary says he worked in wholesale sales with PhilMar Company in Albuquerque.

He was married twice: to Mildred Davis on 14 Sep 1930, and upon her death, to Grace Patterson on 24 Jun 1936.[729] The second marriage resulted in four children and ended in divorce. Between the two marriages, Jesse was hit by a car while crossing the street, resulting in a quite serious head injury. The long term effect was mental decline late in life.

---

[725] Wikipedia: George Washington Truett, http://en.wikipedia.org/wiki/George_Washington_Truett

[726] 22: A. E. "Phil" & Marion Phillips, "*The Descendants of James William McIlhaney*", introduction by Sam McIlhaney, 1987

[727] 630: Funeral program, George T. McIlhaney, 18 Nov 1972, original

[728] 268: Social Security Administration Online Death Index, Ancestry.com paywalled database

[729] 22: A. E. "Phil" & Marion Phillips, "*The Descendants of James William McIlhaney*", introduction by Sam McIlhaney, 1987

Jesse was buried in Resthaven Memorial Park, Lubbock, Texas.[730] Grace is buried in Tecumseh Cemetery, Pottawatomie Co., Oklahoma.[731] Mildred is buried in Lubbock City Cemetery.[732]

Jack McIlhaney

Born 6 May 1910, Tom Green Co., Texas, and died 19 Sep 1984, Otero Co., New Mexico[733]

According to family legend, he was called Sweetie, having never been given an official name by his parents.[734] One day, his father walked through the house and said "*Hi Jack*," as one might say "*Hi pal*," but Jack immediately assumed that he had been assigned a name, and Jack it was thereafter. In addition to working as a foreman at the creamery, Jack worked as a boxer's sparing partner, and the family's assessment was that because of the head injuries, he "*wasn't right*" thereafter.[735] Jack married Lucille Chamness on 29 Dec 1940.[736] They were the parents of two children.

Ollie Louise McIlhaney Deering

Born 26 Jun 1913, Lubbock Co., Texas, and died 20 Jan 2009, Bexar Co., Texas[737]

A talented painter, Louise studied painting in her teens, and attended Texas Tech to study art. On 30 Jun 1935, Louise married Gordon Deering, an educator in Lubbock. They were the parents of three children. Louise was a charter member of the Lubbock Art Association, served as its president, and regularly exhibited her work in Texas and New Mexico.[738] She was also an active member of First Baptist Church of Lubbock. More than one member of the family felt that Louise was afflicted with the family paranoia. Louise died in San Antonio, and is buried in Resthaven Memorial Park in Lubbock.[739]

---

[730] 498: Obituary of Jesse R. McIlhaney, Lubbock Avalanche-Journal, Friday 6 Mar 1998, photocopy of original

[731] 2312: Findagrave.com #20049606

[732] 2551: The City of Lubbock Cemetery, 1892-2002, South Plains Genealogical Society, publ. 2005, Lubbock, TX

[733] 631: Funeral program, Jack McIlhaney, 21 Sep 1984, original

[734] Federal Census: 1910, Tom Green Co., TX, pg 132A. Jack is recorded simply as Baby in this record.

[735] 19: Nancy McIlhaney Rainwater, deceased, (McIlhaney Family), conversations between 1991 and 1997

[736] 22: A. E. "Phil" & Marion Phillips, "*The Descendants of James William McIlhaney*", introduction by Sam McIlhaney, 1987

[737] 2335: Obituary, Louise McIlhaney Deering, Lubbock Avalanche Journal, 23 Jan 2009

[738] 632: Announcement for Lubbock Art Association One Person Show, Louise Deering (featured artist), 11-25 Jan 1987, includes brief bio

[739] 2312: Findagrave.com #62073137

Samuel Frank McIlhaney

Born 13 Jul 1916, Lubbock Co., Texas, and died 27 Sep 1998, Georgia[740]

According to Nancy Rainwater, Sam's middle name was originally Franklin, but he signed all of his World War II military papers with the name Samuel Frank. Discovering that it would be almost impossible to fix the mistake, Sam simply changed his name.

Sam married Marian Grady in 1939, and can be found in the 1940 census as the manager of a creamery in San Antonio.[741] The marriage resulted in three children, and ended in divorce. Sam married Flora Strickland on 16 May 1961.[742] Following the war, Sam entered the insurance business and became a successful agent in Albany, Georgia.[743] He and his second wife are buried in Crown Hill Cemetery in Albany, Georgia.[744]

---

[740] 646: Funeral program, Sam Frank McIlhaney, 29 Sep 1998, transcription

19: Nancy McIlhaney Rainwater, deceased, (McIlhaney Family), conversations between 1991 and 1997

[741] Federal Census: 1940, Mission St, San Antonio, Bexar Co, TX, pg 631B. The Phillips indicate that Sam and Marian were married in Nov 1940, but they are already married in the 1940 census, taken in April of that year.

[742] 22: A. E. "Phil" & Marion Phillips, *The Descendants of James William McIlhaney*, introduction by Sam McIlhaney, 1987

[743] 643: Marketing bulletin, USLC, "McIlhaney Earns Double Megacircle," Jan 1981, original

[744] 2312: Findagrave.com #22783199 and #22783202

John R. Goodrich and Sarah A. Richardson

John R. Goodrich
Born Feb 1830, Tennessee
Died 24 Jun 1902, Washington Co., Arkansas

Married before 1856

Sarah A. Richardson
Born Feb 1830, Missouri
Died after 1910 Oklahoma

John R. Goodrich was born in Tennessee in February 1830. Because he had left home before 1850, it's impossible to use the census to discover the names of his parents, and no family story has been passed down to fill in the gap.

Goodrich had gone west to California, apparently enjoying a youthful adventure before settling down to married life. In the 1850 census, he is recorded in the midst of ten pages of mostly single men as a 20-year-old miner in a mining camp called Logtown in El Dorado Co., California.[745]

We have no reason to believe that John R. Goodrich's career as a gold miner "panned out" because he returned to the midwest within a few years. There he met and married a woman named Sarah A., c. 1855, probably in Missouri.[746]

Sarah's maiden name is a vexing problem. When her son Fulton died, his brother James provided the names of their parents for the death certificate. He gave Richardson as his mother's maiden name. When their sister, JoAnn Atchison died, her son, Elmer Atchison, filled in the names, and gave the name as Roundtree. A Bible passed down in the family of another daughter, Edna Goodrich Ferguson, provides a third option: Daniels.[747] I lean slightly to Richardson because this name was supplied by her son, the others by grandchildren.

John R. Goodrich did not enlist at the start of the Civil War. He was a father with a wife and three children to support. He had a change of heart in the spring of 1863 and enlisted in the Arkansas Confederate Infantry, Company F, 12th Regiment. His service would last only a few months. Company F, known as the Jackson Minute Men, was organized in the Jackson Township of Dallas Co., Arkansas, which provides evidence for where the family lived. The company, part of the 12th Regiment, had been nearly annihilated in 1862 during the Battle of Island Number Ten. Now revitalized with new recruits,

---

[745] Federal Census: 1850, Logtown, El Dorado Co., CA, pg 369A, line 16

[746] Federal Census: 1900, Center Twp., Washington Co., AR, pg 48A. The couple indicates they have been married 45 years.

[747] 360: Death certificate #38843, Fulton Miller Goodrich, Levelland Co., TX, 1949, certified copy
370: Death certificate #23059, Joan Atchison, Levelland Co., TX, 1946, certified copy

the 12th was charged with the unenviable task of holding Port Hudson against the Union Army.

Port Hudson, Louisiana sat on the heights above the Mississippi River about 145 miles south of Vicksburg. As part of a strategy to keep supply lines open during the Vicksburg Campaign, the Confederate Army had fortified a position on the bluffs. On 27 May 1863, Union troops under the command of Major General Nathaniel P. Banks launched an assault against Port Hudson's fortifications. The siege ended with the Confederate surrender on 9 Jul 1863.

Drawing from the diary of Robert Knox Sneden, 1832-1918
Virginia Historical Society

On 14 Jul 1863, John R. Goodrich was paroled by the Union Army on account of his injuries. He had been shot in the back of the head, with a musket ball making an entry near the spine. The wound was infected, and he was not expected to survive. But survive he did.[748]

In civilian life, John R. Goodrich made his living as a miller. He and Sarah were the parents of eight children. In the 1900 census, Sarah Goodrich says she is the mother of eight children, six of whom are still living. Two children had died prior to 1900.

The family never stayed in a county more than ten years. They are found in Porter Township, Christian Co., Missouri in 1860; and had probably moved to Jackson Township, Washington Co., Arkansas by 1863; moved again to Vineyard Township, Washington Co., Arkansas by 1870; then to Jackson, Greene Co., Missouri by 1880; and finally back to Center Township, Washington Co., Arkansas by 1900.[749]

In July 1901, John R. Goodrich applied for a disability pension from the State of Arkansas. Like many divided states, its Union veterans received pensions from the federal government, while the state paid the Confederate veteran benefits.

In his pension application, Goodrich describes himself as partially blind, unable to walk without assistance or perform any manual labor as a result of the wounds received in battle. His physician, Dr. J. R. Johnson, notes in his deposition, that the cause of the disability is an infection of the spinal column. The pension was quickly approved, and Goodrich received $100 per year, one of the larger amounts I have seen granted.

He lived just 11 months after making application, dying on 24 Jun 1902. His widow Sarah filed for her own pension a year later, and was granted $50 per year.[750] Her application was made from Prairie View, Washington Co., Arkansas, suggesting that she was already living with her daughter JoAnn and son-in-law Robert H. Atchison. When Robert died the following year, JoAnn moved her family to Kiowa Co., Oklahoma. Sarah Goodrich moved with them and died in the decade after the 1910 census.

The children of James R. and Sarah Goodrich

Amanda Virginia Goodrich

> Born c. 1856, Missouri, and died 24 Nov 1891, Washington Co., Arkansas
>
> In 1889, Amanda married Confederate veteran, Thomas Jefferson

---

[748] 2629: Civil War Confederate pension application #13599; John R. Goodrich and Sarah A. Goodrich, Washington Co., AR, Arkansas pension rolls, dated 29 Aug 1902 and 15 Jun 1903, abstract from microfilmed original

[749] Federal Census: 1860, Christian Co., MO, pg 457; 1870, Washington Co., AR, pg 253; 1880, Greene Co., MO, pg 69C; 1900, Washington Co., AR, pg 48A; 1910, Kiowa Co., OK, pg 5B

[750] 2629: Civil War Confederate pension application #13599; John R. Goodrich and Sarah A. Goodrich, Washington Co., AR, Arkansas pension rolls, dated 29 Aug 1902 and 15 Jun 1903, abstract from microfilmed original

Shannon, in Washington Co., Arkansas.[751] She died two years later. T.J. died in 1930. Curiously, the date inscribed on his tombstone doesn't exist – November has no 31st. The couple is buried in Vineyard Cemetery in Evansville, Arkansas.[752]

Walter V. Goodrich

Born Sep 1858, Missouri, and died between 1920 and 1930, Oklahoma
Walter married Nancy H. c. 1886. He was a miller and cotton gin engineer, and in later life, a merchant.[753] The couple had no children.

JoAnn Goodrich Atchison

Born 16 Aug 1860, Missouri, and died 9 May 1946, Hockley Co., Texas
JoAnn married Robert Hatch Atchison c. 1882. They were the parents of seven children.[754] They were also the guardians of their niece, Opal Goodrich, after her mother died. Robert Atchison died 1 Jan 1904 and is buried in Prairie Grove, Washington Co., Arkansas. JoAnn then moved her family first to Kiowa Co., Oklahoma[755] and then to Texas. She died in Hockley County and is buried in Levelland City Cemetery with her brother Fulton and son Elmer.[756]

J. Frank Goodrich

Born c. 1866, Arkansas, and died before 1910

James Hamilton Goodrich

Born Feb 1867, Arkansas, and died 1 Jan 1857, Lea Co., New Mexico
See profile of Fulton Miller Goodrich and Callie Kuykendall

Patrick G. H. Goodrich

Born Sep 1869, Arkansas, and died between 1910 and 1920, Oklahoma
In the early 1920s, Patrick G. H. Goodrich, decided to leave Loveland, Oklahoma, in search of better farmland in Texas. He settled in Levelland in Hockley County and in 1922, JoAnn Goodrich Atchison, their families and relations, also moved to Levelland.[757] Patrick was

---

[751] 554: Washington Co., AR Marriages, Books D-I, Lois N. Miller, McDowell Publications, Utica, KY

[752] 2312 Findagrave.com #21389003 and #21390285

[753] Federal Census: 1910, Cherokee Co., OK, pg 4A

[754] Federal Census: 1900, Center Twp., Washington Co., AR, pg 51A

[755] Federal Census: 1910, Kiowa Co., OK, pg 5B

[756] 1417: Goodrich and Atchison tombstones in Levelland City Cemetery, Hockley Co., TX, photos by Susan & R. Steven Rainwater, April 1997

[757] 272: From the Heart of Hockley County – Recollections, Hockley Co., TX Historical Society, pg 272, profile of Oliver and Reba Atchison, publ. 1986, Hockley County Historical Commission,

married to a girl named Belle c. 1893, and by 1910 they were the parents of six children, though the census notes that four others have died.[758] Patrick was a miller and a farmer.[759]

Fulton Miller Goodrich

Born 15 Oct 1871, Arkansas, and died 9 Aug 1949, Hockley Co., Texas
See profile of Fulton Miller Goodrich and Callie Kuykendall

Edna Ann Goodrich Ferguson

Born 24 Nov 1874, Arkansas, and died 20 Dec 1958, Nueces Co., Texas
Edna married James Atchley Ferguson c. 1899, probably in Washington Co., Arkansas. They were the parents of two children, one of whom died in childhood. James was a blacksmith and mechanic. The family lived in Oklahoma until 1920, then moved to Amarillo. James died in 1940.[760] Edna retired to Corpus Christi, and is buried there in Seaside Memorial Park.[761]

Levelland, TX
[758] Federal Census: 1910, Davis Twp., Pottawatomie Co., OK, pg 194B
[759] Federal Census: 1900, Washington Co., AR, pg 48
[760] Federal Census: 1900, Stilwell, Cherokee Nation, Indian Territory (OK), pg 100A; 1910, Tipton, Tillman Co., OK, pg 188A; 1920, Sand Springs, Tulsa Co., OK, pg 57A; 1930, Amarillo, Potter Co., TX, pg 54B-55A
[761] Findagrave.com #71776298 & Nueces Co., Texas death certificate #70876

James Calvin Kuykendall and Mary Frances Strawn

James C. And Mary F. Kuykendall, drawing from photograph

James Calvin Kuykendall

Son of James Kuykendall and Rebecca Norton
Born 18 Dec 1830, Indiana
Died 18 Dec 1907, Wickes, Polk Co., Arkansas

Married before 1850, probably Arkansas

Mary Frances Strawn

Daughter of Rebecca and Greenbury Strawn
Born 5 Jul 1835, Alabama
Died 24 Apr 1915, Wickes, Polk Co., Arkansas

James Calvin Kuykendall was the third James in his line of James Kuykendalls.[762]

His grandparents, James Kuykendall, Sr., and Mary Hambright, were born in North Carolina. They were the parents of at least ten children.[763] The family

---
[762] The surname Kuykendall is Dutch and despite appearances, it's pronounced Kirk-en-doll, and can be spelled a dozen different ways.
[763] Federal Census: Buncomb Co., NC, 1800, pg 57; 1810, no page number; 1820, pg 64

lived in Buncomb Co., North Carolina, until 1820, and were slave owners.[764] James, Sr., is said to have served in the Revolutionary War militia in North Carolina, however, I have been unable to find any evidence that supports this.

His son, James Kuykendall, Jr., was born c. 1794. James, Jr., married Rebecca Norton, probably in North Carolina. Their first son, Peter, was born in Buncomb Co., North Carolina in 1814. Shortly thereafter, they undertook a series of moves: to Georgia, then to McMinn Co., Tennessee, to Knox Co., Indiana, prior to 1830, and then four years later to the outskirts of Memphis, Tennessee. Finally in 1835, the family came to rest in Crawford Co., Arkansas.

The Goodspeed profile of James and Rebecca's son, Peter, says that he had seven siblings, four of whom were deceased at the time of publication in 1889. We know that he had two sisters, Rebecca and Melissa, who were listed in the 1850 census, and a brother, James Calvin.[765] Numerous family trees on Ancestry.com propose names for the other four, but with no credible documentary evidence.

James Kuykendall, Jr., died in 1846, and Rebecca followed in 1866. They are buried in Byers Cemetery, Crawford Co., Arkansas.[766]

James Calvin Kuykendall was born during the family's short stay in Knox Co, Indiana.[767] The identification of Knox County as his birth place is based on the 1830 census, which, of course, lists only the householder's name. James Calvin would be the sole boy under the age of five recorded in this household. In later census years, James identified Indiana as his place of birth, with the exception of the 1850 census where he said Georgia.[768]

In or before 1850, James Calvin Kuykendall married Rebecca Norton. Since the marriage records for Crawford County start in 1877, we can only estimate the date of their marriage from the birth of their first child. In all, the couple were the parents of four children who lived to adulthood.

In 1919, George Benson Kuykendall published his genealogical study, "*The History of the Kuykendall Family*." In this volume, he reprints this excerpt of a letter from Lorenzo Dow Kuykendall:

---

[764] The sources for this section, unless otherwise noted, are:
2074: History of Benton, Washington, Carroll, Madison, Crawford, Franklin, and Sebastian Counties, Arkansas, Profile of Peter Kuykendall Sr., The Goodspeed Publishing Company, publ., 1889, Chicago, IL
2522: George Benson Kuykendall, "*History of the Kuykendall Family*", published by the Kilham Stationery & Printing CO. Portland, Oregon, 1919, transcription

[765] Federal census: 1850, Richland Twp., Crawford Co., AR, pg 323A, household of the widowed Rebecca Kuykendall

[766] 2312: Findagrave.com #68053010 and #68053173

[767] Federal Census: 1830, Knox Co., IN, pg 254B, household of James Kuykendall, Jr.

[768] Federal Census: 1850, Richland Twp., Crawford Co., AR, pg 641A; 1860, Richland Twp., Crawford Co., AR, pg 663B; 1870, Richland Twp., Crawford Co., AR, pg 230B; 1900, Ozark Twp, Polk Co., AR, pg 349B

My father was named James C. Kuykendall, born in North Carolina, December 18, 1830. My grandfather's name was James, don't know the date of his birth, but he died between 1840 and 1850. Grandmother's maiden name was Rebecca Norton, who died in 1866, I think in her 77th year. My father was in the Federal Army, in the 2nd Arkansas Cavalry. He lived until 1907. He married Mary F. Strawn and they raised a family of four children, whose names were Peter, Lorenzo Dow, Mary Jane and Amanda.

James Calvin Kuykendall was thirty when the Civil War erupted. He enlisted in the Union Army on 10 Oct 1863. Two of his nephews, the sons of his brother Peter, served the Confederacy.[769]

Kuykendall enlisted as a Private in Company L of the 2nd Regiment of the Arkansas Volunteer Cavalry.[770] The word *volunteer* is critical in the identification of this unit, because there was also a 2nd Arkansas Cavalry on the Confederate side. Decades later, someone arranged for an official U.S. Veteran's Administration headstone to be placed on James Calvin Kuykendall's grave. It was engraved with the Southern Cross of Honor, which the VA reserves for the gravestones of Confederate veterans.[771] Whoever requested the tombstone got the two 2nd Arkansas Cavalry regiments confused.

The 2nd Arkansas Cavalry was organized at Helena, Arkansas, and Pilot Knob, Missouri, and mustered into service in July 1862. Regimental records show them in Crawford Co., Arkansas on 25 Nov 1863. The regiment was mustered out 20 Aug 1865.[772] They served in a few minor skirmishes, but no significant battles.

The Kuykendall family farmed land in Richland Township, Crawford Co., Arkansas, for at least thirty-five years.[773] Sometime between 1870 and 1900, the family moved to Ozark, Polk Co., Arkansas.[774]

James died in 1907 and is buried in Daniel Cemetery, east of Wickes.[775]

---

[769] 2635: Index to Arkansas Confederate Soldiers, multiple volumes, Desmond Walls Allen, publ. 1990, Arkansas Research Inc.,Conway, AR

[770] 1271: The Roster of Union Soldiers, 1861-1865, all volumes, Janet B. Hewett, publ. 1999, Broadfoot Publishing Co., Wilmington, NC

[771] Wikipedia: Southern Cross of Honor, http://en.wikipedia.org/wiki/Southern_Cross_of_Honor

[772] Wikipedia: 2nd Regiment Arkansas Volunteer Cavalry (Union), http://en.wikipedia.org/wiki/2nd_Regiment_Arkansas_Volunteer_Cavalry_(Union)
Arkansas Cavalry Volunteers, 2nd Regiment, Union,
http://www.couchgenweb.com/civilwar/2ArCavhs.html, list of engagements

[773] Federal Census: Richland Twp., Crawford Co., AR, 1850, pg 641; 1860, pg 663B; 1870, pg 230B

[774] Federal Census: 1900, Ozark Twp, Polk Co., AR, pg 349B

[775] 413: Cemetery Inscriptions of Polk Co., AR, Nixby Daniel Kannady and Loreda Hicks Daniel, publ. 1984, Cove, AR

Mary Frances immediately applied for a Union widow's pension, which makes very clear on which side of the Civil War James served.[776] She died in 1915, and is also buried in Daniel Cemetery.[777]

---

[776] 2638: Arkansas Union Soldiers Pension Application Index, Desmond Walls Allen, publ. 1987, Conway, AR

[777] 907: Arkansas Death Record Index, 1914-1923, Desmond Walls Allen, publ. 1996, Arkansas Research, Conway, AR

413: Cemetery Inscriptions of Polk Co., AR, Nixby Daniel Kannady and Loreda Hicks Daniel, publ. 1984, Cove, AR

Peter D. Kuykendall and Martha Conley

Peter D. Kuykendall
Son of James Calvin Kuykendall and Mary Frances Strawn
Born 17 Nov 1850, Arkansas
Died 13 Apr 1900, Red Oak City, Latimer Co., Oklahoma

Married, 1st wife, before 1869, probably Crawford Co., Arkansas

Elizabeth J.
Born c. 1849, Arkansas
Died before 1872, Arkansas

Married, 2nd wife, before 1872, probably Arkansas

Martha Conley
Daughter of Anna and Thomas Conley
Born 3 Mar 1852, Tennessee
Died 6 Aug 1934, Red Oak City, Latimer Co., Oklahoma

Peter Kuykendall was born 17 Nov 1850 in Arkansas, the eldest of the surviving children of James Calvin Kuykendall and Mary Frances Strawn.[778]

In about 1869, Peter married for the first time. Because Crawford County's marriage records prior to 1877 have been lost, we don't know the exact date or his wife's maiden name. She is identified in the 1870 census only as Elizabeth J., and their young daughter as M. J.[779] Elizabeth died prior to 1872, and M. J. died before 1880.

In about 1872, Peter married his second wife, Martha Conley, again probably in Crawford Co., Arkansas.

Martha Conley was born 3 Mar 1852, in Tennessee, the daughter of Anna and Thomas Conley.[780] The census rolls of the midwest record a flood of Irish immigrants in the 1850s and 1860s, mostly coal miners, and the number named Thomas Conley is daunting. However, only one – Thomas Conley of Howell Co., Missouri – has a daughter, Martha, the right age who was born in Tennessee in the 1860 census.[781] He and his wife, Anna, were the parents of seven children. Tom died between 1863, the year of birth of his last child, and the 1870 census. The other noteworthy event between the two census years is that the family moved to Crawford Co., Arkansas.

---

[778] 203: Red Oak City Cemetery, Latimer Co., OK, Gloryanne Hanbins Young, publ. 1988, G. H. Young, Wister, OK
Federal Census: 1800, Sebastian Co., AR, pg 663C
[779] Federal Census: 1870, Van Buren PO, Richland Twp, Crawford Co., AR, pg 230B
[780] 366: Death certificate #38066, Martha Kuykendall, Latimer Co., OK, 1934, certified copy. Her death certificate names only her father.
[781] Federal Census: 1860, West Plains PO, Howell Co., MO, pg 559

In 1870, the widowed Anna Conley and her seven children are recorded living only a few households from Peter Kuykendall (brother of James Calvin Kuykendall), the uncle of Martha's future husband.[782] This is undoubtedly how the young couple met. Anna Conley died between 1880 and 1900.[783]

Peter and Martha Kuykendall were the parents of eleven children, four of whom died prior to 1900.[784] Found in Sebastian Co., Arkansas, in 1880,[785] they moved into the fringes of Indian Territory (the future Oklahoma) for cheap land. Peter died in Red Oak on 13 Apr 1900 and is buried in Red Oak City cemetery.[786]

Martha carried on as a farmer in Red Oak for twenty years, seeing her new state enter the union in 1907. She had gone to live with her son Lee by 1920, and by 1930 with her daughter, Emma Kuykendall Maddox.[787] Martha died of a stroke in 1934, and is buried beside Peter and their son, James, in Red Oak, Latimer Co., Oklahoma.

The children of Peter D. and Martha Kuykendall

James David Kuykendall

> Born 20 Dec 1872, Crawford Co., Arkansas, and died 12 Jul 1956, Latimer Co., Oklahoma
> James married his wife Mamie c. 1896. They were the parents of three children. James worked as a farmer and tractor driver. He died of leukemia in 1956 and is buried with his wife in Red Oak Cemetery.[788]

Mary Frances Kuykendall

> Born c. 1874, Arkansas, and probably died before 1900

Callie A. Kuykendall Goodrich

> Born Jan 1877, Arkansas, and died c. 1917, Oklahoma
> *See profile of Fulton Miller Goodrich and Callie Kuykendall*

---

[782] Federal Census: 1870, Bellmont PO, Lafayette Twp, Crawford Co, AR, pg 205A

[783] Federal Census: 1880, Lafayette Twp, Crawford Co, AR, pg 536A

[784] Federal Census: 1900, Choctaw Nation, Indian Territory, pg 200B; 1910, Latimer Co., OK, pg 6B

[785] Federal Census: 1880, Dayton Twp., Sebastian Co., AR, pg 31

[786] 1415: Kuykendall tombstones in Red Oak Cemetery, Red Oak, Latimer Co., OK, photos by Susan & R. Steven Rainwater, 26 Apr 1998

[787] Federal Census: 1920, Red Oak, Latimer Co., OK, pg 241B; 1930, Howe, LeFlore Co., OK, pg 165B

[788] 365: Death certificate #010596, James David Kuykendall, Latimer Co., OK, 1956, certified copy

Susan Emma Kuykendall

Born 16 Jan 1879, Arkansas, and died 4 Dec 1951, Kay Co., Oklahoma
Emma married James Oscar Maddox on 24 Dec 1896.[789] Their first two children were technically born in Choctaw Nation, Indian Territory, though later records would say Oklahoma.[790] The family moved to Arkansas between 1900 and 1902, where the next three children were born. They returned to Oklahoma by 1909, where the last two daughters were born.[791] The couple died in Kay Co., Oklahoma, and is buried in the IOOF Cemetery in Ponca City.[792]

Andrew Jackson Kuykendall

Born 25 Nov 1880, Arkansas, and died 21 Oct 1971, Latimer Co., Oklahoma
Jack married Barbara Liller Pitchford on 2 Jul 1902, in Red Oak, Indian Territory.[793] They were the parents of seven children, whom they raised while farming in Red Oak. The couple is buried in Red Oak City Cemetery, Latimer Co., Oklahoma.[794]

Nellie Kuykendall Yandell

Born Feb 1886, Arkansas, and died 23 Dec 1946, Sebastian Co., Arkansas
Nellie married John D. Yandell on 17 Dec 1905, in Red Oak, LeFlore Co., Indian Territory.[795] Yandell was a grocery store proprietor. They were the parents of eight children. The couple moved from Red Oak to Fort Smith, Arkansas, between 1920 and 1930.[796] John died in 1944 in Sebastian Co., Arkansas. Nellie died two years later.[797]

Lee Andrew Kuykendall

Born 2 Dec 1890, Polk Co., Arkansas, and died 16 May 1958, Latimer Co., Oklahoma

---

[789] 2632: Oklahoma Indian Territory, Marriage Book 7, US Court 2nd Division, Choctaw Nation, Jul 1896-Dec 1897, Thurman & Joan Shuller, publ. 1990, McAlester, OK
[790] Federal Census: 1900, Choctaw Nation, Indian Territory, pg 201A
[791] Federal Census 1910, Howe Road South, Howe, Le Flore, OK, pg 198A
[792] 2312: Findagrave.com #78004374 and #78004943
[793] 2631: Marriage Records, US District Court, Central District, South McAlester, Indian Territory, Book 10, 6 Jan 1902-10 Nov 1903, Thurman & Joan Shuller, publ. 1990, McAlester, OK
[794] 2312: Findagrave.com #21060514 and #19256103
[795] 464: LeFlore Co., OK Marriages, Vol. 3, Indian Territory, Jan 1905 - Nov 1907, Poteau Valley Genealogy Society, publ. 1985
[796] Federal Census: 1920, Red Oak, Latimer Co., OK, pg 235A; 1930, Upper Twp., Fort Smith, Sebastian Co., AR, pg 74B
[797] 1563: Arkansas Death Record Index, 1941-1948, pg 668, Desmond Walls Allen, publ. 1996, Arkansas Research, Conway, AR

Lee served his country in World War I as a Private in Company E, 154th Infantry. Lee and his wife, Bessie, raised two children in Red Oak.[798] They are buried in Rock Creek Cemetery, Latimer Co., Oklahoma.[799]

---

[798] Federal Census: 1930, McCurtain Rd, Red Oak, Latimer Co., OK, pg 229B
[799] 2312: Findagrave.com #26449261 and #26449005

Fulton M. Goodrich and Callie Kuykendall

Fulton Miller Goodrich
Son of John R. Goodrich and Sarah A. Richardson/Roundtree
Born 15 Oct 1871, Arkansas
Died 9 Aug 1949, Levelland, Hockley Co., Texas

Married 9 Sep 1906, LeFlore Co., Indian Territory

Callie Kuykendall
Daughter of Peter D. Kuykendall and Martha A. Conley
Born Jan 1877, Arkansas
Died c. 1917, Oklahoma

In the first decade of the twentieth century, Fulton Goodrich met Callie Kuykendall in Red Oak City, Latimer Co., Oklahoma.

On 11 Mar 1901, Callie had taken out a marriage license with Rufus Gowan, but the wedding never took place and the license was returned unused.[800] Now five years later, Callie, age 29 and probably more than ready to marry, accepted the proposal of Fulton Goodrich. They were married on 9 Sep 1906, in LeFlore Co., Indian Territory.[801] They had one child, a daughter, Lillian Opal Goodrich, born 11 Jan 1910, in Red Oak.[802] Seven years later, Callie Kuykendall Goodrich died of Pellegra.[803]

Pellegra is a vitamin B deficiency and can be caused by a diet whose primary component is corn. Corn, not coincidentally, is the crop Oklahoma is known for, and is probably what Fulton had planted in his fields. And Red Oak, despite the word "city" tacked on the end, was merely a wide spot in the road. They probably didn't have access to a doctor, and no money to pay if one had been available. We believe that Callie is buried in Red Oak City Cemetery, but there is no marker.[804]

As a widower, Fulton had little choice but to place his seven-year-old daughter with relatives. She first went to live with her grandmother, Martha Conley Kuykendall in Red Oak,[805] but, after Martha's death, was relocated to the household of her uncle, Sterling Atchison, in Haskell, Oklahoma.[806] Some

---

[800] 204: Marriage Records, US District Court, Central District, South McAlester, Indian Territory, Book 9, 1900-1902, pg 348, Thurman & Joan Shuller, publ. 1990, McAlester, OK. Rufus Gowan may be the farm hand recorded as Rufus Gipson in Martha Kuykendall's 1900 household.

[801] 205: LeFlore Co., OK Marriages, 1897-1907, pg 21, Poteau Valley Genealogical Society, publ. 1985, Poteau, OK

[802] 384: Application for SSI #439-24-6296, Lillian Opal Goodrich Baldridge, copy

[803] 19: Nancy McIlhaney Rainwater, deceased, (McIlhaney Family), conversations between 1991 and 1997. This seems to be the origin of Nancy's belief that *"whole kernel corn will kill you."*

[804] No death certificate was issued for Callie Kuykendall Goodrich, another indication that a doctor was not available in Red Oak.

[805] Federal Census: 1910, Red Oak, Latimer Co, OK, pg 16B

[806] Federal Census: 1920, Loveland, Tillman Co., OK, pg 10B

years later, she was transferred to the care of her aunt, JoAnn Goodrich Atchison, her father's sister.

Fulton, meanwhile, had moved in with his brother, James Hamilton Goodrich. He worked any job he could find – as a day laborer, cotton ginner, mechanic at a flour mill, and saw mill engineer.[807] Between 1910 and 1920, James' first wife, Maggie Laura Hooker, died.[808] Like his brother, James was now a widower with a small child, and remarried quickly, to Elizabeth "Lizzie" Stalnaker. This also allowed Fulton to retrieve his daughter from Levelland. Aunt Lizzie then raised her step-son, Rector Fred Goodrich, and her niece, Opal Goodrich. Fulton and James found employment in Lubbock managing a combination gas station and tourist court motel.[809]

James and Lizzie Goodrich remained in Lubbock through 1930.[810] By 1935, Fulton had moved to Lamb Co., Texas, and by 1940, to Levelland.[811] He died in 1949 of cancer and malnutrition, and is buried beside his sister JoAnn, in Levelland City Cemetery.[812]

Elizabeth Stalnaker Goodrich died in 1937 in Lubbock of an infection related to a blood transfusion.[813] She is buried with her parents in Chico Cemetery in Wise Co., Texas. Her tombstone notes that she was the wife of J. H. Goodrich and includes the sentiment, *"the most wonderful woman I ever knew."*[814] James H. Goodrich died in 1957 and is buried in Tatum Cemetery, Lea Co., New Mexico.[815]

The children of Fulton Goodrich and Callie Kuykendall:

Lillian Opal Goodrich McIlhaney Baldridge

> Born 11 Jan 1910, Latimer Co., Oklahoma, and died Aug 1991
> *See profile of Joe Singleton McIlhaney, Sr. and his two wives*

---

[807] 360: Death certificate #38843, Fulton Miller Goodrich, Levelland Co., TX, 1949, certified copy
    Federal Census: 1910, Latimer Co., OK; 1920, Okfuskee Co., OK; 1930, Lubbock Co., TX, pg 226

[808] 2636: Wise Co., TX Marriage Records, Book I-IA-II, 1881-1893, Frances T. Ingmire, publ. 1995, St. Louis, MO

[809] 20: Conversation with Louise McIlhaney Deering, Apr 1997

[810] Federal Census: 1930, Lubbock Co., TX, pg 48

[811] Federal Census: 1940: Levelland, Hockley Co., TX, pg 145B

[812] 1417: Goodrich and Atchison tombstones in Levelland City Cemetery, Hockley Co., TX, photos by Susan & Steven Rainwater, April 1997

[813] 364: Death Certificate #10458, Elizabeth Goodrich, Lubbock Co., TX, 1937, certified copy

[814] 2098: Stalnaker & Goodrich tombstones in Chico Cemetery, S. Weatherford St. & CR 1540, Chico, Wise Co., TX, Susan Chance-Rainwater & R. Steven Rainwater, 1 Jun 2003

[815] 2312: Findagrave.com #50837520

Richard Singleton and his two wives

Richard Singleton
Born c. 1796, South Carolina
Died between January and May 1880, Clarke Co., Alabama

Married, 1st wife, 8 Sep 1815, Clarke Co., Alabama

Susannah Bradley
Born c. 1800, Alabama
Died c. 1842, Clarke Co., Alabama

Married, 2nd wife, 20 Jan 1849, Clarke Co., Alabama

Elizabeth A. Milstead
Born c. 1812, Clarke Co., Alabama
Died between 15 May and 25 Jun 1880, Clarke Co., Alabama

Richard Singleton, Sr.,[816] was born, according to his many census records, in South Carolina c. 1796.[817] When he was about 19, he went west to Clarke Co., Alabama. Here he met and married Susannah Bradley, on 8 Sep 1815.[818]

Richard's household was taxed by the county in 1816.[819] The couple then returned to South Carolina by 1818, where their first two known children were born. They are recorded in Horry District, South Carolina, in the 1820 census.[820] They may have moved to Florida prior to 1827, based on the birthplace claims of their third known child.[821] By 1830, the couple had returned to Clarke Co., Alabama, where they would remain for the rest of their lives.[822]

In 1834, Richard Singleton was appointed by the county court to act as guardian of Rebecca Watson, the minor daughter of Samuel and Martha Watson. In January 1835, the court asked him to appraise the value of three slaves, who may have been part of the Watson estate.[823]

---

[816] Richard Singleton appears in over 200 family trees on Ancestry.com. You will not be surprised to learn that I think nearly everything found in those trees is wrong. Among the errors is a tendency to credit Richard with the children of two of his sons, and two extra wives, one of whom was actually his ward. He has also been allotted three different middle names, and several different sets of parents.

[817] Federal Census: 1850, Clarke Co., AL, pg 507B; 1860, Clarke Co., AL, pg 614B; 1870, Clarke Co., AL, pg 127B-128A

[818] 950: Early American Marriages: Alabama to 1825, Jordan R., Dodd, Liahona Research, Precision Indexing Publishers, Bountiful, UT

[819] Transcribed tax lists on Clarke Co., AL USGenWeb site, now offline

[820] Federal Census: 1820, Horry District, SC, pg 18. South Carolina did not adopt the county designation until 1868.

[821] Federal Census: 1860, Grove Hill, Clarke Co., AL, pg 645A. William B. Singleton says he was born in Florida, c. 1827.

[822] Federal Census: 1830, Clarke Co., AL, pg 230B

[823] 109: Clarke Co., AL Vital Records, 1814-1885, Marilyn Davis Barefield, publ. 1983, Southern Historical Press, Easley, SC

The court likely called on Singleton's expertise because he was a slave owner. He is recorded owning three slaves in 1840, fifteen slaves in 1850, and six slaves in 1860.[824] He was also a considerable land owner, holding about 440 acres in Clarke County. The Bureau of Land Management patent (deed) database contains five entries for Richard, all in the St. Stephens Land Office, which handled the sale of public land in Clarke County.[825] In 1841, Richard purchased a 40 acre tract in the NW¼SE¼ aliquot (section) that his second wife would claim as her homestead many years later.

Susannah Bradley Singleton died c. 1842. Her last child, Solomon J. Singleton, is recorded in the 1860 census as "*dumb and idiotic,*" the tactless 19th century way of saying that he was mentally handicapped. She apparently died as a result of his birth, and it's possible that his condition was the result of a troubled childbirth.

On 20 Jan 1849, Richard married his second wife, Elizabeth A. Milstead.[826] They were the parents of three children: Lucinda M., Joseph, and Olivia Virginia, all of whom are listed in the 1860 and 1870 census records with their parents.

Richard's children by Susannah are problematic. The handicapped Solomon, and the two youngest daughters, Mary and Julia, are recorded in Richard's 1850 household. But the 1830 and 1840 census records hint at additional daughters who cannot be identified apart from a will, which Richard did not leave. And then there are Richard and Susannah's sons.

Here I have to fall back on proximity. In antebellum census records, the proximity of one family to another is often indicative of relationship; in this case, among Richard Singleton, Sr., and his presumed sons, Richard J. Singleton, Joseph T. Singleton, and William B. Singleton.

In the 1860 census, the enumerator recorded not just the state of birth of each individual, but the county as well. This allows us to track the transit of these individuals, using the counties in which their children were born and other evidence. There is sufficient evidence to say that Richard Sr. lived in Clarke County from 1840 to the end of his life, that Joseph Singleton lived continuously in Pike County from 1843 to 1856, but with Richard J., all I can say is that he was in Covington County in 1845 and then Pike County in 1848. I don't have enough data to say when he moved. However, what I can say is that it appears to me that Richard J. and William B. were relocating

---

171: Alabama Records, Vol. 239, Clarke County (Alabama), Pauline Jones Gandrud

[824] Federal census: 1840, Clarke Co., AL, pg 234B; 1850 and 1860 Slave Schedules, Clarke Co., AL

[825] 1087: Bureau of Land Management land patent database, glorecords.blm.gov/PatentSearch/Default.asp

[826] 109: Clarke Co., AL Vital Records, 1814-1885, Marilyn Davis Barefield, publ. 1983, Southern Historical Press, Easley, SC. The 1846 marriage record of Richard Singleton to Nancy Ann Etheridge refers to a different couple, based on the 1850 and 1860 census records, and her Confederate widow's pension applications.

together. During the 1840s and early 1850s, they synched up with their middle brother, Joseph T. This can't be an accident – these individuals are related.

Date	Richard Sr.	Richard Jr.	William B.	Joseph T.
1840 census	Clarke	Clarke	Clarke	Clarke
1843	"			Pike
1844	"		Covington	"
1845	"	Covington		"
1846	"		Pike	"
1848	"	Pike	Montgomery	"
1850 census	Clarke	Pike, pg 239B	Pike, pg 239B	Pike, pg 239B
1853	"		Montgomery	"
1854	"	Butler		"
1856	"		Butler	"
1857	"			Clarke
1858	"	Clarke	Clarke	"
1860 census	Clarke, pg 614A	Clarke, pg 614A Also BLM land records	Clarke, pg 654A Same page as sister Mary	Clarke, pg 614A

Joseph T. Singleton settled in Clarke County in the 1850s, and remained there for rest of his life. He is profiled in detail in the next chapter.

William B. Singleton married Nancy Ann Davis on 24 Jul 1846, in Pike Co., Alabama.[827] They were the parents of at least eight children. He enlisted in the 32nd Alabama Volunteer Infantry on 1 Feb 1862, and died in Mobile, Alabama, in 1863.[828] His widow, Nancy, applied for a Confederate widow's

---

[827] 111: Marriage Record of Pike Co., AL, 1830-1849, Nell Bass Riggs, publ. 1983, Stewart University Press, Centre, AL

[828] 2662: Confederate widow's pension application of Nancy Ann Davis Singleton (widow of William B. Singleton), Alabama, documents dated 1 Aug 1887 through 20 Jul 1900, scans of

pension in 1887, and was required to reapply about every two years until her death in 1902.[829] She is buried in Forest Springs Baptist Church Cemetery in Marengo Co., Alabama.[830] William is probably buried in an unmarked mass grave in Mobile.

Richard J. Singleton married Matilda Ann Davis on 12 Nov 1845, in Washington Co., Alabama (on the western border of Clarke County).[831] They were the parents of at least ten children, including a pair of twins. Richard does not appear to have enlisted or served during the war. In September 1860, he purchased 640 acres from the St. Stephens Land Office, having chosen an unfortunate moment to establish a plantation.[832] After the Civil War, he relocated to Escambia County by 1870, but had returned to Clarke County by 1880.[833] He died in 1898, and is buried with his wife in Mount Zion Cemetery in Clarke County.[834]

Richard Singleton, Sr., was reduced to dire poverty by the Civil War. He is recorded in the 1860 census as the owner of $5,000 in real estate and $8,760 in personal property, such as tools, furniture, luxury items, and of course, slaves. Asked the same questions in 1870, he reported that he owned $300 in real estate and $200 personal property.

Richard Singleton, Sr., died in early 1880. On 15 May 1880, his widow, Elizabeth, filed to secure her homestead claim to 40 acres previously held by her husband.[835] But a month later, Elizabeth was not recorded in the 1880 census, leading to the conclusion that she had died in the interval.[836]

It is not known where Richard and his wives are buried.

---

originals plus abstract

[829] The state legislature amended the terms of these pensions about once every two years, requiring all applicants to re-apply. The purpose of these amendments was to reduce the number of pensioners on the roll, because the state could not adequately fund its pension obligations. So, for example, under the 1887 act, a widow was allowed $1000 of income or property, but in the 1889 act, she was only permitted $400.

[830] 2312: Findagrave.com #58498355

[831] 110: Early Alabama Marriages, 1813 - 1850, Vol A-Z, publ. 1991, Family Adventures Publishing, Nacogdoches, TX

[832] 1087: Bureau of Land Management land patent database, glorecords.blm.gov/PatentSearch/Default.asp

[833] Federal Census: 1870, Brewton PO, Escambia Co., AL, pg 231B; 1880, McLeods Beat, Clarke Co., AL, pg 347B

[834] 2312: Findagrave.com #34482823 and #34482807

[835] 2662: Application to retain homestead exemption of Elizabeth Singleton, widow of Richard Singleton Sr., 15 May 1880, homestead certificate #503, application #886, Vol 140 pg 377, 40.08 acres under the Homestead Act of 20 May 1862, Bureau of Land Management Database, Clarke Co., AL, Township 006N, Range 002E, scan of original patent.

[836] The 1880 census of the Jackson district was taken on 24 Jun 1880

The children of Richard and Susannah Singleton
Richard J. Singleton, 1818-1898
Joseph T. Singleton, 1820-1883
William B. Singleton, 1827-1863
Mary Singleton Emerson,[837] born c. 1843
Julia Ann Singleton Gill,[838] 1834-1916[839]
Solomon J. Singleton, born c. 1842, died between 1860-1870

The children of Richard and Elizabeth Singleton
Lucinda M. Singleton, born c 1850
Joseph Singleton, born c. 1853
Olivia Virginia Singleton, born c. 1854

---

[837] 112: Clarke Co., AL (Marriages), 1812-1899, Nicholas Russell Murray, publ. 1986, Hunting for Bears Inc., Hammond, LA

[838] 112: Clarke Co., AL (Marriages), 1812-1899, Nicholas Russell Murray, publ. 1986, Hunting for Bears Inc., Hammond, LA

[839] 2312: Findagrave.com #20464066

Rev. Joseph T. Singleton and Delilah Robbins

Delilah Robbins Singleton

Joseph T. Singleton
Son of Richard Singleton and Susannah Bradley
Born 30 Dec 1820, South Carolina
Died 6 Apr 1883, Grove Hill, Clarke Co., Alabama

Married 1841, Alabama

Delilah Robbins
Daughter of Hardy Hubea Robbins
Born 15 Oct 1821, Alabama or Georgia
Died 14 Dec 1912, Clarke Co., Alabama

Joseph T. Singleton was a farmer and a minister in the Primitive (Hardshell) Baptist faith. Primitive Baptists were deeply fundamentalist, but, unlike most Baptists, take their predestinarian beliefs so seriously that they oppose all missionary activity, believing it serves no purpose.[840] His daughter, Mary Jane, would later describe him as "*a high-tempered, fractious man [who] had not been kind to her mother.*" Annie Presnall Wood describes her grandfather as "*proud, overbearing, and worldly-minded,*" who, despite his Baptist beliefs, "*liked his dram and liked his social life.*"[841]

In 1841, Joseph married Delilah Robbins.[842] Annie describes her grandmother Delilah as, "*a perfect angel of mercy...so kind, and always going to see the sick and dying.*"

Delilah Singleton's obituary described her as having been born at Fort Madison on the Flint River in Georgia. The problem with this statement is that the seven historic Forts Madison were neither in Georgia nor on the Flint River.[843] Delilah's census records give both Alabama and Georgia as her birthplace, as do those of her children. If the Fort Madison reference is correct, the most likely choice is the Fort Madison in Clarke Co., Alabama, which was situated between the Alabama and Tombigbee Rivers.[844] Still, this is not at all certain.

There is also a question about Delilah's surname. A note on the back of a photo from the collection of Nancy Rainwater says that Delilah's *adopted* name was Davis, but that her birth name was Robbins. Mary Jane Singleton Umberson's death certificate says her mother's surname was David.[845] A Bible passed down from Delilah's daughter, Elizabeth, that has ended up in the Hahn family says Delilah was the daughter of Hardy Hubea Robbins, which clarifies her surname, but, is silent on her place of birth.[846]

Joe and Delilah lived in Pike Co., Alabama before the war, but after 1860, relocated about 140 miles west to Grove Hill, Clarke Co., Alabama.[847] A 1923 county history notes:

---

[840] Primitive Baptists, pgs 52-53, *The Handbook of Denominations*, New Eighth Edition, Frank S. Mead, revised by Samuel S. Hill, Abingdon Press, Nashville, TN, publ. 1987

[841] 18: Annie Presnall Wood, "*The Autobiography of Annie Presnall Wood*," Preface #2, written c. 1940, photocopy of original.

[842] No marriage record has ever been located.

[843] 1239: Historical Register and Dictionary of the United States Army, Sept 29, 1789 to March 2, 1903, Vols. 1-2, pg 521, Francis B. Heitman, publ. 1903, reprinted by the Genealogical Publishing Co., Baltimore, MD

[844] Fort Madison, Clarke Co., AL was built in Aug 1813 on the Alabama River during the Creek Indians war, alabamatrailswar1812.com. Most sources do say she was born in Georgia; one census record says Florida, and the note on the back of her photo says North Carolina.

[845] 357: Death certificate #33035, Mary J. Umberson, Wilbarger Co., TX, 1922, certified copy

[846] Jim Hahn, conversation via email, Aug 2012. Jim's late mother, Marilyn Davis Hahn Barefield, was a certified professional genealogist whose books you will find frequently cited in any section of this book touching Alabama.

[847] Federal Census, Pike Co., AL, 1850, pg 239B; 1860, pg 614A; Clarke Co., AL, 1870, pg 105B; 1880, pg 322D

Tolbert Spring is situated about seven miles northeast of Jackson. This spring was once known as the Singleton Spring. In 1875, old Mr. Joe T. Singleton lived close to this spring – had lived there many years, and lived there until he died, in the latter part of the seventies or in the early part of the eighties.[848]

Joseph Singleton's father, Richard, was a slaveholder, recorded as the owner of five slaves in the 1860 slave census.[849] There is no evidence that Joseph ever owned slaves, but when the War Between the States erupted, he enlisted, despite being 41 years of age.

Singleton researcher John Ellis says this about Joseph Singleton's Civil War service:

> He joined Company G, 32nd Alabama Infantry 12 on April 1862 "for the war" but was discharged due to sickness on 16 Sep 1862. He was later in Co. B, Clarke County Reserves, State Militia, Home Guard, enlisting 15 Sep 1864. I have also seen him as being in Co. E of the 32nd but don't have that record if it is correct (*I think this is an error produced in Delilah's pension application*). I believe that somebody either remembered wrong at the time of the pension app. or simply misunderstood and heard 'E' when someone actually said 'G'. The only other explanation is that he signed up again in Co. E. His brother, Richard, was in Co. G, 32nd, also. Family members usually served together in those days.[850]

Joseph Singleton died in the home of his son, Francis Napoleon Singleton, on 6 Apr 1833. The cause of death was aggravated quinsy, which we today would call severe tonsillitis.[851]

Delilah moved in with her daughter Susan and son-in-law Jesse Summers, and lived there until her death in 1912.[852] Her obituary noted that she was survived by 52 grandchildren, 83 great-grandchildren, and 9 great-great grandchildren.

The children of Joseph and Delilah Singleton

Emeliza A. Singleton Joiner Thompson Gomillion

> Born 10 May 1843, Pike Co., Alabama, and died 21 Jan 1921, Alabama Emmie married Cornelius E. Joiner on 26 Sep 1860.[853] Joiner enlisted in Company B of the 32nd Alabama Confederate Infantry, and died in

---

[848] 172: History of Clarke County, AL, John Simpson Graham, 1923, Birmingham Printing Company

[849] 1860 Federal Census, Clarke Co., AL, Slave Schedule

[850] 1595: Confederate pension application #27120 of Delilah Singleton, Clarke Co., AL, 25 Jul 1895, 6 Jun 1899 and 11 Jul 1908, copy of microfilmed original

[851] 109: Clarke Co., AL Vital Records, 1814-1885, Marilyn Davis Barefield, publ. 1983, Southern Historical Press, Easley, SC

[852] We have been unable to retrieve a death certificate, though one should have been issued.

service.[854] After his death, Emmie and her son, Jefferson, lived with her parents. On 12 Jan 1867, Emmie married John Thompson.[855] They were the parents of one daughter. Thompson died prior to 1880.[856] Emmie's daughter, Delilah Thompson married Frank Martin Gomillion in 1885, and on 20 Jul 1910, Emmie married Frank's father, Henry Christian Gomillion.[857] The Gomillions are buried in Hollingsworth Cemetery, Clarke Co., Alabama.[858]

Mary Jane Singleton McDonald Presnall Umberson

Born 31 Oct 1844, Pike Co., Alabama, and died 25 Nov 1922, Vernon, Wilbarger Co., Texas
See profile of Mary Jane Singleton and her three husbands

Elizabeth "Mattie" Singleton McLeod

Born 12 Jun 1847, Pike Co., Alabama, and died 31 Mar 1936, Clarke Co., Alabama
Elizabeth married Stephen Wesley McLeod on 22 Mar 1866.[859] They were the parents of five children, and lived in Clarke Co., Alabama, all of their lives.[860] They are buried in Old Camp Ground Cemetery, Clarke Co., Alabama.[861]

Susan Martha Singleton Summers

Born 14 Oct 1849, Pike Co., Alabama, and died, 2 Mar 1926, Alabama
On 24 Dec 1868, Susan Singleton married Jesse E. Summers.[862] They were active Baptists, attending camp meetings in the summer. No

---

[853] 112: Clarke Co., AL (Marriages), 1812-1899, Nicholas Russell Murray, publ. 1986, Hunting for Bears Inc., Hammond, LA
[854] 125: The Roster of Confederate Soldiers, 1861-1865, multiple volumes, Janet B. Hewett, publ. 1995, Broadfoot Pub. Co., Wilmington, NC
[855] 113: Clarke Co., AL Marriage Book B, 1865-1870, Freeda Crumpton, publ. 1987, Cumby, TX
[856] Federal Census: 1880, household of Jesse Summers, Clarke Co., AL, pg 377C
[857] 1463: Frances Marie Gomillion Phillips, (Singleton family)
[858] 109: Clarke Co., AL Vital Records, 1814-1885, Marilyn Davis Barefield, publ. 1983, Southern Historical Press, Easley, SC
[859] 113: Clarke Co., AL Marriage Book B, 1865-1870, Freeda Crumpton, publ. 1987, Cumby, TX
[860] Federal Census: 1870, Grove Hill, Clarke Co., AL, pg 107B; 1880, McLeod's District, Clarke Co., AL, pg 348D; 1900, McLeod's Pct, Clarke Co., AL, pg 104B; 1910, McLeod's Pct, Clarke Co., AL, pg 113B; 1920, McLeod's Pct, Clarke Co., AL, pg 95B
[861] 109: Clarke Co., AL Vital Records, 1814-1885, Marilyn Davis Barefield, publ. 1983, Southern Historical Press, Easley, SC
[862] 112: Clarke Co., AL (Marriages), 1812-1899, Nicholas Russell Murray, publ. 1986, Hunting for Bears Inc., Hammond, LA

children were born to this couple.⁸⁶³ They are buried in Matthews Cemetery, Grove Hill, Clarke Co., Alabama.⁸⁶⁴

Francis Napoleon Singleton

Born 5 Apr 1852, Pike Co., Alabama, and died 28 Feb 1926, Monroe Co., Alabama
F. N. married Mary Calhoun on 3 Dec 1874.⁸⁶⁵ The couple had no children, and Mary died prior to 1887. In or before September 1887, he married Alva Sawyer, and made up for lost time by fathering seven children.⁸⁶⁶ The couple is buried in Shiloh Primitive Baptist Church Cemetery in Frisco, Monroe Co., Alabama.⁸⁶⁷

Richard Singleton

Born c. 1854, Pike Co., Alabama, and died, c. 1883, Texas
Richard Singleton was an artist and photographer.⁸⁶⁸ He never married. He lived in Alabama until the 1880 census, after which he moved to Texas. His 1883 death is mentioned in his mother's obituary.⁸⁶⁹

Minerva A. Singleton Fleming

Born 16 Mar 1858, Clarke Co., Alabama, and died 31 Jan 1930, Alabama
Minerva married Thomas Fleming on 22 Apr 1880.⁸⁷⁰ The couple were the parents of eight children, three of whom died in childhood.⁸⁷¹ Thomas was a farmer and house carpenter. The couple is buried in Pine Level Cemetery, Escambia Co., Alabama.⁸⁷²

---

⁸⁶³ Federal Census: 1900, Grove Hill Clarke Co., AL, pg 148B; 1910, Grove Hill Clarke Co., AL, pg 153B

⁸⁶⁴ 109: Clarke Co., AL Vital Records, 1814-1885, Marilyn Davis Barefield, publ. 1983, Southern Historical Press, Easley, SC

⁸⁶⁵ 112: Clarke Co., AL (Marriages), 1812-1899, Nicholas Russell Murray, publ. 1986, Hunting for Bears Inc., Hammond, LA

⁸⁶⁶ Federal Census: 1900, Claiborne, Monroe Co., AL, pg 36B

⁸⁶⁷ Findagrave.com #24613409 and #24613408

⁸⁶⁸ Federal Census: Grove Hill, Clarke Co., AL, 1880, pg 363C; Jackson, Clarke Co., AL, 1880, duplicate entry, pg 322D

⁸⁶⁹ 109: Clarke Co., AL Vital Records, 1814-1885, Marilyn Davis Barefield, publ. 1983, Southern Historical Press, Easley, SC

⁸⁷⁰ 112: Clarke Co., AL (Marriages), 1812-1899, Nicholas Russell Murray, publ. 1986, Hunting for Bears Inc., Hammond, LA

⁸⁷¹ Federal Census: 1900, Jackson Precinct, Clarke Co., AL, pg 61A; 1910, Terichton, Mobile Co., AL, pg 48A

⁸⁷² 2312: Findagrave.com #69208205 and #69208034

Elizabeth Singleton McLeod

Sarah Singleton

Born c. 1862, Clarke Co., Alabama, and died after 1912
She is mentioned in Annie Presnall Wood's memoir, appears in two census records and is apparently one of the living children mentioned in her mother's 1912 obituary. Other than these scant facts, I have been unable to learn anything about her.

Beulah E. Singleton Murphy

Born 17 Aug 1864, Clarke Co., Alabama and died 6 Sep 1938, Clarke Co., Alabama

Beulah married John Whitfield Murphy on 29 Nov 1885.[873] They were a farm family and produced five children, three of whom died before 1900.[874] Between 1910 and 1920, John suffered some kind of mental collapse and was committed to the Mobile County Poor Asylum, where he spent the rest of his life, dying in 1931.[875] Beulah returned to Grove Hill, taking employment as a housekeeper for a wealthy widow.[876] She died in 1938 and is buried in Hollingsworth Cemetery in Clarke Co., Alabama.[877]

---

[873] 112: Clarke Co., AL (Marriages), 1812-1899, Nicholas Russell Murray, publ. 1986, Hunting for Bears Inc., Hammond, LA

[874] Federal Census: 1900, Monroe Co., AL, pg 243A

[875] Federal Census: 1920, Mobile County Poor Farm, Toulminville, Mobile Co., AL, pg 221A; 1930, Mobile County Poor Farm, Toulminville, Mobile Co., AL, pg 161A. Date of death from Ancestry.com, Alabama, Deaths and Burials Index, 1881-1974.

[876] Federal Census: 1930, Suggsville Rd, Grove Hill, Clarke Co., AL, pg 113A

[877] 2312 Findagrave.com #67277032

Mary Jane Singleton and Her Three Husbands

Mary Jane Singleton McDonald Presnall Umberson

Mary Jane Singleton
Daughter of Joseph T. Singleton and Delilah Robins
Born 31 Oct 1844, Pike Co., Alabama
Died 25 Nov 1922, Wilbarger Co., Texas

Married, 1st husband, 21 Jun 1860, Clarke Co., Alabama

James G. McDonald
Born before 1844
Died 1863, Nashville, Tennessee

Married, 2nd husband, 22 Nov 1865, Clarke Co., Alabama

Caleb Calvin Presnall
Son of Elijah Presnall and Mary Dean
Born Oct 1822, Clarke Co., Alabama
Died 16 Oct 1874, Clarke Co., Alabama

Married, 3rd husband, 18 Jun 1876, Gholson, McLennan Co., Texas

William Franklin Umberson
Son of Jerome George Umberson and Elizabeth Kellum
Born 11 May 1837, Winston Co., Mississippi
Died 24 Oct 1898, Gholson, McLennan Co., Texas

Annie Presnall Wood said of her family, "*I am sure that not one of the second generation could tell who were whole, half, or step-brothers and sisters.*"[878] We quite agree.

Almost six months to the day before South Carolina seceded from the Union, Mary Jane Singleton married James G. McDonald.[879] We know that he was a steward in the Methodist Church, the only description recalled of him by Annie Presnall Wood. McDonald, Annie believed, enlisted in the Confederate Army at the very start of the war, but we have never been able to locate a service record. She had been told by her mother that McDonald had died of measles in an army hospital in Nashville in 1863. Mary Jane had almost immediately become pregnant, but her newborn died at birth. But for Annie's memoir, the marriage would now be forgotten.

On 22 Nov 1864, Mary Jane married a widower twenty-two years older than herself, Caleb Calvin Presnall.[880] He had been a slave owner before the war, and a wealthy man. Union prisoner of war records show that he was captured at Blakely, Alabama, on 9 Apr 1865, imprisoned at Ship Island, Mississippi, and then received at Camp Townsend on 6 May 1865, for exchange. His name appears on a roll of prisoners of war surrendered by Lt. General R. Taylor, paroled at Meridian, Mississippi, on 9 May 1865, conditional upon their return to civilian life at his home in Clarke Co., Alabama.[881]

Presnall's wife, Phoebe Ann McAden[882] had died almost nine months before his release. Their five children had been cared for by her brother James McAden and wife, Jane Lammore,[883] along with their own three children. Upon his return home, it was essential for Presnall to acquire a mother for his children, and the widow McDonald was his choice.

---

[878] 18: Annie Presnall Wood, "*The Autobiography of Annie Presnall Wood*," Preface #2, written c. 1940, photocopy of typed original. We are deeply indebted to her narrative and here summarize her account of the three blended families.

[879] 110: Early Alabama Marriages, 1813 - 1850, Vol A-Z, publ. 1991, Family Adventures Publishing, Nacogdoches, TX

[880] 1566: Marriage record of Caleb Presnall & Mrs. Mary J. McDonald, 22 Nov 1865, Clarke Co., AL, certified copy of original

[881] 125: Roster of Confederate Soldiers, 1861-1865, Janet B. Hewett, publ. 1995, Broadfoot Publishing Co., Wilmington, NC

[882] The name McAden is spelled in every possible way in the available records. The spelling I am using is from James McAden's tombstone in Gholson Cemetery. I generally give tombstones the last word on spelling.

[883] 109: Clarke Co., AL Vital Records, 1814-1885, Marilyn Davis Barefield, publ. 1983, Southern Historical Press, Easley, SC

The original Presnall children were Elizabeth Ann, Elijah Calvin, Robert James, Sallie Erzola, and Martin Thomas. The first child born to the second marriage was Phoebe Ann – whom we know as Annie Presnall Wood. Two sons followed, Joseph Singleton and Caleb Wesley, then two infants who died at birth.

Annie describes her father as a man whose health was broken by the rigors of war, and after steadily declining for several years, Caleb Calvin Presnall died in 1874.

Mary Jane now decided to move to Texas, where James McAden had moved following the war. She didn't write ahead to see what he thought of the idea, she just packed up her blended family and headed for Texas, joining a group of families with the same intentions. Annie notes that the bottom had fallen out of post-war cotton prices, and this was a major factor in so many families moving to Texas. The only one of the children who did not go was Elizabeth Ann Presnall, who had married unhappily the year her father died.[884]

Of the trip, Annie says,

> "I do not think we bought tickets until we reached Mobile. We then bought 'emigrant tickets,' as did all the others. We went by way of New Orleans and Galveston, crossing the Gulf of Mexico. We stayed two days and one night in Mobile, at which place we took the train to New Orleans, leaving Mobile in the afternoon. We took a ship at New Orleans. We embarked about 4 o'clock in the afternoon, and were aboard all night, arriving in Galveston about noon of the following day. We took the H&C[885] train for Waco. We arrived sometime during the night, and went to the Brazos Hotel. It was situated near the suspension bridge, which at that time was new, and was a toll bridge."[886]

Uncle Jim McAden was utterly unprepared for the arrival of eight relatives from Alabama, but he put them up for several months, until he could locate a vacant cabin for them to rent. McAden had married his second wife, Elizabeth Robertson.[887] Aunt Lizzie, says Annie, was a born matchmaker, and she immediately set about finding a husband for Mary Jane Presnall. Her choice was William Franklin Umberson.

---

[884] 112: Clarke Co., AL (Marriages), 1812-1899, Nicholas Russell Murray, publ. 1986, Hunting for Bears Inc., Hammond, LA

[885] We believe she means the H&TC – the Houston & Texas Central, which ran from Galveston to Waco. The line had been completed in 1872. From the Texas State Historical Association website, which references the book, "*Charles Morgan and the Development of Southern Transportation,*" James P. Baughman, publ. 1968, Vanderbilt University Press, Nashville, TN.

[886] 18: Annie Presnall Wood, pgs 45-46

[887] 113: Clarke Co., AL Marriages, Book B, 1865-1870, Freeda Crumpton, publ. 1987, Cumby, TX

William Franklin Umberson

Umberson had come to Texas in the 1850s with his mother and siblings. During the Civil War, he had served the Confederate cause by joining Company K, 15th Texas Infantry. He also served with Company B, 22nd Texas Infantry. He does not appear to have been wounded or captured, and never applied for a pension.[888]

He had fallen in love with a young woman named Ann Ophelia Westmoreland, but she had spurned his offer of marriage, and, in 1860, married James B. Neal.[889] Neal died two years later in Confederate service, leaving his wife and one-year-old daughter, Pernecia Evie, behind.[890]

---

[888] 125: Roster of Confederate Soldiers, 1861-1865, various volumes, Janet B. Hewett, publ. 1995, Broadfoot Publ. Co., Wilmington, NC

[889] 181: McLennan Co., TX Marriage Records, Vol. 1, 1850-1870, Central Texas Genealogical Society, publ. 1963, Waco, TX

[890] 125: Roster of Confederate Soldiers, 1861-1865, various volumes, Janet B. Hewett, publ. 1995, Broadfoot Publ. Co., Wilmington, NC

Umberson's second proposal was more successful. He and Ann Westmoreland Neal were married on 31 Oct 1866, in McLennan County.[891] To this second marriage were born William Thomas Riddle, Smith Elnathan, Mary Ophelia, and Joshua Julius, whom everyone called Frank. Ann Westmoreland Umberson died eleven years later on 13 Dec 1875.[892] She was the first person buried in Gholson Cemetery, the land for which was donated by Umberson as a community graveyard. [893]

Now if you're beginning to hum the theme from *The Brady Bunch*, you're not wrong. Thanks to the efforts of Aunt Lizzie McAden, the widower William F. Umberson proposed to the widow Mary Jane Singleton McDonald Presnall, saying "my *little children are running wild, and need a mother's care.*" They were married on 18 Jun 1876.[894] Their instant family included fifteen children from four different marriages.

On 17 Mar 1877, the Umbersons welcomed into the world their first daughter, Ollie Delilah Umberson.[895] Three children would follow – Emma Florence, Richard Rufus, and Edward Brown – but all died in childhood.[896]

Annie describes her step-father, William Umberson as "*very nervous and excitable in times of danger,*" the principal danger being a chimney that regularly caught fire, though he was also unnerved by the severe storms that regularly swept across the plains. Annie describes him as a very devoted Christian, good and honest, a hard worker, but not very affectionate to his children and step-children.

Umberson had been a plantation overseer before the war, but post-war made his living as a cotton farmer.[897] He also managed extensive vegetable gardens, as well as chickens, milk cows, and hogs raised for use by the family, which Annie describes:

> "Practically everything that we ate was raised at home, such as flour, corn meal, sweet potatoes, sorghum molasses, dried peaches, black-eyed peas, pumpkins, and from twenty-five to thirty big hogs were butchered every winter which were converted into hams, shoulders, sausage, souse,

---

[891] 181: McLennan Co., TX Marriage Records, Vol. 1, 1850-1870, Central Texas Genealogical Society, publ. 1963, Waco, TX

[892] 80: Index to Early McLennan Co., TX Deaths, John M. Usry, Central Texas Genealogical Society, Waco, TX

[893] 317: Texas Historical Commission marker at Gholson Cemetery, FM 1858, Gholson, McLennan Co., Texas (photograph).

126: Gholson Cemetery History, 1871-1981, Lelia McDugal, publ. 1983, Gholson Cemetery Association, Waco, TX

[894] 120: McLennan Co., TX Marriage Records, Vol. 2, 1871-1892, Central Texas Genealogical Society, publ. 1963, Waco, TX

[895] 249: Joseph Singleton Presnall family Bible, transcription provided by Joyce Beardon

[896] 1412: All three are buried in Gholson Cemetery on FM 1858, McLennan Co., TX. We photographed the graves in April 1997.

[897] Federal Census: Waco, McLennan Co., TX, 1860, pg 426B; 1870, pg 61. Annie also notes that he was a cotton farmer.

and lard. Green coffee and salt were bought by the sack. We always had milk and butter, [but] never enough eggs to eat, more than once or twice a week. There was always a big turnip patch, with a lot of mustard greens sown in for good measure."[898]

William Umberson was a deacon in the Baptist church,[899] and hitched up the farm wagon on both Saturday and Sunday to haul his extended family to services. Annie notes that they attended both Methodist and Baptist services, though she eventually chose to be baptized in the Missionary Baptist church.

As a teenager, Annie got crossways with her step-father, and his constant criticism and disapproval drove her into early marriage with a man who had also run afoul of Umberson's temper. Annie tells some of her husband's story as she remembered it, and we have been able to fill in some of the gaps.

Benjamin Carter Wood's father, James William Wood, was born into the aristocracy of Virginia. Annie says this lifestyle didn't suit him, and James went west to Duck Hill, Mississippi, seeking a rough frontier life. He purchased land and slaves, and established a cotton plantation in the care of tenant farmers and overseers, spending his own time hunting and fishing. Wood married Rhoda Ann Williams in 1839,[900] and they were the parents of four children. Upon Rhoda's death, Wood married Samantha Carter, and this union produced two children, a daughter named Rhoda Ann and Benjamin Carter Wood, called Bennie.

During the war, James W. Wood enlisted in the Carroll County Minute Men as a 3rd Lieutenant.[901] Annie recalls that the care of the estate fell to Bennie, and, when the war ended, Bennie immediately left for Texas. He married and lost a wife, before his arrival in Gholson, where he purchased a grocery store from Annie's half-brother, Elijah Presnall. Like Annie, Bennie got crossways with William Umberson, in his case because he carried bitters, a combination of alcohol and aromatic herbs. On 6 Jul 1881, Bennie and Annie were married.[902] Annie would later come to regret the marriage, and expressed her strong disapproval of teenagers marrying too soon.

William Franklin Umberson died on 24 Oct 1898, at the age of 61, leaving no will.[903] His widow, Mary Jane, moved to Vernon, where Annie and her

---

[898] 18: Annie Presnall Wood, pg 57

[899] 468: History of the Waco Baptist Association of Texas, J. L. Walker and C. P. Lumpkin, publ. 1897, Byrne-Hill Printing House, Waco, TX

[900] 1573: Carroll Co., MS Marriage Records, Betty C. Wiltshire, publ. 1990, Pioneer Publishing Co., Carrollton, MS

[901] 883: For Dixie Land I'll Take My Stand: A Muster Listing of All Known Mississippi Confederate Soldiers, Sailors & Marines, 4 volumes, H. Grady Howell Jr., publ. 1998, Chickasaw Bayou Press, Madison, MS

[902] 120: McLennan Co., TX Marriage Records, Vol. 2, 1871-1892, Central Texas Genealogical Society, publ. 1963, Waco, TX

[903] 80: Fall & Puckett Funeral Home Records, Index to Early McLennan Co., TX Deaths, John M. Usry, Central Texas Genealogical Society, Waco, TX

husband Benjamin Carter Wood were living.[904] In 1922, she was overcome by a series of strokes, succumbing to what Annie calls *"creeping paralysis."* She died on 25 Nov 1922. The couple is buried in Gholson Cemetery.[905]

The children of Mary Jane Singleton and James G. McDonald

One child, died at birth

The children of Phobe Ann McAden and Caleb Calvin Presnall

Elizabeth Ann Presnall McVey

Born 17 Dec 1852, Clarke Co., Alabama, and died 22 Apr 1926, Clarke Co., Alabama

Lizzie became the second wife of Matthew T. McVay on 8 Apr 1874.[906] The unhappy union produced ten children, five of whom were still living in 1900. The family moved frequently. Based on the birthplaces of the surviving children, they had moved to Texas by 1875, back to Alabama before 1880, to Mississippi before 1885, and finally back to Alabama by 1888. Matthew died c. 1894, and Lizzie settled in Good Springs, Alabama, where she raised her children.[907] She died in 1926, and is buried in Ulcanush Cemetery in Coffeeville, Clarke Co., Alabama.[908]

Elijah Calvin Presnall

Born Oct 1854, Alabama, and died 19 May 1926, McLennan Co., Texas

Annie Presnall Wood recalls that Elijah was very devoted to his stepmother, and was of great assistance in the move to Texas. Once there, he established himself as a businessman, running a grocery store, grist mill, and cotton gin. He married Martha Euphrasia Philen on 1 Dec 1881, and they were the parents of four children.[909] The couple is buried in Gholson Cemetery, McLennan Co., Texas.[910]

According to the Clerk of the Court of McLennan County, there is no probate file for William Umberson, per letter, Oct 2012.

[904] Federal Census, Wilbarger Co., TX, 1910, pg 195B; 1920, pg 235A

[905] 1412: Umberson, Kellum and Presnall tombstones in Gholson Cemetery, Gholson, McLennan Co., TX, April 1997, photos by Susan & R. Steven Rainwater

[906] 112: Clarke Co., AL (Marriages), 1812-1899, Nicholas Russell Murray, publ. 1986, Hunting for Bears Inc., Hammond, LA

[907] Federal Census: 1900, Good Springs, Clarke Co., AL, pg 103A; 1910, Good Springs, Clarke Co., AL, pg 121A; 1920, Coffeeville, Clarke Co., AL, pg 167A

[908] 2312: Findagrave.com #77060748

[909] 120: McLennan Co., TX Marriage Records, Vol. 2, 1871-1892, Central Texas Genealogical Society, publ. 1963, Waco, TX

Federal Census: 1900, McLennan Co., TX, pg 135A; 1910, Hill Co., TX, pg 1A; 1920, Marlin, Falls Co., TX, pg 43B

Robert James Presnall

Born c. 1857, Alabama, and died between 1910 and 1920

Jimmie was injured as a child in a hunting accident, and walked with a cane. He never married, and lived with relatives for most of his life.[911] Minnie Humberson Guyton recalled that for a while, he ran a grocery store in China Springs, Texas.[912] His last known residence was Alabama. It's not clear when or where he died.

Sally and John H. Humberson and family

Sally Erzola Presnall Humberson

Born 1859, Alabama, and died 7 Aug 1925, McLennan Co., Texas

Sallie married John H. Humberson on 13 Nov 1879.[913] He was the son of Alexander Humberson, the presumed brother of Jerome G. Umberson. The couple had eight children, two of whom died in childhood. They are buried in China Springs Cemetery, McLennan Co., Texas.[914]

---

[910] 1412: Umberson, Kellum and Presnall tombstones in Gholson Cemetery, Gholson, McLennan Co., TX, April 1997, photos by Susan & R. Steven Rainwater

[911] Federal Census: 1880C, McLennan Co., TX, pg 143A, with his sister Sallie; 1900, McLennan Co., TX, pg 131B, with his brother Martin; 1910, Good Springs, Clarke Co., AL, pg 121A, with his nephew Arthur.

[912] 1106: Minnie Humberson Guyton, *"Once Upon A Journey: The descendants of John H. Humberson and Sallie Presnall"*, written pre-1987

[913] 1106: Minnie Humberson Guyton, *"Once Upon A Journey: The descendants of John H. Humberson and Sallie Presnall"*, written pre-1987

[914] 2206: Presnall-Humberson in China Springs Cemetery, Old China Springs Road, China Springs, McLennan Co.,TX, 19 June 2005, Susan & R. Steven Rainwater

Martin Thomas Presnall

Martin Thomas Presnall

Born 2 Oct 1861, Clarke Co., Alabama, and died 4 Jul 1932, McLennan Co., Texas

Tommie married Dieppe Fetzer on 5 Nov 1884.[915] They were the parents of five children, one of whom died in childhood. Dieppe died in 1928, the result of a botched hysterectomy.[916] Tommie married her sister, Sallie, as his second wife, on 15 Aug 1930. Martin worked most of his life as a grocer, but became the McLennan County Treasurer prior to 1930.[917] He died in 1932, and his wife Sallie took over his position for the next ten years[918]. Martin and both wives are buried in China Springs Cemetery, McLennan Co., Texas.[919]

---

[915] 120: McLennan Co., TX Marriage Records, Vol. 2, 1871-1892, Central Texas Genealogical Society, publ. 1963, Waco, TX

[916] 2086: Death certificate #12975; Dieppe (Fetzer) Presnall, 31 Mar 1928, McLennan Co., TX, photocopy of microfilmed original

[917] 2650: Death certificate #13294; Martin Thomas Presnall, 4 Jul 1932, McLennan Co., TX, scan of original

[918] 2651: Death certificate #71198; Sallie Martin Presnall, 29 Jul 1942, McLennan Co., TX, scan of original

[919] 2206: Presnall-Humberson in China Springs Cemetery, Old China Springs Road, China Springs, McLennan Co.,TX, 19 June 2005, Susan & R. Steven Rainwater

The children of Mary Jane Singleton McDonald and Caleb Calvin Presnall

Annie Presnall Wood and son

Phoebe Ann Presnall Wood

Born 11 Oct 1866, Clarke Co., Alabama, and died 23 Nov 1956, Los Angeles, California
Annie married Bennie Wood on 6 Jul 1881.[920] They were the parents of seven children, two of whom died in childhood. By her own account, Annie had about eight years of occasional education. Despite this, she became a county public health nurse, ran an egg business, was a Bible school teacher, and wrote a fine autobiography. Bennie died in 1923 in Vernon, Texas, of cancer, and is buried in Tolbert Cemetery. Annie moved in with her daughter, Ann, in Los Angeles. She died in 1956 and is buried at Forest Lawn Memorial Park, Glendale, California.[921] Annie's grandson, Presnall Hansel Wood was for many years the editor of the Baptist Standard.

Joseph Singleton Presnall

Born 25 Dec 1870, Clarke Co., Alabama, and died 2 Dec 1963, Van Zandt Co., Texas
On 7 Sep 1899, Joe married Elizabeth Moore.[922] They were the parents of three children. Joe was a graduate of a business college, and ran a

---

[920] 120: McLennan Co., TX Marriage Records, Vol. 2, 1871-1892, Central Texas Genealogical Society, publ. 1963, Waco, TX

[921] 2312: Findagrave.com #85551612

[922] 249: Joseph Singleton Presnall family Bible, transcription provided by Joyce Beardon

lumberyard.⁹²³ The couple are buried in White Rose Cemetery, Wills Point, Van Zandt Co., Texas.⁹²⁴

Caleb Wesley Presnall, c. 1895

Caleb Wesley Presnall

Born 21 Jun 1873, Clarke Co., Alabama, and died 25 May 1925, Pueblo Co., Colorado

Life did not go well for Caleb Presnall. He was a sickly child who suffered from migraines, but he eventually recovered his health enough to became an Allopath, having attended both Baylor College and the University of Louisville. Caleb's entry in the Directory of Deceased American Physicians reflects an unsettled life – he practiced medicine in three different states and the territory of Alaska.⁹²⁵ In July 1924, he was found by a passer-by on a remote road outside of Trinidad, Colorado. It appeared that he and his wife, May, had been in a car accident, but a grand jury charged him with murder.⁹²⁶ Found unfit to stand trial, he was committed to a mental hospital, where a year later, he

---

⁹²³ 1920 Federal Census, Navarro Co., TX, pg 131
⁹²⁴ 2312: Findagrave.com #96691175 and #96691261
⁹²⁵ Directory of Deceased American Physicians, 1804-1929, Ancestry.com index and abstract
⁹²⁶ Federal Census: 1910, Kettle Falls, Stephens Co., WA, pg 132B, indicates that his marriage to May James is his second. I have no information on his first marriage.

committed suicide by hanging himself.⁹²⁷ Caleb and May are buried in the Masonic Cemetery in Trinidad, Las Animas Co., Colorado.⁹²⁸

The children of Ann Ophelia Westmoreland and James B. Neal

Evvie Pernecia Neal Walker

Born 22 Apr 1861, McLennan Co., Texas, and died 2 Mar 1887, McLennan Co., Texas

Evvie married Rev. James Lafayette Walker on 15 Jan 1876.⁹²⁹ Tate (or Fate – it's unclear), was a school teacher in his early years, but soon became the pastor of a Baptist church. He was active in the Waco Baptist Association, and co-authored its history in 1897.⁹³⁰ Tate and Evvie were the parents of three children. Evvie died in 1887 and is buried in Gholson Cemetery. Tate married again in 1890.⁹³¹ He, his wife Leila, and his daughter Carrie (from his first marriage) are buried in Oakwood Cemetery, Waco.⁹³²

The children of Ann Ophelia Westmoreland and William Franklin Umberson

William Thomas Riddle Umberson

Born 21 Sep 1867, McLennan Co., Texas, and died 22 Nov 1932, McLennan Co., Texas

---

⁹²⁷ I am grateful to Virginia Humberson Owen for telling me this story and providing the following documents and clippings:
1191: Application for License to Practice Medicine, Caleb W. Presnall, 1 Jul 1913, photocopy
1192: "Coroner's Jury Probes Tragic Death of Mrs. Presnall," 7 Jul 1924, Chronicle-News, Trinidad, CO, photocopy
1193: "Coroner's Jury Reports on Probe of Death of Mrs. C. W. Presnall, 8 Jul 1924, Chronicle-News, Trinidad, CO, photocopy
1194: "Mrs. May J. Presnall Laid to Rest Here This Morning," 8 Jul 1924, Chronical-News, Trinidad, CO, photocopy
1195: "Dr. C. W. Presnall of Trinidad Found Dead Early Friday," 30 May 1925, Pueblo Chieftan Newspaper, Pueblo, CO, photocopy
1196: "Life's Burden Too Great, Wife Slayer Suspect Kills Self: Dr. C. W. Presnall Hangs Himself at Pueblo Hospital," 29 May 1925, Chronicle-News, Trinidad, CO, photocopy
1197: "Military Honors for Funeral of Dr. Presnall," 30 May 1925, Chronical-News, Trinidad, CO, photocopy
1198: Obituary of Caleb W. Presnall, 31 May 1925, unknown Pueblo Co., CO newspaper, photocopy

⁹²⁸ 2312: Findagrave.com #54953707 and #54953858

⁹²⁹ 120: McLennan Co., TX Marriage Records, Vol. 2, 1871-1892, Central Texas Genealogical Society, publ. 1963, Waco, TX

⁹³⁰ 468: History of the Waco Baptist Association of Texas, J. L. Walker and C. P. Lumpkin, publ. 1897, Byrne-Hill Printing House, Waco, TX

⁹³¹ 210: McLennan Co., TX Marriage Records, Vol. 3, Central Texas Genealogical Society, publ. 1963, Waco, TX

⁹³² 217: McLennan Co., TX Cemeteries, Vol. 3, Oakwood, John M. Usry, Central Texas Genealogical Society

On 23 Jan 1895, Billie married Ola E. Chatham.⁹³³ They were the parents of three children, one of whom survived to adulthood. Billie was a farmer and a Baptist. The couple is buried in Gholson Cemetery.⁹³⁴

Smith Elnathan Umberson

Born 11 May 1869, McLennan Co., Texas, and died 17 Jun 1940, Andrews Co., Texas

Smith married Lula Delma Horn on 1 Jan 1896.⁹³⁵ They were the parents of eight children. Smith worked as a farmer and real estate agent, and in 1920 was listed in the census as the county tax assessor-collector.⁹³⁶ Smith is buried in Old Andrews Cemetery in Andrews, Texas, and Delma is buried in Fairview Cemetery in Midland, Texas.⁹³⁷

Mary Ophelia Umberson Garrett

Born 17 Jan 1872, McLennan Co., Texas, and died 8 Feb 1935, McLennan Co., Texas

Mollie married William Thomas Garrett on 25 Nov 1892.⁹³⁸ They were the parents of six children including a pair of twins. William ran a general store, and later a wholesale dry goods business.⁹³⁹ The couple is buried in Oakwood Cemetery, Waco.⁹⁴⁰

Joshua Julius "Frank" Umberson

Born 27 Nov 1873, McLennan Co., Texas, and died 1 Feb 1912, Young Co., Texas

Frank married Mattie Barbara Smith on 24 Mar 1899.⁹⁴¹ They were the parents of six children, one of whom died in childhood. Frank was a grocery and department store clerk. In 1906, the family moved to Graham, Texas, and took up farming. On 1 Feb 1912, Frank walked

---

⁹³³ 210: McLennan Co., TX Marriage Records, Vol. 3, 15 Aug 1892-19 Jan 1901, Central Texas Genealogical Society, publ. 1963, Waco, TX

⁹³⁴ 1412: Gholson, McLennan Co., TX, photographed in April 1997 by Susan and Steven Rainwater

⁹³⁵ 210: McLennan Co., TX Marriage Records, Vol. 3, 15 Aug 1892-19 Jan 1901, Central Texas Genealogical Society, publ. 1963, Waco, TX

⁹³⁶ 1920 Federal Census, Andrews Co., TX, pg 1

⁹³⁷ 2312: Findagrave.com #74680815

⁹³⁸ 210: McLennan Co., TX Marriage Records, Vol. 3, 15 Aug 1892-19 Jan 1901, Central Texas Genealogical Society, publ. 1963, Waco, TX

⁹³⁹ 1920 Federal Census, McLennan Co., TX, pg 279

⁹⁴⁰ 217: McLennan Co., TX Cemeteries, Vol. 3, Oakwood, John M. Usry, Central Texas Genealogical Society, Waco, TX

⁹⁴¹ 210: McLennan Co., TX Marriage Records, Vol. 3, 15 Aug 1892-19 Jan 1901, Central Texas Genealogical Society, publ. 1963, Waco, TX

away from his plow team in mid-morning, barricaded himself in his father-in-law's cotton seed house, and shot himself. Neighbors found him the next day after an extensive search.[942] After Frank's death, Mattie carried on as a farm manager.[943] Frank is buried in Oak Grove Cemetery, Young County. Mattie in Floydada Cemetery, Floyd County.[944]

The children of Mary Jane Singleton McDonald Presnall and William Franklin Umberson

Ollie Delilah Umberson McIlhaney

Born 19 Mar 1877, McLennan Co., Texas, and died 13 Jul 1966, Lubbock, Lubbock Co., Texas
See profile of Ollie Delilah Umberson and John Richardson McIlhaney

Emma Florence Umberson, Richard Rufus Umberson, and Edward Brown Umberson

Died in childhood[945]

---

[942] 2654: "Farmer Found Dead," Dallas Morning News, 3 Feb 1912, scan of original, (J.J. "Frank" Umberson)

[943] Federal Census: McLennan Co., TX, 1910, pg 259B; 1920, 45B; Floyd Co., TX, 1930, pg 163

[944] 256: Joyce Beardon (Umberson family)

[945] 1412: Umberson, Kellum and Presnall tombstones in Gholson Cemetery, FM 1858, Gholson, McLennan Co., TX, April 1997, photos by Susan & R. Steven Rainwater

JEROME GEORGE UMBERSON AND HIS TWO WIVES

Jerome George Umberson
Born between 1800 and 1810, Alabama
Died between 1868 and 1870, probably Texas

Married, 1st wife, 18 Aug 1835, Lowndes Co., Mississippi
Separated between 1854 and 1861

Elizabeth Kellum
Daughter of Edward Kellum and Karenhappuch Tabor
Born 30 Mar 1814, Alabama
Died 19 Nov 1889, McLennan Co., Texas

Married, 2nd wife, between 1854 and 1861

Nancie Jane Holding
Daughter of John Holding and Susan James
Born April 1835, Tennessee
Died 21 May 1921, Little River Co., Arkansas

I know of no one person who has been more thoroughly and fruitlessly researched than Jerome George Umberson. Joyce Beardon and Virginia Humberson Owen have both been on the Humberson/Umberson trail for over thirty years, and still cannot identify more than a theoretical parent for Jerome. He seems to appear out of thin air. The current best guess is that Thomas G. and Sarah Humberson, mentioned in the land records of Alabama,[946] were Jerome's parents. There may never be enough documentary evidence to say for certain.

Jerome G. Umberson was born in Alabama.[947] The old family story that the "H" was dropped from the name on the way to Texas is certainly untrue. His 1840 and 1850 census records both say Umberson, and his marriage license was issued using that spelling. It's much more likely that Jerome simply pronounced his name that way.

On the basis of very slim circumstantial evidence, researchers in this line are persuaded that Jerome George Umberson and Alexander Marion Humberson were brothers. They were both born in Alabama and they moved to Texas around the same time. Alexander's son, John H. Humberson, married Sallie Erzola Presnall, William Umberson's step-daughter. That's pretty much the sum total of the proof. I feel certain the two men are related, far less certain that they are brothers.

---

[946] Based on Joyce Beardon's research. I have been unable to confirm her observation.
[947] Based on the 1880 Federal Census records of two of his children: McLennan Co., TX, pg143A, George Umberson; pg 143B, William F. Umberson

The Handbook of Gholson says that Jerome G. Umberson was an orphan raised by Melinda Tabor Berry and her husband, Uriah Berry.[948] My problem with this is date-related. Melinda Tabor Berry was born in 1803, her husband in 1801. And we know that Jerome G. Umberson was born between 1800 and 1810.[949] It seems unlikely that Melinda could become the guardian of someone who was essentially her own age. You can make this work *only if* Umberson was born in 1810, and Melinda took custody of him when he was 10 and she was 19. So there's a long-shot possibility that this story is correct.

What we know for certain is that Jerome G. Umberson is listed in the 1840 census on the same page with Nathan Tabor, Elijah Tabor, and Edward Kellum, and two pages from William Tabor. These men were his two uncles-in-law, father-in-law, and grandfather-in-law. So it is certain that the Umbersons, Tabors and Kellums were all acquainted.

Bettie Kellum Umberson and son, George Umberson, Jr.

---

[948] 1475: Profile of Elizabeth Kellum Umberson, The Handbook of Gholson, McLennan Co., TX, Gholson Historical Society, 1992. This profile is riddled with mistakes and cannot be taken as any kind of proof.

[949] Federal Census: 1840, Winston Co., MS, pg 254 and 1850, pg 361B.

Jerome G. Umberson married Elizabeth "Bettie" Kellum on 18 Aug 1835, in Lowndes Co., Mississippi.[950] In Feb 1841, he acquired 42 acres of land in Choctaw, Winston Co., Mississippi.[951] The Umbersons had three sons and three daughters. The eldest son was William Franklin Umberson, born in 1837 in Winston County.[952]

In 1854, Bettie Umberson's father, Edward Kellum, and all of his living children, sold out and moved to Texas.

The traditional story[953] is that a number of families packed up their wagons with the intention of heading to the Brazos River valley, where they understand good farm land could be had. On the way, Jerome was caught fooling around with a younger woman, and was sent packing by his eldest son. The embarrassed family dropped the "H" from their name and became Umberson, a detail we've already disproved.

The remainder of the story leaves hanging one key question. Did Jerome and Bettie get divorced, or did they just separate? Elreeta Weathers, a tireless McLennan County researcher, notes that Bettie's tombstone calls her *Mrs. Jerome Umberson*, and certainly no divorce decree has ever been discovered. This would not be of concern but for the rest of the story – the part we learned from researcher Brian Umberson.

The younger woman was named Nancie Jane Holding.[954] According to the version of the story preserved in Brian's family, both Jane and Jerome left the wagon train as it crossed through Arkansas.

Jerome and Jane settled in Crawford Co., Arkansas, until after the birth of their first child, then resettled in Roxton, Lamar Co., Texas, where two additional children were born.[955] No researcher has found a marriage record,[956] and since Jerome does not appear to have obtained a formal divorce, it's likely his arrangement with Jane was common law. Jerome is believed to have died in Roxton between 1866 and 1870.[957] His two sons from the second marriage are buried in the modern Restland Cemetery in Roxton. It's generally thought that Jerome Umberson is buried in an unmarked grave in Old Denton Cemetery with two infant granddaughters (marked), but the cemetery is

---

[950] 1491: Marriage license, 11 Aug 1835, and minister's return, 18 Aug 1835 for Jerome Umberson and Elizabeth Kellum, Lowndes Co., MS, Book 1 pg 127, photocopy of microfilmed original

[951] 1151: Land Patent 13275 for 42.18 acres in Choctaw, Winston Co., MS, issued 27 Feb 1841 to Jerome Umberson, scan of original

[952] 1412: Umberson, Kellum and Presnall tombstones in Gholson Cemetery, Gholson, McLennan Co., TX, April 1997, photos by Susan & R. Steven Rainwater

[953] 20: Conversation with Louise McIlhaney Deering, Apr 1997

[954] 368: Death certificate #37978, Benjamin McCulloch Umberson, Lamar Co., TX, 1933. Jane Holding is named as his mother, Jerome Umberson as his father. His birthplace is listed as Crawford Co., AR.

[955] 1880 Federal Census, Lamar Co., TX, pg 87B

[956] They are likely to have been married in Crawford Co., AR, but the marriage records prior to 1877 have been lost.

[957] The interval between the birth of his third child and his absence in the 1870 Federal Census.

abandoned and no records survive.[958] By 1900, Jane Holding Umberson had taken residence with her daughter, Sudie,[959] and died in Foreman, Little River Co., Arkansas, in 1921.[960] She, too, is buried in Roxton, Texas.[961]

Bettie Kellum Umberson continued on to Texas and settled with her children in Waco, east of the Brazos River.[962] Here, Annie Presnall Wood picks up the story:

> "[William's] mother was never well, especially after her husband left her. She was neither able physically or mentally to be of any benefit to him.[963] Grandma's health had been bad for years. Any kind of excitement brought on what must have been epileptic fits. She had a hard fit the evening after the wedding.[964] When I was thirteen (1879), Grandma came back to live with us. She was so childish and such a care. I'm sure that no one except mother could have gotten along with her. [Mother] paid no attention to [Grandma's] quarrelsome ways." [965]

Only two other records mention Bettie Umberson. First, the Texas Confederate Indigent List, a census taken in 1865, lists E. Umberson with five dependents living in McLennan County. Her inclusion on the list is based on her son William's service in 15th Texas Infantry.[966] The second is from Caledonia Baptist Church, east Waco, whose records mention Elizabeth Umberson and her son William as founding members.[967]

Elizabeth Kellum Umberson died on 19 Nov 1889. She is buried in Gholson Cemetery on FM 1858 in rural McLennan County.[968]

---

[958] 1521: Umberson tombstones in Old Denton Cemetery, Roxton, Lamar Co., TX, photos by Susan & R. Steven Rainwater, 3 Nov 2001

1522: Umberson tombstones in Restland Cemetery, CR 38, Roxton, Lamar Co., TX, photos by Susan & R. Steven Rainwater, 3 Nov 2001

[959] Federal Census: 1900, Morris Co., TX, pg 200B; 1910, Little River Co., AR, pg 24A; 1920, Little River Co., AR, pg 200A.

[960] 907: Arkansas Death Record Index, 1914-1923, Desmond Walls Allen, publ. 1996, Arkansas Research, Conway, AR

[961] 2684: Death certificate #1139; Nancie Jane Holding Umberson, 21 May 1921, Foreman, Little River Co., AR, certified copy

[962] Federal Census, McLennan Co., TX, 1860, pg 426B and 1870, pg 61.

[963] 18: Annie Presnall Wood, "*The Autobiography of Annie Presnall Wood*," pg 53, written c. 1940, photocopy of original

[964] 18: pg 56. Annie is referring to the wedding of her mother to William F. Umberson in June 1876.

[965] 18: Annie Presnall Wood, pg 82

[966] 465: Confederate Indigent Families Lists of Texas, 1863-1865, pg 303, Linda Mearse, publ. 1995, San Marcos, TX

[967] 181: McLennan Co., TX Marriage Records, Vol. 1, 1850-1870, Appendix, pg B-9. Central Texas Genealogical Society, 1963, Waco, TX

[968] 1412: Umberson, Kellum and Presnall tombstones in Gholson Cemetery, Gholson, McLennan Co., TX, April 1997, photos by Susan & R. Steven Rainwater

The children of Jerome G. and Elizabeth Umberson

William Franklin Umberson

Born 11 May 1837, Winston Co., Mississippi and died 24 Oct 1898, McLennan Co., Texas
See profile of William Franklin Umberson and Mary Jane Singleton

Rufus W. Umberson

Born c. 1840, Mississippi, and died between 1860 and 1870, Texas
Rufus served in Company E, 4th Texas Infantry of the Confederate Army.[969] He appears to have died in service.

Sarah Jane Umberson Goza Landrum

Born c. 1842, Mississippi, and died 1876, Gillespie Co., Texas
Sarah Jane married William A. Goza on 24 Dec 1858, in McLennan County.[970] He enlisted in the Texas 6th Cavalry, Company D, 1861, and died of measles at Little Rock, Arkansas, in the same year. She then married Larkin Landrum, c. 1865. Sarah Jane died in Fredericksburg, Texas in 1876 of fever.[971]

Amanda F. Umberson Tabor

Born c. 1844, Mississippi, and died after 1880, Texas
Amanda married William T. Tabor on 11 Sep 1860 in McLennan Co., Texas. He was related to Amanda's grandmother, Karen Tabor Kellum, but I am not certain of the exact relationship. Annie Presnall Wood hints that Tabor was a drunk, but describes her Aunt Amanda as "*a smart woman, very deserving.*" Tabor had served the Confederacy in the Texas 9th Infantry, Company K.[972] The family is listed on the Confederate Indigent List in 1865 in McLennan County.[973]

---

[969] 2554: Texas Confederate Soldiers, 1861-1865, Janet B. Hewett and Joyce Lawrence, 1997, Broadfoot Co., Wilmington, NC

[970] 181: McLennan Co., TX Marriage Records, Vol. 1, 1850-1870, Central Texas Genealogical Society, 1963, Waco, TX. The marriage record says Gasey, but absolutely no other records support this name. Her descendants say the correct surname is Goza.

2554: Texas Confederate Soldiers, 1861-1865, Janet B. Hewett and Joyce Lawrence, 1997, Broadfoot Co., Wilmington, NC

[971] Email from Patricia Morrow and Don Michael Bottoms, unverified

[972] 2554: Texas Confederate Soldiers, 1861-1865, Janet B. Hewett and Joyce Lawrence, 1997, Broadfoot Co., Wilmington, NC

[973] 465: Confederate Indigent Families Lists of Texas, 1863-1865, Linda Mearse, 1995, San Marcos, TX

C. Ann Umberson Messer

Born c. 1846, Mississippi, and died between 1870 and 1880, Texas
Ann married Thomas G. W. Messer on 14 Jun 1867, in McLennan Co., Texas.[974] Annie Presnall Wood describes him contemptuously, saying, *"He was absolutely worthless, goodeasy, good for nothing except to give Aunt Ann children."*[975] They had three children, whom Annie remarks were the most *"uncouth, untrained, ill mannered children it has ever been my misfortune to see."* In the 1870 census, the Messer household is listed next to the Umbersons. Annie notes that Aunt Ann suffered from her own mental problems, describing her as *"not seeming to know how to take hold and be any help about the work, but rather a hindrance."*[976]

Jerome George Umberson, Jr.

Born 11 Jun 1854, Chicksaw Co., Mississippi, and died 21 Aug 1888, McLennan Co., Texas
On 26 Dec 1875, Jerome married Orpha Savannah Kiker.[977] They were the parents of four children. Jerome died in 1888, and is buried in Oakwood Cemetery, Waco.[978]

The children of Jerome G. and Nancie Jane Umberson

Benjamin McCullouch Umberson

Born 29 Sep 1861, Crawford Co., Arkansas, and died 1 Aug 1933, Roxton, Lamar Co., Texas
Benjamin married Brazzie Zora Hattie Josephine Penn on 17 Mar 1892, in Paris, Lamar Co., Texas.[979] They had seven children, six of whom lived to adulthood. Brazzie died of pneumonia in 1908, and on 2 Jul 914, Benjamin married Ida Mae Clark McCoy.[980] They were the parents of two daughters.[981] According to his death certificate, he is buried at Restland in Roxton, under, we believe, the fallen Woodman of the World tombstone next to his brother's.

---

[974] 181: McLennan Co., TX Marriage Records, Vol. 1, 1850-1870, Central Texas Genealogical Society, 1963, Waco, TX

[975] 18: Annie Presnall Wood, pg 82

[976] 18: Annie Presnall Wood, pg 93

[977] 120: McLennan Co., TX Marriage Records, Vol. 2, 1871-1892, Central Texas Genealogical Society, 1963, Waco, TX

[978] 217: McLennan Co., TX Cemeteries, Vol. 3, Oakwood, John M. Usry, Central Texas Genealogical Society, Waco, TX

[979] 2637: Lamar Co., TX Marriage Records, Vol. 3, 1890-1899, Lamar County Genealogical Society, publ. 1995, Paris, TX

[980] 2665: Marriage announcement; B. M. Umberson & Mary McCoy, Dallas Morning News, pg 6, 3 Jul 1913, scan of original

[981] Federal Census: 1930, JP #2, Lamar Co., TX, pg 6A

Sudie M. Umberson Prewitt Thompson

Born Apr 1864, Texas, and died between 1920 and 1930

On 28 Jan 1897, Sudie married widower Spencer H. Prewitt.[982] He had been married twice before; she had been married once, possibly to a man named Kirby.[983] Sudie and Spencer were the parents of three children. The couple lived in Morris Co., Texas in 1900,[984] and moved to Little River Co., Arkansas, thereafter, where Spencer died c. 1903. Sudie married her third husband, William M. Thompson, before 1910.[985] The couple died prior to 1930.

John Arthur Umberson

Born 11 Jul 1866, Roxton, Lamar Co., Texas, and died 30 Jul 1911, Roxton, Lamar Co., Texas

John married Susie Nix on 23 Dec 1888, in Lamar Co., Texas.[986] They were the parents of two daughters who died in childhood and are buried in Old Denton Cemetery, Roxton.[987] According to John's death certificate, the couple was separated prior to his death.[988] John is buried at Restland in Roxton, under an enormous Woodman of the World tombstone that has toppled over. Only the initials on the footstone give any clue to the identity of the grave.[989]

---

[982] 256: Joyce Beardon (Umberson family). No marriage records for this date are available in Morris Co., TX.

[983] Both her 1900 and 1910 census records say she has been married three times, but this cannot be right. If she is on her third marriage in 1910, then 1900 is her second. If she is on her third in 1900, then 1910 is her fourth. In either case, there must have been a first marriage. Her eldest son is named Thomas Kirby Prewitt, giving rise to the idea that her first husband was named Kirby. This may or may not be true.

[984] Federal Census: 1900, Morris Co., TX, pg 200B

[985] Federal Census: 1910, Little River Co., AR, pg 24A; 1920, Little River Co., AR, pg 200A

[986] 950 Rootsweb, http://www.rootsweb.com, unverified

[987] 1521: Umberson tombstones in Old Denton Cemetery, Roxton, Lamar Co., TX, photos by Susan & R. Steven Rainwater, 3 Nov 2001

[988] 369: Death certificate #16091, John Umberson, Lamar Co., TX, 1917, certified copy

[989] 1522: Umberson tombstones in Restland Cemetery, CR 38, Roxton, Lamar Co., TX, photos by Susan & R. Steven Rainwater, 3 Nov 2001

Edward Kellum and Karenhappuch Tabor

Edward and Karenhappuch Kellum

Edward Kellum
Born 28 Feb 1787, Virginia
Died 23 Feb 1864, McLennan Co., Texas

Married 9 Nov 1812, Davidson Co., Tennessee

Karenhappuch Tabor
Daughter of Lt. William Tabor and Susannah Tubb
Born 1795, Tennessee or South Carolina
Died 1869, McLennan Co., Texas

Edward Kellum was born in 1787 in Virginia.[990] As a young man, he settled in Davidson Co., Tennessee, where on 9 Nov 1812, he married Karenhappuch Tabor. Her odd name, Karenhappuch, has been used to support spurious claims of Native American ancestry. In fact, it's biblical. Karenhappuch, along with Jemimah and Keziah, are the three replacement daughters God gave Job as a reward for his faithful suffering.[991] Her name has been mangled in nearly every document in which it appears, but her husband's probate file and her tombstone support the biblical spelling.[992]

---

[990] Kellum says he was born in Virginia in both the 1850 and 1860 censuses. His birthplace is frequently identified as Accomack Co, Virginia, though without supporting evidence. However, his son William's official biography identifies Edward's birthplace as Scotland.
Federal Census: 1850, Chickasaw Co, MS, pg 412A; 1860, McLennan Co., TX, pg 389B
54: A Memorial & Biographical History of McLennan, Falls, Bell & Coryell Counties, TX, 1893, Lewis Publishing Co., Chicago, IL

[991] Job 42:13-15

[992] 1280: Probate file #175, Edward Kellum, 1864, McLennan Co., TX, selected documents, photocopies of originals. Nearly every record gives her a different name, including Cary, Carion, Keren Happy, C.A., Carry, and Karenhappuck.

On 13 Nov 1814, Edward Kellum enlisted in Col. William Metcalf's 1st Regiment of the West Tennessee Militia in Capt. John Barnhart's Company, at Nashville. Shortly thereafter, the regiment began the 600-mile journey to New Orleans, which they reached by boat via the Mississippi River in mid-December. The regiment was assigned to hold the right section of Major General William Carroll's line at the fortifications at Chalmette, just east of New Orleans. The unit engaged in skirmishes in December 1814 and January 1815, but did not participate in any major battles.[993]

Kellum was discharged 13 May 1815, in Davidson County. For his service, he was on 14 Apr 1853, granted a bounty land warrant for 50 acres in Union County, Louisiana.[994] He apparently sold the warrant, since he had moved to Texas the year before the grant was made.

Shortly after their marriage, Edward and Karen moved to Bibb Co., Alabama, and purchased 238 acres of land.[995]

Six of their nine children were born there.[996] By 1840, the family had moved to Winston Co., Mississippi, and by 1850 to Chickasaw Co., Mississippi.[997] In search of better farmland, the entire Kellum clan moved to McLennan Co., Texas, in 1854.[998] Edward became a deacon of the First Baptist Church of Waco, and the family acquired land in east Waco. An acre of that land was set aside for a family cemetery.[999]

Kellum died in 1864, leaving a large estate that included twenty-two slaves and a considerable amount of Confederate currency, both of which became worthless at the end of the Civil War. This caused the estate to be tied up for years in court. Kellum owned a considerable amount of livestock – thirty cattle, thirty sheep, four oxen, fifty hogs, three mules, several horses, at least 240 acres of land, and more furniture and agricultural equipment than was typical for that era. Even with the loss of some of the capital and cash, the

---

[993] Regimental Histories of Tennessee Units During the War of 1812, Tennessee State Library and Archives, http://www.tennessee.gov/tsla/history/military/1812reg.htm

[994] 2560: Bounty Land Warrant #27,264 for 80 acres granted 14 Apr 1853, under the Act of Congress passed 28 Sep 1850 to provide land for veterans of the War of 1812 and various Indian wars, scan of original, Bureau of Land Management database. The dates of service are from the online database of the National Society United States Daughters of 1812, http://www.usdaughters1812.org

[995] Federal Census: 1830, Bibb Co., AL, pg 155B. Surname misspelled Celum.
1087: Bureau of Land Management database shows Kellum purchased 238 acres in Bibb Co. on 1 Dec 1826, patents 5381, 5382, & 5383.

[996] Many researchers include an eleventh daughter named Leiury Jane, for whom I can find no evidence. Ancestry.com indicates that she died in West Chicasaw Co., MS, c. 1850, surnamed Williams, but this information actually describes Susannah Kellum.

[997] Federal Census: 1840, Winston Co., MS, pg 245; 1850, Chickasaw Co., MS, pg 412A

[998] 54: A Memorial & Biographical History of McLennan, Falls, Bell & Coryell Counties, TX, 1893, Lewis Publishing Co., Chicago, IL
Federal Census: 1860, McLennan Co., TX, pg 389B

[999] 316: Texas Historical Commission marker at Kellum Cemetery, East Herring & J.J. Flewellen Roads, Waco, McLennan Co., Texas

executor (his son, William R. Kellum) estimated the value of the estate at $50,000.[1000]

Karen Tabor Kellum died five years after her husband. They are both buried in the now abandoned Kellum Cemetery at the intersection of East Herring and J. J. Flewellen Roads, east Waco.[1001]

The children of Edward and Karen Kellum:

Elizabeth "Bettie" Kellum Umberson

Born 30 Mar 1814, Alabama, and died 19 Nov 1889, McLennan Co., Texas
See profile of Elizabeth Kellum and Jerome George Umberson

Nancy M. Kellum Lockhart Rheuson

Born 1 Dec 1816, Tennessee, and died after 1870, Texas[1002]
On 8 Jan 1831, Nancy married William Lockhart in Bibb Co., Alabama.[1003] They were the parents of at least seven children. They moved to Mississippi between 1834 and 1836, where they were recorded in both the 1840 federal census and the 1841 state census. William died between 1848 and 1850.[1004] Nancy married Louis Rheuson, c. 1854, in Mississippi. They were the parents of one daughter. By 1870, the Rheuson family had moved from Mississippi to McLennan County.[1005] Both Louis and Nancy appear to have died prior to 1880. They are likely among the unmarked graves in Kellum family cemetery, Waco.

William Riley Kellum

Born 27 Dec 1817, Alabama, and died 23 Oct 1890, Waco, McLennan Co., Texas
Referred to in the county history as the "Merchant Prince of Waco," W. R. was a very successful man. He appears to have come to Waco before the rest of the family in 1851, where he purchased 1200 acres near the Brazos River and planted cotton. In March 1867, he opened a general merchandise business, Kellum & Sparks in Waco, and the business ran

---

[1000] 1280: Probate file #175, Edward Kellum, 1864, McLennan Co., TX, selected documents, photocopies of originals
[1001] 1421 Kellum tombstones in Kellum Cemetery, Waco, McLennan Co., TX, photos by Susan & R. Steven Rainwater, 7 Mar 1999
[1002] 54: A Memorial & Biographical History of McLennan, Falls, Bell & Coryell Counties, TX, 1893, Lewis Publishing Co., Chicago, IL
258: Kay Tucker (Kellum family)
[1003] 110: Early Alabama Marriages, 1813 - 1850, Vol A-Z, publ. 1991, Family Adventures Publishing, Nacogdoches, TX
[1004] Federal Census: 1850, Western Division, Chickasaw Co., MS, pg 822A
[1005] Federal Census: 1870, east of the Brazos River, McLennan Co., TX, pg 76B

under various names for the next twenty years. W.R. was a Baptist Deacon, a Mason, a Confederate, a Democrat, and a Justice of the Peace.

Rejected as a soldier, he worked in the Quartermaster's Department during the War. From 1876 to 1888, he served as a director of the Waco Bridge Company. At the time of his death, he was director of a cotton factory.[1006]

W.R. was married twice: first, to Nancy Jane Cooper, whom he married in Winston Co., Mississippi, on 12 Sep 1844,[1007] and second to Mary E. Jurney, whom he married on 15 Jul 1856 in McLennan Co., Texas.[1008] One son survived from the first marriage, five children survived from the second. W.R. and his second wife are buried in Kellum Cemetery.[1009] His first wife is buried in Old 1st Street Cemetery in Waco.[1010]

Polly Ann Kellum Kirkland

Born 9 Apr 1821, Alabama, and died 21 Jun 1893, Coryell Co., Texas Polly married Dr. William Wilson Kirkland on 14 Sep 1837, in Winston Co., Mississippi.[1011] He was a farmer before the war and a country doctor afterward. The couple had eight children, the first seven born in Mississippi and the last born in Arkansas.[1012] They arrived in Texas in the fall of 1863. Polly and William are buried with several of their children in Osage Cemetery in rural Coryell County.[1013]

Both of Polly and William's sons served in the Confederate army. When their eldest son, Edward Pickens Kirkland, returned home from almost four years of service, he was a broken man. During his recovery, he wrote the story of his branch of the family, entitled "*The History & Traditions of the Kirkland Family.*"[1014]

[1006] 54: A Memorial & Biographical History of McLennan, Falls, Bell & Coryell Counties, TX, 1893, Lewis Publishing Co., Chicago, IL

107: Handbook of Waco and McLennan County, Texas, Dayton Kelly, editor, 1972, Waco, Texas

[1007] 855: Marriage Records of Winston Co., MS, Vol. 1, 1834-1880, Winston County Genealogical and Historical Society, 1984, Louisville, MS

[1008] 181: McLennan Co., TX Marriage Records, Vol. 1, 1850-1870, Central Texas Genealogical Society, 1963, Waco, TX

[1009] 1421: Kellum tombstones in Kellum Cemetery, Waco, McLennan Co., TX, photos by Susan & R. Steven Rainwater, 7 Mar 1999

[1010] 2205: Kellums in Old 1st Street Cemetery, 1st Street at I-35, Waco, McLennan Co.,TX, 19 June 2005, Susan & R. Steven Rainwater

[1011] 862: Winston Co., MS Marriage Records, Nicholas Russell Murray, 1981, Hunting for Bears Inc., Hammond, LA

[1012] Federal Census: 1850, Chickasaw Co., MS, pg 350A; 1860, Jackson Co., AR, pg 683A; 1870, Waco, McLennan Co., TX, pg 82A; 1880, Coryell Co., TX, pg 471

[1013] 1420: Carter, Kellum & Kirkland tombstones in Osage Cemetery, Coryell Co., TX, photos by Susan & R. Steven Rainwater, 1 Jan 2000

[1014] 509: Elreeta Weathers (Kellum-Umberson-Parmley-Gibson families)

Thomas Smith Kellum

Born 27 Apr 1823, Alabama, and died 7 Jun 1873, McLennan Co., Texas

Smith, as he was called, married Martha Elizabeth Wilson in Mississippi between 1846 and 1849. They were the parents of six, possible eight children.[1015] Some researchers believe that Smith had a previous wife, Phoebe Lipsey, who was the mother of the first two children. Because the marriage records for Chickasaw Co., Mississippi, were lost in a fire, there is no record for either marriage.[1016] In June 1873, Smith was murdered at the ford of White Rock Creek on Fort Graham Road, in McLennan County.[1017] It is not clear if the crime was ever solved. The couple is buried in Kellum Cemetery.[1018]

Edward D. Kellum, Jr.

Born 19 Jan 1826, Alabama, and died 7 Mar 1891, McLennan Co., Texas

Edward was married three times. In Winston Co., Mississippi, he married Virginia Clementine Moorehead on 1 Mar 1846.[1019] They were the parents of four children. After she died, he married Nancy Cobb Weaver between 1862 and 1870, probably in Texas. They were the parents of two daughters. Upon his second wife's death, he married a widow, Sarah E. Waddington.[1020] Edward and his second wife are buried in Gholson cemetery.[1021]

Susannah M. Kellum Williams

Born c. 1829, Alabama, and died 30 Mar 1847, Mississippi

According to her father's probate file, Susannah married a man surnamed Williams and had a son, Samuel, and daughter, Virginia. The

---

[1015] Federal Census: 1850, Chickasaw Co, MS, pg 306B; 1860, McLennan Co., TX, pg 409A; 1870, Waco, McLennan Co., TX, pg 61A.

[1016] The Smith Kellum, who married Martha Dunn in Bibb Co., AL, in 1838 is a different person, though probably related.

[1017] 179: McLennan Co., TX Cemeteries, Vol. 1, Central Texas Genealogical Society, Waco, TX. The location of his murder is engraved on his tombstone. If you follow the path of Fort Graham Road and White Rock Creek on Google Maps Satellite, the two never actually cross, though they may have crossed in the past. The creek comes closest to Fort Graham Road at Ross Road.

[1018] 1421: Kellum tombstones in Kellum Cemetery, Waco, McLennan Co., TX, photos by Susan & R. Steven Rainwater, 7 Mar 1999

[1019] 862: Winston Co., MS Marriage Records, Nicholas Russell Murray, 1981, Hunting for Bears Inc., Hammond, LA

[1020] 120: McLennan Co., TX Marriage Records, Vol. 2, 1871-1892, Central Texas Genealogical Society, 1963, Waco, TX
Federal Census: 1880, McLennan Co., TX, pg 144D

[1021] Federal Census: 1870, Waco, McLennan Co., TX, pg 59B
1412: Umberson, Kellum and Presnall tombstones in Gholson Cemetery, FM 1858, Gholson, McLennan Co., TX, April 1997, photos by Susan & R. Steven Rainwater

couple appears to have died before the family moved to Texas. An affidavit given by Samuel Williams in 1866 describes Edward Kellum as his grandfather, and names William R. Kellum as his guardian in his minority. Virginia is found in the 1850 household of her uncle, Nathan Tabor.[1022] I have not been able to learn anything more about this family.

Lydia Mariah Kellum Brown Putnam

Born 15 Jul 1833, Chickasaw Co., Mississippi, and died Jan 1893, McLennan Co., Texas

Lydia married James Edward Brown c. 1854, probably in Mississippi. They were the parents of one son, Edward Kellum Brown.[1023] James died within two years of the marriage, and Lydia married Berry P. Putnam on 30 Dec 1868, in McLennan County, and moved briefly to Georgia.[1024] Berry is remarked as "sick" in the 1870 census, and died a few months later.[1025] Lydia and her two children returned to McLennan County.[1026] She died in 1893.[1027] Berry Putnam is buried in Sixes Methodist Church Cemetery, Cherokee Co., Georgia.[1028] It is likely that Lydia and her first husband are among the unmarked graves in the Kellum family cemetery in Waco.

Emma Caroline Kellum Puckett

Born 22 Dec 1837, Mississippi, and died after 1900, McLennan Co., Texas

Emma married John Beard Puckett on 5 Jan 1859, in McLennan County.[1029] They were the parents of nine children, one of whom died in childhood. Annie Presnall Wood refers to her as Aunt Emma Puckett, and describes an incident where Aunt Emma's well-meaning advice caused a misunderstanding between Annie and her step-father, ultimately leading Annie to marry as an escape from her unhappy family situation. John Puckett died prior to 1900, and Emma moved in with her daughter Emma Puckett Story and son-in-law, J. E. Story, a dentist in Midland.[1030]

[1022] Federal Census: 1850, Winston Co., MS, pg 326B
[1023] Federal Census: 1860, Waco, McLennan Co., TX, pg 39
[1024] 181: McLennan Co., TX Marriage Records, Vol. 1, 1850-1870, Central Texas Genealogical Society, publ. 1963, Waco, TX
[1025] Federal Census: 1870, Canton, Wildcat District, Cherokee Co., GA, pg 266B
[1026] Federal Census: 1880, McLennan Co., TX, pg 92A
[1027] 80: Index to Early McLennan Co., TX Deaths, John M. Usry, Central Texas Genealogical Society, Waco, TX
[1028] 2312: Findagrave.com #67998231
[1029] 181: McLennan Co., TX Marriage Records, Vol. 1, 1850-1870, Central Texas Genealogical Society, 1963, Waco, TX
[1030] Federal Census: 1900, Midland, TX, pg 222A

WILLIAM TABOR AND SUSANNAH TUBB

William Tabor
Son of John Tabor and Elizabeth Sharp
Born 4 Jan 1761, Orange Co., North Carolina
Died 4 Jun 1844, Winston Co., Mississippi

Married 5 Jun 1781, Rutherford Co., North Carolina

Susannah Tubb
Daughter of George and Mary Tubb
Born 11 Oct 1761, King's Mountain, Mecklenburg Co., South Carolina
Died 31 Jul 1852, Winston Co., Mississippi

William Tabor[1031] was the son of John Tabor and Elizabeth Sharp; the grandson of William Tabor, Jr., and Rachel Womack; the great-grandson of William Tabor, Sr., and Hagar Stoval; and the great-great-grandson of Stephen Tabor, who was born in Virginia in 1650.

William was born in Orange Co., North Carolina, on 4 Jan 1761.[1032] His family soon moved to Burke Co., North Carolina. In the summer of 1780, Tabor enlisted in Capt. Alexander Irvine's company of light horse (cavalry) in Col. Charles McDowell's regiment. This company was mainly engaged in scouting duties, and, as William would later put it, *"routing little knots and settlements of British and Tories."*[1033] Their service brought the regiment into the line of fire at the Battles of Camden (16 Aug 1870), King's Mountain (7 Oct 1780), and Cowpens (17 Jan 1781). Wounded at King's Mountain, Tabor was nursed by Susannah Tubb, the daughter of one of his comrades-in-arms, George Tubb, who had died in the battle.

[1031] The sources for this section, unless otherwise noted, are:

1593: Revolutionary War service & pension papers of Lt. William Tabor and Susannah Tabor, National Archives file #W6245, scan of originals

74: Genealogical Abstracts of Revolutionary. War Pension Files, Vol 3, N-Z, pg 3411, pension file of William Tabor #W6245, Virgil D. White 1992, National Historical Publishing Co., Waynesboro, TN

232: Hamilton B. Zeigeler, "*The Genealogy of the Tabor Family*", online edition (now offline)

597: Pioneers and Residents of West Central Alabama Prior to the Civil War, pg 268, Madge Pettit, 1988, Heritage Books, Bowie, MD.

2552: Winston Co., MS Cemeteries, Profile of William Tabor, pg 377, Hazel Crenshaw Garrett and Louis Taunton, 1993, G&T Publishers, Louisville, MS

[1032] 1593: 29 Dec 1926 letter of Winfield Scott, Commissioner of Pensions, to Mrs. B. J. Baskin, Cameron, Texas

[1033] 1593: William Tabor's deposition, 16 Oct 1832, Bibb Co., AL

The couple married on 5 Jun 1781, in Rutherford Co., North Carolina.[1034] Years later, their grandson, James Berry, would say that they were married *"before peace was made with England."*[1035]

The frequent skirmishes, small though they were, caused William's father, John, to move the entire family to Rutherford Co., North Carolina, in late 1780 or early 1781.[1036] As a result, Tabor left Irvine's company and in Feb 1781, joined Capt. John Anderson's company in Major Robert (Robin) Porter's regiment. Starting with the rank of ensign, he was promoted after two months to lieutenant, serving for a total of nine months. Porter's regiment was assigned to frontier duties and stayed well out of the way of harm. Tabor was discharged from service in December 1781, but was recalled briefly in 1782 to defend against Indians who were raiding small settlements on North Carolina's western border.[1037]

William's post-war life was punctuated by near-constant moving. He appears to have moved to South Carolina around 1783. By his own account, he lived for fourteen years in the Greenville and Pendleton Districts of South Carolina.[1038] Then after 1805[1039], he moved to Tennessee, living in Dickson, Davidson, Franklin, and Hickman Counties.[1040] He estimates that he lived in Tennessee for six years, though it appears to have been longer.[1041]

Finally, William moved to Shelby Co. and then Bibb Co., Alabama, where on 16 Oct 1832, he first filed for a pension on his Revolutionary War service. He was awarded $100 per year, $80 of which was granted because he had served as an officer. He finally came to rest in Winston Co., Mississippi, in the late 1830s.[1042]

William Tabor died on 4 Jun 1844, at the age of 81. His widow, Susannah, successfully reapplied for her husband's pension on 1 Feb 1847. By 1850,

---

[1034] 1593: This date is given by Susannah in several of the applications, and is supported in the 5 Apr 1847 deposition of Mary Logan, who says she personally attended the wedding. The Clerk of the Court of Rutherford Co., NC, however, wrote that no records could be found in the courthouse, which is to be expected since the marriage records of that era would have been the responsibility of the local churches.

[1035] 1593: James M. Berry deposition, 12 Oct 1855, Holmes Co., MS

[1036] 1593: William Tabor's deposition, 16 Oct 1832, Bibb Co., AL

[1037] 1593: William Tabor's deposition, 16 Oct 1832, Bibb Co., AL and Susannah Tabor's deposition, 1 Feb 1847, Winston Co., MS

[1038] Federal Census: 1800, Pendelton District, SC, pg 34. South Carolina used the term District instead of County until 1868.

[1039] All of the children say in later census records that they were born in South Carolina. The youngest appears to have been Elijah, who was born in 1805, according to the family Bible presented to the Clerk of the Court of Holmes Co., MS on 12 Oct 1855, by Melinda Tabor Berry, who was at that time, her mother's executor.

[1040] Federal Census: 1830, Hickman Co., TN, pg 47

[1041] If he left South Carolina around 1805, and went to Alabama c. 1830, he was in Tennessee fifteen years, not six. Tabor is not listed in NC or SC in 1810, and no census was taken in Tennessee in that year. The William Tabor who appears in the 1820 and 1830 census records of Tennessee appears to be Jr. not Sr., based on his age.

[1042] Federal Census: 1840, Winston Co., MS, pg 258

Susannah had taken up residence with her daughter Melinda, and son-in-law, Uriah Berry.[1043]

Susannah Tubb Tabor died on 31 Jul 1852, at the age of 91.[1044] She and her husband were buried in a private family cemetery on Hawthorn Farm, four miles south of Louisville, Winston Co., Mississippi.[1045]

Establishing the canonical list of William and Susannah's children is something of a challenge.

On 12 Oct 1855, Melinda Tabor Berry, now the administrator of her mother's estate, submitted the Tabor family Bible to the Clerk of the Court of Holmes Co., Mississippi. The clerk certified the Bible as genuine and made a copy to accompany his deposition. The Bible lists the following family members:[1046]

> William Tabor, son of John and Elizabeth Tabor, was born January 4, 1761
> Susannah Tubbs, daughter of George and Mary Tubbs, was born October 11, 1761
> Kerenhappy Tabor, daughter of William and Susannah Tabor, born April 23, 1795
> Nathan Tabor, born August 3, 1797
> Nancy Tabor, born January 8, 1800
> Malindy Tabor, born April 23, 1803
> Elijah Tabor, born October 26, 1805

On 20 Mar 1856, a final payment voucher was issued to pay the pension's remainders to Susannah's heirs. This document states that the "*only children of William Tabor, deceased*" are "*Nathan Tabor, Elijah Tabor, John Tabor, William Tabor (Jr.), Mary Smith, Melinda Barry and Caren Kellum.*"[1047] While this establishes the living children, it does not speak to those who had died before 1856.

The final four children are established by correspondence from the 1920s found in William and Susannah's pension file. These are answers to the requests of applicants to the DAR and SAR for information about William's service. One of these letters, answered in 1926 by the Commissioner of Pensions Winfield Scott, includes four children who have apparently been left out of the family Bible: Elizabeth, John, William Jr. and Susan.[1048] All four

---

[1043] Federal Census: 1850, Winston Co., MS, pg 361B

[1044] 74: Genealogical Abstracts of Revolutionary. War Pension Files, Vol 3, N-Z, pg 3411, pension file of William Tabor #W6245, Virgil D. White 1992, National Historical Publishing Co., Waynesboro, TN

[1045] 2548: Revolutionary War Graves Register, Clovis H. Brakebill, editor, The National Society of the Sons of the American Revolution, 1993, DB Publications, Dallas, TX

[1046] 1593: Certified by Clerk of the Court Clerk of the Court A. G. Otery, Holmes Co., MS

[1047] 1593: Edward L. Matthews of the Second Comptroller's Office of the U. S. Department of the Treasury, final payment voucher

[1048] 1593: 29 Dec 1926 letter of Winfield Scott, Commissioner of Pensions, to Mrs. B. J. Baskin, Cameron, Texas

appear to have either predeceased their mother, or died before her estate was settled in 1856. Scott's letter gives the strong impression that he had access to documents which we do not; that some of the documents from the pension file are now missing.

This leaves one child whom I dispute. Madge Pettit in her book, "*Pioneers and Residents of West Central Alabama Prior to the Civil War*," lists Thomas L. Tabor in her summary of William Tabor's pension file. Having thoroughly examined the Tabors' 92-page pension file, I can say with certainty that Pettit is mistaken.[1049]

The children of William and Susannah Tabor:

John Tabor

Born 18 Apr 1783, South Carolina, and died between 1855 and 1856, Mississippi
On 12 Oct 1855, James Berry mentioned his uncle in a deposition, noting that he had known his uncle John all of his life, and that John was 67 or 68 years old. The 1926 letter from the pensions department gives his official date of birth. He is not included in the final list of surviving children, so he died prior to 1856. I have not been able to learn anything more about him.

William Tabor, Jr.

Born 15 Apr 1786, South Carolina, and died 11 Mar 1856, Hinds Co., Mississippi
According to a family Bible preserved by this branch of the family, William married Lydia Hinds, c. 1807. They were the parents of at least ten children. Several successful applications to the Sons of the American Revolution have been filed by his descendants.[1050]

Mary Tabor Smith

Born before 1790, South Carolina and died after 1856.
Mary Tabor married Thomas Hunt Smith. I have not been able to learn anything more about her.

Karenhappuch Tabor Kellum

Born 23 Apr 1795, South Carolina, and died 1869, McLennan Co., Texas
See profile of Edward Kellum and Karenhappuch Tabor

[1049] 597: Pioneers and Residents of West Central Alabama Prior to the Civil War, Madge Pettit, publ. 1988, Heritage Books, Bowie, MD
[1050] 2680: Sons of the American Revolution membership application database, 1889-1970, Ancestry.com, paywalled

Nathan Tabor

Born 3 Aug 1797, South Carolina, and died 5 Dec 1869, Choctaw Co., Mississippi

Nathan married Maria Henry on 3 Aug 1819, in Bibb Co., Alabama.[1051] They were the parents of at least four children. He served as a Justice of the Peace in Bibb County from 1825 to 1833. He moved to Winston Co., Mississippi, prior to the 1840 census.[1052] On 27 Feb 1841, he purchased 161 acres in the vicinity of Louisville.[1053] He served as Justice of the Peace in Winston County from 1843 to 1849, officiating at several of the weddings of his Kellum and Berry nieces.[1054] Nathan died in 1869 from injuries received in a wagon accident, and is buried in Bankston Cemetery.[1055] Maria moved to Texas with her son, John Washington Tabor.[1056] She died in 1884 and is buried in Bryan City Cemetery, Brazos Co., Texas.[1057]

Nancy Tabor

Born 8 Jan 1800, South Carolina, and died before 1852
I have not been able to learn anything about her.

Melinda Tabor Berry

Born 23 Oct 1803, South Carolina, and died 8 Jun 1880, Franklin Co., Arkansas

On 27 Jan 1819, Melinda married Uriah Berry.[1058] They were the parents of at least five children, probably more. Melinda is alleged to have acted as the guardian to the orphaned Jerome George Umberson (*see his profile for a more complete explanation*).[1059] Melinda and her husband moved to Winston Co., Mississippi, prior to 1840 where they remained for twenty years.[1060] Uriah died in Holmes Co., Mississippi, in 1866 and is buried in Saron Cemetery.[1061] Melinda moved in first

---

[1051] 110: Early Alabama Marriages, 1813 - 1850, Vol A-Z, publ. 1991, Family Adventures Publishing, Nacogdoches, TX

[1052] Federal Census: 1840, Winston Co., MS, pg 254

[1053] 1087: Bureau of Land Management land patent database, glorecords.blm.gov/PatentSearch/Default.asp

[1054] 855: Marriage Records of Winston Co., MS, Vol. 1, 1834-1880, Winston County Genealogical and Historical Society, publ. 1984, Louisville, MS

[1055] 2312 Findagrave.com #13495963

[1056] Federal Census: 1870, Bryan post office, Brazos Co., TX, pg 8A

[1057] 2312 Findagrave.com #85116452

[1058] 110: Early Alabama Marriages, 1813 - 1850, Vol A-Z, publ. 1991, Family Adventures Publishing, Nacogdoches, TX

[1059] 1475: The Handbook of Gholson, McLennan Co., TX, Gholson Historical Society, publ. 1992, McLennan Co., TX

[1060] Federal Census: 1840, Winston Co., MS, pg 254; 1850, Winston Co., MS, pg 361B

[1061] 2312: Findagrave.com #53191711

with her son, James, in Fort Smith, Arkansas, and later with her daughter, Cyrena Mitchell, in Franklin Co., Arkansas.[1062] Melinda died in Franklin County in 1880.[1063]

Elizabeth Tabor Morrow

Born after 1781, South Carolina and died between 1826 and 1844
The Tabor family Bible lists the birth date of William Morrow, and the two children of William and Elizabeth Morrow. Elizabeth's own birth date is not provided. Based on this record, in 1926, Commissioner of Pensions Winfield Scott accepted Elizabeth as one of the canonical children of William and Susannah Tabor.[1064] No other evidence is known to exist.

Susan Tabor Capshaw

Born after 1781, South Carolina, and died before 1852, Alabama
Susan married William W. Capshaw c. 1805, probably in South Carolina. She died prior to his second marriage in 1813. In 1926, Commissioner of Pensions Winfield Scott accepted Susan as one of the canonical children of William and Susannah Tabor.[1065] No other evidence is known to exist.

Elijah Tabor

Born 26 Oct 1805, Tennessee, and died 20 Mar 1864, Union Parish, Louisiana
Elijah married Susan Sims c. 1829. They were the parents of at least six children.[1066] The family moved to Union Parish, Louisiana, in the 1840s, where Elijah acquired about 560 acres of land.[1067] Susan Sims Tabor died in 1851, followed by her husband in 1864. They are buried in Shiloh Cemetery, Union Parish, Louisiana.[1068]

[1062] Federal Census: 1870, Fort Smith, Sebastian Co., AR, pg 200B; 1880, Prairie Twp, Franklin Co., AR, pg 820A

[1063] 1880 Federal Mortality Schedule

[1064] 1593: 29 Dec 1926 letter of Winfield Scott, Commissioner of Pensions, to Mrs. B. J. Baskin, Cameron, Texas

[1065] 1593: 29 Dec 1926 letter of Winfield Scott, Commissioner of Pensions, to Mrs. B. J. Baskin, Cameron, Texas

[1066] Federal Census: 1850, Union Parish, LA, pg 385B; 1860, Union Parish, LA, pg 71

[1067] 1087: Bureau of Land Management land patent database, www.glorecords.blm.gov/PatentSearch/Default.asp

[1068] 2312: Findagrave.com #15181805, #15181811, and #98202726

JOEL HALBERT AND HIS TWO WIVES

Joel Halbert
Son of John Halbert and Susannah Higgins
Born c. 1810, Tennessee
Died 19 Jan 1887, Shelby Co., Texas

Married, 1st wife, 25 Feb 1828, Lincoln Co., Tennessee

Tabitha Elizabeth Cox
Born c. 1814, Lincoln Co., Tennessee
Died 30 Jun 1851, Sabine Co., Texas

Married, 2nd wife, 23 Jan 1852, Limestone Co., Alabama

Emeline Grindle
Born c. 1815, Alabama
Died 8 Mar 1918, Shelby Co., Texas

Joel Halbert was born c. 1810 in Tennessee.[1069] He was the son of John Halbert, born c. 1783 in North Carolina, and his wife Susannah Higgins, born c. 1789 in Kentucky.[1070] We know nothing about their other children because by the time the couple is recorded in the 1850 census of Limestone Co., Alabama, all of their children had left home. In fact, the only reason this couple can be identified at all is that after Susannah died, John took up residence with his son in Sabine Co., Texas.[1071] John Halbert died prior to the 1870 census.

Joel Halbert married Tabitha Elizabeth Cox on 25 Feb 1828, in Lincoln Co., Tennessee.[1072] Their first two daughters, Louisa and Martha, were born in Alabama in 1834 and 1836 respectively. On 28 Sep 1837, the family arrived in the Republic of Texas.[1073] Their son, William Washington Halbert, Sr., was born in 1838, and daughters Amanda, Susan, and Rebecca followed.[1074] There may have been children born between 1828 and 1834, who had either died or left home before the 1850 census, and therefore cannot be identified.

[1069] Federal Census: 1850, Sabine Co., TX, pg 324A
[1070] Federal Census: 1850, Limestone Co., AL, pg 32
2609: Application for membership to the National Society of the Daughters of the American Revolution, #39471, Eva Mae Halbert Hackney, approved 18 Jul 1973, gift of Mary Sims
[1071] Federal Census: 1860, Milam, Sabine Co., TX, pg 319A
[1072] 2603: Her full name is provided by the Confederate pension papers filed by her son, William W.
2609: Application for membership to the National Society of the Daughters of the American Revolution, #39471, Eva Mae Halbert Hackney, approved 18 Jul 1973, gift of Mary Sims
[1073] 2648: The First Settlers of Sabine Co., TX, Gifford White, from the originals in the General Land Office and the Texas State Archives, publ. 1983, Ericson Books, Nacogdoches, TX
[1074] Federal Census: 1870, Sabine Co., TX, pg 11A-11B

Tabitha Cox Halbert died on 30 Jun 1851.[1075] Joel then married his second wife, Emeline Grindle. The couple married on 23 Jan 1852, in Limestone Co., Alabama.[1076] Why Joel returned to Alabama to marry Emeline and how he knew her is unknown. The marriage produced between six and eight children: Tabitha, Theodoshia, Leona, and Mary, who is remarked in the 1880 census as epileptic and died as a young woman. Two, possibly four, additional children were born and died between 1880 and 1887, and their names are not known.[1077]

The 1860 census reveals that Joel Halbert was a substantial slave holder, owning eleven female and five male slaves. His father, John Halbert, also owned one male slave.[1078] Three of these individuals remained with the family after the Civil War. The 1870 census record of the Halbert household includes three free African American servants, Joe, Jane, and Thomas Halbert. Jane and Thomas are also present in the 1880 household.

On 23 May 1839, Halbert was granted 1280 acres by the county in the form of a Republic of Texas 2nd class headright certificate. The 2nd class certificate required the grantee to agree to remain in Texas for three years, and live on the land he had been granted before the title to the land became final. Halbert swore under oath that he had arrived on 28 Sep 1837, which fulfilled nearly two of the required three years. He is recorded in the 1839 tax list, with one taxable – the land itself.[1079] He was recorded the following year in the 1840 census of Texas.[1080]

The land records of Sabine County contain over a dozen transactions in which Joel Halbert is either the seller or buyer. Several are notable for the genealogical information they contain. On 20 Apr 1858, Joel Halbert and his wife, who is identified as Emeline Grindle, sell land on Boreagas Creek to John Halbert. On 22 Jan 1874, Joel Halbert deeded 358 acres to his daughter, Tabitha Halbert Dorsey. And in 1877, he deeded land to the county for a public school.[1081]

Joel served as a County Commissioner in 1856 and 1864, for what appear to be two-year terms. He was also one of the original trustees of Sabine Valley

---

[1075] 2609: Application for membership to the National Society of the Daughters of the American Revolution, #39471, Eva Mae Halbert Hackney, approved 18 Jul 1973, gift of Mary Sims

[1076] 110: Early Alabama Marriages, 1813-1850, Vol A-Z, 1991, Family Adventures Publishing, Nacogdoches, TX

[1077] Federal Census: 1880, Sabine Co., TX, pg 239B; 1910, Shelby Co., TX, pg 59A. The 1910 census says she is the mother of six children, three of whom are living, but her obituary says she is the mother of eight children, three of whom are living.

[1078] Federal Census: 1860, Slave Schedule, Sabine Co., TX, pg 361A-B. Both surnames are spelled Holbert in this record.

[1079] 2648: The First Settlers of Sabine Co., TX, Gifford White, from the originals in the General Land Office and the Texas State Archives, publ. 1983, Ericson Books, Nacogdoches, TX

[1080] 2649: The 1840 Census of the Republic of Texas, Gifford White, publ 1966, The Pemberton Press, Austin, TX

[1081] 2602: Abstract of Deeds, Sabine Co. Archives, Hemphill, TX, pgs 285, 339, & 406, Blanche Toole, 1983, Ericson Books, Nacogdoches, TX.

University, which was chartered on 7 Jun 1879. The school included courses in business, engineering, law, medicine, and theology.[1082]

Sometime after the 1880 census, Joel and Emeline moved to Shelby Co., Texas. Joel died on 19 Jan 1887. Emeline continued to run the family farm, dying at the age of 103, carried off during the 1918 influenza epidemic. The couple is buried in Truitt Cemetery, Shelby Co., Texas.[1083]

[1082] 2606: Sabine Co., TX, The First One Hundred Fifty Years, 1836-1986, pgs 198-199, Robert Cecil McDaniel, 1987, Hemphill, TX

[1083] 2312: Findagrave.com #24963088

William W. Halbert and His Two Wives

William W. Halbert, Sr. and first wife, Mary F. Allen

William Washington Halbert, Sr.
Born 23 Sep 1838, Sabine Co., Texas
Died 11 Jan 1926, Milam, Sabine Co., Texas

Married, 1st wife, 9 Sep 1857, Sabine Co., Texas

Mary Frances Allen
Born 23 Feb 1843, Texas
Died 30 Jun 1900, Milam, Sabine Co., Texas

Married, 2nd wife, 13 Jun 1901, Sabine Co., Texas

Mary Elizabeth Smith
Born 9 Jan 1865, Texas
Died 21 Jan 1839, Milam, Sabine Co., Texas

William Washington Halbert, Sr., appears to have spent his entire life in Sabine Co., Texas. He is called Washington in the 1850 census, and William W. in every census thereafter through 1920. Halbert family historians call him Dick. On 9 Sep 1857, William married Mary Frances Allen.[1084]

[1084] 2603: Sabine Co., TX in the Civil War, pg 44-45, Kathryn Hooper Davis, Linda Ericson Devereaux and Carolyn Reeves Ericson, publ. 2001, Ericson Books, Nacogdoches, TX
2604: Citizen-Soldiers of Sabine Co., TX, 1812-1991, pg 32, Robert Cecil McDaniel, 1992, Texas Press, Waco, TX

Mary Frances Allen was the daughter of Thompson Allen and Elizabeth Wooldridge; the granddaughter of Joel Wooldridge and Martha Ellington; the great-granddaughter of Jeremiah Ellington and Frances Jones. Jeremiah Ellington, on account of his furnishing supplies to the militia in Amelia Co., Virginia, is reckoned a patriot of the Revolutionary War. Ellington's descendants are therefore eligible for membership in the Sons and Daughters of the American Revolution.[1085]

William W. Halbert, Sr., and his first wife, Mary Frances, were the parents of sixteen children, twelve of whom lived to adulthood.[1086]

On 5 Jun 1862, William W. Halbert, Sr., enlisted in Company F, 11th Regiment of the Texas Infantry, CSA, and served honorably as a Private until his discharge on 31 May 1865.[1087] The 11th served primarily in Texas, Arkansas, and Louisiana, and participated in a number of small skirmishes, but no well-known battles.

Mary Frances Halbert died in June 1900, and William married his second wife, Mary Elizabeth Smith, within a year.[1088] They were the parents of three children.[1089]

If you search for this couple on World Connect you will discover that several researchers have confused William Sr.'s second family with that of his son William Jr. That this is entirely incorrect is made clear by the fact that Mary Elizabeth Smith Halbert filed for a Confederate pension and mortuary warrant on the service of her husband in the 11th Regiment.[1090] William W. Halbert, Jr., could not possibly have served in the Civil War, since he was born in 1862.

William left no description of his life, but an article observing the 83rd birthday of his daughter Sudie, published in 1963 by the Sabine County Reporter, contained these observations:

> There was hard work in farming in those early days, but there were high spots, too. There was fishing, hunting, swimming, and during the summer, singing schools. Sudie enjoyed helping her mother with the spinning, weaving, knitting, gardening and caring for the chickens. She

---

[1085] 2609: Application for membership to the National Society of the Daughters of the American Revolution, #39471, Eva Mae Halbert Hackney, approved 18 Jul 1973, gift of Mary Sims

[1086] Federal Census: 1900, Sabine Co., TX, pg 130A. Mary Frances says she is the mother of 16 children, 12 living.

[1087] 2618: Confederate pension application #39670, William Washington Halbert, Sr., dated 20 Aug 1909-18 Jan 1926, Sabine Co., TX

[1088] 2603: Sabine Co., TX in the Civil War, pg 44-45, Kathryn Hooper Davis, Linda Ericson Devereaux and Carolyn Reeves Ericson, publ. 2001, Ericson Books, Nacogdoches, TX

[1089] Federal Census: 1910, Sabine Co., TX, pg 154B

[1090] 2619: Confederate pension application #45388, Mary Elizabeth Smith Halbert, dated 30 Mar 1929-26 Jan 1939, Sabine Co., TX

2605: "Levi Thompson Halbert 90th Birthday," Old Timers of Sabine Co., TX, pgs 47-48, articles from the Sabine County Reporter newspaper, Virgie Speights, 1983, Ericson Books, Nacogdoches, TX

and her mother would take the eggs to the store in Milam and trade for calico and trimmings for Sunday dresses. Eggs sold for 5¢ to 10¢ a dozen. She recalls hog-killing time, with gallons of cracklings being cooked into soap, with lye leached from hardwood ashes. They were a religious family and always went to church on Sunday.[1091]

William died of pneumonia in 1926.[1092] Mary Elizabeth moved in with her widowed daughter, Virgie Russell, and remained there until her death from breast cancer in 1939.[1093] William and both wives are buried in Joel Halbert Cemetery, Milam, Sabine Co., Texas.[1094]

The children of William and Mary Frances Halbert:

Alfred Arva Halbert

Born 23 May 1858, Sabine Co., Texas, and died 20 Oct 1902, Shelby Co., Texas

On 19 Nov 1879, Alfred married Arletha Alford.[1095] They were the parents of five, possibly six, children. They lived in Sabine County for a year or so after their marriage, but then moved to Shelby County with Alfred's grandfather.[1096] Alfred died in 1902 and his second son, Obie, died the following year. Both are buried in Rather Cemetery, Shelby County.[1097] Arletha died on 13 Jun 1935, and is buried in Marshall, TX.[1098] Their eldest son, Dr. William W. Halbert is mentioned in Annie Presnall Wood's memoir as a prominent member of the Waco Baptist community.

Joel Pinkney Halbert

Born 24 Jan 1860, Sabine Co., Texas, and died 2 Dec 1941, Sabine Co., Texas

On 20 Dec 1883, Joel married Susan Evie McGowen. They were the parents of three sons, one of whom died in childhood. Evie died in

---

[1091] 2605: "Sudie Halbert Wilson 83rd Birthday," Old Timers of Sabine Co.,TX, pgs 33-34, articles from the Sabine County Reporter newspaper, Virgie Speights, 1983, Ericson Books, Nacogdoches, TX. This excerpt has been heavily edited.

[1092] 383: Eight transcribed Halbert death certificates, copied from microfilm at the Dallas Public Library, 20 May 2012 & 9 Jun 2012

[1093] 104: Texas Death Record Index, 1903-1940, G-J, Roll #3, Texas State Department of Health Records and Statistics, microfilm

383: Eight transcribed Halbert death certificates, copied from microfilm at the Dallas Public Library, 20 May 2012 & 9 Jun 2012

[1094] 2312: Findagrave.com #52766014, #82032440, and #12249356

[1095] 1031: Sabine Co., TX Marriages, Blanche Toole, 1983, Ericson Books, Nacogdoches, TX

[1096] Federal Census: 1900, Shelby Co., TX, pg 128A

[1097] 2312: Findagrave.com #82039236 and #103097246

[1098] 383: Eight transcribed Halbert death certificates, copied from microfilm at the Dallas Public Library, 20 May 2012 & 9 Jun 2012

1906, and on 10 Mar 1909, Joel married Mary Wessie Rice, a widow.[1099] Joel died in Sabine County in 1941, Mary in 1947.[1100] Joel and both wives are buried in Joel Halbert Cemetery, Milam.[1101]

William Washington Halbert, Jr.

Born 7 Dec 1862, Sabine Co., Texas, and died 7 Feb 1937, Nacogdoches Co., Texas

In 1862, twins named William and Washington, were born to the Halbert family. According to family legend, the twin named William died after being accidentally dropped by a laundress into a vat of lye soap. Upon his twin's death, Washington Halbert was given his brother's name, making him William Washington Halbert, Jr.[1102]

William married Mary Agnes Chambers on 15 Dec 1886.[1103] They were the parents of seven children. A farm family, they lived in Sabine, Bell, and Nacogdoches Counties in the course of their marriage.[1104] William and Agnes are buried in Joel Halbert Cemetery, Milam.[1105]

James Clarence Halbert

Born c. 1864, Sabine Co., Texas, and died c. 1902, Sabine Co., Texas James married Alice Madora Mason on 22 Dec 1886.[1106] They were the parents of two children.[1107] James died between 1900 and 1902, and Dora married William T. Conner on 13 Dec 1902.[1108] They were the parents of four children. The couple divorced prior to 1920 and Dora supported herself by running a boarding house.[1109]

[1099] 2312: Findagrave.com #27215332

995: Sabine Co., TX Marriages, 1880-1930, Vol. 1, Books A-G, Julia Iles Freeman, published 2005, Charcoal Hill Publishing, Hemphill, TX

[1100] 104: Texas Death Record Index, 1903-1940, G-J, Roll #3, Texas State Department of Health Records and Statistics, microfilm

[1101] 2312: Findagrave.com #27215332, #27215383, and #27215273

[1102] Traci Roberts' comment on the entry for the grave of William W. Halbert, Jr. and Wayne Halbert's "Halbert Family Plus, June 2010" family tree on Ancestry.com. Roberts refers to the laundress as a slave; Halbert refers to her as a negro woman. The 1860 Slave Schedules do not record William Washington Halbert, Sr., as a slave owner, but his father certainly was. Accidents with lye soap must have been frighteningly common. My own great-great uncle, Adam Hartmann, died in a similar accident.

[1103] 995: Sabine Co., TX Marriages, 1880-1930, Vol. 1, Books A-G, Julia Iles Freeman, publ. 2005, Charcoal Hill Publishing, Hemphill, TX

[1104] Federal Census: Sabine Co., TX, 1900, pg 129B and 1920, pg 173B; Bell Co., TX, 1910, pg 64B; Nacogdoches Co., TX, 1930, pg 208A.

[1105] 2312: Findagrave.com #12249349 and #27227633

[1106] 995: Sabine Co., TX Marriages, 1880-1930, Vol. 1, Books A-G, Julia Iles Freeman, publ. 2005, Charcoal Hill Publishing, Hemphill, TX

[1107] Federal Census: 1900, Milam, Sabine Co., TX, pg 130A

[1108] 995: Sabine Co., TX Marriages, 1880-1930, Vol. 1, Books A-G, Julia Iles Freeman, publ. 2005, Charcoal Hill Publishing, Hemphill, TX

[1109] Federal Census: 1920, Rockport, Aransas Co, TX, pg 246B

Clara Elizabeth Halbert

Born 27 Jul 1867, Sabine Co., Texas, and died 17 Sep 1938, Nacogdoches Co., Texas

Clara married John Henry King on 1 Jan 1885.[1110] They were the parents of five children, including a pair of twins. John died on 3 Jan 1899, and is buried in King Cemetery, Sabine County.[1111] In 1905, Clara married John S. Goodrich.[1112] They were the parents of one daughter. John and Clara are buried in Hemphill Cemetery, Sabine Co., Texas.[1113]

Nina T. Halbert

Born 13 Aug 1869, Sabine Co., Texas, and died 28 Nov 1902, Sabine Co., Texas

Nina was recorded as Diana in the 1880 census, causing numerous researchers to conclude that Diana was an additional daughter. However, all other records call her Nina T. She married James Dixon King on 24 Nov 1886.[1114] They were the parents of four children. Nina and James died in 1902 within eight days of each other. The couple is buried in King Cemetery, Milam.[1115] The younger three children were taken in by James' spinster sister, Mattie W. King.[1116]

Flora Halbert

Born c. 1872, Sabine Co., Texas, and died between 1889 and 1893, Sabine Co., Texas

Flora married Alexander R. Cooper on 18 Nov 1888.[1117] They were the parents of one daughter. Alex remarried twice, and was the father of five additional children. He and his second and third wives are buried in Cooper-Harris Cemetery, Sabine County.[1118] I have been unable to learn where Flora is buried.

[1110] 995: Sabine Co., TX Marriages, 1880-1930, Vol. 1, Books A-G, Julia Iles Freeman, publ. 2005, Charcoal Hill Publishing, Hemphill, TX
[1111] 2312: Findagrave.com #31464045
[1112] Federal Census: 1910, Sabine Co., TX, pg 151B
[1113] 2312: Findagrave.com #80970328 and #80969233
[1114] 995: Sabine Co., TX Marriages, 1880-1930, Vol. 1, Books A-G, Julia Iles Freeman, publ. 2005, Charcoal Hill Publishing, Hemphill, TX
[1115] 2312: Findagrave.com #31395455 and #31395512
[1116] Federal Census: 1910, Sabine Co., TX, pg 152A
[1117] 995: Sabine Co., TX Marriages, 1880-1930, Vol. 1, Books A-G, Julia Iles Freeman, published 2005, Charcoal Hill Publ., Hemphill, TX
[1118] 2312: Findagrave.com #36921417, #36921631, and #36921599

Levi Thompson Halbert, Sr.

Born 1 Mar 1874, Sabine Co., Texas, and died 10 Dec 1867
See profile of Levi Thompson Halbert, Sr. and Mary Ann Armstrong

John W. Halbert

Born 14 Apr 1876, Sabine Co., Texas, and died 27 Mar 1967, Dallas, Dallas Co., Texas
John married Mary Pearl Mason on 14 Mar 1896.[1119] They were the parents of at least ten children. The couple farmed in Sabine and Nacogdoches Counties.[1120] By 1930, the family had moved to Dallas, where John worked for the rest of his life as a house carpenter.[1121] He died in 1967 of heart disease, and is buried in Restland Cemetery, Dallas, with his wife and several other family members.[1122]

Sam Houston Halbert

Born 2 Jun 1879, Sabine Co., Texas, and died 15 Mar 1970, Sabine Co., Texas
Sam married Mabel B. Allen on 16 Nov 1898. They were the parents of three children and spent their lives on the farm.[1123] The couple is buried in Joel Halbert Cemetery, Milam.[1124]

Susan A. "Sudie" Halbert Wilson

Born 1882, Sabine Co., Texas and died 1970
On 5 Nov 1899, Sudie married William K. Wilson, a farmer. They were the parents of four children, one of whom died prior to 1910.[1125] Her husband died in 1902, leaving her to manage the farm alone.[1126] In 1963, the local newspaper profiled Sudie Wilson, who was then working as a housekeeper. The profile mentioned two additional daughters who are not listed in the census, possibly step-daughters.[1127]

[1119] 1031: Sabine Co., TX Marriages, Blanche Toole, 1983, Ericson Books, Nacogdoches, TX
[1120] Federal Census: 1900, Milam, Sabine Co., TX, pg 130A; 1920, Nacogdoches Co, TX, pg 167A
[1121] 1930 Federal Census, 2903 Shelby St, Dallas, Dallas Co., TX, pg 26B
[1122] 383: Eight transcribed Halbert death certificates, copied from microfilm at the Dallas Public Library, 20 May 2012 & 9 Jun 2012 and
photographs of the Halbert plot in the Fountain View section of Restland, taken 25, Jun 2012
[1123] Federal Census: Sabine Co., TX, 1900, pg 130A, 1910, pg 160B, 1930, pg 34A; San Augustine Co., TX, 1920, pg 9B.
[1124] 2312: Findagrave.com #82032443 and #82032438
[1125] Federal Census: Sabine Co., TX, 1900, pg 135B, and 1910, pg 166B. I could not find Sudie at all in 1920 or 1930.
[1126] 2312: Findagrave.com #27227251
[1127] 2605: "Sudie Halbert Wilson 83rd Birthday," Old Timers of Sabine Co., TX, articles from the Sabine County Reporter newspaper, Virgie Speights, publ. 983, Ericson Books, Nacogdoches, TX

Around 1965, she married William Middleton,[1128] and is buried in Joel Halbert Cemetery as Sudie Wilson Middleton.[1129]

Grover Cleveland Halbert

Born 18 Dec 1882, Sabine Co., Texas, and died 24 Sep 1961, Nacogdoches Co., Texas

Grover married Rosa A. Kirk, c. 1904.[1130] They were the parents of at least five children. They farmed land in both Sabine and Nacodoches Counties. The couple is buried in Joel Halbert Cemetery, Milam.[1131]

Clyde B. Halbert

Born May 1886, Sabine Co., Texas, and died 26 Mar 1973, Sabine Co., Texas

Clyde married Betty Cordray on 3 Dec 1905.[1132] They raised their seven children on a farm in Sabine County, where they spent their entire lives. The couple is buried in Joel Halbert Cemetery, Milam.[1133]

Died in childhood

William Halbert (twin), 7 Dec 1862 – 25 Dec 1863[1134]
Ida Lena Halbert, 27 Dec 1868 – 12 Apr 1876[1135]
Stephen Halbert, 27 Jan 1875 – 28 Jan 1875[1136]

The children of William and Mary Elizabeth Halbert:

Willie Thomas Halbert

Born 14 Jun 1901, Sabine Co., Texas, and died 22 Jun 1996, Sabine Co., Texas

Willie married Dessie Lucille Dent on 31 Dec 1921.[1137] By 1930, they had one daughter.[1138] The couple is buried in Joel Halbert Cemetery, Milam.[1139]

[1128] 268: Social Security Administration Online Death Index, Ancestry.com paywalled database
[1129] 2312: Findagrave.com #52765637
[1130] 1930 Federal Census, Attoyac Village, Nacogdoches Co., TX, pg 200A
[1131] 2312: Findagrave.com #45085460 and #45085529
[1132] 995: Sabine Co., TX Marriages, 1880-1930, Vol. 1, Books A-G, Julia Iles Freeman, published 2005, Charcoal Hill Publ., Hemphill, TX
[1133] 2312: Findagrave.com #27237191 and #27237229
[1134] 2312: Findagrave.com #103099779
[1135] 950: Ancestry.com's Rootsweb and WorldConnect online databases
[1136] 950: Ancestry.com's Rootsweb and WorldConnect online databases
[1137] 995: Sabine Co., TX Marriages, 1880-1930, Vol. 1, Books A-G, Julia Iles Freeman, publ. 2005, Charcoal Hill Publishing, Hemphill, TX
[1138] 1930 Federal Census, Sabine Co., TX, pg 77B
[1139] 2312: Findagrave.com #12249335 and #12249344

Ralph Polley Halbert

Born 25 Jul 1903, Sabine Co., Texas, and died 29 Jul 1984, Sabine Co., Texas

Ralph married Era Elliott on 11 Nov 1922.[1140] They were the parents of two children, both of whom died in childhood.[1141] The couple is buried in Joel Halbert Cemetery, Milam.[1142]

Virgie Lorena Halbert Russell Nethery

Born 4 Nov 1905, Sabine Co., Texas, and died 18 Sep 1991, Sabine Co., Texas

Virgie married Roy Drayton Russell on 29 Dec 1921, in Sabine Co., Texas.[1143] She and her husband were the parents of one son. Roy was stabbed to death by a relation, Al Halbert, on 16 Nov 1929, in a dispute about a pair of mules.[1144] Virgie took over running the family cotton farm.[1145] Between 1935 and 1938, she married Charles O'Neil Nethery, a farmer. She is buried in Joel Halbert Cemetery, as is her first husband.[1146] Charles Nethery died in 1990 and is buried in Milam Cemetery.[1147]

[1140] 995: Sabine Co., TX Marriages, 1880-1930, Vol. 1, Books A-G, Julia Iles Freeman, publ. 2005, Charcoal Hill Publishing, Hemphill, TX

[1141] 950: Ancestry.com, Halbert Family Plus June 2010, Wayne Halbert

[1142] 2312: Findagrave.com #82032442 and #82032432

[1143] 995: Sabine Co., TX Marriages, 1880-1930, Vol. 1, Books A-G, Julia Iles Freeman, publ. 2005, Charcoal Hill Publishing, Hemphill, TX

[1144] San Augustine History for November 1929, Harry P. Noble, San Augustine Tribune, 20 Oct 2005, transcription. The article calls Al Halbert Roy's nephew, but he does not appear to have been an actual nephew. He was probably a cousin at some remove.

[1145] 1930 Federal Census, Sabine Co., TX, pg 76A.

[1146] 2312: Findagrave.com #12249364 and #12249361

[1147] 2312: Findagrave.com #54446969

Levi Thompson Halbert, Sr. and Mary Ann Armstrong

Levi Thompson Halbert, Sr.
Son of William W. Halbert, Sr., and Mary Frances Allen
Born 1 Mar 1874, Milam, Sabine Co., Texas
Died 10 Dec 1967, Milam, Sabine Co., Texas

Married 13 Nov 1895, Milam, Sabine Co., Texas

Mary Ann Armstrong
Born Dec 1878, Milam, Sabine Co., Texas
Died 13 May 1958, Milam, Sabine Co., Texas

Like his father, Levi T. Halbert spent his entire life in Milam, Sabine Co., Texas.

His middle name is the source of some difficulty. Nancy McIlhaney Rainwater recalled it as Thomas, a 1964 newspaper article says Thompson, and his death certificate says Tompkins. What settles this question is a draft registration card he filled out at the age of 44, declaring himself to be Levi Thompson Halbert.[1148]

On 13 Nov 1895, he married Mary Ann Armstrong, the daughter of William Armstrong.[1149] The couple were the parents of eleven children, nine of whom lived to adulthood.

Following the marriage, Levi took up farming, though in the course of his lifetime, he would pursue many occupations, including merchant, saw mill operator, and cotton gin operator. At his 90th birthday party, his daughter-in-law, Genevieve Halbert, designed a cake depicting the themes of his life. The frosting was designed to resemble plowed ground, set with plastic figures of a barn, cattle, horse, and a tractor.[1150]

Both Levi and his sister Sudie claimed that their Halbert ancestors "*landed at Plymouth Rock.*" The original Mayflower expedition passenger lists, which are widely available in printed form and online, contain no Halberts, Holberts, or similar names.[1151] There is no evidence to support this claim.

[1148] 950: Ancestry.com. Draft registration card #42-2-36C, 12 Sep 1918, FHL Roll #1983584
[1149] 1031: Sabine Co., TX Marriages, Blanche Toole, publ. 1983, Ericson Books, Nacogdoches, TX
[1150] 2605: "Levi Thompson Halbert 90th Birthday," Old Timers of Sabine Co., TX, article, pgs 47-48, articles from the Sabine County Reporter newspaper, Virgie Speights, publ. 1983, Ericson Books, Nacogdoches, TX
[1151] http://www.mayflowerfamilies.com/ and Wikipedia, http://en.wikipedia.org/wiki/List_of_Mayflower_passengers

On 13 May 1985, Mary Ann Halbert died of a heart attack.[1152] Her husband survived her by nine years, dying on 10 Dec 1967, at the age of 93 of bronchial pneumonia.[1153]

The children of Levi and Mary Ann Halbert:

Halbert Family, 12 Nov 1955
Back row L>R: Io, Porter, Willie Veda, Basil, Imogene, Levi Jr., Lollie
Front row L>R: Levi Sr. (father), Edith, Mary Ann (mother), Biddie

Mary Arlena Halbert

Born 3 Nov 1896, Sabine Co., Texas, and died 8 Aug 1898, Sabine Co., Texas
According to Nancy McIlhaney Rainwater, Mary Arlena died of diphtheria.

Basil T. Halbert

Born 27 Aug 1899, Sabine Co., Texas, and died Sep 1980, Freestone Co., TX
Basil married Edna Elizabeth Smith c. 1925. They were the parents of

---

[1152] 383: Eight transcribed Halbert death certificates, copied from microfilm at the Dallas Public Library, 20 May 2012 & 9 Jun 2012

[1153] 383: Eight transcribed Halbert death certificates, copied from microfilm at the Dallas Public Library, 20 May 2012 & 9 Jun 2012

four children. Basil was a Baptist minister and a chaplain during World War II. The couple is buried in Joel Halbert Cemetery, Milam.[1154]

Willie Veda Halbert Davidson

Born 13 Feb 1901, Sabine Co., Texas, and died 20 Nov 1993, Beaumont, Jefferson Co., Texas

Veda married Horace Chilton Davidson, Sr., on 9 Sep 1923 in Sabine Co., Texas.[1155] They were the parents of three children. Veda died in 1993, and was joined in death by her husband in 1996.[1156] They are buried in King Cemetery, Milam, Sabine Co., Texas.[1157]

Onie Imogene Halbert

Born c. 1903, Sabine Co., Texas, and died 11 Jun 1979, Nacogdoches Co., Texas

Imogene married William Rufus Miller.[1158] They were the parents of at least one child.[1159]

Lollie Lou Halbert Gunn Lee

Born 9 Aug 1902, Sabine Co., Texas, and died 17 Oct 2007

Lollie married John Charles Claude Gunn after 1930. They were the parents of three children. John died in 1953 and was buried in Oaklawn Cemetery, Decatur, Wise Co, TX.[1160] Lollie worked as a public school teacher in Milam and school councilor.[1161] Late in life she married Alton Lee, and the couple is buried in Joel Halbert Cemetery, Milam.[1162]

Biddie Orlean Halbert Browning

Born 1904, Sabine Co., Texas, and died 26 Feb 1994, Sabine Co., Texas

Biddie married Lacy T. Browning on 29 Dec 1921, in Sabine Co., Texas. They were the parents of five children, one of whom died in

---

[1154] 2607: Joel Halbert Cemetery (formerly Fox Hill Cemetery), Milam, Sabine Co., TX, Rootsweb transcription, Mackie & Kay Parker McCary, 10 Oct 2000

[1155] 995: Sabine Co., TX Marriages, 1880-1930, Vol. 1, Books A-G, Julia Iles Freeman, published 2005, Charcoal Hill Publ., Hemphill, TX

[1156] 268: Social Security Administration Online Death Index, ancestry.com paywalled database

[1157] 2312: Findagrave.com #31355683 and #31354987

[1158] 995: Sabine Co., TX Marriages, 1880-1930, Vol. 1, Books A-G, Julia Iles Freeman, published 2005, Charcoal Hill Publ., Hemphill, TX

[1159] Federal Census: 1930, 122 Star Ave, Nacogdoches, Nacogdoches, Co, TX, pg 18B

[1160] 2312: Findagrave.com #22890508

[1161] Obituary, Sabine County Reporter October 24, 2007, Page 11, transcription, McLemore Strong Genealogy, http://strongfamilytree.org

[1162] 2607: Joel Halbert Cemetery, Milam, Sabine Co., TX, Rootsweb transcription, Mackie & Kay Parker McCary, 10 Oct 2000

childhood.¹¹⁶³ The couple is buried in Joel Halbert Cemetery, Milam.¹¹⁶⁴

Io Halbert McIlhaney

Born 23 Sep 1906, Sabine Co., Texas, and died 3 May 2004, Lubbock, Lubbock Co., Texas
See profile of Joe Singleton McIlhaney, Sr., and his two wives

Levi Thompson Halbert, Jr.

Born 9 Oct 1910, Sabine Co., Texas, and died 4 Oct 1983, Sabine Co., Texas
Levi married Genevieve Muckleroy after 1930. The couple is buried in Joel Halbert Cemetery, Milam.¹¹⁶⁵

Edward Porter Halbert

Born 1913, Sabine Co., Texas and died 22 Jan 1978, Sabine Co., Texas
Edward married Dorothy Nichols after 1930. The couple is buried in Joel Halbert Cemetery, Milam.¹¹⁶⁶

Edith Wesley Halbert Mills

Born 31 Aug 1915, Sabine Co., Texas, and died 7 Nov 1978, Angelina Co., Texas
Edith married Turner Mills after 1930. The couple is buried in Joel Halbert Cemetery, Milam.¹¹⁶⁷

[1163] McLemore Strong Genealogy, http://strongfamilytree.org
[1164] 2312: Findagrave.com #52766608 and #52766515
[1165] 2607: Joel Halbert Cemetery, Milam, Sabine Co., TX, Rootsweb transcription, Mackie & Kay Parker McCary, 10 Oct 2000
[1166] 2607: Joel Halbert Cemetery, Milam, Sabine Co., TX, Rootsweb transcription, Mackie & Kay Parker McCary, 10 Oct 2000
[1167] 2607: Joel Halbert Cemetery, Milam, Sabine Co., TX, Rootsweb transcription, Mackie & Kay Parker McCary, 10 Oct 2000

Joe Singleton McIlhaney, Sr., and His Two Wives

Joe and Io McIlhaney, 20 Oct 1946, on boardwalk at Atlantic City, NJ

Joe Singleton McIlhaney
Son of John Richardson McIlhaney and Ollie Delilah Umberson
Born 18 Oct 1902, Gholson, McLennan Co., Texas
Died 27 Nov 1999, Lubbock, Lubbock Co., Texas

Married, 1st wife, 17 Dec 1927, Lubbock, Lubbock Co., Texas
Divorced 18 Sep 1932, Lubbock, Lubbock Co., Texas

Opal Lillian Goodrich
Daughter of Fulton Miller Goodrich and Callie Kuykendall[1168]
Born 11 Jan 1910, Red Oak, Latimer Co., Oklahoma
Died Aug 1991

Married 2nd wife, 1 Sep 1934, Lubbock, Lubbock Co., Texas
Divorced 30 Mar 1979, Lubbock, Lubbock Co., Texas

Io Halbert
Daughter of Levi Tompkins Halbert, Sr. and Mary Ann Armstrong
Born 23 Sep 1906, Milam, Sabine Co., Texas
Died 3 May 2004, Lubbock, Lubbock Co., Texas

[1168] 384: Application for SSI #439-24-6296, Lillian Opal Goodrich Baldridge, copy

Joe Singleton McIlhaney was a driven man. Driven to succeed, where his ne'er-do-well father had not, driven to control all of the circumstances of his life, after a childhood of uncertainty. At his funeral, his descendants remembered him with gentle humor as a man of notoriously thrifty "Scotch" temperament.

At the age of 21, he had gone to Trinidad, Colorado, to study butter-making.[1169] He had not completed high school because, at his father's insistence, he had gone to work at age 16 in one of his father's many business ventures – a used cooking oil and grease collection service.[1170] Joe found this employment embarrassing, and was frequently taunted by his former schoolmates. His father had once worked as a dairyman, and Joe must have looked back at this as a more acceptable form of employment. So after his apprenticeship in Trinidad, he returned to Lubbock and founded the McIlhaney Creamery in 1925. His obituary would note that *"sales offices were located in Lubbock, Beaumont, San Antonio, and El Paso. He ultimately shipped butter as far as the West Coast and Chicago."*[1171] The Lubbock buildings were located at 1803-1805 Avenue H.[1172]

The McIlhaney Creamery, Lubbock, Texas

The creamery employed nearly all of Joe's brothers at one time or another. The 1930 census lists George T. McIlhaney and William U. McIlhaney as dairymen.[1173] The 1935 Lubbock City Directory lists Jesse R. McIlhaney as a

---

[1169] Conversation with David McIlhaney, Nov 1999. David recalled that he studied with a Mr. Peterson. The 1921 R. L. Poll City Directory for Trinidad, CO suggests that this might have been the Hey-Patterson Meat & Dairy Company, which appears to have been the largest in the county, or at least, the most prominent advertiser. The 1920 census does not list any Mr. Peterson who is a dairyman, so this is our best guess.

[1170] Conversations with Joe S. McIlhaney, Jr.

[1171] 624: Obituary of Joe Singleton McIlhaney Sr., Lubbock Avalanche-Journal, 29 Nov 1999

[1172] 118: Lubbock City Directory, pages from the 1935 & 1943 editions, photocopied in the Lubbock Public Library

[1173] 1930 Federal Census, Lubbock, Lubbock Co., TX, pg 227

milkman and Jack McIlhaney as the creamery foreman.[1174] Even his daughter, Nancy, worked as a secretary at the creamery while she was in high school and college.

The creamery originally produced only butter, but the growing popularity of margarine cut into the butter sales. Other products were added, including cream and milk in "cream top" bottles with tiny tin ladles that allowed you to easily skim the cream before using the milk. The creamery eventually leased railroad cars to ship their product[1175], with an advertising banner on the side carrying the somewhat disingenuous slogan, *From the Cool, Breezy Plains of Texas*. McIlhaney Creamery offered home delivery, like most dairies of that era, which was accomplished in horse-drawn wagons driven by formally attired deliverymen. They were the last Lubbock dairy to discontinue this practice.[1176]

Around 1927, Joe met Lillian Opal Goodrich. She attended the same high school as Joe's sister, Louise, and the two girls often hitched rides on one of the creamery's delivery wagons to the local movie theater. Joe complained that this was costing him money – delivering the girls must have taken the wagon off its regular route – and suggested that he date Opal instead.[1177]

Opal came from difficult family circumstances. She was born in Oklahoma, where her parents had been tenant corn farmers. When Opal was seven, her mother had died of Pellegra.[1178] Opal would later remember:

> I was an only child and was awfully lonesome sometimes. The only very happy days I remember as a child were before mother died. I was about seven then, altho for a year before her death, she was too sick to notice me. After she died, I was left to board with various relatives.[1179]

Unable to adequately care for a small child, her father had placed Opal with her grandmother, Martha Kuykendall,[1180] and later with her aunt, JoAnn Goodrich Atchison.[1181] In her early teens, she came to live in Lubbock with her father, Fulton, his brother Jim, and Jim's second wife Lizzie. The years of being passed around from one relative to another had left Opal withdrawn and guarded.

It's not clear what Joe saw in Opal. She was eight years younger, not yet out of high school. He was a Baptist, active in his church, and she had been raised

---

[1174] 118: Lubbock City Directory, pages from the 1935 & 1943 editions, photocopied in the Lubbock Public Library

[1175] 1863: The McIlhaney Creamery Company, Margie O'Neill, The Newsletter of the Lubbock Model Railroad Association, July 2001. The company leased two BREX cars on the Fort Worth & Denver, and five Reefers on the Burlington & Quincey.

[1176] 624: Obituary of Joe Singleton McIlhaney Sr., Lubbock Avalanche-Journal, 29 Nov 1999

[1177] 20: Conversation with Louise McIlhaney Deering, Apr 1997

[1178] 20: Conversation with Louise McIlhaney Deering, Apr 1997

[1179] 623: Pg 4, Letter from Opal McIlhaney Baldridge to Grace Patterson McIlhaney (Mrs. Jesse), 1942, photographs of original

[1180] 1910 Federal Census, Red Oak Twp., Latimer Co., OK, pg 16B

[1181] 1920 Federal Census, Tillman Co., OK, pg 10B

with no particular religious beliefs. Joe would later tell his daughter Nancy that he had been *"seduced by Opal's attractive legs."*[1182]

In December 1927, Joe and Opal went down to the Lubbock County Courthouse for a marriage license. They were accompanied by Opal's aunt, Lizzie Goodrich, because Opal was only 17 and needed the permission of a relative. Aunt Lizzie's tart assessment of her niece did not bode well for the marriage – telling Joe that *"I could do nothing with her, and I hope you have better luck than I did."*[1183] The couple was married in the office of Rev. W. A. Bowen, the pastor of First Baptist Church of Lubbock on December 17th, with only their witnesses in attendance.[1184] They announced the marriage at a family Christmas party later that evening, apparently to the family's astonishment. Opal complained over dinner that everyone was staring at her. It was not an auspicious beginning.[1185]

The couple had two children, JoAnn, born 28 Sep 1928, and Nancy Jane, born 14 Sep 1930. They bought a small brick bungalow at 2006 17th Street in Lubbock.

JoAnne and Nancy McIlhaney, c. 1948

The marriage lasted four years. Joe's cold, controlling behavior and constant criticism of Opal took a deep toll on the insecure young woman. He was frequently absent from home, often failing to come home from work at all.

[1182] 19: Conversations with Nancy McIlhaney Rainwater, between 1991 and 1997

[1183] 20: Conversation with Louise McIlhaney Deering, Apr 1997

[1184] Marriage record; Joe S. McIlhaney, Sr., and Lillian Opal Goodrich, 17 Dec 1927, Lubbock, Lubbock, Co., TX, certified copy

[1185] 20: Conversation with Louise McIlhaney Deering, Apr 1997

By 1932, she could take no more. Opal decided to leave her husband, and moved with the children into an apartment owned by a friend of the McIlhaney family. About a month later, the time frame is now impossible to pin down more accurately, Joe arrived at the apartment to demand her return. What he discovered, described in detail in a later chapter, resulted in the couple's divorce on 18 Sep 1932.[1186]

Joe's sister Louise took over the care of the children for the next two years, developing a life-long surrogate mother relationship with Nancy.

Despite the fact that the divorce decree allowed Opal visitation rights, she was never permitted to use them. She continued to live in Lubbock until 1935, the last year she is found in the Lubbock City Directory.[1187] Nancy would later recall that Opal came to the backyard fence and asked to speak to the girls. Nancy, only five-years-old, was too frightened, but JoAnn agreed. Opal told JoAnn that she was leaving Lubbock to remarry. She attempted to make contact one more time in 1942, but was rebuffed by both girls.[1188]

Joe frequently made sales trips to promote the creamery's products and one of these trips took him to Milam, Texas, where he met Io Halbert.[1189] They married on 1 Sep 1934.[1190] The marriage resulted in three sons: Joe Singleton, Jr., Richard Gale, and David Lee. Io would later say that she had married Joe because she fell in love with his two young daughters, and while she loved her three sons, Joe Sr. was a mean old man whom she otherwise wished she hadn't married.[1191]

In the early days of the creamery's existence, Joe had maintained a cattle ranch near the current location of Maxey Park, transporting the raw milk to the creamery by rail. The city of Lubbock eventually condemned the buildings in order to take the land, forcing Joe to cut his herd and buy milk from other ranchers.[1192] Now in the 1950s, he found himself in another protracted fight over eminent domain issues, this time with the highway department. When it became clear that the battle was lost, Joe sold the business.[1193] He donated

---

[1186] 495: Divorce Decree #5208, Joe S. McIlhaney, Sr., v. Opal McIlhaney, 99th District Court, Lubbock Co., TX, 6 Sep 1932, photocopy of original

[1187] 118: Lubbock City Directory, pages from the 1935 & 1943 editions, photocopied in the Lubbock Public Library

[1188] 623: Letter from Opal McIlhaney Baldridge to Grace Patterson McIlhaney (Mrs. Jesse), 1942, photographs of original

[1189] Email from David McIlhaney, 2012

[1190] 22: A. E. "Phil" & Marion Phillips, *"The Descendants of James William McIlhaney"*, introduction by Sam McIlhaney, 1987

[1191] 30 Nov 1999, Io Halbert McIlhaney's spontaneous remarks at the luncheon following Joe Sr.'s funeral.

[1192] 1863: The McIlhaney Creamery Company, Margie O'Neill, The Newsletter of the Lubbock Model Railroad Association, July 2001

[1193] The buildings are no longer standing, but would have stood at what is now the intersection of Buddy Holly Avenue and 19th Street. It appears to us that the eminent domain case was involved with the development of I-27.

some of the equipment to Texas Tech.[1194] But he never recovered from the loss of his beloved creamery.

Now in his fifties, Joe purchased land on the outskirts of Lubbock, and started farming and raising chickens. Steve recalls finding horned toads among the rows of corn. The isolated life in the primitive farmhouse took a toll on Io. She eventually moved back into the Lubbock bungalow, but found that Joe was unwilling to provide financial support. Io's sons finally convinced her that divorce was the only way she could require Joe to provide her with an income.[1195] The couple divorced in 1979.[1196]

Joe was remembered by his daughter, Nancy, as a man who liked the outdoors, especially fishing and deer hunting.[1197] His obituary mentioned his civic involvement in Scottish Rite Children's Hospital, Texas Boy's Ranch, Masonic Blue Lodge, Texas Tech Dad's Club, and the First Baptist Church where he served as a deacon.[1198] Steve recalls his keen interest in reading history. But as he aged, the Joe described by these accolades was being overshadowed by his unfortunate tendency to paranoia. Attempts to coax him into seeking help failed. His paranoid behavior contributed significantly to both divorces.

Some kind of mental illness stalked this family. Elizabeth Kellum Umberson was chronically depressed and suffered fits. William Umberson had panic attacks. His sister Ann seemed chronically disorganized and helpless. Ollie Umberson McIlhaney was nervous and hysterical, and her husband, John McIlhaney, seemed to live in some sort of alternate reality. At least four of Ollie and John's children have been described to us as ranging from "*not quite right*" to "*barking mad.*" And Joe's daughter, Nancy McIlhaney Rainwater, would exhibit lifelong problems with paranoia. Whether these were learned behaviors passed from one generation to the next, or inherited traits, is impossible to say.

Opal Goodrich McIlhaney married Fred C. Baldridge, probably around 1935. We know his name from Opal's 1942 Social Security application, and from a heartbreaking letter she sent to Grace Patterson McIlhaney (Mrs. Jesse McIlhaney), also in 1942.[1199] The letter speaks for itself:

[1194] 624: Obituary of Joe Singleton McIlhaney, Sr., Lubbock Avalanche-Journal, 29 Nov 1999
[1195] Conversations with Joe S. McIlhaney, Jr.
[1196] Texas Divorce Index, Ancestry.com, 30 Mar 1979, Lubbock Co., TX
[1197] 19: Conversations with Nancy McIlhaney Rainwater, between 1991 and 1997
[1198] 624: Obituary of Joe Singleton McIlhaney Sr., Lubbock Avalanche-Journal, 29 Nov 1999
[1199] Nancy had cryptically mentioned this letter on several occasions. In Feb 1998, we asked Nancy if we could see it. When Nancy left the room to take a phone call, we placed the letter under a desk lamp and photographed every page. The letter has since vanished, and our photographed copy may be the only evidence that it ever existed.

2671 Gladiolus
New Orleans, LA
April 16, 1942

My dear Grace,

Even though I say "Thank you" most sincerely with all my heart, it isn't nearly enough, but I know and so must you, that someday and somehow we'll be rewarded for every kind deed. Certainly I know how sure and thorough is the punishment for mistakes.

Grace, I don't know if I'm equal to writing this letter, or not, but I know I must try. If Nancy or JoAnne want to know, it's got to be told as completely and truthfully as I can. You'll understand I can't just pick out one event and explain it, or make it sound at all reasonable. There's always the background and the things leading up to it. So maybe I'd better just start as far back as I can remember and tell the whole story of my life. It will probably be boring to you, Grace, in spots, but I'll be writing mostly for Nancy, and since you've already been so kind, you'll have to be a little kinder still and "listen," too. Some of this is pretty foolish and even worse, – but I was – so why wouldn't it! This is sort of like taking a dose of castor oil – I just keep trying to make conversation so I can delay it a little bit longer. I had to take a lot of castor oil when I was a little girl, so I would think of that.

I was an only child and was awfully lonesome sometimes. The only very happy days I remember as a child were before mother died. I was about seven then, altho for a year before her death, she was too sick to notice me. After she died, I was left to board with various relatives. I can understand now, that I must have been a nuisance to them and when one bunch got tired of me I was sent to some of the others. None of them was ever really mean to me. I'm sure they did the best they could and I probably wasn't a very loveable child, but I never felt at home anywhere. After I was about fifteen, I kept house for my father most of the time until I was married. I don't know if you've met my father. I never knew him very well or felt at all close to him myself. I met Joe while I was living with Dad. In about a year, we were married. I think I loved him, but I didn't know much about love or anything else. I knew about the physical facts of sex and marriage, not because anyone had talked to me and told me about it, but because I was curious and interested enough to find books on the subject. I neither knew or thought about the duties and responsibilities of being a wife and mother. JoAnne was born about 9½ months after we were married, and Nancy almost two years later.

I did feel very deeply the responsibility of their care and I read baby books and followed exactly the doctor's advise. He said, I remember, that I was "a perfect little mother." (I wonder what he's thought since then.) They were lovely babies. Just the sort of little girls I had dreamed of having.

I guess Joe was doing what he felt to be his duty by working all day and most of the night. I didn't see him very much and when he did come home, of course, he was tired and needed to rest. But I didn't think of it that way, as I should have. I had thought that when I got married that I'd always have a companion, someone who was really all mine for the first time in my life, and that I'd never be lonesome anymore. But I was very mistaken. I don't know whether Joe loved me or not, but I began little by little to feel sure that he didn't. I was even jealous of his relatives. They were always having secrets and doing things they thought I didn't know about. Of course this wouldn't have bothered me if I'd been sure he loved me best. Well, things began to get worse and worse. We were always quarreling about something. I hated housekeeping and did a very bad job of it, and of course he had a right to fuss about that. Deema knows I never had any clothes or any money, but I could have put up with everything and straightened it all out if I had just had a little common sense. Or maybe a little religion. But I had none of either.

Finally, when I couldn't stand it any longer, I jumped out of the "frying pan into the fire" to put it mildly. I have no excuse. I just didn't have the courage to stick to my job. I took JoAnne and Nancy and left. We lived about a month in an apartment by ourselves. Then one night, I left the children with the colored girl and Joe came and got them while I was gone. He never let me see them anymore except a few times for an hour or two. Finally, not even that. He said that he could prove that I was not morally fit to have them. Probably he could have, and if there had been a trial and anything had happened, it would have been worse for JoAnne and Nancy.

I didn't know what to do. I knew I had made some bad mistakes and I thought, maybe he is right. I felt completely beaten and willing to do whatever I was told. So I have tried to stay away and let him bring them up as he said was best. He said they would be happier if they forgot me completely. I finally promised to do whatever he thought was best for them. I thought then, that he meant it only for their good and not just to punish me.

I remember the house on 16th Street, too. Mrs. Roberts lived there. She was good to me. She used to cry with me sometimes, though I guess her tears were mostly for her husband, who had died. There's a big grandfather clock downstairs in the hall, and lots of nights when I couldn't sleep, I've sat at the top of those stairs and listened to the clock tick. It was comforting, in a way, to know that time was going on just the same as ever.

I must quit. I'm making this such a long letter and maybe not very clear in places, but I want to hurry so you'll get it as soon as possible. This is the first time I've ever tried to write all this on paper and to a woman I've never met. I wouldn't have believed I'd ever do it. Deema has told me a little about you in her letters. I've thought I would like you but never imagined I'd have any reason to be so grateful to you as I am. I keep wondering how Jesse got such a nice wife. He must be better than I know. (I don't mean anything bad about Jess. I liked him better than most of the other in-laws).

I'm sorry you have to be away from your baby son for a while, but I'll bet your mother will take good care of him. I heard from two friends in Dallas the other day and both of them have sons in the army. They are so worried, but brave about it, too. I'll try to stop now – at last. Please remember that if my prayers and loving thoughts will be of any help to you or yours, you have them.

Sincerely,

Opal

P.S. I loved every word of your letter. There just couldn't be too many details for me about JoAnne and Nancy.

Of course, as you said, I do love Nancy and JoAnne so very much. Every night and morning, I think of them and hope they are well and happy. I never wanted them to miss me enough to make them cry because of me but I'm almost hysterically happy to know that haven't forgotten. And there's something else I'd like you to tell them, if you will – that if they're ever in trouble or need me, they can write or telegraph or phone collect and that Deema or you will know the address. Maybe this is asking too much of you. I don't want you to quarrel with anyone or make them mad at you. Deema has always said she would let me know if they were very sick or anything like that, and I'm sure she would. But I wish they knew I would come if they needed me. You have the address and the phone number is Crescent 6567. There's nothing in the world I'd like better than to have them write to me – except of course to see them. Surely I've said enough for this time. I hope you will write again.

Opal Goodrich McIlhaney Baldridge died in August 1991, having never seen her daughters again.[1200] She and her second husband are not listed in the 1940

[1200] 268 Social Security Administration Online Death Index. Her social security number was issued in Louisiana, but does not say where she died. Our research has so far eliminated Texas, California and Louisiana as possibilities.

census.[1201] We have been unable to learn where she died or where she is buried.

In extreme old age, Joe returned to the 17th Street house, where he was cared for by a day nurse. He died of pneumonia on 27 Nov 1999, and is buried in Resthaven Memorial Park in Lubbock.[1202]

Io Halbert McIlhaney continued to reside in Lubbock. She died on 3 May 2004, and is buried in Resthaven Memorial Park in Lubbock with her husband.[1203]

The children of Joe and Opal McIhaney

JoAnne McIlhaney Conely

> Born 28 Sep 1928, Lubbock Co., Texas, and died 20 Apr 1992, Taylor Co., Texas
> JoAnne attended the University of North Texas for a year, before transferring to Texas Tech. On 15 Nov 1951, she married John Riley Conely. They were the parents of two children. JoAnne died of cancer in 1992 and is buried in Elmwood Memorial Park in Abilene with her husband.[1204]

Nancy Jane McIlhaney Rainwater

> Born 14 Sep 1930, Lubbock Co., Texas, and died 4 Feb 2010, Dallas Co., Texas
> *See profile of Clois Miles Rainwater and Nancy Jane McIlhaney*

The children of Joe and Io McIlhaney
> Joe Singleton McIlhaney, Jr.
> Richard Gale McIlhaney
> David Lee McIlhaney
>
> *Living*

[1201] Searching for first name Opal and last name Goodrich, McIlhaney or Baldridge

[1202] 333: Death certificate #142-99-130464; Joe Singleton McIlhaney, Sr., 28 Nov 1999, Lubbock, Lubbock Co., TX, certified copy

629: Funeral program, Joe S. McIlhaney Sr., 30 Nov 1999, original

[1203] 334: Death certificate #142-04-047766; Io McIlhaney, 3 May 2004, Lubbock, Lubbock Co., TX, certified copy

[1204] Correspondence with John Riley Conely

How We Became the World's Leading Experts on Dr. DeZita

I met Nancy McIhaney Rainwater for the first time at Thanksgiving 1987. It had already been made clear that she did not approve of me as potential marriage material for Steve and the atmosphere was tense. Which is why, when across the kitchen's breakfast bar, she said to me "*I was kidnapped as a child, you know,*" I was dumbstruck. Etiquette guides do not offer much advice on how one should respond in this situation.

Nancy would repeat this story to me and Steve nearly a dozen times in the next ten years, and he had heard it many times before. The details varied considerably, but we eventually identified the core of the story that Nancy always included. It goes like this:

> When Nancy was two-years-old, her mother, Opal, left her father, Joe. They moved several blocks away from Joe's 17th Street home into an apartment owned by a family friend.[1205] On the day the move occurred, a man with a big green car drove Opal and the children to the apartment. Nancy was frightened by the man and tried to run away. He chased her down and put her in the green car.
>
> About a month later, Opal had an affair with a magician. Around that same time, Joe arrived at the apartment to confront Opal about the separation. He found the children in the care of the housekeeper and demanded to know Opal's whereabouts. The housekeeper refused to tell him, but Joe noticed a slip of paper on a table with an address of a Plainview motel and got the housekeeper to admit that this was where Opal had gone.
>
> He then rounded up a Lubbock County deputy sheriff, crossed county lines into Hale Co., went to a motel in Plainview, and found his wife and a magician *in flagrante delicto*. Opal and the magician were arrested and sent to jail. The next day, Joe offered to drop the charges if Opal would give up all claim to their daughters, and agree to divorce.
>
> To Joe's horror, a front page story about the arrest appeared the next day in the Lubbock newspaper. Joe would later tell Nancy that she had been kidnapped the same year as the Lindbergh baby.

[1205] 118: Lubbock City Directory, pages from the 1935 & 1943 editions, photocopied in the Lubbock Public Library. Page 229 of the 1935 directory lists Opal's residence at 1201 17th Street, and we assume that this is the same apartment. Joe lived at 2006 17th Street. In some versions of the story, Nancy told us that Opal had moved to Plainview, though at other times, Nancy said that Opal moved to a nearby apartment in Lubbock. We are here telling the Lubbock version, because Opal had no family in Plainview and no apparent reason to move there, and the newspaper article covering the arrest refers to Opal as a "Lubbock woman." On the other hand, her moving to Plainview does simplify the question of how she ended up being arrested there. Either version is possible, and does not substantially change the basic facts.

Several things should be immediately clear from a careful reading of this account. First, this is two stories, not one. The big green car story is Nancy's own memory of being frightened by being chased by a stranger. But the second story is Nancy's memory of a story *she has been told* – because there is no possible way she experienced these events herself as a two-year-old child.[1206] The only part that could be Nancy's own memory is Joe's confrontation with the housekeeper. Finally, it should be obvious that no kidnapping took place. Nancy's parents simply separated,

In April 1997, Steve and I took a trip to Lubbock, for three reasons.[1207] We wanted to see Steve's grandfather, the nonagenarian Joe McIlhaney; we wanted to visit Joe's sister, Aunt Louise; and we wanted to plunder the genealogical resources of the Lubbock Public Library.

We started with the assumption that Nancy's basic premise was correct – that she was two-years-old and that an article had appeared in the newspaper. So we sat down at the microfilm readers with the first rolls of 1932 of the The Lubbock Daily Journal and The Lubbock Morning Avalanche, and began to scroll through them, page by page.

It was Steve who found the first clue – a small article on the bottom of page one in the 5 Jul 1932, edition of The Lubbock Daily Journal, whose headline said, "*Dr de Zita, Woman Arrested.*" It read as follows:

> Doctor de Zita, whose blindfolded automobile driver act almost ended disastrously here recently, and a Lubbock woman were arrested Saturday in Plainview, after officers found them in a room together, the Lubbock County Sheriff's Department has reported. Lubbock County officers assisted in the arrest.
>
> A former officer in the French Foreign Legion, Doctor de Zita presented a hypnotic act here, in addition to completing an automobile drive while blindfolded. The Lubbock woman arrested with him was said to be separated from her husband.

This essentially put to rest Nancy's claim that her father's good name had been dragged through the mud by newspapers. Opal is not named in this article, nor in the follow-up article two days later.[1208]

[1206] Nancy claimed in one retelling that she had been in the hotel room at the time of her mother's adultery. This seems absolutely impossible, and the arrest record makes no mention of a minor child being in the room.

[1207] In the fall of 1996, we told Steve's parents that we wanted to join them in Lubbock for Thanksgiving. Steve had not seen his grandfather in many years, and this seemed a good opportunity. The Tuesday before Thanksgiving, Steve received a panicked phone call from Nancy. A terrible blizzard was headed towards Lubbock, she said, and it was too dangerous to drive. They weren't going, and we mustn't, either. Steve agreed to this on the phone, but when we checked later, we realized that no such storm was headed to Lubbock – that for some reason, Nancy didn't want us there. Realizing that we would never be able to get official permission, we made the trip the following April, telling no one in advance. As a research trip it was highly successful, but Nancy was furious.

[1208] 659: "Dr DeZita, Woman Arrested," Lubbock Daily Journal, pg 1, 5 Jul 1932

By working our way backward through the papers, we collected our first evidence on the man Nancy inaccurately called "*the magician*," Dr. DeZita. And here, we take a bit of a detour.

Dr. de Zita, publicity photo, Lubbock Daily Journal, 7 June, 1932

His name was William Michael Achilles de Orgler, or so he claimed. Since he spent his life as a con man, it's hard to say how much of what he claimed for himself was true and how much was invention. From the very first article, dated 1914 to his end in a Los Angeles hospital in 1955, he always said William Michael Achilles.[1209] The surname varied – sometimes de Orgler, sometime de Zita, and sometimes both.

Based on our collection of newspaper articles, we believe that de Orgler, as he originally called himself, arrived in the United States between 1906 and 1914.[1210]

661: "DeZita and Local Woman Are Charged," Lubbock Daily Journal, pg 1, 7 Jul 1932

[1209] Except for a brief period in 1917, when he was claiming to be Baron Francis de Orgler of Austria.

2597: "Suspect the Baron," pg 2, 9 Nov 1917, Lawrence Daily Journal-World, Lawrence, KS

2598: "The Baron in Jail: Is held in Tulsa for Obstructing War Policies," pg 1, 19 Dec 1917, Lawrence Daily Journal-World, Lawrence, KS

2599: "Baron is Unauthorized," pg 14, 19 Jul 1917, The Decatur Review, Decatur, IL

During the First World War, he supported himself by running a speakers bureau con, claiming that he was a representative of the American Red Cross or National Security League.[1211] He would arrive in town, hire a hall, speak dramatically in support of American involvement in the war, then collect donations, which he pocketed. Sometimes it worked (21 Aug 1917, Toledo, Ohio), sometimes he was ordered out of town by the authorities (10 Jun 1916, Reading, Pennsylvania), sometimes he spent the night in jail (9 Apr 1918 , Nevada, Missouri). [1212]

There's a gap after the Armistice, but De Orgler would later claim to have gone to Hollywood and worked as a technical adviser on the many foreign legion-themed films of the silent era. He was, he claimed, a former World War I-era officer of the Austrian Royal Dragoons, a veteran of the French Foreign Legion (1908-1912), and had served in Casablanca and Tangier, French Morocco; and Tetuan, Spanish Morocco.[1213] Among the films on which he claimed credit were *Beau Geste* (1926) with Ronald Coleman, *Beau Sabreur* (1928) with Gary Cooper,[1214] Sigmund Romberg's operetta *Desert Song* (1929), *Morocco* (1930) with Gary Cooper, and *Renegades* (1930) with Warner Baxter. In this latter film, he claimed to have been the double for Baxter. The most I believe is that he worked as an extra in movies that needed exotic-looking cannon fodder charging down the sand dunes in the battle scenes.

By the start of the 1930s, he was on to a new career in small time vaudeville with a new stage name, Dr. DeZita. The heyday of vaudeville was 1890-1932, so DeZita had joined up just in time for the medium to decline.[1215] He traveled a circuit of movie theaters in small and mid-sized towns with a hypnotist-seer of the future act, but with a couple of business-savvy twists.

A week before DeZita was to arrive, an ad would appear in the newspaper under a headline like "*Why Worry About the Future?*" suggesting that if you

---

[1210] The first article we have found is dated 1914. In the 1930 census, he says he emigrated from Austria in 1906, which obviates his claim of service in the French Foreign Legion and Austrian army.

[1211] Wikipedia: National Security League, http://en.wikipedia.org/wiki/National_Security_League. Similar to the John Birch Society in philosophy, the real NSL would have been apoplectic at his representation of himself as their agent.

[1212] 2547: "Baron Pleads For Recruits for U.S. Army," pg 7, Toledo Bee, Toledo, OH, 21 Aug 1917

2493: "Mayor orders Count to get out of Reading," page 1, The Reading Eagle, Reading, PA, 10 Jun 1916

2459 "The Baron has been given his freedom," The Nevada Daily Mail and The Evening Post, Nevada, MO, 9 Apr 1918

[1213] 1930 Federal Census, Atascadero, San Luis Obispo Co., CA, pg 66A. He claimed to be a World War I veteran, though he also said he had emigrated to the United States in 1906, which presents something of a conflict. His profession was listed as Astrological Lecturer.

657: "Hypnotist Will Appear At Ritz Theatre Tonight", Plainview Evening Herald, pg 3, 14 Jun 1932

2597: "Suspect the Baron: Topeka People Exhibit Distrust of Dr. DeOgler" [sic], pg 2, 9 Nov 1917, Lawrence Daily Journal-World, Lawrence, KS, scan of original

[1214] According to film historians, the trailer contains the only frames of this film still in existence.

[1215] Wikipedia: Vaudeville, http://en.wikipedia.org/wiki/Vaudeville

filled out the coupon and mailed it into the newspaper, you would receive a private reading with Dr. DeZita, the famed astrologist.[1216] A day or two before his arrival, the newspaper would run stories about DeZita's upcoming activities – a blindfolded drive through town using a car from a local dealership, serving customers blindfolded at a department store or diner, hypnotizing a pretty college girl to believe she was royalty, or putting her to sleep in the department store window.[1217] The businesses where these demonstrations were to occur would then take out a full page ad promoting the schedule of events and no doubt, Dr. DeZita got a kickback from the ads. In the evening, he would appear on stage between features, dressed in a Sheik of Araby costume, and perform hypnotism, mind reading, and other fakery. He would provide personal readings and cast horoscopes in the lobby.

This, then, is the pattern of events as they occurred in Lubbock. DeZita gave an interview on the subject of Hollywood immorality on June 7th, 1932.[1218] On June 8th, the full page ad appeared in the Lubbock papers.[1219] On June 9th, an article ran promoting the hypnotist act[1220], and on the 10th, a follow-up article reported on the adventures of the hypnotized girl.[1221] On the 12th, an article described DeZita's not entirely successful blindfolded drive through town (he hit a parked car).[1222] And on June 14th, a full-page ad appeared in the Plainview Evening Herald, promoting DeZita's upcoming appearance in their town.[1223]

[1216] 660: "Why Worry About the Future?", 2 column ad, Plainview Evening Herald, pg 5, 24 Jun 1932

[1217] 654: "Young Woman To Be Hypnotized Here By Former Foreign Legion Captain," Lubbock Morning Avalanche, pg 9, 5 Jun 1932

663: "Man to Drive Blindfolded," San Francisco Chronicle, pg 3, 16 Aug 1934

2546: "Blindfold Driver Will Amaze City Tomorrow," pg 1, The Oxnard Daily Courier, Oxnard, CA, 23 Aug 1935

2512: "Girl Snoozing in Window Under Hypnotist's Care," Los Angeles Times, 22 Dec 1944, page A1

There is evidence that these girls were hired in advance. David Wilkinson writing about the history of local movie theaters (Daily Democrat, Woodland, CA, 11 Feb 2007), mentions that DeZita advertised in the local newspaper for a pretty 120-130 lb girl to act as a stage assistant about a week before he appeared in Woodland. So even the hypnotism act was utterly fake.

[1218] 647: "Hypnotist Takes Issue With Movie Actor Over Hollywood Immorality," Lubbock Daily Journal, pgs 1 & 7, 7 Jun 1932. Some weeks earlier, local boy turned Hollywood supporting player, John Arledge, had said in an interview that reports of Hollywood immorality were "*all tommyrot and malicious gossip.*" DeZita disputes Arledge's claim, and gleefully elaborates on the sex, drugs, and wild party scene in Tinseltown.

[1219] 648 "Dr DeZita Appearing in Person," full page ad, Lubbock Morning Avalanche, pg 5, 8 Jun 1932

[1220] 649: "Texas Tech Graduate to Substitute as Subject for Hypnotic Exhibition," Lubbock Morning Avalanche, pg 9, 9 Jun 1932

[1221] 651: "Duchess of Lubbock, Under Spell of Hypnotist, Gives Out Interview," Lubbock Daily Journal, pgs 1 & 7, 10 Jun 1932

[1222] 655 "Hypnotist Runs Into Parked Truck On Blindfold Drive On Lubbock Streets," Lubbock Daily Journal, pg 5, 12 Jun 1932

[1223] 656 "Ritz Theatre Tonight and Tomorrow," full page ad, Plainview Evening Herald, pg 2, 14 Jun 1932

We theorize, though we certainly cannot prove, that Opal filled out one of the coupons for a private reading. She was only twenty, her life was falling apart, her marriage had failed, she was a poorly educated girl with, as she would say later, no particular religious convictions. When she received her reading, DeZita probably marked her as the sort of girl he could take advantage of, and did.

In Nancy's telling of the story, DeZita was the driver of the big green car. But the date evidence should make clear that this simply isn't possible. If Joe and Opal were separated for a month before Opal's arrest, how could a man who was only in town from June 7th to June 13th have been the driver of the big green car? This would also require DeZita to have taken a personal interest in Opal, which seems very unlikely, given the man's almost complete lack of scruples. So no, Dr. DeZita did not kidnap Nancy. In all likelihood, one of Opal's male relatives – her father Fulton, her Uncle Jim, or her cousin Rector – drove the big green car.

When DeZita left Lubbock for Plainview, Opal took the one irrational step that would lead to her undoing – she insisted on seeing DeZita one more time, failing I think, to grasp that his interest in her was strictly carnal. She left her children with the housekeeper and went to Plainview. She apparently did not have a car of her own, so she must have either borrowed a car or made the trip by bus.

We drove that same 48 mile trip up I-27 and found the Hale county courthouse. Armed with the date, we requested DeZita and Opal's arrest record, and any other records pertaining to the case. Records of that era, we were informed, were stored across the street in a condemned building. We would have to wait until someone had time to go across the street to retrieve them.

About an hour later, the clerk returned. Opal and DeZita had been arrested on 2 Jul 1932, and the clerk had found the booking ledger. Other records followed. For each individual, the clerk found a Complaint, an Information, and a Capias (warrant).[1224] Opal had spent the night in jail, and was released the next day when the charges against her were dropped, presumably when she agreed to give up her daughters to their father. DeZita cooled his heels for at least three days, possibly longer, but ultimately was never prosecuted. The charges were officially dismissed in August 1932.[1225]

[1224] 665 Complaint, Hale Co., TX, names Mrs. Joe McIlhaney, 2 Jul 1932, photocopy of original
666 Information, Hale Co., TX, names Mrs. Joe McIlhaney, 2 Jul 1932, photocopy of original
667 Capias (warrant), Hale Co., TX, names Mrs. Joe McIlhaney, 2 Jul 1932, photocopy of original
668 Complaint, Hale Co., TX, names Dr. DeZita, 2 Jul 1932, photocopy of original
669 Information, Hale Co., TX, names Dr. DeZita, 2 Jul 1932, photocopy of original
670 Capias (warrant), Hale Co., TX, names Dr. DeZita, 2 Jul 1932, photocopy of original
[1225] 671: Hale Co., TX Court Minutes, Aug 1932 Term, list of cases dismissed, photocopy

We returned to Lubbock, and the next day went to the Lubbock courthouse to get the divorce papers. Nancy always maintained that her father had gotten the court to seal the divorce records, so we expected an argument, especially since Joe was still living. The clerk took our $10 and returned about twenty minutes later with a photocopy of the divorce decree.

Joe had received sole custody of both daughters. The court placed a $5,000 value on the creamery and a $3,100 value on the house, neither of which was considered in the determination of a settlement. Opal received what furniture she had taken with her to the duplex, visiting rights (of which she was eventually deprived), and a cash settlement of $2500, to be paid in $25/month payments. The judgment states that the court felt the "*material allegations in the plaintiff's petition are true,*" but does enumerate them.[1226]

We returned to the clerk and asked for the sealed records. "*What sealed records?*" she wanted to know, "*These are the only records we have.*" So were the records ever actually sealed? Apparently not.

Our naïve hope was that Nancy, given what we had learned about these events, would gain some peace...that she would be able to move on. But presented with the blurry photocopy of the newspaper photo of Dr. DeZita, she became almost rigid with fear, and burst into tears. Far from seeing that the facts demolished at least half of the story, Nancy believed we had confirmed her worst nightmares. Not long after, Nancy went entirely silent as a genealogical source, and we later learned that she had written to several relatives asking them not to cooperate with our research.[1227] But she continued to tell the kidnapping story. The last time I witnessed the telling was at the dinner after the viewing of her father's casket, where she latched onto a startled relative and said, "*Did you know I was kidnapped as a child?*"

It's impossible to know how many lives DeZita ruined as he did Opal's and Nancy's. He managed to make the vaudeville act pay for about 15 years. But the circuit collapsed at the end of World War II, and DeZita undertook a new career as a booking agent for strippers.[1228] His final movie role was as Satan in Ed Wood's schlocky *Glen or Glenda*. He is utterly forgotten today, by all but die-hard Ed Wood fans, and ironically, by us.[1229]

[1226] 495: Divorce Decree #5208, Joe S. McIlhaney vs. Opal McIlhaney, 99th District Court, Lubbock Co., TX, 6 Sep 1932

[1227] I learned this from Betty Rainwater Parker, after we visited her in Colorado Springs. Nancy implied to us that she had made the same request of Louise McIlhaney Deering.

[1228] "*Film Scratches: One critic's favorite onscreen devils, from Tim Curry to Buster Keaton,*" Richard von Busack, metroactive.com, 2 Nov 1995. The article quotes George Weiss, Wood's producer, who recalled him as "Captain DeZita," his first name completely forgotten. DeZita's entry in the Internet Movie Database appeared shortly after I published a short biography on findagrave.com (#50884347).

[1229] He is buried in an unmarked grave in Valhalla Cemetery in North Hollywood.

Clois Miles Rainwater
and Nancy Jane McIlhaney

Clois and Nancy Rainwater

Clois Miles Rainwater
Son of Roscoe Rainwater and Gertrude Alice Caughron
Born 12 Mar 1923, Oklaunion, Wilbarger Co., Texas
Died 9 Jan 2010, Clyde Cosper Veterans Home, Bonham, Fannin Co., Texas

Married 1 Oct 1949, Lubbock, Lubbock Co., Texas

Nancy Jane McIlhaney
Daughter of Joe Singleton McIlhaney and Opal Lillian Goodrich
Born 14 Sep 1930, Lubbock, Lubbock Co., Texas
Died 4 Feb 2010, Irving, Dallas Co., Texas

Clois Miles Rainwater was born in Oklaunion, Texas, a small farming hamlet about 10 miles east of Vernon. He was the fifth child born to Roscoe C. Rainwater and Gertrude Caughron. His name, Clois, was pronounced as a single syllable that rhymes with "Joyce". His middle name, Miles, has been passed down in every branch of the Rainwater family, originally in honor of

Rev. Miles Rainwater of South Carolina (1787-1826). By the time Clois was born, this tradition had been forgotten, and his middle name was bestowed in honor of his uncle. In the army, Clois acquired the nickname "Drip," the name by which many of his adult acquaintances knew him.

Clois told few anecdotes about his childhood, but one he did recall was particularly sweet. As a boy of perhaps five or six, Clois accompanied his father, Roscoe, on a visit to C. V. Compton, his mother Gertrude's uncle. Compton lived in a Highland Park mansion and employed a staff of live-in servants.[1230] It was luxury beyond anything Clois had experienced. When the family sat down to lunch, a servant brought out crackers and butter. Clois assumed this course was the entire meal. When the next course arrived, he was too full of buttered crackers to eat anything else.

By 1930, the family had moved to Vernon, and Clois grew up in the house at 2128 Mesquite Street.[1231] He attended Vernon High School, graduating in 1940, and was taking classes at the community college when World War II broke out. On 1 Apr 1941, Clois enlisted in the Army Air Corps as a Private. His enlistment record describes him a high school graduate, 5'8" and 137 lbs.[1232]

Clois took basic training at Lowery Field, Denver, Colorado. A skilled mechanic, he was quickly promoted to the position of Sergeant Air Mechanic 2nd Class, then to Staff Sergeant on 1 Aug 1942. He was stationed at Foster Field, Victoria, Texas, until Aug 1943, where he worked as an aircraft armorer and mechanic on fighter planes, including the P61 Nightfighter. He was responsible for the proper functioning and loading of the P61's guns, armoring the plane, and other mechanical issues.[1233]

When I asked him to describe his service, Clois recalled being stationed at Randolph Field in San Antonio; Lowrey Field, Denver; at Victoria, Texas; at the Texas Gunnery Range on Matagorda Island (1942); and at Visalia Army Air Field, California (25 Aug-2 Nov 1944) where he joined the 550th Nightfighter Squadron. In December 1944, his unit was transferred to the south Pacific, to the forward base at Morotai, Dutch East Indies. He later served on New Guinea; Tacloban on the island of Leyte, Phillipines,[1234] and Sanga-Sanga, Borneo.[1235] In the summer of 1945, he was assigned to the forces preparing for the invasion of Japan, when the atomic bomb was dropped,

---

[1230] Federal Census: 1930, 4900 Lakeside Drive, Highland Park, Dallas Co., TX, pg 57A

[1231] Federal Census: 1930, 2128 Mesquite Street, Vernon, Wilbarger Co., TX, pg 126B

[1232] 950: Ancestry.com's Abstract of U.S. World War II Army Enlistment Records, 1936-1946, paywalled

[1233] US Army Separation Qualification Record, scan of original, undated, Rainwater family archives

[1234] This particular location is confirmed by a photo Clois took of the capital building, Rainwater family archives

[1235] This location is confirmed by a note on the back of one of Clois' photos, Rainwater family archives

ending the Pacific war. Clois was discharged at Fort Sam Houston, San Antonio, Texas, on 28 Dec 1945.[1236]

A letter from Douglas D. Rappley, Captain Air Corps Adjutant, sent from the Headquarters of the 550th Nightfighter Squadron APO 76, states that Clois was entitled to wear Bronze Battle Stars for New Guinea (24 Jan 1945), Southern Philippines (23 Jul 1945), Air Combat Borneo (28 Aug 1945); the Philippines Liberation Ribbon (5 Feb 1945), the Asiatic-Pacific Theater Ribbon (1944); and Good Conduct Medal (15 Jul 1943).[1237] Clois's discharge papers also qualify him to wear the World War II Victory Medal, American Defense Service Medal, American Theater Campaign Medal, one service stripe and two overseas service bars.[1238]

Clois used his veteran's benefits to attend Texas Tech in Lubbock, Texas. He purchased a sporty car with a rumble seat and began dating.[1239] After dating several other girls, he asked out one of his Tech classmates, Nancy McIlhaney. Their meeting was accidental. Clois was volunteering as a set carpenter in the drama department, when Nancy noticed him and asked friends who he was. The friends later introduced them. Clois decided he wanted a photo of Nancy, so on one of their early dates, Clois arranged things so that a friend *just happened* to need a lift, and *just happened* to have a camera. The resulting photo, of the couple in the front seat of Clois' convertible, ended up in the family album.

Nancy was the daughter of Joe Singleton McIlhaney, Sr., a local creamery owner, and his first wife Lillian Opal Goodrich. The marriage had ended in divorce in 1932, and Nancy was raised first by her Aunt Louise, and then by her step-mother, Io Halbert. Nancy attended Lubbock High School, graduating in May 1947. She worked during high school and college as a secretary in her father's creamery.

Nothing was more important to Nancy than her Christian faith. In a talk given in the 1970s to a Bible study class, she described her conversion experience:

> As an 8-year-old, sitting in church on a Wednesday night, I realized that Christ wanted to be the guiding light of my life, but I did not accept Him at this time. That night, my Mother set me on her lap, Daddy pulled a chair close by, and they explained to me that receiving Christ was personal and something they wanted for me more than

---

[1236] Conversation with Clois Rainwater about his military service in Jul 1993

[1237] Undated letter from from Douglas D. Rappley, Captain Air Corps Adjutant, scan of original, Rainwater family archives

[1238] Enlisted Report of Separation, issued 28 Dec 1945, recorded 3 Jan 1946, Vol 4 page 87, Wilbarger Co., TX, scan of original, Rainwater family archives

[1239] The car was remembered by Nancy's younger brother Joe, who also described Clois as "a lot of fun."

anything else. As I snuggled under the warm cover in my bed that night, I prayed, inviting Jesus Christ into my life.[1240]

Clois graduated from Texas Tech in June 1949 with a Bachelor of Business Administration. Nancy attended Texas Tech as a home economics major for one year, a classic case of attending college for an "Mrs. degree." The couple was married on 1 Oct 1949, in Lubbock at First Baptist Church. Nancy was given her grandmother Ollie's wedding ring to wear as her own.[1241]

Nancy McIlhaney Rainwater had been raised in the circle of a close-knit extended family of fundamentalist Baptists. The McIlhaneys, Umbersons, and other kin were Nancy's entire affinity. Now in Vernon, probably for the first time in her life, she was exposed to a completely different type of family – the boisterous extended family of the Rainwater clan.

While the Rainwaters were also deeply sincere Baptists, they were not quite as dour about their faith as Nancy. In the Rainwater clan, it was possible to be a believing Christian and still have a good time. Their exuberance made Nancy uncomfortable, and she frequently refused to attend family gatherings or attended but withdrew into a back room with her children, declining to interact with the Rainwaters. Georgia Rainwater, Gene's wife, told me that Gertrude had asked her to try to draw Nancy into the group and make her feel included, but Georgia's efforts were rebuffed. Any one of a number of factors might have contributed to Nancy's behavior, including her shyness or her tendency to overreact to the perceived threats of the outside world.

Nancy clearly wanted to create the ideal family, secure from the upheaval she had experienced as a child when her parents' marriage collapsed. Sadly, this wholly admirable desire seemed to degenerate into the belief that nearly everything outside of the immediate family posed some kind of threat. Thus the children were told that this or that relative said things that were not true or were told not to be in the presence of particular relatives unless Nancy was present. By the time I met the family in the late 1980s, Clois barely had any contact with his brothers. Nancy told me that this was because they had "*been mean to him as a child*," but I have come to believe that she, more than Clois, cut off contact. Eventually, her paranoia would extend to her children's spouses, who were also seen as a threat to the unity of the family.

Clois took employment with the Boy Scouts as an Executive, or troop organizer. This employment required frequent relocation, and the couple's first move was to Texas City on the gulf coast. Their first son, Randy, was born there in 1950. By 1951, they had moved back to Vernon, where their first two daughters, Linda and Vicki, were born.[1242]

[1240] Notecards for "*The Reality of Christianity in a Woman's World*," a talk given by Nancy Rainwater to a Bible study group in 1971, Rainwater family archives

[1241] Ollie Delilah Umberson McIlhaney, called Mother Ollie by the younger members of the family

[1242] 2326: Ancestry.com, Texas Birth Index, 1903-1997, paywalled

During their Vernon years, Clois briefly left the Boy Scouts to work with his father in the insurance business,[1243] but was ultimately unhappy with his choice and returned to the Scouts. The four positions he held in his years with the Scouts were District Scout Executive, Director of Special Projects (Inter-City and Rural), Assistant Director of Field Services, and Field Director.[1244]

In 1956, Clois was in serious auto accident. An evening sandstorm, one of the worst the area had experienced in years, created poor visibility conditions, causing Clois to rear-end a stalled tractor trailer. The driver had set out flares, which had been extinguished or simply blown away in the wind. A passing driver stopped to help, getting Clois out of his car, then going to check on the driver of the truck. When he returned, Clois was nowhere to be found, having somehow slipped under the truck. Once Clois was located, the good Samaritan drove him to the hospital in Childress, where he was attended to by a plastic surgeon. Clois had suffered quite serious lacerations, a broken jaw, broken ribs and wrist, and numerous other injuries.[1245]

The children woke the next morning to discover their Uncle Johnie and Aunt Kay in their parents' bed – Johnie Rainwater and his wife had been asked to look after the children while Nancy stayed at the hospital with her husband. Clois recovered completely, but shaved with an electric razor for the rest of his life because of the scars. Photos taken after the accident show him with a different jawline than in earlier years. The damage had been significant.

After a five-year stay in Vernon, the Rainwaters relocated to Santa Fe, New Mexico, where their third daughter, Kelly, was born.[1246] By 1962, they found themselves in Tyler, Texas, where Steve, their fifth child, was born.[1247]

In the summer of 1964, the family moved to Vienna, Illinois. This would prove to be the high point in Clois' career with the Boy Scouts.

Clois was assigned to conduct a study of how scout troops might be developed in rural, underprivileged areas. Vienna in southern Illinois was chosen as the location for this four-year study. Clois quickly realized that the traditional methods of organizing scout troops simply would not work in Vienna and improvised his own. The results of his efforts were included in a 1970 report entitled "*Boypower '76 Development Program Success Stories."* The preface to the section on Clois' work in southern Illinois was entitled "*He not only threw away the book, he wrote a new one.*" I am including a lengthy excerpt because it so completely expresses the man Clois Rainwater was, and how different he was from the man I met twenty years later.

[1243] Nov 1951 to Feb 1953, resume of Clois M. Rainwater, dated Apr 1982, original, Rainwater family archives

[1244] Resume of Clois M. Rainwater, dated Apr 1982, original, Rainwater family archives

[1245] Randy Rainwater has expressed the belief that his father's purchase of a 1954 Mercury saved his life. The car was twice as heavy as the previous car, a 1952 Nash Rambler.

[1246] Santa Fe City Directory, 1959, scan of original in Ancestry.com's City Directory Project

[1247] 2326: Ancestry.com, Texas Birth Index, 1903-1997, paywalled

One of the greatest difficulties in bringing Scouting into such areas is that no structure for creating the activity exists. There are no troop committees, no sponsoring institutions, no Scoutmasters. Moreover, there are usually no interested adults with which to build a structure. This was the situation facing District Scout Executive, Clois Rainwater, in the 'Little Egypt' area of Illinois – isolated, insulated, out of the mainstream of American life.

His solution was to work from the bottom up. He started by recruiting boys for a small troop. For these, he served as Scoutmaster himself, teaching the boys the rudiments of Scoutcraft, organizing them, securing their steady, interested attendance. Then, he asked the boys to name a local man they wanted to be their regular Scoutmaster – and sent the boys themselves to recruit the man.

One of two things then happened. Most often, the man chosen, pleased that the boys had selected him, agreed to become Scoutmaster. But sometimes there was unwillingness, whereupon Clois Rainwater sent the boys to tell their story to the women of the community. The women then could frequently induce the nominee to serve.

What Clois Rainwater had done, in essence, was to interest previously uninterested people on the basis of an already-functioning activity. The Scoutmaster came in because the boys wanted him. The second father came in because the boys and the Scoutmaster selected him. The sponsor was found because the troop already existed. Committees were formed of people who saw troop, Scoutmaster, parents, and sponsors all involved. Single-handed, Clois succeeded in throwing the entire regional organizational structure of the Boy Scouts of America into reverse – and making it work![1248]

All five of the children attended school in Vienna, with the eldest son, Randy, graduating from Vienna High School in 1968.

In the summer of 1969, the family moved to Irving, Texas, where the national Boy Scouts organization was headquartered. The family purchased a home on Yellowstone Street[1249] and joined Plymouth Park Baptist Church. Clois also joined a number of civic organizations, including Rotary and Kiwanis, where his sunny good-old-boy personality endeared him to the other members.

Nancy joined Bible Study Fellowship, and quickly became a discussion leader. Ultimately, this was one of her proudest accomplishments. Every member of the family became a Bible Study Fellowship member sometime during the 1970s. Both Nancy and Clois also volunteered with Campus Crusade for Christ. Nancy frequently included the Campus Crusade's *Four Spiritual Laws*

[1248] Preface to Section 12 of "*Boypower '76 Development Program Success Stories*," Feb 1970, Boy Scouts of American internal report, Ivan B. Stafford and Ray Neal, editors

[1249] 1969 Irving, Texas, R. L. Polk Directory, Ancestry.com City Directory Project

tract when she handed out Halloween candy. All of the family members attended Bill Gothard's Basic Youth Conflicts seminars.

With a family of seven to feed, Clois became an expert bargain hunter. Steve recalls trailing around with his Dad at stores like Treasure City and Woolco. Clois would often bring home cases of bargain soda – every can a different flavor – and the kids would delight in trying the crazy flavors. However, this also meant the kids got knockoff Christmas presents as Clois, born before modern marketing, could not really see the point of buying a name-brand toy when he could buy a cheap look-alike.

Randy would later recall his mother as a fine cook, turning out wonderful family meals despite the limited budget.

> One of my memories of my mom from growing up, as simple as it may sound, was that my mom was a wonderful cook. We never had lots of money, but she was always able to take what our Dad provided and turn that into dishes that I loved. She made wonderful dishes in her electric skillet: hot dogs in tomato sauce with chopped onions; round steak with tomatoes and onions with rice and peas. She made great casseroles: tuna casserole or pork chop casserole, and meat loaf to die for. Desserts for special occasions: cherry pie, oatmeal-chocolate chip cookies, pound cake with dates and pecans. No matter how short money was, or how crazy or difficult things were otherwise, she always saw to it that we were fed well and with love.[1250]

Three events in the early 1970s changed the family's lives.

As a result of their exposure to the structured theology both of Bible Study Fellowship and Dallas Theological Seminary, the Rainwaters had become increasingly disenchanted with the pastor of Plymouth Park Baptist Church, whom they perceived as expressing an unclear, lightweight theological position. Eventually an unrelated incident proved the tipping point that led the family to the growing Bible church movement.

The Plymouth Park board had presented for approval an extensive building plan at a Sunday evening congregational meeting, but the congregation voted against proceeding with the plan. At the next congregational meeting, a poorly-attended Wednesday evening service, those in charge used a parliamentary trick to reverse the previous vote. They asked the congregation to approve the minutes of the last meeting, having altered the minutes to reflect a positive vote at the previous meeting, which effectively approved the building plan retroactively. When Randy and Clois asked the church for copies of both sets of minutes, the request was refused. This experience, combined with the family's concern over the pastor, caused the Rainwaters to leave Plymouth Park and join Irving Bible Church.[1251]

[1250] Randy Rainwater, Thoughts on Our Mom and Dad, email, 7 Feb 2010

At almost the same point, Clois found himself in a similar position with the Boy Scouts. Now employed by the Circle Ten Council based in Irving, Texas, Clois objected to the organization's falsifying their enrollment numbers. The purpose of this membership inflation was to increase the matching funds they received from United Way and other charitable organizations. Thirty years later, the membership inflation scandal became public knowledge and an investigation was undertaken by the FBI.[1252] All of this was too late for Clois, who had been quite vocal in his opposition to these tactics. In 1972, he was fired from his position with Circle Ten.[1253]

The third event was a crisis in the marriage of close friends of the Rainwaters. Steve's recollection is that his parents received a phone call from the distressed wife, and went to her house to find her frantic about her husband's recently disclosed infidelity. Clois was deeply affected by these events and told Nancy that he felt *convicted* about his own faults as a husband. The experience provoked a mid-life crisis for Clois, and eventually the couple began to try to work through their problems together behind closed doors. Despite their discussions, Nancy became convinced that Clois had been unfaithful. She had first made this accusation in Tyler in the early 1960s. Nancy would suspect Clois of infidelity during his insurance adjusting travels, but, as far as anyone can tell, there was never any substance to it. Nancy's apparent paranoia is reminiscent of Joe McIlhaney, Sr.'s, accusations against his second wife.

These events were a sea change in the family dynamics. Prior to these events, Clois seemed to his children to be very much the head of the household. Now Nancy seemed to be the dominant half of the marriage. However much the couple tried to keep their discussions behind closed doors, the problems spilled over into the family's daily life. Nancy began regularly haranguing Clois for his perceived failings and openly speculating to the two children still living at home that their father was having an affair. Clois, who was stubborn but not confrontational, appeared to ignore her.

Frustrated by the family's financial insecurity, Nancy insisted that Clois take a job at the mall. He took a position in a shoe store, but loathed it. One day on his lunch break, he told the manager he had to water his lawn, left, and never returned.

The Rainwater's eldest son, Randy, had qualified for his real estate sales license and joined Emken Realty's commercial division in 1972.[1254] Clois, who had an insurance license from his years working for Rainwater Insurance in Vernon,

---

[1251] Linda Rainwater, who was by this time already living in her own apartment and had transferred her membership to First Baptist Church of Dallas, was not involved in these events at Plymouth Park Baptist Church.

[1252] "Boy Scouts Suspected of Inflating Rolls," Manuel Roig-Franzia, Washington Post, 29 Jan 2005, pg A1

[1253] With the 2012 release of the Boy Scouts of America's "perversion files," we have been able to determine that, thankfully, his name is not included.

[1254] "May We Introduce Emken Realty's Commercial, Land & Industrial Department," 1 Oct 1972, Irving News, Rainwater family archives

joined the George Gray Agency, an independent insurance agency, which soon became over-extended and went under.[1255] In the meantime, Clois had earned a real estate license, and joined Bud Archer Real Estate, where he remained until 1975.[1256] By 1975, Randy started Rainwater Real Estate and invited his father to go into partnership with him.

Years of working in the relatively laid-back environment of the Boy Scouts, did not outfit Clois with the skills for the highly competitive real estate business. Randy would later describe his frustration with his father's less than pro-active approach. When issues with a property arose, Clois preferred to let the problems solve themselves, which they frequently didn't. Eventually, Randy dissolved the partnership. In 1979, Clois took a class in insurance adjusting, and added the service to the renamed Rainwater Real Estate and Rainwater Adjusters.[1257]

Clois simply wasn't making enough money to make ends meet. Through one of the church or civic organizations he had joined, Clois had developed a relationship with a local banker and was able to take large signature loans with no collateral. When the Texas banking laws changed in the mid-1980s, he was deeply in debt with insufficient income.

Then financially, they caught a break. Leonard Lee, husband of Clois' sister Cristine, had found employment as a FEMA catastrophe adjuster, and suggested that Clois join him. Clois' real estate background made him a natural, and for the first time since the Boy Scouts, he seemed to find real success and work he enjoyed. The work involved frequent travel to disaster areas, and Nancy often went along. His resumes from that era mention working numerous earthquakes, hurricanes, and hail storms.

It wasn't enough. To repay the loans, Clois sold the family home in Irving in 1986. At the same time, he located a large turn-of-the-century, four-square house in the tiny Fannin County community of Honey Grove that the owner was willing to sell on a monthly payment basis with no formal mortgage. This solved their immediate housing problem, and fulfilled Clois' dream of owning a large house in a small town where the entire family could gather.

It never really worked out. They found the local Baptist church bland after so many years as members of a Bible church, and found company in only one or two of the neighbors. Now starting their own lives, the Rainwater children were rarely gathered as a group in Honey Grove, really only at holidays.[1258] Eventually, living 75 miles from Dallas left Clois and Nancy quite isolated.

[1255] "Gray Agency Celebrates With Open House," undated newspaper clipping, Rainwater family archives

[1256] Resume of Clois M. Rainwater, dated Apr 1982, original, Rainwater family archives

[1257] Resume of Clois M. Rainwater, dated 1987, original, Rainwater family archives

[1258] Up to the year of the family split, individual children, mostly the daughters, did occasionally visit on weekends, but my point here is that the happy gatherings of the entire family that Clois imagined were not a common occurrence. In the years that I attended the holiday gatherings (1987-1999), the friction among the children that made these gatherings unpleasant.

I met the Rainwaters in the late 1980s. Clois seemed to me to be a man who was running on empty, unable to carry on any sort of meaningful conversation. He seemed to ignore most of what was said to him, and his responses were often generic catch phrases like, "*Yeah, I know it.*" I have suspected in the years since that this was a harbinger of the Alzheimer's that would claim his mind. I would eventually learn from his children and relations that Clois had been a charming person in decades past, but by the time I met him, he seemed withdrawn.

Nancy seemed to me, to put it bluntly, neurotic. Every holiday was marred by some sort of drama, generally with Nancy at the center. Every member of the family was at some point accused of doing something they hadn't done. Each one of the children who wanted to marry found him or herself the target of a campaign of disinformation; the future spouses the targets of outright lies. Eventually the atmosphere at the holidays became so poisonous that Steve and I declined to attend. Randy and Linda, for reasons different from ours, made the same choice. Nancy would characterize these events as our "*breaking up the family,*" unwilling or unable to acknowledge that her own behavior had played any part.

By the late-1990s, Nancy had begun to believe that Clois was going deaf, and clearly his communication problems were getting worse. Even speaking quite loudly, it was often impossible to get an answer from Clois that matched the question. Nancy eventually told us that she had accepted that Clois had a more serious problem in 1994 when she had a lumpectomy. Clois had became disoriented in the hospital and could not understand where he was or why he had to pay the bill. But, rather than sharing this observation with her children, Nancy continued to insist that Clois was merely deaf.

Clois' decline after that point was slow but steady. He could no longer drive the two blocks to the gas station and find his way home, could not do his quarterly taxes, and certainly could not work. The couple were dependent on Social Security for their income and on the two daughters they had not alienated for emotional support.

Eventually, in July 2008, Nancy admitted to us that Clois had been diagnosed with Alzheimer's, though two of the daughters had known years earlier. The deteriorating situation had caused daughters Kelly and Vicki to arrange for Clois to be moved into the Clyde Cosper Veteran's Home in Bonham. This lasted exactly one day, after which, Nancy became so distraught by the loss of her lifelong companion that she retrieved him from the Cosper Home despite entreaties from both daughters.[1259] In 2007, Nancy and Clois informally moved in with Vicki, where they would live for over a year. Clois had developed a tendency common among individuals with Alzheimer's – a strong belief that home was somewhere else, and he needed to get there. As a result,

---

[1259] Conversation with Kelly Rainwater Kovar at Irving Hospital, Nov 2009

he required constant supervision and on a couple of occasions, he simply wandered out the front door and down the street.

He was briefly moved into an Irving assisted living facility, but the facility was not appropriate for Alzheimer's patients, and his stay lasted only a couple of months. Eventually, Nancy agreed to return Clois to the Cosper Home in Bonham where he would live for the remaining year of his life. Nancy sold the house in Honey Grove, and purchased a refurbished ranch house in Irving.

Clois broke a hip several months prior to his death, leading to the inevitable decline that often accompanies this kind of injury. He died at the Clyde Cosper Veteran's Home in Bonham, Texas, on 9 Jan 2010.

Nancy was scheduled to drive up to the funeral home with Steve on 24 Jan 2010, to retrieve Clois' ashes. An unexpected business emergency prevented Steve's driving, and it turned out that I was the only person available to make the drive. For an hour and a half, Nancy and I had the most pleasant conversation we had ever had in the 23 years of my knowing her.

Towards the end of the drive, she asked what Steve and I had discovered regarding her mother. I was surprised by the question because Nancy had previously expressed such unforgiving disapproval of Opal. I was sincerely sorry that all I could tell her was the date of Opal's death – that we had not been able to learn where she had died or was buried. Nancy seemed content to know we had tried.

We parted with a hug. It was the last time I saw her alive. Ten days later, Nancy died of an unsuspected aneurysm and was found the next day, lying on her bed.

The couple's ashes were interred on 30 Mar 2010, in the Rainwater family plot in Wilbarger Memorial Park, Lockett, Wilbarger Co., Texas.

The children of Nancy and Clois Rainwater
    William Randy Rainwater
    Linda Anne Rainwater Davis
    Vicki Lynn Rainwater Floyd
    Kelly Jane Rainwater Kovar
    Robert Steven Rainwater

    Living

Back row L>R: Randy, Linda, Vicki, Kelly
Front row L>R: Clois, Nancy, Steve
Photos from Plymouth Park Baptist Church Directory, c. 1973

They Served Their Country

Should you ever wish to join a heritage organization that requires you to prove the military record of an ancestor, these individuals have served their country in the following conflicts:

Colonial Militia
  James Rainwater
  John Rainwater

Revolutionary War
  Jeremiah Ellington
  William Tabor
  William Tribble

War of 1812
  Edward Kellum
  John Milton Weddle

Civil War / Union
  Blatchley C. W. Caughron
  Erasmus Compton
  James Calvin Kuykendall
  Josiah Rainwater

Civil War / Confederacy
  John R. Goodrich
  William W. Halbert, Sr.
  William James Gibson McIlhaney
  William Franklin Umberson

World War II
  Clois Miles Rainwater

Cause of Death

A growing number of experts recommend undertaking genealogy to discover, not how your ancestors lived, but how they died. Knowing what diseases ended the lives of ones ancestors can point to patterns that will affect their descendants. This cause of death summary was included at the request of Linda Rainwater Davis.

RAINWATER	
William Rainwater	Gangrene, from failing to have a foot amputated
Bartholomew Rainwater	Stroke
Nancy McLaughlin	Flux (severe diarrhea)
Josiah Rainwater	Cardiac dysfunction
Elizabeth J. Weddle	Bronchitis and pneumonia
Roscoe Rainwater	Hepatitis, caused by a blood transfusion during surgery
Gertrude A. Caughron	Cardiac arrest during surgery for broken jaw
Clois Rainwater	Broken hip, end stage Alzheimer's disease
Nancy J. McIlhaney	Aneurysm near the optic nerve
Adam Rexroat	Old age
Jacob Tarter	Fell off a wagon and died of the resulting injuries
Mary McDaniel Weddle	Flux (severe diarrhea)
Josiah W. Duck, Jr.	Enteritis (swelling of the small intestine, resulting in lethal dehydration)
Erasmus Compton	Cardiovascular crisis, arteriosclerosis, high blood pressure
Martha J. Duck	Apoplexy (cerebral hemorrhage or stroke)
T. W. Caughron	Heart failure and cardiac insufficiency, in his sleep; possible Alzheimer's disease
Arzona Compton	Thrombosis of the femoral artery and arteriosclerosis; was diabetic

McILHANEY	
James W. McIlhaney	Drowned in rain-swollen creek
John R. McIlhaney	Hepatitis, related to a gall bladder operation
Ollie D. Umberson	Arteriosclerosis, heart disease and senility
Martha A. Conley	Paralysis of the right side (stroke)
Elizabeth Kellum	Senility, epilepsy
John R. Richardson	Infection of the spine, war injuries
Fulton M. Goodrich	Metastatic carcinoma and severe malnutrition
Callie Kuykendall	Pellegra
Joseph Singleton	Aggravated quinsy (tonsillitis)
Mary J. Singleton	Stroke and paralysis
Emeline Grindle	1918 influenza epidemic & extreme old age
William W. Halbert, Sr.	Pneumonia
Mary E. Smith	Influenza and breast cancer
Levi T. Halbert, Sr.	Bronchial pneumonia
Mary Ann Armstrong	Acute myocardial infarction (heart attack)
Joe S. McIlhaney	Pneumonia and respiratory arrest
Io Halbert	Congestive heart failure, dementia, atrial fibrillation

The Family Bible of William and Martha Rainwater

Gift of Frances Aderholt Smith
The current owner of the original is unknown.

> William Howard Rainwater Sone of Dito was Borne June the 17: 1813
>
> Susannah Rainwater Daughter Borne Septembr the 28" 1815 —
>
> Miles Rainwater sone of Dito May the 15 Day 1818
>
> Elisabeth Rainwater was born October the 1
>
> Patsey Rainwater daughter of dito was born March 15" 1823

Bible of William & Patsy Rainwater

Lydda Rainwater Daughter of William Rainwater and Patty his wife was borned May the 8D 1802

Burtholomew Rainwater Son of Ditto was Borned the 28 of Janunary 1804

James Rainwater Son of Ditto was Borned the 9 of February 1806

Abraham Rainwater Son of Ditto was Borned the 3 of April 1808

John Rainwater and Nancy Rainwater Son and Daughter of Ditto was Borned March the 5 1810

Bible of William & Patsy Rainwater

The Family Bible of Bartholomew and Nancy Rainwater

Included by Roscoe Rainwater in "*Here's the Plan of the Rainwater Clan*"
The current owner of the original is unknown.

Bartholomew Rainwater his Holy B[ible]

FAMILY RECORD.

Births.

Bartholomew Rainwater was born January the 20 day 1804 – Died June 25 1889

Nancy McLaughlin was born August the 2 day – 1807 – died Jan 20 1889

Births

Anne Rainwater Daughter of Bartholomew and Nancy Rainwater was born April the 18 day of 1826 –

Emily Rainwater was born May the 17 day 1827 on Thursday

Daniel M. Rainwater was born November the 10 day 1828 on Monday

Samantha Jane Rainwater was born January the 19 1830

Sally Rainwater was born February the 16 day 1832 on Thursday

June the 17, 1840

FAMILY RECORD.

BIRTHS.

Susannah Rainwater was born February the 12 day 1834 — on Tuesday

Two girls Born and Deceased March the 15 day 1835

Milo Rainwater was Born April the 5 day 1836 — on Friday

Polly Rainwater was born December the 28 day 1837

Ciota Rainwater was born December the 28 day 1839

Zarelda ann Rainwater was Born December 5 day on Sunday 1841

Josiah W. W. Rainwater was born October 18 day 1843 on Wednesday

Galen E. Weddle was Borned May the 10 1829

G. E. Weddle married to Sally Rainwater July the 6 = 1847

Lucy Isadore Holbrook was born March 5 1860

Francis M. Holbrook was born July 14 1861

Nancy Belle Holbrook was born May 1st 1863

FAMILY RECORD.

MARRIAGES.

Bartholomew Rainwater was married To Nancy McLaughlin February 24th day 1825

Alexandria Eastham & Emily Rainwater was Married Sept. the first day 1844

Daniel Weddle and Anne Rainwater was Married July the 26 day 1846

Daniel W[?] [?] married [?] the 14 day December 1848

MARRIAGES.

[?]alex [?] was married [?] Sally [?]ain[water] July the 6 day 18[?]

Thomas D. [Hay?] was married to Susannah Rainwater January the 16 day 185[?]

[?]rachia Chumn[?] [?] [?] [?] [?] [?] [?] [?] [?] 185[?]

J. W. Rainwater Elisoveir [?] Weddle Married January 11th

FAMILY RECORD.

BIRTHS.

John Perry Chumney was born January the 10 day 1860

Jams M Chumbly was Born May 7th 1862

Miles R Chumbly was Born 27 March 1864

George A Chumbly was born Dec 2 1866

Nancy Jane Chumbly was Born Sep. 17- 1869

Bartholonew Chumbly was born Apr 5th 1872

Robert Chumbly was born January 12th 1885

Margaret Ann Chumbly was born march 27 1877

Lewis Milton Chumbly was born July 8th 1879

[illegible] Chum[illegible]
[illegible] June 19 1883
[illegible] Chumbly [illegible]
[illegible] November 3rd 1886

DEATHS.

[illegible] Eastham departed this life 65 [illegible] the 4th day 1859

Polly Holbrook daughter of Bartholomew & Nancy Rainwater departed this life in Linn county Kansas, Janiy 20th 1865 — aged 24 years 4 months

[illegible]
[illegible] 1883 —
[illegible]

Bart[holomew] [illegible]
departed this life Ju[ly]
28. 1889. aged 85 [years]
5 months & 8 d[ays]

Bartholomew & Nancy Rainwater Bible

Daniel Weddle was born March
the 14th day 1817
Anne Weddle his wife was born
April 15th day 1826
Wm. N. Weddle was born June
the 10th day 1840
Daniel G. Weddle was born April
the 10, 1842
Nancy Jane Weddle was born
May 31st day 1844
Francis Marion Weddle was born
June 12th 1847
Joseph Milton Weddle was born
Oct. 25th 1848
Sarah Elen Weddle was born
February 24 day 1850
John Perry Weddle was born
February the 6th day 1852
James Madison Weddle was born
January 12th day 1854
Millard Fillmore Weddle was born
July the 3rd day 1856
Bartholomew Franklin Weddle
was born November 18th day 1857

25

Bartholomew & Nancy Rainwater Bible

1 Martha O. Weddle was Borned October the 6th 1848.

2 Mary Jane Weddle was Borned May the 27th 1850

3 George H M D Weddle was Borned December the 14th 1853

4 Miles R Weddle was Borned Aprile the 4th 1855

Emily C. Weddle was Borned December the 10th 1856

6 Daniel F. Weddle was Borned April the 20th 1859

7 F. B. Weddle was Borned Sept the 17th 1861

Senetta Bell Weddle was Borned November 18th 1863

Madison Weddle was Born April 1867

S E. Weddle

1. Elisabeth M Eastham was Born July the 25th day 1845
2. Polly ann S Eastham was Born July the 8th day 1847
3. Zachary Taylor Eastham was Born December the 15th day 1848
4. Nancy J Eastham was Born May the 9th day 1850
5. Obediah Eastham was Born September the 10 day 1851
6. Lucinda Frances Eastham was Born November 27 day 1852
7. Susannah Eastham was Born October the 2nd day 1854
8. John Foster Eastham was Born July the 5th day 1857
9. Talitha Isabel Eastham was Born February the 6th day 1859

The Family Bible of Josiah and Elizabeth Jane Rainwater

Included by Roscoe Rainwater in *"Here's the Plan of the Rainwater Clan"*. The current owner of the original is unknown.

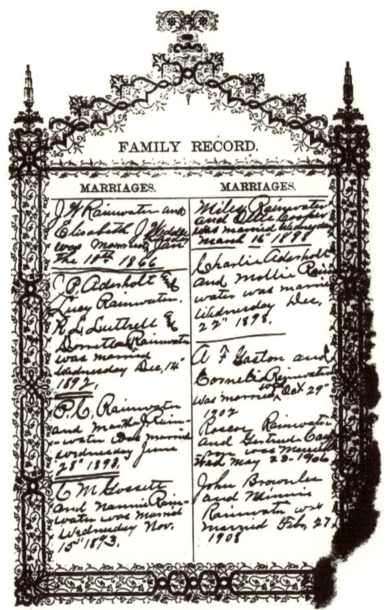

Josiah & Elizabeth Jane Rainwater Bible

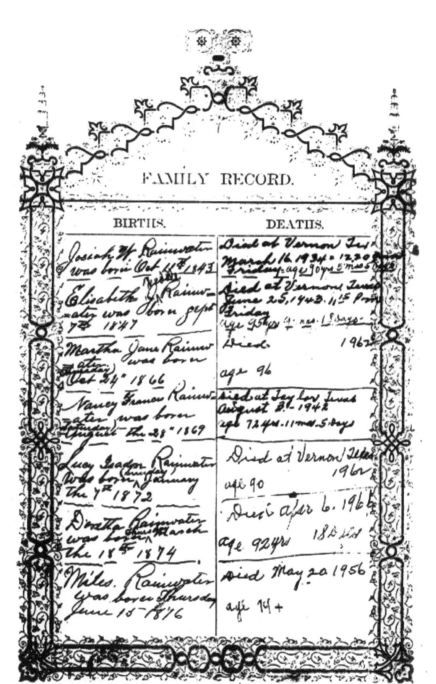

Josiah & Elizabeth Jane Rainwater Bible

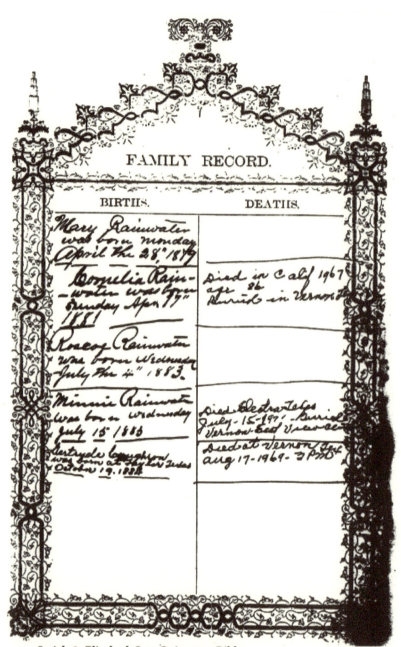

Josiah & Elizabeth Jane Rainwater Bible

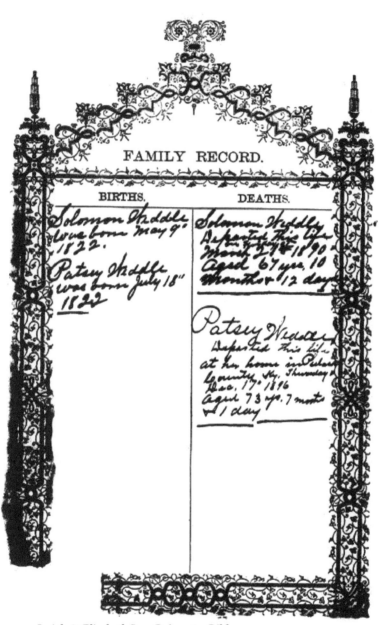

Josiah & Elizabeth Jane Rainwater Bible

The Family Bible of John P. and Lucy Rainwater Aderholt

Gift of Polly Thorne Flory
In December 2007, Polly Thorne Flory noticed this Bible at an estate sale, purchased it and donated it to the *The Rainwater Collection*.

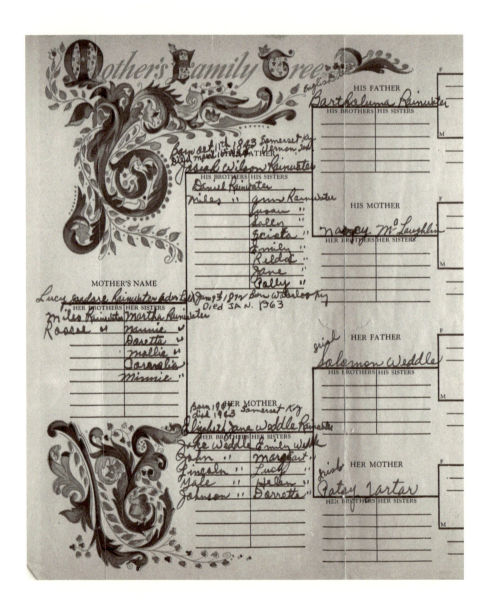

Father's Family Tree

FATHER'S NAME
John Pink Aderholt
Born 1870 Springville Ala
Died 1946 Wedmon Tex.

HIS BROTHERS: Fletcher Aderholt, Adam ", Forrest ", Charlie ", Bud ", Porter "
HIS SISTERS: Annie, Emma, Florence, Nellie

HIS FATHER
Emanuel Aderholt
Born 1846 Oct 9th St Clair Co Ala.
Died July 3

HIS BROTHERS: Bob Aderholt, Dave ", John "

HIS MOTHER
Saphronia E. Jones
Born Dec 17th 1854
Died St Clair Co

Letter from Josiah W. Rainwater to Miles Rainwater, 1889

Original owned by Mark Sanborn

from uncle Jos keep this

Waterloo Ky.
July 9" 1889,

Miles Rainwater
  Mehama Oregon
Dear brother!—

You have no doubt before this have noticed in the Republican of the sickness and death of father, He was stricken down on the night of the 20" of June and continued to get worse until he died, he was unconscious almost all the time from the first stroke He made but very little complaint, the greater part of the time appeared to be entirely easy,

He went to sleep about 5 oclock om on Wednes- and could not be aroused any more, he apparently slept natural and easy from the time mentioned up to friday, June 28 at 10 Oclock a,m, when he breathed his last, without a struggle,

Every thing was done for him that could be done, but human power could not save him Will write you more soon, we are all in moderate health. Hope this will find you all well, write soon

Yours &c
J W Rainwater

Letter from John Levi Elder to Josiah W. Rainwater, 1876

Original owned by Steve and Susan Rainwater

P.1

August 6. 1876

dear brother & family i sete my self this morning to inform you that we are all well and harty and i hope these few lines may reach yo and find yo all well yo must excuse me for not writing soon i expect yo thought i was ded but it is a grand miss the sir i am helthier than i ever was in my life and sciota has ben tolerbly good and all of the children i mean all 7 of them times is vary hard her about money but we hav corn and wheat plenty but no money corn worth 20 cts per bushel wheat worth 60 cts bushel bacon 14 cts lbs calico u to 5 cts per yard
i left hold co last fall and moved to Johnson Co Kansas rite on the line between Kansas and Missouri rite at the corner of cass Co me just 18 miles dew south from Kans citty

p-2

a good wattered country and as helthy a cauntry as yu ever saw i no it is a heap helthier than kentuckey i liv on the black bob reserve so cald it belongs to some indens that never gave up ther land tell her of late and the people think it will come in in the corse of twelve months this land is ritch and yu can buy a claim her from 300 to 500 dollars 160 acres. men that has got pore land and stock would do well to turn it all in to stock and come out her and buy nerly all of the connection lives her that lived in holt i live on what is cald the lige blew river it is a nice little streeme and i can ketch fish when i pease and that is pretty often i rented a farm from an old man from verginna he lives with us no boddy of his family but him self in. this country and he wants me to still remain on his farm

P-3

i gave him the third of what
i make and his land lais rite in
the blew bottom and and just as
rich as can bee old corn is only worth 20 cts
per bushel and we hav got fine
crops her and yo may no that corn
will be cheepe we hav had a heap of
rain her this summer i lost all of my
crop last yer on the acount of the
grasshoppers   before it got ripe
it frosed and all shoit and i
lost it all and they eat all of my
wheat up but i hav got fine corn
this year

the 2 day of september 1875
my mother died she was well and harty
as common eate her super and went
to bed and a bout 10 oclock she cald me
and it seamed as tho she could not get
her breth good and in 30 minuits
she was a corps just seemed as though
she went of to sleep she was burried in

P. 4

the semetry in oregon holt Co
i still live in th christian
church and am trying to live the
christian life and i want usall to live
so for we shal soon all pass a way
and if we are prepard to dye we will
all meete again whar we can enjoy each
others society in piece So fare well for
a while but we will meat again
gave my best respects to all enquireing
friends if any rite soon and fail not
So i must close
                John L. Elder and family
to D. W. rainwater and family
father and mother all so

        direct your letters
to belton cass Co missouri

Belton Cass Co Mo

Register Report: Descendants of William Rainwater

The following is a summary of four generations of the descendants of William Rainwater and Martha "Patsy" Hodges. This information presented in the register report style, which is a standard genealogical format developed by the New England Historical and Genealogical Society in 1870.

First Generation

1. William Rainwater. Son of James Rainwater Sr. Born between 1765/1775 in North Carolina. Died 1825 in Faubush, Pulaski Co, KY. Buried in Rainwater Cemetery, Pulaski Co., KY.

He married **Martha "Patsy" Hodges**, daughter of Bartholomew Hodges & Elizabeth, c. 1802 in Surry Co., NC. Born c. 1785 in Surry Co., NC. Died between 1841/1850 in Pulaski Co., KY. Buried in Rainwater Cemetery, Pulaski Co., KY.

They had the following children:

	i.	Lydia Rainwater (never married); 8 May 1802 in NC. Died after 1880 in MN.
2	ii.	Bartholomew Rainwater
3	iii.	James Rainwater
4	iv.	Abraham Rainwater
5	v.	John R. Rainwater (twin)
6	vi.	Nancy Rainwater (twin)
7	vii.	William Howard Rainwater Sr.
	viii.	Susanna Rainwater (never married); 28 Sep 1815 -14 Apr 1858 in Pulaski Co., KY.
8	ix.	Miles Rainwater
9	x.	Elizabeth Rainwater
10	xi.	Martha Rainwater (twin)
	xii.	infant Rainwater, Born & died 15 Mar 1823 in Pulaski Co., KY.

Second Generation

2. Bartholomew Rainwater. Son of William Rainwater & Martha "Patsy" Hodges. Born 20 Jan 1804 in North Carolina. Died 28 Jun 1889 in Waterloo, Pulaski County, KY. Buried in Rainwater Cemetery, Pulaski Co., KY.

He married **Nancy McLaughlin**, daughter of Jane & Daniel McLaughlin, 24 Feb 1825 in Adair Co., KY. Born 20 Aug 1807 in Russell Co., KY. Died 20 Jan 1883 in Pulaski Co., KY. Buried in Rainwater Cemetery, Pulaski Co., KY.

They had the following children:

11	i.	Anne Rainwater
12	ii.	Emily Rainwater
13	iii.	Daniel McDaniel Rainwater

	iv.	Samantha Jane Rainwater (never married); 19 Jan 1830 - after 1860, Pulaski Co., KY
14	v.	Sarah Rainwater
15	vi.	Susannah Rainwater
	vii.	infant twins Rainwater (died at birth), Born & died 13 Mar 1835 in Pulaski Co., KY
16	viii.	Miles Rainwater
17	ix.	Mary Rainwater
18	x.	Sciota Bethene Rainwater
19	xi.	Sarelda Ann Rainwater
20	xii.	Josiah Wilson Rainwater
	xiii.	infant Rainwater (died at birth), Born & died 7 Nov 1853 in Pulaski Co., KY

3. James Rainwater. Son of William Rainwater & Martha "Patsy" Hodges. Born 8 Feb 1806 in North Carolina. Died c. 1862 in Pulaski Co., KY.

He married **Mary McDaniel**, daughter of William McDaniel & Elizabeth Weaver, 19 Apr 1826 in Pulaski Co., KY. Born Before 1810 in KY. Died 9 Dec 1880 in Pulaski Co. KY.

They had the following children:

21	i.	Elizabeth W. Rainwater
22	ii.	William H. Rainwater
	iii.	Martha Rainwater; Born c. 1833 in KY. Died between 1850/1860 in KY.
23	iv.	Enoch Rainwater
24	v.	John Rainwater
	vi.	Mary Rainwater (never married); Born 14 Feb 1842 in KY. Died 2 Aug 1918 in KY.
25	vii.	Sarah Rainwater
26	viii.	Amanda C. Rainwater
27	ix.	Samantha Rainwater
28	x.	Alethia Rainwater

4. Abraham Rainwater. Son of William Rainwater & Martha "Patsy" Hodges. Born 3 Apr 1808 in North Carolina. Died c. 1875 in Brown Co., IN.

He married **Anna McLaughlin**, daughter of Jane & Daniel McLaughlin, 16 Apr 1829 in Russell Co., KY. Born c. 1810 in North Carolina. Died c. 1875 in Brown Co., IN.

They had the following children:

29	i.	Jeremiah Stanton Rainwater
	ii.	Joycia Rainwater; Born c. 1832 in KY. Married Louis R. Lemon, 8 Aug 1867 in Lawrence Co., IN
30	iii.	Ephraim R. Rainwater

31	iv.	Ira Hardin Rainwater	
32	v.	Sarah Ann Rainwater	
	vi.	Abram Rainwater (never married); Born c. 1845 in KY. Died after Jun 1865	
	vii.	Nancy Elizabeth Rainwater; Born c. 1847 in Kentucky.	
	viii.	Susan Rainwater; Born Jan 1850 in Kentucky. Died Before 1860.	

5. John R. Rainwater. Son of William Rainwater & Martha "Patsy" Hodges. Born 5 Mar 1810 in Surry Co., NC. Died 1889 in Casey Co., KY. Buried in Grave Hill, Mintonville, Casey Co., KY.

He married **Elizabeth Lawless**, daughter of Frances & James Lawless, 2 Dec 1837 in Pulaski Co., KY. Born c. 1817 in North Carolina. Died Aug 1860 in Pulaski Co., KY. Buried in Cedar Point Cemetery, Pulaski Co., KY.

They had the following children:

33	i.	Nancy Rainwater	
34	ii.	Giles R. Rainwater	
	iii.	Squire Mitchell Rainwater; Born c. 1843 in KY. Died 10 Sep 1852 in KY.	
35	iv.	George Alfred Rainwater	
36	v.	Susannah Rainwater	
	vi.	Mary Rainwater; Born & died in 1852 in KY.	

6. Nancy Rainwater. Daughter of William Rainwater & Martha "Patsy" Hodges. Born 5 Mar 1810 in Surry Co., NC. Died 10 Aug 1891 in Fulton Co., IL.

She married **William Merritt Roy** , son of Thomas Roy & Mary Phipps, 22 Feb 1834 in Pulaski Co. KY. Born c. 1814 in NC. Died 27 Aug 1889 in Fulton Co., IL.

They had the following children:

37	i.	Melissa Roy	
	ii.	Clarissa Roy (Oaks); Born c. 1837 in Lawrence Co., IN.	
	iii.	Martha Roy; Born c. 1839 in Indiana.	
	iv.	Thomas J. Roy; Born c. 1841 in Indiana.	
38	v.	Elizabeth Roy	
39	vi.	John Roy	
40	vii.	Ralph N. Roy	
	viii.	Nancy Jane Roy (Bowers); Born Mar 1850 in Lawrence Co., IN.	
	ix.	William P. Roy; Born c. 1852 in Indiana.	
	x.	Miranda Roy (Carlton) (twin); Born c. 1855 in Lawrence Co., IN.	
	xi.	Amanda Roy (Orendorff) (twin); Born c. 1855 in Indiana.	

7. William Howard Rainwater Sr. Son of William Rainwater & Martha "Patsy" Hodges. Born 17 Jun 1813 in Pulaski Co., KY. Died c. 1889 in Brown Co., IN.

He first married **Nancy Ann Hodge**, 2 Oct 1831 in Casey Co., KY. Born Before 1815. Died After 1837. They were divorced 13 Jan 1837.

They had the following children:

| | | i. | James B. Rainwater (never married); Born 21 Jul 1832 in KY. Died Between 1850/1860. |

He second married **Minerva Ann Rayborn**, daughter of John Rayborn & Margaret Rayborn or Rainwater, 4 May 1838 in Pulaski Co., KY. Born c. 1813 in Pulaski Co., KY. Died After 1895 in Brown Co., IN.

They had the following children:

41	i.	Martha Rainwater
42	ii.	John Raleigh Rainwater
43	iii.	Miles Rainwater
	iv.	Mary D. Rainwater; Born 11 Sep 1845 in Pulaski Co., KY. Died in Oklahoma City, OK. Married Wallace N. Markwell, son of John W. Markwell & Sarah, 11 Feb 1869 in Brown Co., IN.
	v.	Sarah Rainwater; Born 25 Oct 1847 in Co., KY. Died Jul 1852 in KY.
44	vi.	William Howard Rainwater Jr.
45	vii.	Matthew F. Rainwater
46	viii.	Mark Rainwater
	ix.	Luke Rainwater; Born 7 May 1858 in Pulaski Co., KY. Died between 1891/1900 Arkansas. He married Mary Ann Legan, 13 Feb 1888 in Brown Co., IN. They were divorced 1891.
47	x.	George Washington Rainwater

8. Miles Rainwater. Son of William Rainwater & Martha "Patsy" Hodges. Born 15 May 1818 in Faubush, Pulaski Co., KY. Died 9 Jan 1884 in Pulaski Co., KY. Buried in Rainwater Family Cemetery, Pulaski Co., KY.

He married **Frances Chaney**, daughter of Hiram Chaney & Mary Ellen Wetter, 29 Jul 1843 in Pulaski Co., KY. Born 27 Mar 1823 in Pulaski Co., KY. Died 26 Dec 1911 in Waterloo, Pulaski Co., KY. Buried 28 Dec 1911 in Rainwater Family Cemetery, Pulaski Co., KY.

They had the following children:

	i.	Silas Rainwater (never married); Born c. 1844 in Pulaski Co., KY. Died 20 Sep 1863 in Battle of Chickamauga Creek, TN
48	ii.	Terrell Rainwater
49	iii.	David Rainwater

	iv.	Erasmus M. Rainwater (never married); Born c. 1850 in KY. Died After 1884 in South Dakota.
50	v.	Mary Elizabeth Rainwater
51	vi.	Fountain Rainwater
	vii.	infant Rainwater (died at birth); Born & died 11 Dec 1855 in Pulaski Co., KY.
52	viii.	Frances Jane Rainwater
	ix.	Coatney Ellen Rainwater; Born 10 Sep 1859 in Pulaski Co., KY. Died 12 Sep 1888 in Pulaski Co., KY. She married John R. Haney, 6 Feb 1881 in Pulaski Co., KY.
53	x.	Sarah Ann Rainwater
54	xi.	James Rainwater

9. Elizabeth Rainwater. Daughter of William Rainwater & Martha "Patsy" Hodges. Born 1 Oct 1819/1822 in Pulaski Co. KY. Died After 1880 in Faribault Co., MN. Buried in Loveall family farm, Faribault Co., MN.

She first married **Isaac Roberts**, 24 Nov 1843 in Pulaski Co. KY. Born Before 1827 in North Carolina. Died between 1850/1854 in Indiana.

They had the following children:

i.	William H. Roberts; Born c 1844 in Indiana.
ii.	Abraham M. Roberts; Born c. 1847 in Indiana.
iii.	Drury W. Roberts; Born c. 1849 in Indiana.

She second married **Zachariah Loveall Sr.**, 15 Oct 1854 in Bedford, Lawrence Co., IN. Born c. 1812 in Kentucky. Died after 1880 in Faribault Co., MN. Buried in Loveall family farm, Faribault Co., MN.

They had the following children:

i.	Miles Loveall; Born 18 Sep 1856 in Indiana.
	He married Hattie Carttick, Jul 1887.
ii.	Kelsey Loveall; Born 22 Apr 1857 in Indiana.
	He first married Clara Smith.
	He second married Mattie Seymore.
iII.	Zachariah Asa Loveall Jr.; Born 22 Nov 1859 in Indiana.
	He married Jessie Carttick.

10. Martha Rainwater. Daughter of William Rainwater & Martha "Patsy" Hodges. Born 15 Mar 1823 in Pulaski Co., KY. Died Before 1859.

She married **Tilman Devenport**, 14 Dec 1841 in Pulaski Co. KY. Born c. 1815 in Kentucky. Died Before 1870.

They had the following children:

i.	Henry Devenport; Born c. 1842 in Kentucky.
ii.	Perry A. Devenport; Born c. 1844 in Kentucky.
iii.	John A. Devenport; Born c. 1846 in Kentucky.

	iv.	Thomas Devenport; Born c. 1849 in Kentucky.
	v.	Martha A. Devenport; Born c. 1856 in Greene Co., IL.
	vi.	Lycaonia Devenport; Born c. 1858 in Greene Co., IL.

Third Generation

11. Anne Rainwater. Daughter of Bartholomew Rainwater & Nancy McLaughlin. Born 15 Apr 1826 in Pulaski Co., KY. Died between 1890/1900 in Pulaski Co., KY.

She married **Daniel S. Weddle**, son of John Milton Weddle Sr. & Mary McDaniel, 26 Jul 1846 in Pulaski Co., KY. Born 14 Mar 1817 in Pulaski Co., KY. Died 17 Sep 1885 in Pulaski Co. KY. Buried in Cedar Point Cemetery, Pulaski Co., KY.

They had the following children:

55	i.	Francis Marion Weddle
	ii.	Joseph Milton Weddle; Born 5 Oct 1848 in Kentucky.
	iii.	Sarah Ellen Weddle; Born 24 Feb 1850 in Kentucky.
56	iv.	John Perry Weddle
	v.	James Madison Weddle; Born 12 Jan 1854 in Pulaski Co., KY. Died 24 Mar 1919 in Kentucky.
	vi.	Millard Filmore Weddle; Born 3 Jul 1856 in Kentucky. Died 22 Aug 1873 in Kentucky.
57	vii.	Bartholomew Franklin Weddle
58	viii.	Lincoln Weddle
59	ix.	Josiah Weddle
	x.	Debby Weddle; Born c. 1864 in Pulaski Co. KY.
		She married John S. Pitman, 17 Aug 1879 in Pulaski Co. KY. Born c. 1861 in Pulaski Co., KY.
60	xi.	Spencer Grant Weddle
	xii.	Mary Ann Weddle; Born 18 Mar 1869 in Pulaski Co., KY.
		She married Aaron Jasper Roy, son of Isaac N. Roy & Elzira Combest, 3 Nov 1890 in Pulaski Co., KY. Born c. 1864 in Pulaski Co. KY.

12. Emily Rainwater. Daughter of Bartholomew Rainwater & Nancy McLaughlin. Born 17 May 1827 in Pulaski Co., KY. Died 1914 in Danville, Boyle Co., KY.

She first married **Alexander Eastham**, son of John Eastham & Mary Denham, 1 Sep 1844 in Pulaski Co., KY. Born 1819 in Kentucky. Died 4 Dec 1859 in Pulaski Co. KY.

They had the following children:

61	i.	Elizabeth Martha Eastham
	ii.	Mary A. Eastham; Born 8 May 1847 in Pulaski Co., KY.
62	iii.	Zachary Taylor Eastham
63	iv.	Nancy P. Eastham
64	v.	Obediah James Eastham

	vi.	Lucinda Eastham; Born 27 Nov 1852 in Pulaski Co., KY.
65	vii.	Susannah Eastham
	viii.	John F. Eastham; Born 10 Sep 1857 in Pulaski Co., KY.
	ix.	Talitha I. Eastham; Born 6 Feb 1859 in Pulaski Co., KY.

She second married **Zachariah Eastham**, son of John Eastham & Mary Denham, 17 Jul 1877 in Pulaski Co. KY. Born Jul 1818 in Pulaski Co., KY. Died After 1900 in Kentucky. They were divorced before 1883.

13. Daniel McDaniel Rainwater. Son of Bartholomew Rainwater & Nancy McLaughlin. Born 10 Nov 1828 in Pulaski Co., KY. Died between 1909/1910 in Pulaski Co., KY. Buried in New Hope Cemetery, Pulaski Co., KY.

He married **Ann Whitaker**, 14 Dec 1848 in Pulaski Co., KY. Born 22 Mar 1829 in Wayne Co., KY. Died 28 Aug 1898 in Pulaski Co., KY. Buried in New Hope Cemetery, Pulaski Co., KY.

They had the following children:

66	i.	Milford Enoch Rainwater
	ii.	Polly Jane Rainwater; Born c. 1851 in Kentucky.
		She married Leon Woolridge, 4 Dec 1870 in Pulaski Co. KY. Born c. 1841 in Russell Co., KY.
	iii.	Sarah E. Rainwater; Born 27 Aug 1853 in Pulaski Co., KY. Died 16 Dec 1919.
		She married Eli Barnes, 23 Jul 1899 in Pulaski Co., KY. Born 22 Mar 1848 in Pulaski Co., KY. Died 3 Jan 1928 in Pulaski Co., KY.
67	iv.	Lucy Ann Rainwater
	v.	Mary Elizabeth Rainwater; Born & died between 1859/1860.
68	vi.	Anderson Warren Rainwater
69	vii.	Bartholomew Rainwater
70	viii.	Francis M. Rainwater
71	ix.	Palmira Marie Rainwater (twin)
	x.	Elzaria Rainwater (twin); Born Jan 1871 in KY. Died 2 Jun 1941 in Pulaski Co. KY.
		She married Wesley R. Huff, 14 Oct 1894 in Pulaski Co., KY. Born c. 1871 in Wayne Co., KY.
	xi.	Terrell Rainwater; Born c. 1878 in Kentucky.

14. Sarah Rainwater. Daughter of Bartholomew Rainwater & Nancy McLaughlin. Born 16 Feb 1832 in Pulaski Co., KY. Died 3 Apr 1906 in Monroe Co., IN. Buried in Pleasant View Baptist Cemetery, Monroe Co., IN.

She married **Galen Edward Weddle**, son of John Milton Weddle Sr. & Mary McDaniel, 6 Jul 1847 in Pulaski Co., KY. Born 10 May 1829 in Kentucky. Died 25 Feb 1914 in Martinsville, Morgan Co., IN. Buried in Pleasant View Cemetery Monroe Co., IN.

They had the following children:

    i.   Martha Ellen Weddle; Born 6 Oct 1848 in KY. Died between 1850/1860 in KY.

    ii.   Mary Jane Weddle; Born 27 May 1850 in Kentucky.

    iii.   George Marion Weddle; Born 14 Dec 1852 in Pulaski Co. KY. Died 22 Feb 1938 in Martinville, IN. He first married Mollie Ferrand, 5 Dec 1876 in. Born 23 Feb 1857. Died 5 Aug 1879.

        He second married Ida Ellen Shively, 6 Apr 1888 in. Born 22 Oct 1872 in Kentucky. Died 24 Jan 1940.

    iv.   Miles Rainwater Weddle; Born 4 Apr 1855 in Pulaski Co., KY.

        Died 5 Feb 1905 in Monroe Co, IN.

    v.   Emily Evelyn Weddle; Born 10 Dec 1856 in Pulaski Co., KY. Died 1926 in Morgan Co., IN.

        She married James Henry Owen.

    vi.   Daniel Francis Weddle; Born 20 Apr 1859 in Pulaski Co., KY.

72   vii.   Thomas Bramletter Weddle

    viii.   Jenette Belle Weddle; Born 18 Nov 1863 in KY. Died 30 May 1898.

        She married David Taylor.

    ix.   James Madison Weddle; Born Apr 1867 in Kentucky. Died 21 Jan 1941 in Indiana.

    x.   Sciota A. Weddle; Born May 1870 in Casey Co., KY.

    xi.   Cornelia Weddle; Born c. 1871 in Kentucky.

    xii.   Willard A. Weddle; Born c. 1874 in Indiana.

    xiii.   Leora Weddle; Born c. 1876 in Indiana.

    xiv.   Henry Clay Weddle; Born Jun 1879 in Indiana. Died 11 Nov 1911.

15. Susannah Rainwater. Daughter of Bartholomew Rainwater & Nancy McLaughlin. Born 12 Feb 1834 in Kentucky. Died 29 Apr 1912 in Casey Co., KY. Buried in Cedar Point Cemetery, Pulaski Co., KY.

She first married **Thomas D. Hainey**, son of Martha (Hainey) , 16 Jan 1856 in Pulaski Co., KY. Born before 1840. Died before Aug 1870.

They had the following children:

    i.   Martha H. Hainey; Born c. 1857 in Kentucky.

73   ii.   Daniel M. Hainey

    iii.   Josiah E. Hainey; Born c. 1862 in Kentucky. Died c. 1940 in Mintonville, KY.

She second married **William Pitman Sr.**, 23 Feb 1871 in Pulaski Co., KY. Born c. 1822. Died 10 Sep 1893 in Pulaski Co. KY.

They had the following children:

74	i.	Silas Green Pitman (born prior to marriage)
	ii.	Julia Pitman; Born c. 1872 in Kentucky.
75	iii.	Enoch Pitman
76	iv.	Charles H. Pitman

16. Miles Rainwater. Son of Bartholomew Rainwater & Nancy McLaughlin. Born 7 Apr 1836 in Pulaski Co., KY. Died 22 Dec 1914 in Ontario, San Bernardino, CA. Buried 23 Dec 1914 in Bellview Cemetery, Ontario, San Bernardino Co., CA.

He married **Cornelia Ellen Sawyer**, daughter of John Sawyer & Mary A. Brown, 13 Aug 1865 in Centerville, Linn Co., KS. Born 28 Jun 1848 in Farmer, Defiance Co., OH. Died 6 Mar 1922 in Upland, San Bernardino, CA. Buried 11 Mar 1922 in Bellview Cemetery, Ontario, San Bernardino Co., CA.

They had the following children:

	i.	Mary Ellen Rainwater (never married); Born 23 Nov 1866 in KS. Died 5 Jun 1886 in Linn Co., OR.
	ii.	Josephine W. Rainwater (never married); Born 16 Aug 1883 in Linn Co., OR. Died 8 Oct 1908 in San Bernardino Co., CA.

17. Mary Rainwater. Daughter of Bartholomew Rainwater & Nancy McLaughlin. Born 20 Dec 1837 in Pulaski Co., KY. Died 20 Jan 1865 in Mound City, Linn Co., Kansas. Buried in Wesley Chapel Cemetery, Bradley, Linn Co., KS.

She married **Alfred Joseph Holbrook**, 31 May 1859 in Linn Co., KS. Born c. 1826 in Massachusetts. Died 19 Jun 1908 in Lyons, Linn Co., OR.

They had the following children:

77	i.	Lucy Isadore Holbrook
	ii.	Francis Marion Holbrook; Born 14 Jul 1861 in Kansas.
		He married Cora Waymire, 20 Jun 1886 in Mound City, Linn Co., KS. Born Feb 1870 in Tipton Co., IN.
	iii.	Nancy Belle Holbrook; Born 1 May 1863 in Kansas.
		She married James Miles, Dec 1880 in Linn Co., KS.

18. Sciota Bethene Rainwater. Daughter of Bartholomew Rainwater & Nancy McLaughlin. Born 26 Dec 1839 in Pulaski Co., KY. Died 7 Jun 1908 in Oregon, Holt Co., MO. Buried in Maple Grove Cemetery, Holt Co., MO.

She married **John Levi Elder**, son of Mary Ellen and Jesse P. Elder, 24 Feb 1859 in Pulaski Co., KY. Born 4 Dec 1837 in Pulaski Co. KY. Died 17 Aug 1905 in Oregon, Holt Co., MO. Buried in Maple Grove Cemetery, Holt Co., MO.

They had the following children:

78	i.	Nancy Belle Elder
	ii.	Mary Jane Elder; Born 4 Nov 1861 in Pulaski Co., KY. Died 16 Aug 1937 in Creston, IA.

	iii.	Sarah F. Elder; Born 8 Nov 1863 in Pulaski Co. KY. She married Seth Judd, 18 Aug 1883 in Holt Co., MO.
	iv.	Amanda Emaline Elder; Born 7 Nov 1865 in Pulaski Co. KY. Died 16 Apr 1925 in Holt Co., MO. She married John Lane, 10 Aug 1887 in Holt Co., MO.
79	v.	Cornelia Ellen Elder
80	vi.	James Riley Elder
	vii.	David Allen Elder; Born 6 Nov 1872 in Holt Co., MO. Died 22 Apr 1928 in Oregon, Holt Co., MO
	viii.	Sabrina Alice Elder; Born 13 Mar 1875 in Missouri. She married Richard D. Sipes, 3 Oct 1893.
	ix.	Infant Elder; Born 20 Jan 1878. Died 1878/
	x.	Jesse Levi Elder; Born 18 Jan 1879 in Johnson Co., KS. Died 29 Mar 1945 in Holt Co., MO. He married Elassie Chance.
	xi.	Dora Myrtle Elder; Born 1 Dec 1883 in Missouri or Kansas. Died in Oregon, Holt Co., MO. She married William M. McDermott, 3 Jul 1904 in Holt Co., MO.

19. Sarelda Ann Rainwater. Daughter of Bartholomew Rainwater & Nancy McLaughlin. Born 9 Dec 1841 in Pulaski Co., KY. Died 16 Oct 1927 in Whitewright, Grayson Co., TX. Buried 17 Oct 1927 in Vittitoe Cemetery, Grayson Co., TX.

She married **Alexander Chumbley**, son of Britain Chumbley & Margaret Russell, 6 Feb 1859 in Pulaski Co., KY. Born 19 Feb 1838 in Claborn Co., TN. Died 1 Jan 1895 in Hunt Co., TX. Buried in Hope Cemetery, Ladonia, Hunt Co., TX.

They had the following children:

81	i.	John Perry Chumbley
82	ii.	James Marion Chumbley
83	iii.	Miles Rainwater Chumbley
84	iv.	George A. Chumbley
	v.	Nancy Jane Chumbley; Born 17 Sep 1869 in Kentucky.
	vi.	Bartholomew Chumbley; Born 3 Apr 1872 in Kentucky.
85	vii.	Robert R. Chumbley
86	viii.	Margaret Ann Chumbley
87	ix.	Lewis Milton Chumbley
	x.	Malinda C. Chumbley; Born 12 Jun 1883.
88	xi.	Josiah Wilson Chumbley Sr.

20. Josiah Wilson Rainwater. Son of Bartholomew Rainwater & Nancy McLaughlin. Born 10 Oct 1843 in Waterloo, Pulaski County, KY. Died 16 Mar 1934 in Vernon,

WIlbarger County, TX. Buried Mar 1934 in East View Cemetery, Vernon, Wilbarger Co., TX.

He married **Elizabeth Jane Weddle**, daughter of Solomon Weddle Sr. & Martha "Patsy" Tarter, 11 Jan 1866 in Pulaski Co., KY. Born 7 Sep 1847 in Pulaski Co., KY. Died 25 Jun 1943 in Vernon, Wilbarger County, TX. Buried Jun 1943 in East View Cemetery, Wilbarger Co., Vernon, TX.

They had the following children:

89	i.	Martha Jane Rainwater
90	ii.	Nancy Frances Rainwater
91	iii.	Lucy Isadore Rainwater
92	iv.	Doretta Rainwater
93	v.	Miles Rainwater
94	vi.	Mary Rainwater
95	vii.	Cornelia Rainwater
96	viii.	Roscoe Conklin Rainwater
97	ix.	Minnie Rainwater

21. Elizabeth W. Rainwater. Daughter of James Rainwater & Mary McDaniel. Born c. 1827 in Kentucky.

She married **William Newton Cooper**, son of Levi Cooper & Nancy Jones, 19 Aug 1844 in Pulaski Co. KY. Born c. 1821 in KY.

They had the following children:

i.	Elizabeth Ellen Cooper; Born c. 1846 in Kentucky.
ii.	Mary Cooper; Born c. 1848 in Kentucky.
iii.	Oliver Cooper; Born c. 1849 in Kentucky.
iv.	Franklin G. Cooper; Born 1 Apr 1852 in Pulaski Co. KY.

22. William H. Rainwater. Son of James Rainwater & Mary McDaniel. Born 11 May 1831 in Pulaski Co., KY. Died 2 Aug 1871 in Pulaski Co., KY. Buried in Hopeful Baptist Cemetery, Pulaski Co., KY.

He married **Nancy Jane Russell**, daughter of David Russell, 29 Oct 1851 in Pulaski Co., KY. Born 22 Jul 1834 in Tennessee. Died 19 Jun 1897. Buried in Hopeful Baptist Cemetery, Pulaski Co., KY.

They had the following children:

98	i.	Sarah E. Rainwater
	ii.	John Rainwater; Born 8 May 1854 in Pulaski Co., KY. Died Before 1860.
	iii.	James F. Rainwater; Born 17 May 1856 in Pulaski Co., KY. Died Before 1860.
99	iv.	Leonidas Breckenridge Rainwater
100	v.	Lubantus B. Rainwater

	vi.	Enoch D. Rainwater; Born 9 Mar 1866 in Pulaski Co., KY. Died 2 Apr 1918 in Pulaski Co., KY.
		He married Laura B. Land, 21 Aug 1902 in Pulaski Co., KY. Born 10 Dec 1858 in Pulaski Co., KY. Died 25 Aug 1946 in Cains Store, Pulaski Co. KY.
101	vii.	Rufus F. Rainwater
	viii.	George Rainwater; Born c. 1870 in Kentucky.
	ix.	Electa Rainwater; Born c. 1872 in Kentucky.

23. Enoch Rainwater. Son of James Rainwater & Mary McDaniel. Born 25 May 1836 in Pulaski Co., KY. Died 12 Jul 1906 in Pulaski Co. KY. Buried in New Hope Cemetery, Pulaski Co., KY.

He first married **Martha E. Compton**, daughter of Micajah Compton & Margaret Rexroat, 22 Dec 1852 in Pulaski Co., KY. Born 7 Jun 1836 in Pulaski Co., KY. Died 16 Aug 1898 in Pulaski Co., KY. Buried in New Hope Cemetery, Pulaski Co., KY.

They had the following children:

102	i.	China Paralee Rainwater
	ii.	Mary Elizabeth Rainwater (never married); Born 2 Nov 1855 in Pulaski Co., KY. Died 4 Oct 1941 in Oil Center, Pulaski Co., KY.
103	iii.	Amanda E. Rainwater
	iv.	infant Rainwater; Born 27 Nov 1859 in Pulaski Co., KY. Died before 1860.
104	v.	Adaliza E. Rainwater
105	vi.	William Harrison Rainwater
106	vii.	Silas Monroe Rainwater
	viii.	Caldonia Rainwater; Born c. 1869 in Pulaski Co., KY.
		She married C. C. Tate, 26 Nov 1884 in Pulaski Co., KY. Born c. 1867 in Casey Co., KY. Died 18 Mar 1953 in Breckenridge Co., KY.
	ix.	Ada R. Rainwater (twin); Born 2 Mar 1873 in Pulaski Co., KY. Died 25 Jan 1961 in Pulaski Co. KY. She married Simeon Simpson, 10 Sep 1905 in Pulaski Co., KY. Born c. 1847 in KY.
107	x.	Terressa Rainwater (twin)
108	xi.	Virgil M. Rainwater
109	xii.	Carl B. Rainwater

He second married **Mary E. (Roy)**, 27 Oct 1903 in Pulaski Co. KY. Born c. 1868 in Russell Co., KY. Died before 1910 in Kentucky.

They had the following children:

	i.	Bertha Rainwater; Born c. 1905 in Kentucky.

24. John Rainwater. Son of James Rainwater & Mary McDaniel. Born 5 Oct 1838 in Pulaski Co., KY. Died 6 Feb 1863 of measles in Nashville while serving in the Illinois

73rd Infantry, Company D of the Union Army. Buried in National Cemetery, Nashville, Davidson Co., TN.

He married **Sarah Elizabeth Porter**, daughter of Rev. William L. Porter Sr., 23 Dec 1857 in Pulaski Co., KY. Born 26 Sep 1842 in Pike Co., IL KY. Died 9 Feb 1892 in Pike Co., IL.

They had the following children:

110	i.	James Henry Rainwater
111	ii.	Enoch John Rainwater
	iii.	Mary Frances Rainwater; Born & died Apr 1863 in Pratt Co., IL.

25. Sarah Rainwater. Daughter of James Rainwater & Mary McDaniel. Born 20 Sep 1843 in Pulaski Co., KY. Died 23 Oct 1883 in Pulaski Co., KY. Buried in Compton Family Cemetery, Pulaski Co., KY.

She married **Harrison A. Compton**, son of Micajah Compton & Margaret Rexroat, 1 Sep 1860 in Pulaski Co., KY. Born 16 Feb 1839 in Pulaski Co., KY. Died 30 May 1909 in Pulaski Co., KY. Buried in Compton Family Cemetery, Pulaski Co., KY.

They had the following children:

i.	John D. Compton; Born 1861 in Kentucky. Died 1948 in Pulaski Co., KY.
	He married Lula P. Born 1875. Died 2 Mar 1956 in Daves Co., KY.
ii.	Permelia Isabell Compton; Born 1863 in Pulaski Co., KY. Died 5 Sep 1916 in Pulaski Co., KY.
	She married Thomas W. Wilson, 28 Sep 1879 in Pulaski Co., KY. Born 1856 in Pulaski Co., KY. Died 15 Oct 1943 in Pulaski Co., KY.
iii.	Erasmus Compton; Born c. 1864 in Kentucky.
iv.	Dora A. Compton; Born 1865 in Pulaski Co., KY.
	She married William Mills, 29 Jul 1885 in Pulaski Co., KY. Born 1863 in Pulaski Co., KY.
v.	Calanza Compton; Born 1867 in Pulaski Co., KY.
	She married James McGahan, 4 Mar 1883 in Pulaski Co., KY. Born 1862 in Pulaski Co., KY.
vi.	Ida Compton; Born c. 1873 in Kentucky.
vii.	Mary Compton; Born c. 1875 in Kentucky.

26. Amanda C. Rainwater. Daughter of James Rainwater & Mary McDaniel. Born c. 1844 in Pulaski Co. KY. Died 17 Jun 1918 in Casey Co., KY. Buried in New Hope Cemetery, Nancy, Pulaski Co., KY.

She married **Robert Marshall Dick**, son of Archibald Dick & Sarah Wesley, 8 Mar 1866 in Pulaski Co., KY. Born c. 1845 in Pulaski Co., KY. Died 2 Sep 1915 in Pulaski Co., KY. Buried in New Hope Cemetery, Nancy, Pulaski Co., KY.

They had the following children:

	i.	Martha J. Dick; Born c. 1867 in Kentucky.
	ii.	Caldona A. Dick; Born c. 1869 in Kentucky.
	iii.	Veantus Dick; Born 3 Sep 1871 in Pulaski Co., KY.
		He married Lizzie Luttrell, 27 Nov 1904 in Pulaski Co., KY. Born c. 1874 in Pulaski Co., KY.
	iv.	James W. Dick; Born Feb 1872 in Kentucky. Died 28 Nov 1933 in Pulaski Co., KY.
	v.	Lorenzo Dow Dick; Born c. 1873 in Pulaski Co. KY.
		He married Levonia E. Cooper, daughter of Isaac E. Cooper & Mary Ann Bastin, 5 Mar 1895 in Pulaski Co. KY. Born c. 1869 in Pulaski Co., KY.
	vi.	Eliza Dick; Born 28 Oct 1875 in Kentucky. Died 23 Jun 1893.
	vii.	Zelotus Dick; Born 29 Sep 1879 in Kentucky. Died 20 Oct 1923 in Jefferson Co., KY.
		He married Ever E. Cooper, daughter of Isaac E. Cooper & Ginay Lizzy Hendricks (Meece).
		Born 15 Jul 1886 in Kentucky. Died 18 Jun 1970 in Pulaski Co., KY.
	viii.	Stellah Dick; Born 23 Jun 1882. Died 6 Jun 1897.
	ix.	Emma Dick; Born Sep 1886 in Kentucky.

27. Samantha Rainwater. Daughter of James Rainwater & Mary McDaniel. Born c. 1846 in KY. Died Before 1911.

She had the following children out of wedlock:

	i.	Montenia Rainwater; Born c. 1868 in Pulaski Co., KY.
		She married Thomas Harrison, 30 Dec 1882 in Pulaski Co. KY. Born c. 1862 in Barren Co., KY.

She first married **John Jackson Sawyer**, 28 Aug 1892 in Pulaski Co. KY. Born c. 1828 in Wayne Co., KY.

28. Alethia Rainwater. Daughter of James Rainwater & Mary McDaniel. Born c. 1849 in Pulaski Co., KY. Died between 1870/1880 in Pulaski Co., KY.

She married **John Dick**, son of Archibald Dick & Sarah Wesley, 28 Jan 1866 in Pulaski Co. KY. Born c. 1843 in Pulaski Co. KY.

They had the following children:

112	i.	Mary Frances Dick
	ii.	Cornelia C. Dick; Born c. 1872 in Kentucky.
113	iii.	Rutherford Columbus Dick

29. Jeremiah Stanton Rainwater. Son of Abraham Rainwater & Anna McLaughlin. Born c. 1831 in Casey Co., KY. Died before 1900 in Kentucky.

He first married **Eve Tarter**, daughter of Peter C. Tarter & Mary Sullivan, 10 May 1852 in Wayne Co., KY. Born c. 1832 in Pulaski Co., KY. Died before 1890.

They had the following children:

114	i.		Perry Milton Rainwater
115	ii.		Oliver Wesley Rainwater
116	iii.		Laura B. Rainwater
117	iv.		Peter Christopher Rainwater
118	v.		George Willis Rainwater
	vi.		Eliza D. Rainwater; Born c. 1868 in Kentucky.
	vii.		Margaret A. Rainwater; Born c. 1870 in Kentucky.
	viii.		Effie O. Rainwater; Born c. 1874 in Kentucky.
	ix.		John E. Rainwater; Born c. 1877 in Kentucky.
			He married Hulda, before 1900. Born Sep 1874 in Kentucky.

He second married **Martha J. "Mattie" Barnes**, before 1890. Born c. 1867 in Virginia. Died After 1910.

They had the following children:

119	i.	Lorenzo Dow Rainwater
120	ii.	Thomas Arnold Rainwater
121	iii.	David Gentry Rainwater
	iv.	Sallie M. Rainwater; Born c. 1901 in Kentucky.

30. Ephraim R. Rainwater. Son of Abraham Rainwater & Anna McLaughlin. Born c. 1835 in Kentucky. Died 26 Dec 1899 in Indiana. Buried in Fairview Cemetery, Stockton section, Greene Co., IN.

He married **Melissa Roy**, daughter of William Merritt Roy & Nancy Rainwater, 15 Feb 1857 in Lawrence Co., IN. Born c. 1835 in Pulaski Co., KY. Died between 1870/1880 in Indiana. They were divorced before 1880.

They had the following children:

	i.	Clifford Rainwater; Born c. 1855 in Indiana. Died between 1860/1870.
	ii.	Milford E. Rainwater; Born c. 1858 in Indiana.
	iii.	Hugh Alonzo Rainwater; Born c. 1859 in Indiana.
		He married Margaret, 1880. Born c. 1862 in Indiana.
	iv.	Luther Rainwater; Born Apr 1862 in Indiana.
	v.	Melissa Rainwater; Born c. 1864 in Indiana.
		She married James M. Bedwell, 1885 in Sullivan Co., IN.
	vi.	Nancy A. Rainwater (Tannahill); Born c. 1866 in Indiana.
122	vii.	Ephriam Rainwater Jr.
	viii.	Martha Bell Rainwater (Hawk); Born c. 1872 in Indiana.

        ix.   Nettie Rainwater; Born c. 1873 in Indiana. She married Thomas Owen, son of Preston Owen & Sarah Rogers, 12 Sep 1900 in Brown Co., IN. Born c. 1869 in Illinois.

31. Ira Hardin Rainwater. Son of Abraham Rainwater & Anna McLaughlin. Born Mar 1835 in Kentucky. Died c. 1902 in Missouri.

He married **Caroline Raisor**, 9 Sep 1869 in Lawrence Co., IN. Born Mar 1847 in Indiana. Died after 1900.

They had the following children:

        i.   Opal Rainwater; Born Feb 1871 in Indiana.

        ii.   Dayton W. Rainwater; Born Nov 1874 in Kansas.

        iii.   Orra Rainwater; Born c. 1876 in Missouri.

        iv.   Blanche Rainwater; Born Mar 1879 in Missouri.

        v.   Denver Rainwater; Born Dec 1883 in Missouri.

32. Sarah Ann Rainwater. Daughter of Abraham Rainwater & Anna McLaughlin. Born c. 1841 in Kentucky. Died Apr 1896.

She married **Moses S. Cunningham**, 25 Mar 1860 in Lawrence Co., IN. Born c. 1937 in Indiana. Died After 1880.

They had the following children:

        i.   Eugene Cunningham; Born c. 1869 in Indiana.

        ii.   Lily M. Cunningham; Born c. 1870 in Indiana.

        iii.   Byron Cunningham; Born c. 1872 in Indiana.

        iv.   Uriah Cunningham; Born c. 1875 in Indiana.

        v.   Emery W. Cunningham; Born c. 1876 in Indiana.

        vi.   Charles C. Cunningham; Born 1880 in Indiana.

33. Nancy Rainwater. Daughter of John R. Rainwater & Elizabeth Lawless. Born 17 Jun 1839 in Pulaski Co., KY. Died Feb 1883.

She married **Milton Emerson**, son of John M. Emerson & Matilda Daws, 26 Jul 1860 in Pulaski Co., KY. Born 17 Mar 1841 in Pulaski Co., KY North Carolina. Died 1918 in Casey Co., KY. Buried in Grave Hill Cemetery, Mintonville, Casey Co., KY.

They had the following children:

        i.   James Franklin Emerson; Born 10 Jul 1861 in KY. Died 3 Apr 1890.

                He married Mary Jasper, 9 Dec 1879 in Casey Co., KY.

123   ii.   George Alfred Emerson

        iii.   Jacob E. Emerson; Born 4 May 1876 in KY. D ied 7 Jul 1921 in Pulaski Co., KY.

        iv.   Welcome Giles Emerson; Born 25 May 1869 in KY. Died 10 May 1944 in Casey Co., KY.

                He married Sallie A. Spaw, 3 Sep 1889 in Casey Co., KY. Born 30 Sep 1872. Died 15 Jan 1957.

124	v.	John Perry Emerson
	vi.	Robert Marion Emerson; Born 20 Oct 1875. Died 20 Jun 1933 in Casey Co., KY.
		He married Patsey E. Spaw, 13 Aug 1897 in Casey Co., KY. Born 15 Jan 1879. Died 28 Sep 1920.

34. Giles R. Rainwater. Son of John R. Rainwater & Elizabeth Lawless. Born 3 Apr 1841 in Pulaski Co., KY. Died 17 Dec 1920 in Mintonville, Casey Co., KY. Buried in Mintonville Methodist Church Cemetery, Casey Co., KY.

He married **Sarah Jane Emerson** , daughter of John M. Emerson & Matilda Daws, 19 Sep 1861 in Pulaski Co., KY. Born 13 Feb 1845 in Pulaski Co., KY. Died 6 May 1911 in Mintonville, Casey Co., KY. Buried in Mintonville Methodist Church Cemetery, Casey Co., KY.

They had the following children:

125	i.	Tilitha J. Rainwater
126	ii.	Daniel Francis Rainwater
127	iii.	Matilda E. Rainwater
	iv.	Patsy J. Rainwater; Born 12 Nov 1869 in Casey Co., KY. Died 18 Jan 1886 in Casey Co., KY.
128	v.	John Silas Rainwater Sr.
129	vi.	Milton Durham Rainwater
130	vii.	George Mitchell Rainwater
131	viii.	Herbert F. Rainwater

35. George Alfred Rainwater. Son of John R. Rainwater & Elizabeth Lawless. Born 1846 in Pulaski Co., KY. Died 13 Jul 1924 in Caintown, Pulaski Co., KY. Buried 14 Jul 1924 in Cedar Point Cemetery, Pulaski Co., KY.

He married **Permelia Susan Garner**, daughter of George Washington Garner Sr. & Mary Watson, 6 Mar 1867 in Pulaski Co., KY. Born 29 Dec 1846 in Pulaski Co., KY. Died 1 Jul 1929. Buried in Cedar Point Cemetery, Pulaski Co., KY.

They had the following children:

132	i.	Mary Elizabeth Rainwater
133	ii.	John Madison Rainwater
	iii.	George Vincent Rainwater (never married); Born 3 Jun 1872 in KY. Died 10 Oct 1933.
	iv.	James Howard Rainwater (never married); Born 1 Jan 1874 in KY. Died 24 Jan 1891 in Texas.
134	v.	Charles Elliott Rainwater
135	vi.	Frances Maria Rainwater
	vii.	Margaret Isabel Rainwater (never married); Born 9 Dec 1879 in KY. Died 17 Apr 1903 in KY.
136	viii.	Giles Alfred Rainwater
137	ix.	Millie Catherine Rainwater

138	x.	William Frederick Rainwater
139	xi.	Susan Jane Rainwater

36. Susannah Rainwater. Daughter of John R. Rainwater & Elizabeth Lawless. Born c. 1848 in Kentucky.

She married **Abraham H. Roysden**, son of Jacob Roysden & Levanna, 5 Sep 1872 in Casey Co., KY. Born c. 1852 in KY.

They had the following children:

	i.	Elizabeth F. Roysden; Born c. 1874 in Kentucky.
	ii.	John C. Roysden; Born c. 1875 in Kentucky.
	iii.	Nancy E. Roysden; Born c. 1879 in Kentucky.
140	iv.	Dollie Mae Roysden

37. Melissa Roy. Daughter of William Merritt Roy & Nancy Rainwater. Born c. 1835 in Pulaski Co., KY. Died between 1870/1880 in Indiana.

She married **Ephraim R. Rainwater**, son of Abraham Rainwater & Anna McLaughlin, 15 Feb 1857 in Lawrence Co., IN. Born c. 1835 in Kentucky. Died 26 Dec 1899 in Indiana. Buried in Fairview Cemetery, Stockton section, Greene Co., IN. They were divorced before 1880.

They had the following children:

	i.	Clifford Rainwater (never married); Born c. 1855 in Indiana.
	ii.	Milford E. Rainwater; Born c. 1858 in Indiana.
	iii.	Hugh Alonzo Rainwater; Born c. 1859 in Indiana.
		He married Margaret, 1880. Born c. 1862 in Indiana.
	iv.	Luther Rainwater; Born Apr 1862 in Indiana.
	v.	Melissa Rainwater; Born c. 1864 in Indiana.
		She married James M. Bedwell, 1885 in Sullivan Co., IN.
	vi.	Nancy A. Rainwater (Tannahill); Born c. 1866 in Indiana.
122	vii.	Ephriam Rainwater Jr.
	viii.	Martha Bell Rainwater (Hawk); Born c. 1872 in Indiana.
	ix.	Nettie Rainwater; Born c. 1873 in Indiana.
		She married Thomas Owen, son of Preston Owen & Sarah Rogers, 12 Sep 1900 in Brown Co., IN. Born c. 1869 in Illinois.

38. Elizabeth Roy. Daughter of William Merritt Roy & Nancy Rainwater. Born 4 Mar 1843 in Indiana. Died 8 Apr 1925 in Culver, Ottawa Co., KS. Buried in Culver Union Cm, Culver, Ottawa Co., KS.

She married **Jonathan Jasper Pierce**, 6 Aug 1863 in Lawrence Co., IN. Born 7 Jul 1841 in Lawrence Co., IN. Died 28 Feb 1920 in Culver, Ottawa Co., KS.

They had the following children:

	i.	Nancy M. Pierce; Born c. 1865 in Indiana.

	ii.	Miranda J. Pierce; Born c. 1869 in Indiana.
	iii.	Cyrus L. Pierce; Born c. 1871 in Indiana.
	iv.	William H. Pierce; Born c. 1873 in Illinois.
	v.	Mary E. Pierce; Born c. 1875 in Kansas.
	vi.	Eliza A. Pierce; Born Feb 1880 in Kansas.

39. John Roy. Son of William Merritt Roy & Nancy Rainwater. Born c. 1845 in Lawrence Co., IN. Died Before Nov 1890.

He married **Nancy**, Before 1866. Born c. 1848 in Indiana.

They had the following children:

	i.	Thomas E. Roy; Born c. 1866 in Illinois.
	ii.	James H. Roy; Born c. 1868 in Illinois.
	iii.	Ida A. Roy; Born c. 1871 in Illinois.
	iv.	Jessimine Roy; Born c. 1876 in Kansas.

40. Ralph N. Roy. Son of William Merritt Roy & Nancy Rainwater. Born c. 1847 in Lawrence Co., IN. Died After Nov 1890.

He married **Nancy**, before 1869. Born in Virginia.

They had the following children:

	i.	William H. Roy; Born c. 1869 in Illinois.
	ii.	Mary C. Roy; Born c. 1875 in Illinois.
	iii.	Nancy Roy; Born c. 1879 in Kansas.

41. Martha Rainwater. Daughter of William Howard Rainwater Sr. & Minerva Ann Rayborn. Born 12 May 1939 in Pulaski Co., KY.

She married **William Dove**, son of John Dove, 18 Feb 1856 in Pulaski Co., KY. Born Dec 1838 in Kentucky.

They had the following children:

		i.	Maureen Minerva Dove; Born c. 1857 in Kentucky.
	141	ii.	Miles L. Dove.
		iii.	Mary Emma Dove; Born 1864 in Minnesota.
		iv.	Emily Dove; Born 1865 in Minnesota.

42. John Raleigh Rainwater. Son of William Howard Rainwater Sr. & Minerva Ann Rayborn. Born 5 Apr 1841 in Pulaski Co., KY. Died 5 Apr 1910 in Adair Co., KY. Buried on the Rainwater family farm on Barnett Creek, Adair Co, KY.

He first married **Genetta Thomas**, 29 Nov 1858 in Casey Co., KY. Born Oct 1838 in Kentucky. Died c. 1918 in Clinton, Van Buren Co., AR. They were divorced 23 Sep 1897.

They had the following children:

	i.	James Christopher Rainwater; Born 3 Apr 1860 in KY. Died 26 Mar 1940 in Pulaski Co., AR.
		He married Ella, between 1910/1920 in Arkansas. Born c. 1856 in Arkansas.

142	ii.	Miles Evan Rainwater
143	iii.	Margaret Ellen Rainwater
144	iv.	Charles Thomas Rainwater
145	v.	William Rainwater Sr.
146	vi.	Henry T. Rainwater
	vii.	Mary Jane Rainwater; Born 10 Sep 1879 in Casey Co., KY. Died 17 Jun 1887 in IL.

He second married **Rhoda Ann Brown**, daughter of Daniel Brown & Ruth Watson, 16 May 1898 in Adair Co., KY. Born c. 1859 in Casey Co., KY. Died 5 Mar 1915 in Adair Co., KY. Buried on Rainwater family farm, Barnett Creek, Adair Co, KY.

They had the following children:

147	i.	Giles R. Rainwater
	ii.	Charles R. Rainwater; Born Apr 1884 in Adair Co., KY. Died 25 Aug 1966 in Hopkins Co., KY.
	iii.	Martha M. Rainwater; Born Jun 1885 in Adair Co., KY.
		She married William Holt, 1 Sep 1900 in Adair Co., KY. Born c. 1879 in Jackson Co., KY.
	iv.	Harrison Rainwater; Born May 1889 in Adair Co., KY. Died 18 Apr 1967 in Casey Co., KY.
		He first married Lucy Carter, daughter of Albert Carter & Mary Copley, 20 Jun 1908 in Casey Co., KY. Born 1 Nov 1888 in KY. Died 15 Nov 1933 in Liberty, Casey Co., KY.
		He second married Bertha Knight (Tedder), daughter of Jeremiah Knight & Catherine Lawless, 14 Mar 1947 in Adair Co., KY. Born c. 1897 in Taylor Co., KY. Died Jun 1987 in Casey Co., KY.
148	v.	Scott Rainwater
	vi.	Dink Rainwater; Born 11 May 1896 in Adair Co., KY. Died 15 Jan 1938 in Morgan Co., IL.
	vii.	Alfred Rainwater; Born Aug 1899 in Kentucky. Died 18 Apr 1958 in Mason Co., OH.
	viii.	Noah L. Rainwater; Born c. 1902. Died 25 Jan 1962 in Adams Co., OH.

43. Miles Rainwater. Son of William Howard Rainwater Sr. & Minerva Ann Rayborn. Born 21 Oct 1843 in Pulaski Co., KY. Died 26 Sep 1927 in Four Mile Twp., Wayne Co., IL. Buried in Egbert Cemetery, Wayne Co., IL.

He first married **Permelia Emily Cain**, daughter of William R. Cain & Permelia McClendon, 18 Oct 1866 in Pulaski Co., KY. Born c. 1846 in Pulaski Co., KY. Died between 1890/1892 in Illinois.

They had the following children:

149	i.	Minerva Ann Rainwater

150	ii.		William Riley Rainwater
	iii.		Ida May Rainwater; Born 1 Mar 1873 in Brown Co., IN.

She married Alexander Forth, son of R. T. Forth & M. J. Polless, 23 Mar 1869 in Wayne Co., IL. Born c. 1869 in Wayne Co., IL.

        iv.   Lucille Elizabeth Rainwater; Born 28 Jul 1875 in KY.

She married B. D. Braddock, 13 Jan 1907 in IL.

151   v.   Isaac Asbury Rainwater

        vi.   Minda Cordelia Rainwater; Born Sep 1881 in Jefferson Co., IL. Died 1947.

She married A. J. Buchanan, son of S. W. Buchanan & Rachel Brown, 12 Apr 1905 in Wayne Co., IL. Born c. 1856 in Wayne Co., IL.

        vii.   Fannie C. Rainwater; Born 8 Aug 1882 in Brown Co., IN. Died 27 May 1940.

She married Oscar Haynes, 2 Jul 1902 in Wayne Co., IL. Born c. 1875 in IL. Died 1963 in IL.

He second married **Elizabeth M. Waters**, 3 Nov 1892 in Wayne Co., IL. Born Mar 1852 in Illinois. They were divorced before 1900.

He third married **Rebecca Olive Davis (Reed)**, 13 Apr 1900 in Wayne Co., IL. Born c. 1854 in Crawford Co., IL. Died 27 Apr 1939 in Wayne Co., IL. Buried in Thomason Cemetery, Wayne City, IL.

They had the following children:

        i.   Rebecca J. Rainwater; Born 16 Oct 1902 in Wayne City, Wayne Co., IL. Died 24 May 1980 in Mt. Vernon, IL. She married Herbert Stevens.

44. William Howard Rainwater Jr. Son of William Howard Rainwater Sr. & Minerva Ann Rayborn. Born 5 Mar 1850 in Somerset, Pulaski Co., KY. Died 22 Nov 1925 in Four Mile Twp., Wayne Co., IL. Buried in Bruce Cemetery, Four Mile Twp., Wayne Co., IL.

He first married **Julia G. Markwell**, daughter of John W. Markwell & Sarah, 7 Jun 1869 in Brown Co., IN. Born c. 1843 in Indiana. Died between 1870/1871.

They had the following children:

152   i.   Henry Clarence Rainwater

He second married **Ellen Victoria Pool**, daughter of Luther A. Pool & Clarinda Peak, 27 Feb 1872 in Brown Co., IN. Born Dec 1835 in Indiana. Died After 1900. They were divorced c. 1877.

They had the following children:

153   i.   William Luther Rainwater

He third married **Mary Ann Buffington**, daughter of Abraham C. Buffington & Mary Ann Garrison, 22 Dec 1877 in Wayne Co., IL. Born 10 Nov 1857 in Long Prairie, Wayne Co., IL. Died 21 Apr 1944 in Mt. Vernon, Jefferson Co., IL. Buried in Bruce Cemetery, Four Mile Twp., Wayne Co., IL.

They had the following children:

| | | i. | Etta Nora Rainwater; Born 2 Jan 1876 in Wayne Co., IL. Died 19 Dec 1940. |

She married Elza Richards, son of Elzaphan Richards & Nancy E. Lee, 23 Oct 1900 in Wayne Co., IL. Born 30 Jun 1872 in Wayne Co., IL. Died 21 Jul 1935.

154 ii. Harvey L. Rainwater

155 iii. Emery Columbus Rainwater

     iv. Oria Caroline Rainwater; Born 12 Jan 1885 in Wayne Co., IL. Died 11 Nov 1962 in Wayne Co., IL. She married Pink A. Lane.

     v. Mary Elizabeth Rainwater; Born 15 Sep 1887 in Four-Mile, Wayne Co., IL. Died 13 May 1946 in Ogle Co., IL. She married J. Albert Lane, son of L. R. Lane & M. S. Marimus Newby, 25 Dec 1904 in Wayne Co., IL. Born c. 1880 in Jefer Co., IL.

156 vi. Oliver Philip Rainwater

     vii. Maggie May Rainwater; Born 29 Jan 1892 in Wayne Co., IL. Died 6 May 1972 in Mt. Vernon, Jefferson Co., IL. She married Logan William Lane, 15 Mar 1913 in Wayne Co., IL.

     viii. Evey Rainwater; Born 12 May 1894 in Wayne Co., IL. Died 28 Jan 1897 in Wayne Co., IL.

     ix. Mark Rainwater; Born 13 Jun 1895 in Wayne Co., IL. Died 20 Apr 1973 in Milwaukee Co., WI.

He married Leo Nadine Padgett, 27 Jan 1920 in Wayne Co., IL.

45. Matthew F. Rainwater. Son of William Howard Rainwater Sr. & Minerva Ann Rayborn. Born 21 Apr 1852 in Pulaski Co., KY. Died between 1920/1930.

He first married **Adeline**, Before 1878. Born 1855 in Ohio. Died 1881 in Wayne Co., IL. Buried in Attenberry Cemetery, Wayne Co., IL.

They had the following children:

     i. Rose Rainwater; Born c. 1874 in Illinois.

She married A. G. Williams, 2 Jul 1891 in IL.

157 ii. Charles Edward Rainwater

     iii. James W. Rainwater; Born 25 Jul 1878 in Four-Mile, Wayne Co., IL.

He married Jane (Moore), c. 1902. Born c. 1877 in Missouri.

He second married **Susan**, c. 1907. Born c. 1878 in Missouri.

46. Mark Rainwater. Son of William Howard Rainwater Sr. & Minerva Ann Rayborn. Born 7 Mar 1856 in Pulaski Co., KY. Died between 1920/1930 in Arkansas. Buried in Culpepper Cemetery, Van Buren Co., AR.

He married Sarah Caroline Jones, c. 1870. Born 9 Aug 1859 in Indiana. Died 21 Jul 1922 in Van Buren Co., AR. Buried in Culpepper Cemetery, Van Buren Co., AR.

They had the following children:

	i.	Sam M. Rainwater; Born Apr 1871 in Arkansas.
	ii.	Sarah D. Rainwater; Born Mar 1876 in Illinois.
158	iii.	Louie M. Rainwater

47. George Washington Rainwater. Son of William Howard Rainwater Sr. & Minerva Ann Rayborn. Born 20 Sep 1863 in Pulaski Co., KY. Died 24 Dec 1943 in Four Mile Twp., Wayne Co., IL. Buried in Egbert Cemetery, Wayne Co., IL.

He married **Emma Rosetta Fox**, daughter of John Fox & Louiza Pike, 23 Dec 1887 in Brown Co., IN. Born Apr 1871 in Tennessee. Died 30 Dec 1950 in Wayne Co., IL. Buried in Egbert Cemetery, Wayne Co., IL.

They had the following children:

	i.	John William Rainwater; Born Mar 1888 in Indiana. Died 1969 in Illinois.
		He married Stella Gingrich, Before 1920. Born 1895 in Illinois. Died 1969 in Illinois.
	ii.	Matthew Floyd Rainwater; Born Jan 1891 in Indiana.
		He married Nellie, Before 1920. Born c. 1899 in Illinois.
	iii.	Ethel Belle Rainwater; Born Jan 1894 in Illinois.
159	iv.	Thomas Marion Rainwater
	v.	Louisa Frances Rainwater; Born Jan 1899 in Illinois.
	vi.	Raymond Rainwater; Born c. 1902 in Illinois.
	vii.	Henry Rainwater; Born c. 1905 in Illinois.
	viii.	Earl Rainwater; Born 21 May 1908 in Illinois. Died 21 Sep 1989 in Bluford, Jefferson Co., IL.
	ix.	Donald Rainwater; Born c. 1911 in Indiana.
	x.	Mabel May Rainwater; Born 27 Jul 1913 in Illinois. Died 24 May 1914 in Illinois.

48. Terrell Rainwater. Son of Miles Rainwater & Frances Chaney. Born 10 Feb 1846 in Somerset, Pulaski Co., KY. Died 4 Nov 1913 in Mexia, Limestone Co., TX. Buried in Old City Cemetery, Sulpher Springs, Hopkins Co, TX.

He married **Esther Shoe**, daughter of Christopher Shoe & Nancy Forgerty, 1879 in Appleton City, St. Clair Co., MO. Born Nov 1853 in Iowa. Died 26 Aug 1941 in Trinity Co., TX. Buried in Old City Cemetery, Sulpher Springs, Hopkins Co, TX.

They had the following children:

	i.	Ethel Frances Rainwater; Born 2 Mar 1884 in Appleton City, St. Clair Co., MO. Died 14 Mar 1899 in Sulphur Springs, Hopkins Co, TX.

		ii.	Jessie Mae Rainwater; Born Mar 1887 in Hopkins Co., TX.
			She married John F. Largin, c. 1906. Born c. 1888 in Texas.
160		iii.	Jennie Lee Rainwater
161		iv.	Walter Terrell Rainwater Sr.

49. David Rainwater. Son of Miles Rainwater & Frances Chaney. Born 30 Nov 1847 in Pulaski Co., KY. Died 25 May 1871 in Pulaski Co., KY. Buried in Rainwater Family Cemetery, Pulaski Co., KY.

He married **Annice Mariah Garner**, daughter of George Washington Garner Sr. & Mary Watson, 21 Feb 1869 in Pulaski Co., KY. Born 8 Feb 1849 in Pulaski Co., KY. Died 5 Mar 1922.

They had the following children:

162	i.	John Silas Rainwater

50. Mary Elizabeth Rainwater. Daughter of Miles Rainwater & Frances Chaney. Born c. 1852 in Pulaski Co., KY. Died between 1884/1900 in Pulaski Co., KY. Buried in Rainwater Family Cemetery, Pulaski Co., KY.

She married **Robert Tilman Gossett**, 1 Nov 1871 in Pulaski Co. KY. Born Oct 1850 in Pulaski Co., KY. Died After 1900.

They had the following children:

	i.	Rosetta A. Gossett; Born c. 1873 in Kentucky.
		She married Isaac C. Roysden, son of Jacob Roysden & Levanna, 24 Nov 1892 in Pulaski Co. KY. Born c. 1858 in Pulaski Co. KY.
163	ii.	Elizabeth F. Gossett
	iii.	Neal W. Gossett; Born c. 1878 in Kentucky.
	iv.	Mary N. Gossett; Born Nov 1882 in KY.
	v.	Erasmus R. Gossett; Born Aug 1884 in KY.
	vi.	Cassie S. Gossett; Born Feb 1887 in KY.
	vii.	Coatney F. Gossett; Born Jan 1889 in KY.
	viii.	John S. Gossett; Born May 1891 in KY.
	ix.	Ethel R. Gossett; Born Jun 1895 in KY.

51. Fountain Rainwater. Son of Miles Rainwater & Frances Chaney. Born 12 Jan 1854 in Pulaski Co., KY. Died 20 Dec 1944 in Pulaski Co., KY. Buried in New Hope Cemetery, Pulaski Co., KY.

He married **China Paralee Rainwater**, daughter of Enoch Rainwater & Martha E. Compton, 19 Nov 1889 in Pulaski Co., KY. Born 5 Jan 1854 in Pulaski Co., KY. Died 11 Jul 1937 in Pulaski Co., KY. Buried in New Hope Cemetery, Pulaski Co., KY.

They had the following children:

	i.	Carthel Spurgeon Rainwater; Born 9 Sep 1890 in Pulaski Co., KY. Died 16 Jun 1967 in Pulaski Co., KY.

52. Frances Jane Rainwater. Daughter of Miles Rainwater & Frances Chaney. Born 8 Feb 1857 in Pulaski Co., KY. Died c. 1885 in Pulaski Co., KY. Buried in private family cemetery, Pulaski Co., KY.

She married **James Willis Tarter**, son of Ivey Tarter & Emily Dunbar, 24 Jan 1878 in Pulaski Co., KY. Born 25 Nov 1857 in Pulaski Co., KY.

They had the following children:

164	i.		Erasmus M. Tarter
	ii.		Christopher Columbus Tarter; Born between 1880/1883.
165	iii.		John Virgil Tarter

53. Sarah Ann Rainwater. Daughter of Miles Rainwater & Frances Chaney. Born 10 Jan 1862 in Pulaski Co., KY. Died 8 Dec 1942 in Pulaski Co. KY. Buried in New Hope Cemetery, Pulaski Co., KY.

She married **Benjamin Franklin Dawes**, son of Joseph Dawes & Mary Owens, 5 Aug 1890 in Pulaski Co. KY. Born 6 Mar 1858 in Pulaski Co. KY. Died 9 Jun 1939 in Pulaski Co. KY. Buried in New Hope Cemetery, Pulaski Co., KY.

They had the following children:

166	i.	Mary Etter Dawes

54. James Rainwater. Son of Miles Rainwater & Frances Chaney. Born 17 Jun 1865 in Pulaski Co., KY. Died 26 Oct 1917 in Pulaski Co., KY. Buried in New Hope Cemetery, Pulaski Co., KY.

He first married **Martha J. McQuary**, daughter of William McQuary & Sarah Jane Ray, 6 Nov 1890 in Pulaski Co., KY. Born 27 Mar 1869 in Pulaski Co., KY. Died 3 Nov 1911 in Pulaski Co., KY. Buried in New Hope Cemetery, Pulaski Co., KY.

He second married **Amanda Belle Wheat**, daughter of Levi Wheat & Sarah F. Cravens, 18 Jun 1913 in Russell Co., KY. Born c. 1892 in Russell Co., KY. Died 7 Apr 1940. Buried in White Cemetery, Adair Co., KY.

They had the following children:

- i. Dortha B. Rainwater; Born 11 Apr 1914 in Pulaski Co. KY.

    She married Cecil Allen, son of David T. Allen & Matilda Parker, 24 Dec 1928 in Pulaski Co. KY. Born c. 1907 in Pulaski Co. KY.

- ii. Sarah Frances Rainwater; Born 25 Jun 1916 in Pulaski Co. KY. Died 2 Oct 1996.

    She married Brent W. Gosser, 27 May 1936 in Ingle, Pulaski Co., KY. Born c. 1916 in Pulaski Co. KY. Died 1 Jan 1957 in Jefferson Co., KY.

Fourth Generation

55. Francis Marion Weddle. Son of Daniel S. Weddle & Anne Rainwater. Born 12 Jun 1847 in Kentucky.

He married **Matilda C. Cox**, 11 Oct 1866 in Pulaski Co. KY. Born c. 1848 in Missouri KY.

They had the following children:

		i.	Jeremiah Weddle
		ii.	Edward Weddle

56. John Perry Weddle. Son of Daniel S. Weddle & Anne Rainwater. Born 6 Feb 1852 in Pulaski Co., KY. Died in Scipio, Pittsburg Co., OK.

He married **Martha J. Campbell**, 19 Feb 1871 in Pulaski Co. KY. Born c. 1854 in Pulaski Co., KY.

They had the following children:

	i.	Victor E. Weddle
	ii.	Banthora F. Weddle
	iii.	Minnie A. Weddle
	iv.	Grant Weddle

57. Bartholomew Franklin Weddle. Son of Daniel S. Weddle & Anne Rainwater. Born 13 Nov 1857 in Kentucky. Died 26 Apr 1934 in Pulaski Co. KY.

He married **Celia E. Sharp**, 24 Feb 1879 in Pulaski Co., KY. Born c. 1862 in Pulaski Co., KY. Died 8 Apr 1939.

They had the following children:

	i.	Cornelius Weddle
167	ii.	Mary Melinda Weddle
168	iii.	Christopher Columbus Weddle Sr.
169	iv.	Killus Green Weddle
	v.	Livonia Weddle
	vi.	Leo Weddle Sr.
170	vii.	Sarah Jane Weddle

58. Lincoln Weddle. Son of Daniel S. Weddle & Anne Rainwater. Born 13 Jun 1860 in Kentucky. Died 10 Mar 1891 in Arkansas.

He married **Nancy Lucy Roy**, daughter of Isaac N. Roy & Elzira Combest, 16 Oct 1879 in Pulaski Co. KY. Born 17 Feb 1862 in Pulaski Co. KY. Died 7 May 1935. Buried in Cedar Point Baptist Cemetery, Pulaski Co., KY.

They had the following children:

171	i.	Ollie M. Weddle
172	ii.	Finley Weddle
173	iii.	Electa Bell Weddle

59. Josiah Weddle. Son of Daniel S. Weddle & Anne Rainwater. Born 18 Sep 1862 in Pulaski Co. KY. Died 31 Oct 1900 in Pulaski Co. KY. Buried in Cedar Point Cemetery, Pulaski Co., KY.

He married **Sarah Melvina Pitman**, daughter of John Frederick Pitman Sr. & Martha Ann Emerson, 1 Aug 1882 in Pulaski Co. KY. Born 2 Nov 1859 in Pulaski Co., KY. Died 27 Jul 1941. Buried in Cedar Point Cemetery, Pulaski Co., KY.

They had the following children:

	i.	Elbert L. Weddle

174	ii.	John D. Weddle
	iii.	Marion W. Weddle
	iv.	Milton Weddle

60. Spencer Grant Weddle. Son of Daniel S. Weddle & Anne Rainwater. Born 28 Aug 1867 in Kentucky. Died 18 Jan 1931 in Victory, Jackson Co., OK. Buried in Rock Cemetery, Duke, Jackson Co., OK.

He married **Martha Frances Sharp**, 14 Jun 1888 in Boonesville, Logan Co., AR. Born 1871. Died 1958 in Oklahoma. Buried in Rock Cemetery, Duke, Jackson Co., OK.

They had the following children:

175	i.	Amster Attenborough Weddle
176	ii.	Beulah Ann Weddle
	iii.	Ruth Ostiley Weddle
	iv.	Beatrice Weddle
177	v.	Lee Corbett Weddle
	vi.	Bertha Theodore Weddle
	vii.	Flora May Weddle
178	viii.	Oscar Jack Weddle

61. Elizabeth Martha Eastham. Daughter of Alexander Eastham & Emily Rainwater. Born 25 Jul 1845 in Kentucky.

She married **Willis Fountain Harris**, 1865 in Russell Co., KY. Born Aug 1835 in Kentucky. Died c. 1901 in Pulaski Co., KY.

They had the following children:

	ii.	Jesse M. Harris
	iii.	Burnetta Harris

62. Zachary Taylor Eastham. Son of Alexander Eastham & Emily Rainwater. Born 15 Dec 1848 in Kentucky.

He married **Mary McQueary**.

They had the following children:

179	i.	James Riley Eastham

63. Nancy P. Eastham. Daughter of Alexander Eastham & Emily Rainwater. Born 9 May 1850 in Pulaski Co., KY. Buried in New Pleasant Point Baptist Church Cemetery, Pulaski Co. KY.

She married **George A. C. Bland**, 22 May 1881 in Pulaski Co. KY. Born c. 1850 in Pulaski Co., KY.

They had the following children:

	i.	Clemy Bland (died at birth)
180	ii.	Luetta Bland

64. Obediah James Eastham. Son of Alexander Eastham & Emily Rainwater. Born 10 Sep 1851 in Pulaski Co., KY. Died 3 Apr 1931 in Boyle Co., KY.

He married **Nancy J. Bray**, daughter of Nathan Bray & Elvira Ellen, 12 Dec 1875 in Pulaski Co., KY. Born c. 1853 in Tennessee.

They had the following children:

	i.	Daniel Eastham
181	ii.	Surilda Margaret Eastham

65. Susannah Eastham. Daughter of Alexander Eastham & Emily Rainwater. Born 2 Oct 1854 in Pulaski Co. KY. Died 1937. Buried in New Pleasant Point Church Cemetery, Pulaski Co., KY.

She married **Thomas Surber Roy**, son of Zachariah Roy & Hannah C. J. Stephens, before 1874 in Kentucky. Born 5 Dec 1853 in Pulaski Co., KY. Died 1930. Buried in New Pleasant Point Cemetery, Pulaski Co., KY.

They had the following children:

	i.	Zachariah C. Roy
182	ii.	Emily E. Roy
	iii.	Hannah C. J. Roy
183	iv.	William T. Roy Sr.
	v.	John Wesley Roy
184	vi.	Alexander Roy
	vii.	Ollie May Roy

66. Milford Enoch Rainwater. Son of Daniel McDaniel Rainwater & Ann Whitaker. Born Aug 1850 in Pulaski Co., KY. Died 15 Jul 1932 in Hays Co., TX. Buried 18 Jul 1932 in Murray Cemetery, Milam Co, TX.

He married **Permelia Ellen Garner**, daughter of Dearborn Garner & Elizabeth Evans, 24 Oct 1867 in Pulaski Co., KY. Born c. 1849 in Pulaski Co., KY. Died 4 Feb 1924 in Milam Co., TX. Buried in Pleasant Grove Cemetery, Milam Co., TX.

They had the following children:

185	i.	Joseph D. Rainwater
186	ii.	John L. Rainwater
187	iii.	George Alford Rainwater
	iv.	Mary E. Rainwater
	v.	Balzory M. Rainwater
	vi.	Permelia Jane Rainwater
188	vii.	James B. Rainwater
	viii.	Sarah Rainwater
	ix.	Nannie Rainwater
	x.	Cloda Rainwater (never married)
	xi.	Julia Rainwater

67. Lucy Ann Rainwater. Daughter of Daniel McDaniel Rainwater & Ann Whitaker. Born 29 Dec 1856 in Pulaski Co., KY.

She married **James C. Hammonds**, 6 Jan 1875 in Pulaski Co. KY. Born c. 1854 in Pulaski Co. KY.

They had the following children:

      i.   Thomas Hammonds

68. Anderson Warren Rainwater. Son of Daniel McDaniel Rainwater & Ann Whitaker. Born 7 Jul 1863 in Pulaski Co., KY. Died 13 Nov 1938 in Nancy, Pulaski Co., KY. Buried in New Hope Cemetery, Pulaski Co., KY.

He married **Mary Jane Morris**, 10 Oct 1881 in Pulaski Co. KY. Born 9 Jul 1865 in Wayne Co., KY. Died 12 Jun 1962. Buried in New Hope Cemetery, Pulaski Co., KY.

They had the following children:

	i.	Louise Wilmurth Rainwater
189	ii.	Loretta B. Rainwater
	iii.	Mollie Rainwater
	iv.	Clarence E. Rainwater
	v.	Delilah Audrey Rainwater

69. Bartholomew Rainwater. Son of Daniel McDaniel Rainwater & Ann Whitaker. Born 6 Mar 1865 in Pulaski Co., KY. Died 9 Dec 1923 in Cains Store, Pulaski Co., KY. Buried 11 Dec 1923 in New Hope Cemetery, Pulaski Co., KY.

He first married **Elizabeth Dawes**, daughter of Joseph Dawes & Mary Owens, 30 Apr 1885 in Pulaski Co., KY. Born c. 1862 in Pulaski Co., KY. Died Before 1899.

They had the following children:

	i.	Julia A. Rainwater
	ii.	Elmira Rainwater
190	iii.	William Chester Rainwater
191	iv.	Louis F. Rainwater
	v.	Roscoe R. Rainwater
192	vi.	Thomas E. Rainwater
	vii.	Flora M. Rainwater

He second married **Louellan Hansford**, 14 Oct 1899 in Russell Co., KY. Born Mar 1878 in Pulaski Co. KY. Died 9 Mar 1914 in Pulaski Co., KY. Buried in Tarter Cemetery, Pulaski Co., KY.

They had the following children:

i.	Florence Rainwater
ii.	Daniel Rainwater
iii.	James E. Rainwater
iv.	Bartholomew Rainwater
v.	Infant Rainwater (died at birth)

He third married **America Minton (Dye)**, daughter of Isaac N. Minton and Rachel Gadberry, 25 Apr 1915 in Pulaski Co. KY. Born c. 1874 in Casey Co., KY.

70. Francis M. Rainwater. Son of Daniel McDaniel Rainwater & Ann Whitaker. Born Nov 1867 in Kentucky.

He married **Amanda E. Rainwater**, daughter of Enoch Rainwater & Martha E. Compton, 27 Nov 1887 in Pulaski Co., KY. Born Nov 1857 in Kentucky. Died 1940 in Illinois. Buried in Bethel Cemetery, Vermilion Co., IL. They were separated before 1920.

They had the following children:

193	i.		Albert Rainwater
194	ii.		Alta Rainwater

71. Palmira Marie Rainwater. Daughter of Daniel McDaniel Rainwater & Ann Whitaker. Born Jan 1871 in Somerset, Pulaski Co., KY. Died 22 Dec 1947 in Post, Garza Co., TX. Buried 23 Dec 1947 in Terrace Cemetery, Post, Garza Co., TX.

She first married **James F. Anderson**, 14 Jan 1897 in Pulaski Co., KY. Born Feb 1870 in Tennessee. Died between 1903/1905.

They had the following children:

- i. Wesley Omar Anderson
- ii. Walter W. Anderson
- iii. Gertrude Anderson

She second married **Rev. Morris J. Osborne**, c. 1905 in Texas. Born c. 1853 in Alabama. Died Before 1930 in Texas.

They had the following children:

- i. Cecil M. Osborne

She third married **Jesse Thomas Sybert**, after 1930 in Texas. Died 1 Mar 1947 in Bailey Co., TX. Buried in Rains Co., TX.

72. Thomas Bramletter Weddle. Son of Galen Edward Weddle & Sarah Rainwater. Born 11 Sep 1861 in Kentucky. Died 17 Jan 1912 in Martinsville, Morgan Co., IN. Buried in New South Park Cemetery, Martinsville, Morgan Co., IN.

He married **Elmira Catherine Hubbard**. Born 3 Nov 1867. Died 17 Feb 1939. Buried in New South Park Cemetery, Martinsville, Morgan Co., IN.

They had the following children:

195	i.		Harold P. Weddle

73. Daniel M. Hainey. Son of Thomas D. Hainey & Susannah Rainwater. Born 6 Mar 1858 in Linn Co., KS. Died 21 Jan 1927 in Pulaski Co. KY. Buried in New Pleasant Point Baptist Church Cemetery, Pulaski Co., KY.

He married **Nancy Margaret Wilson**, daughter of Willis N. Wilson Sr. & Nancy Combest, 1 Dec 1880 in Pulaski Co., KY. Born 20 Feb 1864 in Pulaski Co., KY. Died 28 Mar 1924 in Pulaski Co., KY. Buried in New Pleasant Point Baptist Church Cemetery, Pulaski Co., KY.

They had the following children:

196	i.		Josiah Willis Hainey
	ii.		Mary L. Hainey
197	iii.		Samuel D. Hainey

	iv.	Victoria Hainey
	v.	Thomas B. Hainey
198	vi.	Miranda Walker Hainey
	vii.	Smith G. Hainey

74. Silas Green Pitman. Son of William Pitman Sr. & Susannah Rainwater. Born 27 Apr 1868 in Pulaski Co., KY. Died 3 Mar 1926 in Pulaski Co., KY. Buried 6 Mar 1926 in Cedar Point Cemetery, Pulaski Co., KY.

He married **Judy Josephine Louden**, before 1887. Born 15 Oct 1872 in Pulaski Co., KY. Died 30 Mar 1947, Randolph Co., IN. Buried in Cedar Point Cemetery, Pulaski Co., KY.

They had the following children:

199	i.	Martin Luther Pitman
200	ii.	Daniel Gaither Pitman
	iii.	Verdyia Pitman
	iv.	Virgil D. Pitman
	v.	John Simpson Pitman
	vi.	Albert O. Pitman
	vii.	Vidia L. Pitman
	viii.	James Arthur Pitman
	ix.	Arnold Edgar Pitman

75. Enoch Pitman. Son of William Pitman Sr. & Susannah Rainwater. Born 21 Mar 1875 in Kentucky. Died 14 Aug 1957. Buried in Shady Grove Cemetery, Pulaski Co., KY.

He married **Colotha**, c. 1894. Born Dec 1877 in Kentucky.

They had the following children:

	i.	Rhoda Pitman
	ii.	William Pitman
	iii.	Chester Pitman

76. Charles H. Pitman. Son of William Pitman Sr. & Susannah Rainwater. Born Apr 1882 in Kentucky.

He married **Nannie F.**, c. 1904. Born c. 1885 in Kentucky.

They had the following children:

	i.	GIlbert L. Pitman
	ii.	Elford Pitman
	iii.	Susan Pitman

77. Lucy Isadore Holbrook. Daughter of Alfred Joseph Holbrook & Mary Rainwater. Born 5 Mar 1860 in Kansas.

She married **Charles Franklin Ashley**, son of John Ashley & Lucy Walden, 28 Nov 1880 in Linn Co., KS. Born 22 Oct 1857 in Kansas.

They had the following children:

        i.   Leo Franklin Ashley

78. Nancy Belle Elder. Daughter of John Levi Elder & Sciota Bethene Rainwater. Born 6 Feb 1860 in Pulaski Co., KY. Died 5 Nov 1928 in St. Joseph, Buchanan Co., MO. Buried in Mt. Auburn Cemetery, Buchanan Co., MO .

She married **George Calvin Lewellen**, 16 Jun 1880 in Holt Co., MO. Born 16 Jun 1821 in Pennsylvania. Died 27 Feb 1917 in St Joseph, Buchanon Co., MO.

They had the following children:

201	i.		Sciota Belle Lewellen
	ii		Josaphine Lewellen
	iii.		Gertrude Lewellen
	iv.		Bessie Lewellen
	v.		Sarah J. Lewellen
	vi.		Ruth Lewellen
	vii.		George Calvin Lewellen, Jr.
	viii.		Eva Blanche Lewellen

79. Cornelia Ellen Elder. Daughter of John Levi Elder & Sciota Bethene Rainwater. Born 7 Jan 1868 in Pulaski Co. KY. Died 27 Jun 1907 in Forest City, Holt Co., MO.

She married **Samuel Robert Ford**, 21 Jan 1903 in Holt Co., MO.

They had the following children:

        i.   Nellie Leona Ford

80. James Riley Elder. Son of John Levi Elder & Sciota Bethene Rainwater. Born 4 Apr 1870 in Pulaski Co., KY. Died 1937 in Oregon, Holt Co., MO. Buried in Maple Grove Cemetery, Oregon, Holt Co., MO.

He married **Mittie J. Hahn**, 21 Feb 1894 in Missouri. Born 1875. Died 1961 in Oregon, Holt Co., MO. Buried in Maple Grove Cemetery, Oregon, Holt Co., MO.

They had the following children:

    i.   George L. Elder
    ii.   Robert F. Elder
    iii.   Russell R. Elder
    iv.   Glenn C. Elder
    v.   Ken C. Elder

81. John Perry Chumbley. Son of Alexander Chumbley & Sarelda Ann Rainwater. Born 10 Jan 1860 in Russell Co., KY. Died 12 Sep 1935 in Whitewright, Grayson Co., TX. Buried in Oak Hill Cemetery, Fannin Co., TX.

He first married **Almarinda J. Trimble**, 30 Oct 1878 in Pulaski Co. KY. Born 22 Aug 1859 in Kentucky. Died 30 Sep 1894 in Whitewright, Grayson Co., TX. Buried in Oak Hill Cemetery, Fannin Co., TX.

They had the following children:

    202   i.   Rev. Cleophas Chumbley

ii.	Nannie Chumbley
iii.	Angelina Chumbley
iv.	Alta Chumbley
v.	Sarelda Chumbley
vi.	Cloda Chumbley
vii.	Debbie Chumbley
viii.	Lela Chumbley

He second married **Mahala Ann Richardson**, c. 1896 in Texas. Born 11 Oct 1862 in Tennessee. Died 25 May 1924 in Whitewright, Grayson Co., TX. Buried in Oak Hill Cemetery, Fannin Co., TX.

They had the following children:

i.	George Chumbley
ii.	Robert Chumbley
iii.	Ethel Chumbley

82. James Marion Chumbley. Son of Alexander Chumbley & Sarelda Ann Rainwater. Born 7 May 1862 in Kentucky. Died 1943 in Arizona.

He first married **Mattie Lelia Fitzgerald**, before 1884 in Kentucky. Born 1865. Died c. 1897 in Texas.

They had the following children:

i.	Elbert Chumbley
ii.	Miles Rainwater Chumbley
iii.	George Alexander Chumbley
iv.	Vessie Chumbley
v.	Effie May Chumbley
vi.	Grace Chumbley (Harkey)

He second married **Alcienia Elizabeth Magnum**, daughter of Alcienia (Magnum), c. 1900 in Texas. Born c. 1866 in Arkansas.

They had the following children:

i.	Dorothy Chumbley
ii.	Alma Jon Chumbley

83. Miles Rainwater Chumbley. Son of Alexander Chumbley & Sarelda Ann Rainwater. Born 27 Mar 1864 in Pulaski Co., KY.

He married **Susan H. Tarter**, daughter of Caleb M. Tarter & Mary Gaines, 3 Jan 1893 in Pulaski Co. KY. Born c. 1874 in Pulaski Co., KY.

They had the following children:

i.	Alex Chumbley
ii.	Sallie Chumbley
iii.	Caleb Milton Chumbley
iv.	John Chumbley

v.	Robert Chumbley
vi.	Elizabeth Chumbley
vii.	James Chumbley

84. George A. Chumbley. Son of Alexander Chumbley & Sarelda Ann Rainwater. Born 2 Dec 1866 in Kentucky. Died 26 Feb 1920 in Klondike, Delta Co., TX. Buried Feb 1920 in Old Klondike Cemetery, Delta Co., TX.

He married **Lula M. Hunt**, c. 1899 in Texas. Born 12 Nov 1878 in Texas. Died 7 Nov 1926.

They had the following children:

i.	James J. Chumbley
ii.	Cemura B. Chumbley
iii.	Selma J. Chumbley
iv.	Cleophas Chumbley
v.	Delbert Chumbley
vi.	Sam B. Chumbley

85. Robert R. Chumbley. Son of Alexander Chumbley & Sarelda Ann Rainwater. Born 12 Jan 1875 in Kentucky. Died 1 Jan 1969 in Sherman, Grayson Co., TX. Buried in Vittitoe Cemetery, Kentuckytown, Grayson Co., TX.

He married **Sallie**, c. 1901 in Grayson Co., TX. Born 1878 in North Carolina. Died 1948. Buried in Vittitoe Cemetery, Kentuckytown, Grayson Co., TX.

They had the following children:

i.	Sarelda Ann Chumbley
ii.	John B. Chumbley
iii.	Charles M. Chumbley
iv.	Joe W. Chumbley
v.	Miles B. Chumbley
vi.	David Chumbley
vii.	James H. Chumbley

86. Margaret Ann Chumbley. Daughter of Alexander Chumbley & Sarelda Ann Rainwater. Born 27 Mar 1878 in Kentucky. Died 10 Aug 1950 in Sherman, Grayson Co., TX. Buried in Old Church Cemetery, Bennington, Bryan Co., OK.

She married George W. Dobbs, 21 Dec 1894 in Hunt Co., TX.

They had the following children:

i.	Joe Dobbs
ii.	Ben Dobbs
iii.	Bartie Dobbs
iv.	William Dobbs

87. Lewis Milton Chumbley. Son of Alexander Chumbley & Sarelda Ann Rainwater. Born 8 Jul 1879 in Kentucky.

He married **Helen Magdelena Cowen**, 16 Aug 1906 in Hunt Co., TX. Born c. 1889 in Kentucky.

They had the following children:

		i.	Avil Walker Chumbley
		ii.	Jim Chumbley (twin)
		iii.	Robert Chumbley (twin)
	203	iv.	Willie Allen Chumbley
	204	v.	Alcienia Elizabeth Chumbley
		vi.	Mary Helen Chumbley

88. Josiah Wilson Chumbley Sr. Son of Alexander Chumbley & Sarelda Ann Rainwater. Born 3 Nov 1886 in Somerset, Pulaski Co., KY. Died 28 Feb 1953 in Sherman, Grayson Co., TX. Buried in West Hill Cemetery, Sherman, Grayson Co., TX.

He married **Mamie Rea Weaver**, daughter of W. E Weaver & Ada May, 15 Dec 1912 in Kondike, Delta Co., TX. Born 5 Apr 1895 in Delta Co., TX. Died May 1968. Buried in West Hill Cemetery, Sherman, Grayson Co., TX.

They had the following children:

i.	Josiah Wilson Chumbley Jr.
ii.	Ilene Chumbley
iii.	Winston A. Chumbley

89. Martha Jane Rainwater. Daughter of Josiah Wilson Rainwater & Elizabeth Jane Weddle. Born 24 Oct 1866 in Somerset, Pulaski Co., KY. Died 2 Aug 1961 in Vernon, Wilbarger Co., TX. Buried in East View Cemetery, Vernon, Wilbarger Co., TX.

She married **Peter Christopher Rainwater**, son of Jeremiah Stanton Rainwater & Eve Tarter, 28 Jun 1893 in Waterloo Williamson Co., TX . Born 12 Sep 1859 in Dalton, GA. Died 19 Dec 1949 in Vernon, Wilbarger Co., TX. Buried in East View Cemetery, Vernon, Wilbarger Co., TX.

They had the following children:

	i.	Eva Rainwater (Kirk)
205	ii.	Hobart Rainwater
	iii.	Vivian Rainwater, Born 1901, died 1904
	iv.	Bristow Rainwater
206	v.	Elizabeth Rainwater (Arnold)

90. Nancy Frances Rainwater. Daughter of Josiah Wilson Rainwater & Elizabeth Jane Weddle. Born 28 Aug 1869 in Waterloo, Pulaski Co., KY. Died 3 Aug 1942 in Taylor, Williamson Co., Texas. Buried 3 Aug 1942 in Taylor City Cemetery, Taylor, Williamson Co., TX.

She married **Charles Mercer Gossett**, son of Joel Thomas Gossett & Selina Duck, 15 Nov 1893 in Williamson Co., TX. Born 20 Jan 1870 in Kentucky. Died 23 May 1941. Buried 25 May 1941 in Taylor City Cemetery, Taylor, Williamson Co., TX.

They had the following children:

i.	Itha Gertrude Gossett (Hamilton)

207	ii.	Charles Carroll Gossett
	iii.	Zella Gossett (died at birth)
	iv.	Louise Gossett (Word)
	v.	Josephine Winifred Gossett (Warren)

91. Lucy Isadore Rainwater. Daughter of Josiah Wilson Rainwater & Elizabeth Jane Weddle. Born 7 Jan 1872 in Waterloo, Pulaski Co., KY. Died 12 Jan 1963 in Vernon, Wilbarger County, TX. Buried 13 Jan 1963 in East View Cemetery, Vernon, TX.

She married **John Pinkney Aderholt Sr.**, son of Emanuel M. Aderholt & Saphronia Elizabeth Stone, 14 Dec 1892 in Taylor, Williamson Co., TX. Born 22 Jun 1870 in Springville, St. Clair Co., AL. Died 6 Jul 1946 in Vernon, Wilbarger County, TX. Buried Jul 1946 in East View Cemetery, Vernon, Wilbarger Co., TX.

They had the following children:

208	i.	Joseph Walter Aderholt
209	ii.	Esta Mary Aderholt (Lemon)
	iii.	Howard Wilson Aderholt
	iv.	John Pinkney Aderholt Jr.
210	v.	Charlie Morris Aderholt

92. Doretta Rainwater. Daughter of Josiah Wilson Rainwater & Elizabeth Jane Weddle. Born 18 Mar 1874 in Waterloo, Pulaski Co., KY. Died 6 Apr 1966 in Electra, Wichita Co., TX. Buried 8 Apr 1966 in East View Cemetery, Vernon, Wilbarger Co., TX.

She married **Ranza Lee Luttrell**, son of James Madison Luttrell & Sarah Jane Taylor, 14 Dec 1892 in Taylor, Williamson Co., Texas. Born 15 Aug 1870 in Dunnville, Casey Co., KY. Died 12 May 1962 in Wilbarger Co., TX. Buried in East View Cemetery, Vernon, Wilbarger Co., TX.

They had the following children:

211	i.	Edward Edgar Luttrell
212	ii.	Ira Bryan Luttrell
213	iii.	Alva Otis Luttrell
	iv.	Gilbert Cecil Luttrell
214	v.	James Roscoe Luttrell
	vi.	infant Luttrell (died at birth)

93. Miles Rainwater. Son of Josiah Wilson Rainwater & Elizabeth Jane Weddle. Born 15 Jun 1876 in Waterloo, Pulaski County, KY. Died 20 May 1956 in Vernon, Wilbarger County, TX. Buried in Eastview Cemetery, Vernon, Wilbarger Co., TX.

He married **Ollie Frances Cooper**, daughter of William Thomas Cooper & Martha Jane Floyd, 16 Mar 1898 in Taylor, Williamson Co., TX. Born 27 Nov 1878 in Kentucky. Died 7 Mar 1965 in Wilbarger Co., TX. Buried in Eastview Cemetery, Vernon, Wilbarger Co., TX.

They had the following children:

	i.	Clarence Rainwater

215	ii.	Hellen Rainwater (Stallings/Jackson)
216	iii.	Lucille Rainwater (Koontz)
217	iv.	Roscoe William Rainwater
218	v.	Lloyd Elmo Rainwater
219	vi.	Dorothy Rainwater (Eure)
220	vii.	Joe T. Rainwater
221	viii.	Betty Jo Rainwater (Floyd)

94. Mary Rainwater. Daughter of Josiah Wilson Rainwater & Elizabeth Jane Weddle. Born 28 Apr 1879 in Waterloo, Pulaski Co., KY. Died 4 Nov 1984 in Taylor, Williamson Co., TX. Buried 6 Nov 1984 in Taylor City Cemetery, Taylor, Williamson Co., TX.

She married **Charles A. Aderholt**, son of Emanuel M. Aderholt & Saphronia Elizabeth Stone, 22 Dec 1898 in Taylor, Williamson Co., TX. Born 14 Dec 1875 in Springville, St. Clair Co., AL. Died 9 Jul 1953 in Taylor, Williamson Co., TX. Buried 11 Jul 1953 in Taylor City Cemetery, Taylor, Williamson Co., TX.

They had the following children:

222	i.	Irene Aderholt (Skinner)
223	ii.	Ruth Aderholt (Guyton)
224	iii.	Ruby Aderholt (Harrod)
225	iv.	Bess Aderholt (Clark)
	v.	Mary Adele Aderholt (Smith)
	vi.	infant Aderholt (died at birth)

95. Cornelia Rainwater. Daughter of Josiah Wilson Rainwater & Elizabeth Jane Weddle. Born 17 Apr 1881 in Waterloo, Pulaski Co., KY. Died 17 Oct 1967 in Long Beach, Los Angeles Co., CA. Buried in East View Memorial Cemetery, Vernon, TX.

She married **Alva Fenton Gaston**, son of Joseph Liman Gaston & Matilda Turner, 29 Oct 1902 in Taylor, Williamson Co., TX. Born 8 Jun 1872 in Missouri. Died 21 Nov 1949 in Vernon, Wilbarger Co., TX. Buried in East View Memorial Cemetery, Vernon, Wilbarger Co., TX.

They had the following children:

	i.	Louise Gaston (Partlow)
226	ii.	Ada Frances Gaston
227	iii.	Edgar Joseph Gaston
	iv.	Robert E. Gaston
228	v.	Miles Warren Gaston
229	vi.	Effie Doretta Gaston (Moon)
230	vii.	Nola Gayle Gaston (Pirkle)

96. Roscoe Conklin Rainwater. Son of Josiah Wilson Rainwater & Elizabeth Jane Weddle. Born 4 Jul 1883 in Waterloo, Pulaski County, KY. Died 8 Nov 1972 in Vernon, Wilbarger County, TX. Buried Nov 1972 in Wilbarger Memorial Park, Lockett, Wilbarger Co., TX.

He married **Gertrude Alice Caughron**, daughter of Theophilus Walter Caughron & Arzona Belle Compton, 23 May 1906 in 1st Baptist Church, Taylor, TX. Born 19 Oct 1884 in Taylor, Williamson Co., TX. Died 17 Aug 1969 in Vernon, Wilbarger County, TX. Buried 19 Aug 1969 in Wilbarger Memorial Park, Lockett, Wilbarger Co., TX.

They had the following children:

231	i.	Roscoe Compton Rainwater
	ii.	Cristine Minnie Rainwater (Fletcher/Lee)
232	iii.	Johnie Wayne Rainwater
233	iv.	Walter Eugene Rainwater
234	v.	Clois Miles Rainwater

97. Minnie Rainwater. Daughter of Josiah Wilson Rainwater & Elizabeth Jane Weddle. Born 15 Jul 1885 in Waterloo, Pulaski Co., KY. Died 15 Jul 1971 in Electra, Wichita Co., TX. Buried in East View Cemetery, Vernon, Wilbarger Co., TX.

She first married **John H. Brownlee**, son of James Andrew Brownlee & Sallie J. Fitzgerald, 27 Feb 1908 in Taylor, Williamson Co., TX. Born 12 Oct 1883 in TX. Died 19 Jun 1939 in Temple, Bell Co., TX. Buried 21 Jun 1939 in East View Cemetery, Vernon, Wilbarger Co., TX.

They had the following children:

	i.	John H. Brownlee, Jr. (died at birth)
	ii.	Frances Eloise Brownlee (died two months after birth)
	iii.	Wilma Brownlee (adopted)
	iv.	Robert Maurice Brownlee (adopted)
	v.	Jack C. Brownlee

98. Sarah E. Rainwater. Daughter of William H. Rainwater & Nancy Jane Russell. Born 2 Dec 1853 in Pulaski Co., KY. Died 31 Jul 1931. Buried in New Hope Cm, Pulaski Co., KY.

She married **Alexander Hunley**, 10 Aug 1876 in Pulaski Co. KY. Born 31 Mar 1855 in KY. Died 28 Nov 1936. Buried in New Hope Cemetery, Pulaski Co., KY.

They had the following children:

	i.	George A. Hunley
	ii.	Edward Hunley
235	iii.	William H. Hunley
	iv.	Nancy J. Hunley
	v.	Sarah E. Hunley

99. Leonidas Breckenridge Rainwater. Son of William H. Rainwater & Nancy Jane Russell. Born 15 Jun 1859 in Pulaski Co., KY. Died 10 Sep 1910 in Pulaski Co., KY. Buried in New Hope Cemetery, Pulaski Co., KY.

He married **Rosetta Harber**, daughter of Naomia & John Harber, 2 Jan 1887 in Pulaski Co., KY. Born 30 Oct 1867 in KY. Died 18 Mar 1908 in Pulaski Co., KY. Buried in New Hope Cemetery, Pulaski Co., KY.

They had the following children:

	i.	Elwood Rainwater
236	ii.	Mary Fannie Rainwater
	iii.	Belzie B. Rainwater
	iv.	Robert F. Rainwater
	v.	Cornelius Rainwater

100. Lubantus B. Rainwater. Son of William H. Rainwater & Nancy Jane Russell. Born 11 Oct 1860 in Kentucky. Died 10 Apr 1934 in Red River Co., TX. Buried in Bluff Cemetery, Red River Co., TX.

He first married **Nancy J. Morris**, 23 Jan 1896 in Pulaski Co., KY. Born Sep 1868 in Pulaski Co., KY. Died before 1900/1910 in KY. They were divorced before 1899.

They had the following children:

    i.   Thomas W. Rainwater

He second married **Ella**, before 1910. Born c. 1889 in Kentucky.

101. Rufus F. Rainwater. Son of William H. Rainwater & Nancy Jane Russell. Born 1 Apr 1869 in Pulaski Co., KY. Died 15 Jan 1939 in Linville, Pulaski Co., KY. Buried 16 Jan 1939 in West Somerset Cemetery, Pulaski Co., KY.

He married **Martha J. Sharp**, 27 Dec 1891 in Pulaski Co. KY. Born 18 Jun 1874 in Pulaski Co. KY. Died 30 Mar 1963. Buried in West Somerset Cemetery, Pulaski Co., KY.

They had the following children:

    i.   William L. Rainwater

    ii.   Robert R. Rainwater

102. China Paralee Rainwater. Daughter of Enoch Rainwater & Martha E. Compton. Born 5 Jan 1854 in Pulaski Co., KY. Died 11 Jul 1937 in Pulaski Co., KY. Buried in New Hope Cemetery, Pulaski Co., KY.

She married **Fountain Rainwater**, son of Miles Rainwater & Frances Chaney, 19 Nov 1889 in Pulaski Co., KY. Born 12 Jan 1854 in Pulaski Co., KY. Died 20 Dec 1944 in Pulaski Co., KY. Buried in New Hope Cemetery, Pulaski Co., KY.

They had the following children:

    i.   Carthel Spurgeon Rainwater

103. Amanda E. Rainwater. Daughter of Enoch Rainwater & Martha E. Compton. Born Nov 1857 in Kentucky . Died 1940 in Illinois. Buried in Bethel Cemetery, Vermilion Co., IL.

She married **Francis M. Rainwater**, son of Daniel McDaniel Rainwater & Ann Whitaker, 27 Nov 1887 in Pulaski Co., KY. Born Nov 1867 in Kentucky. Died After 1920. They were separated Before 1920.

They had the following children:

193	i.	Albert Rainwater
194	ii.	Alta Rainwater

104. Adaliza E. Rainwater. Daughter of Enoch Rainwater & Martha E. Compton. Born Dec 1863 in Pulaski Co., KY. Died 1906. Buried in New Hope Cemetery, Pulaski Co., KY.

She married **James Wright Ware**, 31 Dec 1882 in Pulaski Co., KY. Born Jan 1863 in Pulaski Co., KY. Died 1946. Buried in New Hope Cemetery, Pulaski Co., KY.

They had the following children:

	i.	Bertha B. Ware
	ii.	Mollie G. Ware
	iii.	Mary M. Ware
	iv.	Terressa L. Ware
	v.	Oteley R. Ware
	vi.	Hobart E. Ware
	vii.	Zula E. Ware

105. William Harrison Rainwater. Son of Enoch Rainwater & Martha E. Compton. Born 29 Nov 1863 in Pulaski Co., KY. Died 29 Jan 1909 in Pulaski Co. KY. Buried in New Hope Cemetery, Pulaski Co., KY.

He married **Martha Ann Redmond**, daughter of William Redmond & Mary Dodson, 19 Dec 1880 in Pulaski Co., KY. Born 20 Apr 1865 in Pulaski Co., KY. Died 14 Jun 1919 in Pulaski Co., KY. Buried 15 Jun 1919 in New Hope Cemetery, Pulaski Co., KY.

They had the following children:

237	i.	Hoy E. Rainwater Sr.
238	ii.	Myrtle L. Rainwater
239	iii.	Oscar Rainwater
240	iv.	Herchel McKinley Rainwater
241	v.	Herbert E. Rainwater
	vi.	Bertha Rainwater
	vii.	Willie Rainwater

106. Silas Monroe Rainwater. Son of Enoch Rainwater & Martha E. Compton. Born 31 Jan 1866 in Pulaski Co., KY. Died 18 Apr 1934 in Patterson, Casey Co., KY. Buried 19 Apr 1934 in New Hope Cemetery, Pulaski Co., KY.

He first married **Nancy Perdaneese Melton**, c. 1885 in Kentucky. Born Jul 1865 in Kentucky. Died 5 Aug 1908 in Hartley Co., TX. Buried in Channing Cemetery, Channing, Hartley Co., TX.

They had the following children:

242	i.	Alta Beatrice Rainwater
243	ii.	Robert T. Rainwater
	iii.	Ressa Myrtle Rainwater
	iv.	Ada May Rainwater

He second married **Mary E. Burton**, 13 Dec 1908 in Pulaski Co., KY. Born 1 Mar 1881 in Pulaski Co., KY. Died 12 Jan 1960. Buried in New Hope Cemetery, Pulaski Co., KY.

They had the following children:

	i.	Edith D. Rainwater

	ii.	Lela V. Rainwater
	iii.	Zena M. Rainwater
	iv.	Clifford C. Rainwater
	v.	Hermionie / Minnie P. Rainwater

107. Terressa Rainwater. Daughter of Enoch Rainwater & Martha E. Compton. Born 1873 in Pulaski Co., KY. Buried in New Hope Cemetery, Pulaski Co., KY.

She married **William L. Porter Jr.** , son of Rev. William L. Porter Sr. & Henrietta Rayburn, 16 Dec 1894 in Pulaski Co. KY. Born c. 1868 in Pulaski Co. KY. Died 21 Aug 1943 in Russell Co., KY.

They had the following children:

| | i. | Roscoe Porter |
| | ii. | Martha Porter (Wilson) |

108. Virgil M. Rainwater. Son of Enoch Rainwater & Martha E. Compton. Born Nov 1876 in Pulaski Co., KY. Died 28 Mar 1959 in Pulaski Co., KY. Buried in New Hope Cemetery, Pulaski Co., KY.

He married **Dora E. Cooper**, daughter of Isaac E. Cooper & Mary Ann Bastin, 18 Jan 1893 in Pulaski Co., KY. Born 21 Jul 1873 in Pulaski Co. KY. Died 26 Sep 1915 in Hickory Nut, Pulaski Co., KY. Buried 28 Sep 1915 in New Hope Cemetery, Pulaski Co., KY.

They had the following children:

| | i. | Orval Rainwater |

109. Carl B. Rainwater. Son of Enoch Rainwater & Martha E. Compton. Born 7 Apr 1881 in Pulaski Co., KY. Died 13 Dec 1962 in Nancy, Pulaski Co., KY. Buried in New Hope Cemetery, Pulaski Co., KY.

He married **Ethie D. Popplewell**, daughter of Milton Popplewell & Lucy Johnson, 27 Mar 1910 in Pulaski Co., KY. Born 28 Mar 1886 in Russell Co., KY. Died 16 Feb 1968. Buried in New Hope Cemetery, Pulaski Co., KY.

They had the following children:

| | i. | Eda Rainwater |

110. James Henry Rainwater. Son of John Rainwater & Sarah Elizabeth Porter. Born 11 Dec 1858 in Somerset, Pulaski Co., KY. Died 13 May 1917 in New Canton, Pike Co., IL.

He married **Sarah E. Crews,** daughter of Fleming H. Crews & Elizabeth White, 9 Jul 1884 in Quincy, Adams Co., IL. Born 16 Nov 1862 in Middletown, Montgomery Co., MO. Died 15 Feb 1950 in Pike Co., IL.

They had the following children:

244	i.	Pearl H. Rainwater
	ii.	Merle Rainwater
	iii.	Fern Rainwater
245	iv.	Russell C. Rainwater

111. Enoch John Rainwater. Son of John Rainwater & Sarah Elizabeth Porter. Born 27 Jan 1861 in Pratt Co., IL. Died 30 Nov 1942 in St. Louis, St Louis Co., MO.

He married **Mary Ann Foote**, 13 Nov 1883 in Pike Co., IL. Born 23 Feb 1862 in Pittsfield, Pike Co., IL. Died 16 Feb 1944 in Hynes, Los Angeles Co., CA.

They had the following children:

	i.	Clarence Elmer Rainwater
246	ii.	Julius Henry Rainwater Sr.
247	iii.	Ethel Elizabeth Rainwater
248	iv.	John P. Rainwater
249	v.	Ida Mae Rainwater

112. Mary Frances Dick. Daughter of John Dick & Alethia Rainwater. Born 22 Nov 1866 in Pulaski Co., KY. Died 19 Jul 1943 in Pulaski Co. KY. Buried in West Somerset Baptist Church Cemetery, Pulaski Co., KY.

She married **William H. Rexroat**, son of George Rexroat & Mary Gosser, 23 Aug 1885 in Pulaski Co. KY.

They had the following children:

250	i.	Alatha Jane Rexroat
251	ii.	JoAnnia Rexroat

113. Rutherford Columbus Dick. Son of John Dick & Alethia Rainwater. Born 19 Nov 1876. Died 22 Nov 1956. Buried in Cedar Point Cemetery, Pulaski Co., KY.

He married **Laura Austin**, Before 1898. Born 2 May 1880 in Russell Co., KY. Died 8 Dec 1955. Buried in Cedar Point Cemetery, Pulaski Co., KY.

They had the following children:

	i.	Elmer L. Dick

114. Perry Milton Rainwater. Son of Jeremiah Stanton Rainwater & Eve Tarter. Born 1 May 1853 in Pulaski Co., KY. Died 11 Jun 1913 in Pulaski Co., KY. Buried in Tarter Hudson Cm, Pulaski Co., KY.

He first married **Polly Ann Stewart**, daughter of Phoebe (Stewart), 10 May 1874 in Pulaski Co. KY. Born c. 1847 in Pulaski Co. KY. Died before 1892.

They had the following children:

	i.	Charles Oland Rainwater
	ii.	William P. Rainwater

He second married **Matilda Foster**, daughter of William Foster & Polly, 1 May 1892 in Pulaski Co., KY. Born 11 Jun 1874 in Wayne Co., KY. Died 15 Jan 1945 in Monticello, Piatt Co., IL. Buried in Goose Creek/DeLand Cemetery, Piatt Co., IL.

They had the following children:

252	i.	Samuel P. Rainwater

115. Oliver Wesley Rainwater. Son of Jeremiah Stanton Rainwater & Eve Tarter. Born Apr 1855 in Green Co., KY. Died 9 May 1924 in Pulaski Co., KY. Buried 10 May 1924 in Cundiff Cemetery, Pulaski Co., KY.

He married **Margaret Ellen LeFaver**, 7 Oct 1883 in Pulaski Co. KY. Born 30 Jun 1859 in Tennessee. Died 29 Sep 1917 in Pulaski Co., KY. Buried in Cundiff Cemetery, Pulaski Co., KY.

They had the following children:

253	i.	Levera Rainwater
	ii.	Archibald Rainwater
	iii.	Louise Rainwater
254	iv.	Jesse Rainwater
	v.	Charles Rainwater
255	vi.	Francis Pierce Rainwater

116. Laura B. Rainwater. Daughter of Jeremiah Stanton Rainwater & Eve Tarter. Born Mar 1865 in KY. Died after 1900.

She had the following children out of wedlock:

	i.	Willie B. Rainwater (illegitimate)

117. Peter Christopher Rainwater. Son of Jeremiah Stanton Rainwater & Eve Tarter. Born 12 Sep 1859 in Dalton, GA. Died 19 Dec 1949 in Vernon, Wilbarger Co., TX. Buried in East View Cemetery, Vernon, Wilbarger Co., TX.

He married **Martha Jane Rainwater**, daughter of Josiah Wilson Rainwater & Elizabeth Jane Weddle, 28 Jun 1893 in Waterloo Williamson Co., TX. Born 24 Oct 1866 in Somerset, Pulaski Co., KY. Died 2 Aug 1961 in Vernon, Wilbarger Co., TX. Buried in East View Cemetery, Vernon, Wilbarger Co., TX.

They had the following children:

	i.	Eva Rainwater
205	ii.	Hobart Rainwater
	iii.	Vivian Rainwater
	iv.	Bristow Rainwater
206	v.	Elizabeth Rainwater

118. George Willis Rainwater. Son of Jeremiah Stanton Rainwater & Eve Tarter. Born 1 Jun 1862 in Kentucky. Died 22 Jan 1936. Buried in Slate Branch Cemetery, Pulaski Co., KY.

He married **Elvira McClendon**, 23 Jul 1889 in Russell Co., KY. Born 8 Apr 1870 in Kentucky. Died 17 Apr 1952. Buried in Slate Branch Cemetery, Pulaski Co., KY.

They had the following children:

	i.	Lucy Rainwater
	ii.	Oras Lee Rainwater
256	iii.	Dona Rainwater
257	iv.	Oliver Leonard Rainwater
258	v.	George Willis Rainwater Jr.
	vi.	Edward P. Rainwater
259	vii.	Virgil Rainwater Sr.
	viii.	Eva A. Rainwater
	ix.	Octavia Rainwater

    x. Orville Rainwater

119. Lorenzo Dow Rainwater. Son of Jeremiah Stanton Rainwater & Martha J. Barnes. Born c. 1890 in Kentucky.

He married **Rose**, before 1914. Born c. 1894 in Kentucky.

They had the following children:

    i. Georgia Rainwater
    ii. Arnold Rainwater
    iii. Leonard Rainwater

120. Thomas Arnold Rainwater. Son of Jeremiah Stanton Rainwater & Martha J. Barnes. Born 14 Feb 1896 in Kentucky. Died 29 Jul 1952 in Logan Co., WV. Buried in Foley Cemetery, Melville, Logan Co., WV.

He married **Effie**, c. 1919. Born 1904 in West Virginia.

They had the following children:

    i. Noah Rainwater
    ii. Okey Rainwater
    iii. Dorothy Rainwater
    iv. Estelle Rainwater
    v. Ruth Rainwater
    vi. Jewell Rainwater
    vii. Viola Rainwater

121. David Gentry Rainwater. Son of Jeremiah Stanton Rainwater & Martha J. Barnes. Born c. 1895 in Kentucky.

He married **Pearl Lawson**.

They had the following children:

    i. Raymond Rainwater
    ii. Arnetta Rainwater
    iii. Opal Rainwater

122. Ephriam Rainwater Jr. Son of Ephraim R. Rainwater & Melissa Roy. Born c. 1869 in Indiana.

He married **Ella Hammond**, 24 Aug 1896 in Knox Co., IL. Born c. 1870 in Missouri.

They had the following children:

  260 i. Raymond Rainwater
    ii. Essie Rainwater
    iii. Marie Rainwater
    iv. Ephriam Rainwater Jr.

123. George Alfred Emerson. Son of Milton Emerson & Nancy Rainwater. Born 28 Mar 1864 in KY.

He married **Aquilla Wall**, daughter of Madison Wall & Elizabeth Ann, 10 Oct 1886 in Casey Co., KY.

They had the following children:

    261   i.   Flonnie Emerson

124. John Perry Emerson. Son of Milton Emerson & Nancy Rainwater. Born 25 Oct 1872. Died 27 May 1950 in Pulaski Co., KY. Buried in Cedar Point Cemetery, Pulaski Co., KY.

He married **Millie Catherine Rainwater**, daughter of George Alfred Rainwater & Permelia Susan Garner, 7 Oct 1902 in Helenwood, TN. Born 9 Jan 1884 in Kentucky. Died 20 Nov 1966 in Cains Store, Pulaski Co., KY. Buried in Cedar Point Cemetery, Pulaski Co., KY.

They had the following children:

            i.   Euphia Emerson
            ii.   Everett Emerson
            iii.   Waldo Emerson
    262   iv.   James Emery Emerson
            v.   John Cloyd Emerson

125. Tilitha J. Rainwater. Daughter of Giles R. Rainwater & Sarah Jane Emerson. Born 6 Mar 1863 in Mintonville, Casey Co., KY.

She married **James P. Wells**, son of Francis Wells & Mahala, 31 Dec 1882 in Casey Co., KY. Born Nov 1856 in Kentucky.

They had the following children:

            i.   Zilah J. Wells
            ii.   Ada L. Wells
            iii.   Arma B. Wells
            iv.   Ella M. Wells
            v.   Mary C. Wells

126. Daniel Francis Rainwater. Son of Giles R. Rainwater & Sarah Jane Emerson. Born 26 Apr 1865 in Casey Co., KY. Died 26 Oct 1913 in Mintonville, Casey Co., KY. Buried in Mintonville Cemetery, Casey Co., KY.

He first married **Serena Henson**, daughter of Joseph Henson & Sarah Jane Ware, 4 Mar 1885 in Casey Co., KY. Born 12 Feb 1865 in South Fork Green River, Casey Co., KY. Died 6 Jan 1910 in Mintonville, Casey Co., KY. Buried in Mintonville Methodist Church Cemetery, Casey Co., KY.

They had the following children:

            i.   Elbert Lee Rainwater
    263   ii.   John Rainwater
    264   iii.   Hettie Jane Rainwater
    265   iv.   Joseph Rainwater
            v.   Everett Rainwater (twin)
    266   vi.   Ella Rainwater (twin)
    267   vii.   Sarah F. Rainwater (Greenwell)

		viii.	Ruth Rainwater
268			

He second married **Josephine Gosser**, daughter of Levi B. Gosser & Sally Ann Taylor, 22 Nov 1911 in Casey Co., KY. Born 10 Mar 1875 in Missouri. Died 30 Oct 1945 in Casey Co., KY. Buried in Mintonville Cemetery, Casey Co., KY.

They had the following children:

	i.	Ralph W. Rainwater (never married)

127. Matilda E. Rainwater. Daughter of Giles R. Rainwater & Sarah Jane Emerson. Born 22 Apr 1867 in Mintonville, Casey Co., KY. Died between 1910/1920 in Arkansas.

She first married **John J. Henson**, son of Joseph Henson & Sarah Jane Ware, 10 May 1883 in Casey Co., KY. Born c. 1863 in Kentucky. Died before 1889 in Kentucky.

They had the following children:

269	i.	Oscar C. Henson
	ii.	Margaret Jane Henson (Lyons)

She second married **John L. Wells**, son of Mahala & Francis Wells, 3 Mar 1889 in Casey Co., KY. Born Jan 1954 in Kentucky. Died between 1910/1920 in Kentucky.

They had the following children:

i.	James F. Wells
ii.	Joseph L. Wells
iii.	Giles M. Wells
iv.	Silas McKinley Wells
v.	Lola M. Wells
vi.	Alla M. Wells

128. John Silas Rainwater Sr. Son of Giles R. Rainwater & Sarah Jane Emerson. Born 21 Apr 1872 in Mintonville, Casey Co., KY. Died 29 Aug 1960 in Okmulgee OK. Buried in Morris Cemetery, Okmulgee Co., OK.

He married **Nancy Catherine Vest**, daughter of John William Vest Sr. & Mary J. Cravens, 19 Oct 1894 in Casey Co., KY. Born 18 Jan 1882 in Casey Co., KY. Died 10 Jun 1955 in Okmulgee Co., OK. Buried in Morris Cemetery, Okmulgee Co., OK.

They had the following children:

270	i.	Dovie Rainwater
271	ii.	Arthur L. Rainwater
	iii.	Orval R. Rainwater
	iv.	Arlis D. Rainwater
	v.	Joe Earl Rainwater
	vi.	Charles Edward Rainwater
	vii.	Ruby E. Rainwater (Flanagan)
	viii.	Mary Juanita Rainwater (Williams)
272	ix.	John Silas Rainwater Jr.

129. Milton Durham Rainwater. Son of Giles R. Rainwater & Sarah Jane Emerson. Born 18 May 1874 in Casey Co., KY. Died 12 Aug 1944 in Pulaski Co., KY. Buried in Bradley's Pleasure Cemetery, Pulaski Co., KY.

He married **Hattie Vest**, daughter of John William Vest Sr. & Mary J. Cravens, 11 Jan 1900 in Casey Co., KY. Born 13 Jan 1884 in Kentucky. Died 7 Feb 1956. Buried in Bradley's Pleasure Cemetery, Pulaski Co., KY.

They had the following children:

273	i.	Bertha Rainwater
	ii.	Ernest Rainwater
274	iii.	Clarence Clay Rainwater
275	iv.	Cecil L. Rainwater
	v.	Ulen C. Rainwater
	vi.	Eunice M. Rainwater (Lane)
	vii.	Hazel G. Rainwater (Delk)
	viii.	Vertis V. Rainwater
	ix.	Ollie Ethridge Rainwater
	x.	Grace Aldena Rainwater (Norfleet)
	xi.	Orville D. Rainwater

130. George Mitchell Rainwater. Son of Giles R. Rainwater & Sarah Jane Emerson. Born 22 May 1879 in Casey Co., KY. Died 22 Jul 1959 in Pulaski Co., KY. Buried in Mintonville Methodist Church Cemetery, Casey Co., KY.

He first married **Sarah Jane Weddle**, daughter of Bartholomew Franklin Weddle & Celia E. Sharp, 4 Jan 1903 in Pulaski Co., KY by Rev. C.L. Bradley. Born 20 Oct 1885 in Pulaski Co., KY. Died 29 May 1913 in Pulaski Co., KY. Buried in Tilman Tarter Cemetery, Ingle, Pulaski Co., KY.

They had the following children:

	i.	Howard Rainwater
276	ii.	Edith Rainwater
	iii.	Jason Rainwater
	iv.	Velber Rainwater

He second married **Eva Effie Roy**, daughter of John Newton Roy & Cynthia Ann Floyd, 5 Jul 1914 in Pulaski Co. KY. Born 16 Sep 1892 in Pulaski Co. KY. Died 1 Oct 1944 in Casey Co., KY. Buried in Mintonville Methodist Church Cemetery, Casey Co., KY.

They had the following children:

	i.	Marie R. Rainwater
	ii.	Woodrow C. Rainwater
277	iii.	Merlie B. Rainwater
278	iv.	Eva Katherine Rainwater
	v.	Effie Rainwater

| | | vi. | Elbert Lee Rainwater |

131. Herbert F. Rainwater. Son of Giles R. Rainwater & Sarah Jane Emerson. Born 16 Jul 1882 in Casey Co., KY. Died 1 Mar 1957. Buried in Mintonville Methodist Church Cemetery, Casey Co., KY.

He married **Julia Idella Gosser**, Before 1906. Born 8 Jul 1885 in Russell Co., KY. Died 26 May 1960. Buried in Mintonville Methodist Church Cemetery, Casey Co., KY.

They had the following children:

		i.	Alma Violet Rainwater (Meece)
		ii.	Alpha Mae Rainwater
		iii.	Myrtle Rainwater
		iv.	Winnie Dew Rainwater (Collins)
	279	v.	Edward Vernon Rainwater
		vi.	Mazie Maxine Rainwater (Jasper)
		vii.	Beecher F. Rainwater
	280	viii.	Richard Lee Rainwater

132. Mary Elizabeth Rainwater. Daughter of George Alfred Rainwater & Permelia Susan Garner. Born 18 Dec 1867 in Kentucky. Died 20 Oct 1950 in Pulaski Co., KY. Buried in Science Hill Cemetery, Pulaski Co., KY.

She married **William Silas Campbell**, 22 Mar 1893 in Pulaski Co., KY. Born 6 Oct 1867 in Pulaski Co., KY. Died 4 Oct 1947 in Pulaski Co., KY.

They had the following children:

		i.	Albert Campbell
		ii.	Ellor Campbell (Vaught)

133. John Madison Rainwater. Son of George Alfred Rainwater & Permelia Susan Garner. Born 1 Apr 1870 in Pulaski Co., KY. Died 17 Aug 1940 in Houston, Harris Co., TX. Buried in Woodlawn Cemetery, Houston, Harris Co., TX.

He married Bertha Sharp, daughter of John Gilbert Sharp & Martha Weddle, 21 Nov 1897 in Pulaski Co., KY. Born 16 Aug 1878 in Pulaski Co., KY. Died 11 Apr 1949 in Dallas, Dallas Co., TX. Buried in Houston, Harris Co., TX.

They had the following children:

		i.	Grace M. Rainwater
	281	ii.	Jesse Bryan Rainwater Sr.
		iii.	Lula H. Rainwater Stephens
	282	iv.	William Cody Rainwater

134. Charles Elliott Rainwater. Son of George Alfred Rainwater & Permelia Susan Garner. Born 30 Jan 1876 in Pulaski Co., KY. Died 14 Jun 1962 in Cape Fair, Barry Co., MO. Buried in Carney Cemetery, Barry Co., MO.

He married **Lydia Jane Smith**, daughter of Francis Marion Smith & Sarah Margaret Still, 18 Dec 1901 in Osa, Barry Co., MO. Born 30 May 1882 in Green Co., TN. Died 26 Jun 1965 in Barry Co., MO. Buried in Carney Cemetery, Barry Co., MO.

They had the following children:

	i.	infant Rainwater (died at birth)
	ii.	infant Rainwater (died at birth)
283	iii.	Loyal George Rainwater
	iv.	Maud Lee Rainwater (Skouby)
	v.	Ruby Edna Rainwater
284	vi.	Vernon Claude Rainwater
285	vii.	Ralph Raymond Rainwater
286	viii.	Beatrice Rainwater

135. Frances Maria Rainwater. Daughter of George Alfred Rainwater & Permelia Susan Garner. Born 3 Jan 1878 in Pulaski Co., KY. Died 31 Jan 1903 in Mintonville, KY.

She married **Gideon Wesley Jasper**, son of Tyler Jasper & Elizabeth F. Gossett, 26 Feb 1899 in Pulaski Co., KY. Born c. 1875 in Casey Co., KY. Died 4 Jun 1955 in Pulaski Co. KY. Buried in Science Hill Cemetery, Pulaski Co., KY.

They had the following children:

287	i.	Velber Jasper Rainwater

136. Giles Alfred Rainwater. Son of George Alfred Rainwater & Permelia Susan Garner. Born 24 Dec 1881 in Kentucky. Died 26 Feb 1945 in Oklahoma.

He married **Myrtle Lupton**.

They had the following children:

	i.	Lucy Rainwater (Pradmore)
	ii.	Susie Rainwater (Wilson)

137. Millie Catherine Rainwater. Daughter of George Alfred Rainwater & Permelia Susan Garner. Born 9 Jan 1884 in Kentucky. Died 20 Nov 1966 in Cains Store, Pulaski Co., KY. Buried in Cedar Point Cemetery, Pulaski Co., KY.

She married **John Perry Emerson**, son of Milton Emerson & Nancy Rainwater, 7 Oct 1902 in Helenwood, TN. Born 25 Oct 1872. Died 27 May 1950 in Pulaski Co., KY. Buried in Cedar Point Cemetery, Pulaski Co., KY.

They had the following children:

	i.	Euphia Emerson
	ii.	Everett Emerson
	iii.	Waldo Emerson
262	iv.	James Emery Emerson
	v.	John Cloyd Emerson

138. William Frederick Rainwater. Son of George Alfred Rainwater & Permelia Susan Garner. Born 6 Jul 1887 in Pulaski Co., KY. Died 26 Apr 1969. Buried in Cedar Point Cemetery, Pulaski Co., KY.

He married **Lottie Margaret Garner**, daughter of Joseph Roy Garner & Margaret Donnelley, 19 Sep 1915 in Pulaski Co. KY. Born 28 May 1890 in Dorrance, Russell Co., KS. Died 28 Jan 1965. Buried in Cedar Point Cemetery, Pulaski Co., KY.

They had the following children:

    288   i.   Ruric Rainwater

139. Susan Jane Rainwater. Daughter of George Alfred Rainwater & Permelia Susan Garner. Born 20 Dec 1889 in Kentucky. Died 28 Aug 1974 in Fayette Co., KY. Buried in Birdie Russell Cemetery, Windsor, Casey Co., KY.

She married **Thomas Jasper**, before 1918. Buried in Birdie Russell Cemetery, Windsor, Casey Co., KY.

They had the following children:

    i.   Robert L. Jasper
    ii.   Vernal Jasper
    iii.   Eugene Jasper
    iv.   Jason Jasper
    v.   Susie T. Jasper

140. Dollie Mae Roysden. Daughter of Abraham H. Roysden & Susannah Rainwater. Born 23 Sep 1883 in Casey Co., KY.

She married **William Henry Lancaster**, son of John Newton Lancaster & Nancy Ann Ford. Born 15 Jun 1867 in Falmouth, Pendleton Co., KY.

They had the following children:

    289   i.   Abe Newton Lancaster

141. Miles L. Dove. Son of William Dove & Martha Rainwater. Born Apr 1860 in Kentucky. Buried in Bruce Cemetery, Wayne Co., IL.

He married **Mary Lane**, c. 1888. Born Jan 1867 in Illinois. Buried in Bruce Cemetery, Wayne Co., IL.

They had the following children:

    i.   Carrie Dove (Shook)
    ii.   Effie D. Dove

142. Miles Evan Rainwater. Son of John Raleigh Rainwater & Genetta Thomas. Born 14 May 1863 in Casey Co., KY. Died 4 Jan 1941 in Heavener, Le Flore Co., OK. Buried in Muse Cemetery, Le Flore Co., OK.

He first married **Harriett Elizabeth Davidson**, 24 Feb 1885 in Casey Co., KY. Born 7 Feb 1869 in Phil, Casey Co., KY. Died 17 Jan 1922 in Whitesboro, LeFlore Co., OK. Buried in Muse Cemetery, Le Flore Co., OK.

They had the following children:

    i.   Alfred Rainwater (died at birth)
    ii.   Emmer Elizabeth Rainwater
    iii.   Gerta Ulso Rainwater
    iv.   Earthy Ellen Rainwater
    290   v.   Jonas Otto Rainwater
    291   vi.   Noah Earl Rainwater
    292   vii.   Choice Rainwater

293	viii.	Dolphis Rainwater
	ix.	Betty Pearl Rainwater
	x.	Genetta Gladys Rainwater
	xi.	Odare Rainwater

He second married **Verdella**, c. 1922. Born c. 1901 in Oklahoma.

They had the following children:

	i.	Oleta Rainwater
	ii.	Gladys Rainwater

143. Margaret Ellen Rainwater. Daughter of John Raleigh Rainwater & Genetta Thomas. Born May 1868 in Indiana. Died 28 Jan 1949.

She first married **M. G. Partain**, 28 Sep 1890 in Van Buren Co., AR. Born in Kentucky. Died Before 1896 in Arkansas.

They had the following children:

	i.	Ida M. Partain

She second married **Marion Calloway Eoff**, 25 Oct 1896 in Van Buren Co., AR. They were divorced c. 1900.

They had the following children:

	i.	Roy Eoff

She third married **Thomas Harrell**, Before 1910. Born c. 1871 in North Carolina.

144. Charles Thomas Rainwater. Son of John Raleigh Rainwater & Genetta Thomas. Born 24 Jan 1870 in Casey Co., KY. Died 1957 in Kansas. Buried in Hunt Cemetery, Kingman Co., KS.

He married **Alta Hunter**, daughter of James M. Hunter, 24 Jun 1900 in Van Buren Co., AR. Born c. 1870 in Arkansas. Died 30 Jan 1918 in Arkansas. Buried in Hunter Hill Cemetery, Van Buren Co., AR.

They had the following children:

	i.	Durward Rainwater
	ii.	Gordon M. Rainwater
	iii.	Ross Rainwater
294	iv.	Sherman Rainwater
	v.	Nettie M. Rainwater
	vi.	James E. Rainwater
	vii.	Hettie Pearl Rainwater (Millard)

145. William Rainwater Sr. Son of John Raleigh Rainwater & Genetta Thomas. Born 11 Sep 1873 in Casey Co., KY. Died 23 Oct 1895 in Arkansas. Buried in Hunter Hill Cemetery, Van Buren Co., AR.

He married **Mary Elizabeth Shannon**, daughter of Samuel Shannon & Sarah C., 16 Dec 1894 in Van Buren Co., AR. Born 28 Oct 1878 in Arkansas. Died 5 Mar 1934 in Arkansas. Buried in Hunter Hill Cemetery, Van Buren Co., AR.

They had the following children:

        i.   William R. F. Rainwater Jr. (never married)

146. Henry T. Rainwater. Son of John Raleigh Rainwater & Genetta Thomas. Born Jan 1878 in Casey Co., KY. Died between 1916/1920.

He married **Cassie Maddox**, 23 Dec 1900 in Van Buren Co., AR. Born c. 1881 in Arkansas. Died between 1916/1920.

They had the following children:

        i.   Cecil Rainwater

        ii.   Willie M. Rainwater

        iii.   Gertrude Rainwater

        iv.   Homer Rainwater

        v.   Herbert C. Rainwater

        vi.   Sylvia E. Rainwater

147. Giles R. Rainwater. Son of John Raleigh Rainwater & Rhoda Ann Brown. Born 1 Apr 1880 in Casey Co., KY. Died 27 Apr 1927 in Adair Co., KY. Buried in Caldwell Chapel Cemetery, Knifley, Adair Co., KY.

He married **Martha Cheek**, daughter of Ed Cheek & Matilda Billings, 23 Aug 1906 in Casey Co., KY. Born c. 1887 in North Carolina. Died 26 Apr 1929 in Casey Creek, Adair Co., KY. Buried in Caldwell Chapel Cemetery, Knifley, Adair Co., KY.

They had the following children:

        i.   Hila M. Rainwater

        ii.   Willie R. Rainwater

        iii.   Minnie O. Rainwater

        iv.   Leila B. Rainwater

        v.   Artie Elizabeth Rainwater (died at birth)

        vi.   James R. Rainwater

        vii.   Zencch P. Rainwater

148. Scott Rainwater. Son of John Raleigh Rainwater & Rhoda Ann Brown. Born 4 Nov 1890 in Adair Co., KY. Died 2 Mar 1936 in Hamilton Co., OH. Buried in Salem UMC Cemetery, Casey Co., KY.

He married **Nancy Linda Carter**, 5 Mar 1911 in Casey Co., KY. Born 1887 in Kentucky. Died 1926. Buried in Salem UMC Cemetery, Casey Co., KY.

They had the following children:

        i.   Rosco Rainwater

        ii.   William Rainwater

        iii.   Marietta Rainwater

        iv.   Marie Rainwater

149. Minerva Ann Rainwater. Daughter of Miles Rainwater & Permelia Emily Cain. Born 1868 in Kentucky. Died 1921. Buried in Egbert Cemetery, Wayne Co., IL.

She married **John E. Burriss**, 13 Sep 1884 in Brown Co., IN. Born 1859. Died 1914. Buried in Egbert Cemetery, Wayne Co., IL

They had the following children:

    i. Margaret Burriess

150. William Riley Rainwater. Son of Miles Rainwater & Permelia Emily Cain. Born Sep 1872 in Indiana. Died 15 Dec 1951 in Illinois. Buried in Egbert Cemetery, Wayne Co., IL.

He first married **Margaret M. Pool**, daughter of Luther A. Pool & Clarinda Peak, 24 Sep 1892 in Brown Co., IN. Born 14 Jul 1871 in Indiana. Died 9 Feb 1949 in Indianapolis, Marion Co., IN. Buried in Rest Haven Cm, Edinburg, IN. They were divorced 1898.

They had the following children:

  295 i. Charles Luther Rainwater

He second married **Nora B.**, c. 1907. Born c. 1872 in Illinois. They were divorced before 1920.

151. Isaac Asbury Rainwater. Son of Miles Rainwater & Permelia Emily Cain. Born 28 Jul 1878 in Illinois. Died After 1920.

He married Zetta Braddock, 14 Jul 1901 in Wayne Co., IL. Born c. 1883 in Illinois.

They had the following children:

    i. Minerva Rainwater
    ii. Virgil Rainwater
    iii. Riley Rainwater

152. Henry Clarence Rainwater. Son of William Howard Rainwater Jr. & Julia G. Markwell. Born 25 Apr 1870 in Brown Co., IN. Died 8 Feb 1943 in Mt. Vernon, Jefferson Co., IL. Buried in Egbert Cemetery, Keene, Wayne Co., IL.

He married **Mary Emily Lane**, daughter of William M. Lane & Mary Ann Davis, 10 Nov 1892 in Keenes, Wayne Co., IL. Born 4 Oct 1870 in Wayne Co., IL. Died 19 Jun 1948 in Mt. Vernon, Jefferson Co., IL. Buried in Egbert Cemetery, Keene, Wayne Co., IL.

They had the following children:

    i. Oma Lee Rainwater
    ii. Mary Edith Rainwater
  296 iii. Raymond Otto Rainwater
  297 iv. William Roy Rainwater
    v. Charles Homer Rainwater
    vi. Jaley Rainwater (died at birth)
    vii. Reathia Marie Rainwater (twin)
    viii. Ruth Rainwater (twin)
    ix. Clarence Rainwater

153. William Luther Rainwater. Son of William Howard Rainwater Jr. & Ellen Victoria Pool. Born Dec 1872 in Indiana. Died Aug 1937 in Morgantown, Morgan Co., IN.

He first married **Josephine Beach**, 15 Feb 1895 in Brown Co., IN. Born Before 1879 in Indiana. Died Before 1900 in Indiana.

They had the following children:

    298   i.   Leroy M. Rainwater

He second married **Cordia Watson**, daughter of William Watson & Rachel Parsley, 15 Jun 1900 in Nashville, Brown Co., IN. Born 1 Jul 1873 in Nashville, IN. Died 24 Jun 1954 in Morgantown, Morgan Co., IN. Buried in East Hill Cm, Morgan Co., IN.

They had the following children:

    i.   William Raymond Rainwater
    ii.   Dorothy E. Rainwater
    iii.   Emory Carl Rainwater
    iv.   Luther Paul Rainwater

154. Harvey L. Rainwater. Son of William Howard Rainwater Jr. & Mary Ann Buffington. Born 15 Oct 1878 in Wayne Co., IL. Died After 1910.

He married **Ettie Brent**, 10 Sep 1901 in Wayne Co., IL. Born c. 1888 in Illinois.

They had the following children:

    i.   William A. Rainwater
    ii.   infant Rainwater (died at birth)
    iii.   Elmer Rainwater
    iv.   Everett Rainwater

155. Emery Columbus Rainwater. Son of William Howard Rainwater Jr. & Mary Ann Buffington. Born 6 Mar 1880 in Wayne Co., IL. Died 1962 in Centralia, Marion Co., IL. Buried in Egbert Cemetery, Keene, Wayne Co., IL.

He married **Anna C. Cates**, daughter of Richard L. Cates & Loretta Egbert, 22 Oct 1900 in Wayne Co., IL. Born 1880 in Wayne Co., IL. Died 1916. Buried in Egbert Cemetery, Keene, Wayne Co., IL.

They had the following children:

    i.   Hazel M. Rainwater
    ii.   Mabel L. Rainwater
    iii.   Lula Rainwater
    iv.   Harry Rainwater
    v.   Elvin Rainwater
    vi.   Loraine Rainwater
    vii.   Grace Rainwater

156. Oliver Philip Rainwater. Son of William Howard Rainwater Jr. & Mary Ann Buffington. Born 1 Mar 1889 in Wayne Co., IL . Died 27 Mar 1975 in Monroe Center, Ogle Co., IL. Buried in Roseland Cemetery, Monroe Center, Ogle Co., IL.

He married **Margaret Elizabeth Fry**, 2 Dec 1909 in Jefferson Co., IL. Born 19 Jan 1888 in Wayne Co., IL. Died Feb 1968 in Texas. Buried in Roseland Cemetery, Monroe Center, Ogle Co., IL.

They had the following children:

    i.   Bonnie Rainwater
    ii.   Bernie Marie Rainwater
    iii.   Nellie Alberta Rainwater
    iv.   William Willard Rainwater
    v.   Oren B. Rainwater
    vi.   Gail Rainwater
    vii.   Virginia Rainwater
    viii.   Ross Rainwater
    ix.   Thomas Howard Rainwater
    x.   Virgene Rainwater
    xi.   Kathleen Rainwater

157. Charles Edward Rainwater. Son of Matthew F. Rainwater & Adeline. Born 20 Nov 1876 in Illinois. Died 2 Jun 1964. Buried in Sunset Memorial Park, Perry Co., IL.

He married **Minnie Belle Fraiser**, 10 Jun 1900 in Jefferson Co., IL. Born 22 Oct 1880 in Illinois. Died 18 Dec 1955. Buried in Sunset Memorial Park, Perry Co., IL.

They had the following children:

    i.   Nona E. Rainwater
    ii.   Mabel E. Rainwater
    iii.   Jesse Ray Rainwater (twin)
299   iv.   Bessie M. Rainwater (twin)
    v.   Edward O. Rainwater (twin)
    vi.   Freddie Olen Rainwater (twin)
    vii.   Glenn Oral Rainwater

158. Louie M. Rainwater. Son of Mark Rainwater & Sarah Caroline Jones. Born c. 1890 in Arkansas.

He married **Nancy E.**, Before 1911 in Arkansas. Born c. 1889 in Arkansas.

They had the following children:

    i.   Villa G. Rainwater
    ii.   Mark Rainwater
    iii.   William T. Rainwater

159. Thomas Marion Rainwater. Son of George Washington Rainwater & Emma Rosetta Fox. Born Mar 1896 in Illinois. Buried in Salem Cemetery, Wayne Co., IL.

He married **Oda M.**, before 1930. Born 1900 in Illinois. Buried in Salem Cemetery, Wayne Co., IL.

They had the following children:

    i.   Lonnie Rainwater

| | | ii. | Howard E. Rainwater |

160. Jennie Lee Rainwater. Daughter of Terrell Rainwater & Esther Shoe. Born 18 Jan 1890 in Hopkins Co., TX.

She married **Robert Lee McDonald**, Before 1913. Born c. 1887 in Texas.

They had the following children:

| | | i. | Felix L. McDonald |

161. Walter Terrell Rainwater Sr. Son of Terrell Rainwater & Esther Shoe. Born 15 Jul 1895 in Hopkins Co., TX. Died Apr 1974 in Trinity Co., TX. Buried in Cedar Grove Cemetery, Trinity, Trinity Co., TX.

He married **Iva M. Moore**, Before 1907. Born 31 Jul 1907. Died 4 Jul 1993 in Trinity Co., TX. Buried in Cedar Grove Cemetery, Trinity, Trinity Co., TX.

They had the following children:

| | | i. | Walter Terrell Rainwater Jr. |
| | 300 | ii. | John Lester Rainwater |

162. John Silas Rainwater. Son of David Rainwater & Annice Mariah Garner. Born 15 Dec 1869 in Somerset, Pulaski Co., KY. Died 11 Jan 1962 in Adair Co., KY.

He married **Martha Jane Bault**, 15 Dec 1890 in Adair Co., KY. Born 26 Aug 1867 in Columbia, Adair Co., KY. Died 14 Dec 1949 in Taylor Co., KY. Buried in Brookside Cemetery, Campbellsville, Taylor Co., KY.

They had the following children:

		i.	David Neil Rainwater
	301	ii.	Alvin Rainwater
	302	iii.	Ada Frances Rainwater
		iv.	Lora Eunice Rainwater
	303	v.	Jewel Haskel Rainwater
	304	vi.	Ras Manford Rainwater
	305	vii.	Walter A. Rainwater
	306	viii.	Millie Annice Rainwater

163. Elizabeth F. Gossett. Daughter of Robert Tilman Gossett & Mary Elizabeth Rainwater. Born 7 Jun 1874 in Pulaski Co., KY. Died 2 Feb 1949 in Pulaski Co., KY. Buried in Cedar Point Baptist Cemetery, Pulaski Co., KY.

She married **John Wyatt Kissee**, son of William F. Kissee & Serena Roberts, 16 Nov 1892 in Pulaski Co. KY. Born 28 Dec 1872 in Casey Co., KY. Died 29 Dec 1960 in Pulaski Co., KY. Buried in Cedar Point Baptist Cemetery, Pulaski Co., KY.

They had the following children:

	307	i.	Demonia Kissee
		ii.	Mavona Kissee
	308	iii.	Belonia Kissee
	309	iv.	Lydia Kissee (Tarter)
	310	v.	Robert William Kissee

   vi. Charles W. Kissee

164. Erasmus M. Tarter. Son of James Willis Tarter & Frances Jane Rainwater. Born c. 1879 in Kentucky.

He married **Ethel A. Scott**, 29 Sep 1901 in Oklahoma. Born c. 1885 in Kansas.

They had the following children:

   i. Lester Tarter
   ii. Earl Manford Tarter
   iii. Lewis Tarter

165. John Virgil Tarter. Son of James Willis Tarter & Frances Jane Rainwater. Born between 1880/1883.

He married **Maude O'Dell**.

Children:

   i. Beulah Tarter (Petrell)
   ii. Ruth Tarter (Shearer)
   iii. Abbie Tarter (Portner)
   iv. Roy L. Tarter
   v. Willis Tarter

166. Mary Etter Dawes. Daughter of Benjamin Franklin Dawes & Sarah Ann Rainwater. Born 11 Nov 1894 in Kentucky. Died 29 Jun 1970 in Pulaski Co., KY. Buried in New Hope Cemetery, Pulaski Co., KY.

She married **John Ed Jasper**, son of Thomas P. Jasper & Priscilla Malvira Huffaker, 14 Sep 1916. Born 8 Oct 1888 in Kentucky. Died 14 Jun 1972 in Pulaski Co., KY. Buried in New Hope Cemetery, Pulaski Co., KY.

They had the following children:

    i. Ezra K. Jasper
 311 ii. Thelma Jasper
    iii. Anna E. Jasper
    iv. Lottie M. Jasper

Register Report: Descendants of James W. McIlhaney

The following is a summary of three generations of the descendants of James William McIlhaney and Mary Jane Gibson. This information presented in the register report style, which is a standard genealogical format developed by the New England Historical and Genealogical Society in 1870.

First Generation

1. James William McIlhaney. Son of William McIlhaney & Mary Cunningham. Born 1795 in Ireland. Died 3 Dec 1869 in Coryell Co., TX. Buried in Coryell Baptist Church Cemetery, Coryell Co., TX.

He married **Mary Jane Gibson**, before 1828 in Tennessee. Born 10 Mar 1803 in Kentucky or Tennessee. Died 18 Dec 1891 in Coryell Co., TX. Buried in Coryell Baptist Church Cemetery, Coryell Co., TX.

They had the following children:

2	i.	Margaret McIlhaney
3	ii.	Catherine McIlhaney
4	iii.	Rebecca Jane McIlhaney
5	iv.	Manervia Ann McIlhaney
6	v.	William James Gibson McIlhaney
	vi.	Randall H. McIlhaney; Born 1842 in Tippah Co., MS. Died 4 Apr 1863 in POW Camp Douglas in Illinois. Buried in Oak Woods Cemetery, Chicago, IL.
	vii.	Henry Clay McIlhaney; Born 1844 in Tippah Co., MS. Died 4 Jul 1862 in Little Rock, AK. Buried in Little Rock National Cemetery, Little Rock, AK.

Second Generation

2. Margaret McIlhaney. Daughter of James William McIlhaney & Mary Jane Gibson. Born 17 Jan 1829 in Tennessee. Died 15 May 1879 in McLennan Co., TX. She was was originally buried in Speegleville Cemetery, and was moved to Chapel Hill Cemetery when Lake Waco was created.

She married widower **John William Wiggins**, between 1855/1860. Born 18 May 1825 in Tennessee. Died 27 Nov 1877 in McLennan Co., Texas. He was originally buried in Speegleville Cemetery, and was moved to Chapel Hill Cemetery when Lake Waco was created.

They had the following children:

	i.	Mary E. Wiggins; Born c. 1851 in Texas (first wife)
	ii.	James D. Wiggins; Born c. 1853 in Texas. (first wife)
	iii.	Michael T. Wiggins; Born c. 1855 in Texas. (first wife)
	iv.	Thomas L. Wiggins; Born c. 1858 in Texas. (mother unclear)

	v.	Frances Louisiana Wiggins (Walters); Born c. 1864 in Texas; Died 1929 in Texas.
	vi.	Charles Wiggins; Born c. 1866 in Texas.
	vii.	Jane Wiggins; Born c. 1869 in Texas.

3. Catherine McIlhaney. Daughter of James William McIlhaney & Mary Jane Gibson. Born c. 1830 in Tennessee. Died 28 Jul 1912 in Texas.

She married **Jesse James**, son of Isaac James & Rachel, between 1850/1853 in Tippah Co., MS. Born c. 1829 in Tennessee. Died after 1861.

They had the following children:

	i.	Minerva J. James; Born c. 1854.
		She married Jesse Givins, 17 Aug 1870.
7	ii.	Rachel A. James
8	iii.	Maggie James
	iv.	Sarah J. James; Born c. 1861 in Texas.

4. Rebecca Jane McIlhaney. Daughter of James William McIlhaney & Mary Jane Gibson. Born 26 Apr 1833 in Tennessee. Died 28 Jul 1912 in Hamilton Co., TX. Buried in Carlton Cemetery, Hamilton Co., TX.

She married **Ephriam Parmley Gibson**, son of Jesse Gibson & Elizabeth Parmley, 19 Oct 1851 in Mississippi. Born 25 Sep 1817 in Kentucky. Died 9 Aug 1907 in Coryell Co., TX. Buried in Coryell Baptist Church Cemetery, Coryell Co., TX.

They had the following children:

	i.	James Henry Gibson; Born 17 May 1852 in Tennessee. Died 8 Jan 1865.
9	ii.	Mary Jane Gibson
	iii.	George Franklin Gibson; Born 22 Jul 1854. Died 3 Apr 1864 in Texas. Buried in Coryell Baptist Church Cemetery, Coryell Co., TX.
10	iv.	Jesse Thomas Gibson
11	v.	Elizabeth Ann Gibson
12	vi.	Randolph Hunter Gibson
13	vii.	John Parmley Gibson
14	viii.	Marcus Layfette Gibson
15	ix.	Ira Jackson Gibson
16	x.	Martin David Gibson
	xi.	Ephriam Alonzo Gibson; Born 29 Sep 1874 in Texas. Died 15 Dec 1908.
	xii.	William Archibald Gibson; Born Sep 1876. Died 11 Dec 1889.

5. Manervia Ann McIlhaney. Daughter of James William McIlhaney & Mary Jane Gibson. Born 9 Feb 1839 in Tippah Co., MS. Died 18 Nov 1873 in Coryell Co., TX. Buried in Coryell Baptist Church Cemetery, Coryell Co., TX.

She first married **Isham F. Johnson**, 16 Jan 1861 in Coryell Co., TX. Born c. 1831 in Alabama or Georgia. Died after 1870 in Texas.

They had the following children:

17	i.	William Cidney Johnson
	ii.	Cicero Judson Johnson; Born 15 Apr 1865 in Texas. Died 14 Jul 1939.

She second married **Patrick Doyle**. Born May 1827 in Ireland. Died 1 Mar 1902 in McLennan Co., TX. Buried in Coryell Baptist Church Cemetery, Coryell Co., TX.

6. William James Gibson McIlhaney. Son of James William McIlhaney & Mary Jane Gibson. Born 8 May 1839 in Tippah Co., MS. Died 30 Jul 1904 in Waldo, Coryell Co., TX. Buried in Coryell Baptist Church Cemetery, Coryell Co., TX.

He married **Mary Charlesana Elizabeth Carter**, daughter of James Carter & Salina Roxanna Dean, 12 Feb 1867 in Austin, Travis Co., TX. Born Sep 1844 in Tippah Co., MS Texas. Died Oct 1911 in Waldo, Coryell Co., TX. Buried in Coryell Baptist Church Cemetery, Coryell Co., TX.

They had the following children:

18	i.	James M. McIlhaney
19	ii.	Lula Belle McIlhaney
20	iii.	John Richardson McIlhaney
	iv.	Annie Ester McIlhaney; Born 9 Apr 1875 in Coryell Co., TX. Died 12 Feb 1876 in Coryell Co., TX
21	v.	William Arthur McIlhaney
22	vi.	Oliver Lee McIlhaney
	vii.	Selena Jane McIlhaney; Born 3 Dec 1880 in Coryell Co., TX. Died 18 Oct 1881 in Coryell Co., TX
23	viii.	Frank B. McIlhaney
	ix.	Ida May McIlhaney; Born 30 Nov 1884 in Coryell Co., TX. Died 21 Sep 1886 in Coryell Co., TX.
24	x.	Ethel Elizabeth McIlhaney

Third Generation

7. Rachel A. James. Daughter of Jesse James & Catherine McIlhaney. Born 12 Jul 1855 in Texas. Died 11 Sep 1941 in Johnson Co., TX. Buried in Grandview Cm, Johnson Co., TX.

She married **Henry C. Polson**, before 1875. Born 13 Apr 1852 in Mississippi. Died 30 Dec 1895. Buried in Grandview Cm, Johnson Co., TX.

They had the following children:

i.	Rosa B. Polson; Born c. 1875 in Texas.
ii.	Thomas J. Polson; Born c. 1877 in Texas.
iii.	Annie J. Polson; Born Jul 1879 in Texas.

8. Maggie James. Daughter of Jesse James & Catherine McIlhaney. Born Sep 1857 in Texas. Died 20 Oct 1899. Buried in Coryell Baptist Ch Cm, Coryell Co, TX.

She married **William M. Fowler**, 20 Apr 1884. Born 25 Sep 1861 in Mississippi. Died 17 Jan 1925. Buried in Coryell Baptist Ch Cm, Coryell Co, TX.

They had the following children:

    i.   Maude M. Fowler; Born Jul 1885 in Texas.

    ii.   Thomas W. Fowler; Born Nov 1887 in Texas.

    iii.   Elmer L. Fowler; Born May 1890 in Texas.

    iv.   Clara E. Fowler; Born Sep 1892 in Texas.

    v.   Oscar L. Fowler; Born Sep 1895 in Texas.

9. Mary Jane Gibson. Daughter of Ephriam Parmley Gibson & Rebecca Jane McIlhaney. Born 3 May 1853 in Tennessee. Died 25 Jun 1928. Buried in Vernon, Wilbarger Co., TX.

She married **Rev. Charles Pinkney Osborne**, son of Thomas Osborne, 19 Jul 1868 in Coryell Co., TX. Born 21 Jun 1845 in Winston Co., MS.

They had the following children:

    i.   Mary Ellen Osborne; Born 14 Dec 1869 in Coryell Co., TX.

        She married Thomas Edward Lee, 8 Jan 1891 in Callihan Co., TX. Born in Texas.

    ii.   Ira Jackson Osborne; Born 21 Apr 1871 in Texas. Died 5 Dec 1934 in Dallas, Dallas Co., TX.

        He married Gertrude Jones, 23 Sep 1903 in Dallas, Dallas Co., TX.

    iii.   Elizabeth Josephine Osborne; Born 1 Dec 1870 in Texas. Died 2 Aug 1914 in Texas.

        She married James E. Lee, 11 Nov 1897 in Texas. Born 11 Mar 1864. Died 11 Jul 1929 in Texas.

    iv.   William Lafayette Osborne; Born 24 Sep 1874 in Coryell Co., TX. Died 11 Jul 1936.

        He married Annie Laura Curry, 8 Sep 1895 in Texas.

    v.   Martha Frances Osborne; Born 1 Sep 1876 in Hamilton Co., TX. Died 3 Aug 1959.

        She married Rev. John Franklin Curry, son of Rev. H. F. Curry & Margaret Long. Born 15 Jul 1869 in Hernando, MS. Died 25 Dec 1943.

    vi.   Nancy Rebecca Osborne; Born 2 Aug 1878 in Burnet, Burnet Co., TX. Died 15 Dec 1936.

        She married C. Evan Hunter, 7 Jun 1902 in Texas.

    vii.   Delula Ann Osborne; Born 12 Jun 1880 in Lampasas, Lampasas Co., TX.

        She married Oscar Smith, 7 Jul 1901 in Texas.

    viii.   Thomas Ephriam Osborne; Born 18 Jan 1882 in Lampasas, Lampasas Co., TX.

	He married Willie Cooper, 5 May 1907 in Texas.
ix.	Florence Belzora Osborne; Born 29 Feb 1884 in Calliham, McMullen Co., TX.
	She married Frank Ridgeway, 23 May 1909 in Texas.
x.	David Nathaniel Osborne; Born 7 Feb 1887 in Calliham, McMullen Co., TX.
	He married Bertha Moore, 26 Mar 1910 in Texas.
xi.	Eva Eudora Osborne; Born 3 Nov 1888 in Calliham, McMullen Co., TX.
	She married Sam Moore, 1 Mar 1906 in Texas.
xii.	Carroll Osborne ; Born 19 Sep 1890 in Texas. Died 3 Nov 1890 in Texas.
xiii.	Pinkney Haseltine Osborne; Born 7 Jun 1892 in Calliham, McMullen Co., TX.
	He married Seth Woodson, 22 Jul 1907 in Texas.
xiv.	Charles Parmley Osborne; Born 26 Mar 1897 in Ft. Bend Co., TX. Died 1976.
	He married Jewell McKroxie, 28 Jun 1920 in Texas.

10. Jesse Thomas Gibson. Son of Ephriam Parmley Gibson & Rebecca Jane McIlhaney. Born 19 Sep 1859 in Texas. Died 10 Jul 1918 in New Castle, Young Co., TX. Buried in Carlton Cemetery, Hamilton Co., TX.

He married **Laura Seals**, daughter of Jemima & John Seals, c. 1884. Born Oct 1864 in Mississippi.

They had the following children:

i.	Elbert L. Gibson; Born Dec 1884 in Texas.
ii.	Aubrey C. Gibson; Born 17 Sep 1886 in Texas. Died 15 Aug 1965.
iii.	Grace T. Gibson; Born Aug 1891 in Texas.
iv.	Thomas J. Gibson; Born Dec 1893 in Texas.
v.	Ruth Gibson; Born Jan 1897 in Texas.
vi.	George W. Gibson; Born c. 1901 in Texas.
vii.	William W. Gibson; Born c. 1903 in Texas.
viii.	Geneva Gibson; Born c. 1905 in Texas.
ix.	Eunice Gibson; Born c. 1907 in Texas.

11. Elizabeth Ann Gibson. Daughter of Ephriam Parmley Gibson & Rebecca Jane McIlhaney. Born 6 Dec 1860 in Texas. Died 7 Aug 1931. Buried in Carlton Cemetery, Hamilton Co., TX.

She married **John Barnett**. Born 11 Jan 1863. Died 11 Jan 1938. Buried in Carlton Cemetery, Hamilton Co., TX.

They had the following children:

	i.	Myrtle Barnett;
	ii.	Mittie May Barnett; Born 2 Feb 1897. Died 15 Mar 1954.
	iii.	Johnny Barnett;
	iv.	Arthur Barnett;
	v.	Carroll Barnett;
	vi.	Ruth Barnett;

12. Randolph Hunter Gibson. Son of Ephriam Parmley Gibson & Rebecca Jane McIlhaney. Born 22 Feb 1863 in Texas. Died 1 Sep 1946 in Hamilton Co., Texas. Buried in Carlton Cemetery, Hamilton Co., TX.

He married **Mary Lenora Cauthen**, 12 Dec 1882. Born 25 Jun 1868 in Alabama. Died 26 May 1955. Buried in Carlton Cemetery, Hamilton Co., TX.

They had the following children:

	i.	Mary Lou Gibson (Kelly) ; Born Oct 1884 in Texas.
	ii.	Elmer W. Gibson; Born Feb 1886 in Texas.
25	iii.	Vora Dell Gibson (McKinzie)
	iv.	Ernest Randolph Gibson; Born Sep 1889 in Texas.
	v.	Mayme Rebecca Gibson (Wells) ; Born Jan 1892 in Texas.
	vi.	Oscar Porter Gibson; Born Aug 1894 in Texas.
	vii.	Henrietta Gibson (Sprang) ; Born Dec 1897 in Texas.
	viii.	Opal Gibson (Blackwell) ; Born c. 1904 in Texas.
	ix.	Harvey Carroll Gibson (twin); Born c. 1907 in Texas.
	x.	George Truitt Gibson (twin); Born c. 1907 in Texas.
	xi.	Connor Brooks Gibson; Born c. 1912 in Texas.

13. John Parmley Gibson. Son of Ephriam Parmley Gibson & Rebecca Jane McIlhaney. Born 21 Jun 1865 in Oglesby, Coryell Co., TX. Died 7 Jun 1948 in Texas. Buried in Lamesa, Dawson Co., TX.

He married **Louise Victoria Seals**, daughter of Jemima & John Seals, 24 Nov 1889 in Killen, Bell Co., TX. Born 2 May 1868 in Lauderdale, MS. Died 16 Apr 1948. Buried in Lamesa, Dawson Co., TX.

They had the following children:

	i.	Ross Emerson Gibson; Born 16 Aug 1890 in Hamilton Co., TX. Died Dec 1986 in Hobbs, Lea Co., NM. He married Cora Inez Austin, daughter of S. Dick Austin & Katie Ross Crowley, 3 Jun 1923 in Lamasa, Dawson Co., TX. Born 17 Aug 1894 in Ardolpha, AR.
	ii.	Horace Parmley Gibson; Born 26 Feb 1892 in Coryell Co., TX. Died 4 Oct 1949 in Texas.
		He married Vivian Cornelia Abernathy, daughter of Ira Elbert Abernathy & Fannie Eulalee Mayfield, 24 Aug

	1916 in Spur, Dickins Co., TX. Born 5 Sep 1896 in Edge, Brazos Co., TX. Died 21 Jan 1984 in Texas.
iii.	Hester Ella Gibson; Born 8 Nov 1893 in Hamilton Co., TX.
	She married James Alexander Hinson, 27 Dec 1917 in Lamasa, Dawson Co., TX. Born 17 Dec 1884. Died 19 Sep 1962.
iv.	Gordon P. Gibson ; Born 28 Feb 1896 in Erath Co., TX. Died 26 Sep 1897 in Erath Co., TX.
v.	James Pilant Gibson Sr.
vi.	Ethel Faye Gibson; Born 1 Jan 1900 in Hamilton Co., TX. Died 18 Jan 1969.
	She married William Ellis Love, son of William Volney Love & Anne Margaret Dean, 1 Jan 1922 in Dawson Co., TX. Born 27 Aug 1894 in Williamson Co., TX. Died 17 Jul 1962.
vii.	Clyde Winston Gibson; Born 5 Jul 1902 in Coryell Co., TX. Died 3 Oct 1972 in Dawson Co., TX.
	He married Alma Ruth Arnett, daughter of D. Arnett & Martha Matilda Hudson, Dec 1928 in Dawson Co., TX. Born Sep 1902. Died 3 Jul 1949.
viii.	Mildred Mae Gibson; Born 29 Apr 1904 in Hamilton Co., TX. Died 16 Feb 1975.
	She married Robert Sidney Stansfield, 18 Jan 1925 in Dawson Co., TX. Born 17 Feb 1897. Died 16 Feb 1975.
ix.	infant Gibson (died at birth); Born 4 Feb 1906. Died 5 Feb 1906.
x.	Homer Gibson ; Born 1 May 1907 in Erath Co., TX. Died 5 Sep 1908 in Erath Co., TX.
xi.	Hazel Irene Gibson; Born 2 Jan 1909 in Hamilton Co., TX. Died 1 May 1972.
	She married James Hezekiah Ragsdale, 5 Jan 1935 in Roswell, NM. Born 28 Jun in Lawton, OK.

14. Marcus Layfette Gibson. Son of Ephriam Parmley Gibson & Rebecca Jane McIlhaney. Born 22 Aug 1867 in Coryell Co., TX. Died 17 Jun 1942 in Stephenville, Erath Co., TX. Buried in Carlton Cemetery, Hamilton Co., TX.

He married **Lula Etta Raby**, 17 Nov 1887 in Carlton, Hamilton Co., TX. Born 27 Dec 1867. Died 8 Jul 1946 in Erath Co., TX. Buried in Carlton Cemetery, Hamilton Co., TX.

They had the following children:

i.	Clara M. Gibson; Born 27 Apr 1890. Died 12 Apr 1936.
ii.	Althea W. Gibson; Born 14 May 1892.
iii.	Alonzo Gibson;

	iv.	Jesse Ella Gibson; Born 30 Jul 1896. Died 7 Mar 1918.
	v.	Ora Lucille Gibson; Born 4 Apr 1899.
	vi.	Hardy Gibson; Born 13 Oct 1901. Died 1973.

15. Ira Jackson Gibson. Son of Ephriam Parmley Gibson & Rebecca Jane McIlhaney. Born 16 Dec 1869 in Coryell Co., TX. Died 28 Nov 1931 in Carlton Cemetery, Hamilton Co., TX. Buried in Carlton Cemetery, Hamilton Co., TX.

He married **Jeanetta Elzora Graves**, 8 Nov 1890 in Carlton Cemetery, Hamilton Co., TX. Born 29 Aug 1872 in Statesville, TN. Died 22 May 1946 in Dublin, Erath Co., TX. Buried 23 May 1946 in Carlton Cemetery, Hamilton Co., TX.

They had the following children:

	i.	Audie Lee Gibson; Born 20 Aug 1891. Died 16 Dec 1932 in Carlton, Hamilton Co., TX.
		He married Clora Laura DeVolin, 8 Jun 1913 in Hamilton Co., TX.
	ii.	Claude Gibson; Born 18 Oct 1893 in Texas.
	iii.	Lewis Parmley Gibson; Born 15 Nov 1895 in Texas. Died 20 Dec 1937 in Erath Co., TX.
		He married Susie Virginia Crockett, 12 Mar 1917. Born 2 Mar 1895. Died 1969.
27	iv.	Clarence Houston Gibson
	v.	Wilma Elizabeth Gibson; Born Apr 1900 in Texas.

16. Martin David Gibson. Son of Ephriam Parmley Gibson & Rebecca Jane McIlhaney. Born 25 Mar 1872 in Coryell Co., TX. Died 1933/1938 in Ellis Co., TX. Buried in Old Bethel Cemetery, Canton, Van Zandt Co., TX..

He married **Levada Amanda Cary**, daughter of Francis Brook Cary & Anna Belle Carter. Born Sep 1876 in Texas. Died 1962 in Texas. Buried in Old Bethel Cemetery, Canton, Van Zandt Co., TX.

They had the following children:

	i.	Edith Gibson; Born Feb 1898 in Texas.
	ii.	Jewel Gibson; Born May 1900 in Texas.
	iii.	Hansell Gibson;

17. William Cidney Johnson. Son of Isham F. Johnson & Manervia Ann McIlhaney. Born Feb 1864 in Texas. Died 21 Dec 1945 in Coryell Co., TX. Buried in McGregor Cemetery, McGregor, McLennan Co., TX.

He first married **Maggie Allen**, 1 Jan 1887 in Gatesville, Coryell Co., Texas. Born 1 Mar 1868 in Alabama. Died 29 Dec 1914. Buried in McGregor Cemetery, McGregor, McLennan Co., TX.

They had the following children:

	i.	King Johnson; Born Feb 1889 in Texas.
	ii.	Allen Johnson; Born May 1890 in Texas.
	iii.	Tull Johnson; Born Aug 1891 in Texas.

		iv.	Parker Johnson; Born Dec 1892 in Texas.
		v.	Floy Johnson; Born Feb 1894 in Texas.
		vi.	Paul Johnson; Born Sep 1896 in Texas.

He second married **Mittie Irene Nelms (Edwards)**, between 1920/1930. Born 13 Apr 1874 in Alabama. Died 24 Jan 1933 in Waco, McLennan Co., TX. Buried in Coryell Baptist Church Cemetery, Coryell Co., TX.

18. James M. McIlhaney. Son of William James Gibson McIlhaney & Mary Charlesana Elizabeth Carter. Born 24 Jan 1868 in Waldo, Coryell Co., TX. Died 14 Feb 1916 in Bell Co., TX. Buried in Coryell Baptist Church Cemetery, Coryell Co., TX.

He married **Bettie Hardin**, daughter of William Henry Harrison Hardin & Zara Adlee Kuykendall, 7 Jul 1886 in Texas. Born 8 Jun 1871 in Texas. Died 12 Dec 1966 in Waco, McLennan Co., TX. Buried in Harris Creek Cemetery, McGregor, McLennan Co., TX.

They had the following children:

		i.	infant McIlhaney; Born and died before 1900.
		ii.	Thomas Elbert McIlhaney; Born 20 Jan 1887 in Coryell Co., TX. Died 25 Feb 1887 in Coryell Co., TX.
		iii.	Addie Lee McIlhaney (Holcomb); Born Mar 1888 in Texas. Died Dec 1977.
	28	iv.	William Edgar McIlhaney
		v.	Grace Monue McIlhaney; Born 21 Jun 1892 in Coryell Co., TX. Died 20 Dec 1892 in Coryell Co., TX.
		vi.	Millie Edith McIlhaney; Born 7 Mar 1894 in Coryell Co., TX. Died 20 Mar 1900 in Coryell Co., TX.
		vii.	Myrtie McIlhaney ; Born 1 Jan 1896 in Texas. Died 22 Oct 1910 in Tolbert, Wilbarger Co.,TX.
		viii.	James Roy McIlhaney; Born 29 Dec 1897 in Texas. Died 16 Jun 1966 in Upton Co., TX.
			He married Hallie Jennette Sloan. Born 4 Oct 1901. Died Mar 1987 in McCamey, Upton Co., TX.
		ix.	Fannie Elizabeth McIlhaney; Born 26 Jan 1900 in Texas. Died 6 Jul 1993 in McLennan Co., TX.
			She married Dolpha Warren, son of Abijah Warren & Ella V. Geyer, 14 Dec 1919 in. Born 15 Oct 1894. Died 14 Feb 1981 in McGregor, McLennan Co., TX.
	29	x.	Ola McIlhaney
	30	xi.	Gladys Velma McIlhaney
		xii.	Truman Hugh McIlhaney; Born 1907 in Texas. Died 30 Jul 1994 in Tatum, Lea Co., NM.
			He married Ruby Fay Mitchell, 15 Jul 1931 in Tatum, Lea Co., NM. Born 16 Dec 1906. Died 13 Oct 1996 in Tatum, Lea Co., NM.

	xiii.	Guy Weldon McIlhaney Sr.; Born 8 Jul 1909 in Texas. Died 22 Feb 2001 in Lorena, McLennan Co., TX. He married Velma Odel, after 1930.

19. Lula Belle McIlhaney. Daughter of William James Gibson McIlhaney & Mary Charlesana Elizabeth Carter. Born 12 Sep 1870 in Waldo, Coryell Co., TX. Died 25 Jul 1929 in McLennan Co., TX. Buried in Coryell Baptist Church Cemetery, Coryell Co., TX.

She married **James Monroe Smith**, 10 Mar 1892 in Texas. Born 1 Feb 1862 in Mississippi. Died 4 Jul 1932. Buried in Coryell Baptist Church Cemetery, Coryell Co., TX.

They had the following children:

	i.	Mary Essie Smith; Born Aug 1893 in Texas.
	ii.	Jessie A. Smith; Born c. 1901 in Texas.
	iii.	George W. T. Smith; Born c. 1905 in Texas.

20. John Richardson McIlhaney. Son of William James Gibson McIlhaney & Mary Charlesana Elizabeth Carter. Born 5 Jul 1873 in Waldo, Coryell Co., TX. Died 25 Sep 1949 in Lubbock, Lubbock Co., TX. Buried 27 Sep 1949 in Resthaven Memorial Park, Lubbock, TX.

He married **Ollie Delilah Umberson**, daughter of William Franklin Umberson & Mary Jane Singleton, 16 Sep 1897 in Gholson, McLennon Co., TX. Born 19 Mar 1877 in Gholson, McLennan County, TX. Died 13 Jul 1966 in Lubbock, Lubbock Co., TX. Buried 15 Jul 1966 in Resthaven Memorial Park, Lubbock, TX. They were divorced before 1930.

They had the following children:

31	i.	William Umberson McIlhaney
32	ii.	Johnye Mae McIlhaney
33	iii.	Joe Singleton McIlhaney Sr.
34	iv.	George Truett McIlhaney
35	v.	Jesse Roland McIlhaney Sr.
36	vi.	Jack McIlhaney
37	vii.	Ollie Louise McIlhaney
38	viii.	Samuel Frank McIlhaney Sr.

21. William Arthur McIlhaney. Son of William James Gibson McIlhaney & Mary Charlesana Elizabeth Carter. Born 5 Dec 1876 in Waldo, Coryell Co., TX. Died Mar 1963 in Temple, Bell Co., TX. Buried in Temple Masonic Cm, Cotton Co., OK.

He married **Addie May Davis**, 27 Jun 1897 in McLennon Co., TX. Born 1 Nov 1881 in Alabama. Died 16 Jun 1938. Buried in Temple Masonic Cm, Cotton Co., OK.

They had the following children:

	i.	Ruby L. McIlhaney; Born c. 1899 in Texas.
	ii.	Mollie M. McIlhaney (Chennault); Born c. 1901 in Texas. Died 4 Aug 1975 in Wilbarger Co., TX.
	iii.	Myrtle Lee McIlhaney; Born c. 1903 in Texas.

    iv.   Opal L. McIlhaney; Born c. 1907 in Texas.

    v.   Ethel McIlhaney; Born c. 1908 in Texas.

    vi.   William Arthur McIlhaney Jr.; Born c. 1916 in Texas.

    vii.   Joe King McIlhaney; Born 12 Jun 1920 in Texas. Died 30 Oct 1948.

22. Oliver Lee McIlhaney. Son of William James Gibson McIlhaney & Mary Charlesana Elizabeth Carter. Born 7 Nov 1878 in Coryell Co., TX. Died 24 Sep 1956 in Vernon, Wilbarger Co., TX. Buried in Eastview Memorial Park, Wilbarger Co., TX.

He married **Minnie Era Holcomb**, 24 Feb 1901 in Texas. Born 1 Feb 1881 in Georgia. Died 29 Jul 1963. Buried in Eastview Memorial Park, Wilbarger Co., TX.

They had the following children:

    i.   Eunice J. McIlhaney; Born c. 1902 in Texas.

    ii.   Leona L. McIlhaney; Born c. 1908 in Texas.

23. Frank B. McIlhaney. Son of William James Gibson McIlhaney & Mary Charlesana Elizabeth Carter. Born 20 Oct 1882 in Waldo, Coryell Co., TX. Died 14 Mar 1962 in McCamey, Upton Co., TX. Buried in Mertzon Cemetery, Irion Co., TX.

He married **Bertha Ellen Hancock**, 6 Oct 1918 in Texas. Born 4 Jul 1893 in Texas. Died 1969 in El Paso, El Paso Co., TX. Buried in Mertzon Cemetery, Irion Co., TX.

They had the following children:

    i.   Faye McIlhaney; Born c. 1914 in Texas.

    ii.   Frank B. McIlhaney Jr.; Born Nov 1919 in Texas. Died 7 Aug 1995 in Burnet, Burnet Co., TX.

    iii.   William McIlhaney; Born c. 1924 in Texas.

    iv.   Raymond Roy McIlhaney; Born 1925 in Dickens Co., TX. Died 1932 in Pecos Co., TX.

    v.   David Ray McIlhaney; Born 6 Apr 1926 in Dickens Co., TX. Died 29 Apr 1995 in Brown Co., TX.

    vi.   Jackie Gayle McIlhaney (twin); Born and died in 1933

    vii.   Glen Harrison McIlhaney (twin); Born and died in 1933

24. Ethel Elizabeth McIlhaney. Daughter of William James Gibson McIlhaney & Mary Charlesana Elizabeth Carter. Born 4 Dec 1887 in Waldo, Coryell Co., TX. Died 12 Nov 1960. Buried in Restland, Gatesville, Coryell Co., TX.

She married **Mack McGruder Davis**, c. 1902. Born 25 Dec 1878 in Alabama. Died 10 Oct 1948. Buried in Restland, Gatesville, Coryell Co., TX.

They had the following children:

    i.   Ruth Davis; Born c. 1904 in Texas.

    ii.   Joseph W. Davis; Born c. 1907 in Texas.

    iii.   Harman Davis; Born Oct 1909 in Texas.

    iv.   Cullen Davis; Born c. 1903 in Texas.

Fourth Generation

25. Vora Dell Gibson (McKinzie). Daughter of Randolph Hunter Gibson & Mary Lenora Cauthen. Born 28 Nov 1887 in Texas. Died 30 Jan 1973. Buried in Llano Cemetery, Amarillo, Potter Co., TX.

She married **Jackson Carleton McKenzie**, 25 Feb 1906 in Hamilton Co., TX. Born 1 Jan 1882. Died 20 Jan 1965. Buried in Llano Cemetery, Amarillo, Potter Co., TX.

They had the following children:

   i. James Randolph McKenzie

26. James Pilant Gibson Sr. Son of John Parmley Gibson & Louise Victoria Seals. Born 18 Feb 1898 in Hico, Hamilton Co., TX. Died 20 Mar 1953. Buried in Lamesa, Dawson Co., TX.

He married **Eva Josephine Dean**, daughter of Lemuel I. Dean & Ida Glazner, 6 Apr 1924 in Dawson Co., TX. Born 28 Aug 1902 in Anson, Jones Co., TX. Died 19 Feb 1995 in Lubbock Co.,TX.

They had the following children:

   i. James Pliant Gibson Jr.

27. Clarence Houston Gibson. Son of Ira Jackson Gibson & Jeanetta Elzora Graves. Born 11 Jan 1897 in Texas. Died 22 Jan 1984 in Stephensville, Erath Co., TX. Buried in West End Cemetery, Stephensville, Erath Co., TX.

He married **Poland E. Edwards**, 26 May 1923 in Hamilton Co., TX.

They had the following children:

   i. Willie Beatrice Gibson

   ii. Paul Franklin Gibson

   iii. Minnie Mabel Gibson

   iv. Wilma Elizabeth Gibson

   v. Mary Rebecca Gibson

28. William Edgar McIlhaney. Son of James M. McIlhaney & Bettie Hardin. Born Apr 1890 in Texas. Died 4 Mar 1981. Buried in Twin Oaks Memorial Park, Artesia, Eddy Co, NM.

He married **Mary Y.**, before 1920. Born 18 Oct 1926 in Texas. Died 24 Mar 1998 in Loco Hills, Eddy Co., NM. Buried in Twin Oaks Memorial Park, Artesia, Eddy Co, NM.

They had the following children:

   i. Fay McIlhaney

29. Ola McIlhaney. Daughter of James M. McIlhaney & Bettie Hardin. Born 11 Jun 1902 in Texas. Died 31 Jan 1989 in Mountain Home, Baxter Co., AR. Buried in West Plains City Cemetery, Howell Co., MO.

She married **Robert Wesley Floyd**, 11 Sep 1924. Born 5 Jan 1902 in San Angelo, Tom Green Co., TX. Died 1972 in West Plains, Howell Co., MO. Buried in West Plains City Cemetery, Howell Co., MO.

They had the following children:

   i. James Floyd (died at birth)

   ii. Robert William Floyd

iii. Kenneth Wesley Floyd

iv. Jefferson Hugh Floyd

30. Gladys Velma McIlhaney. Daughter of James M. McIlhaney & Bettie Hardin. Born 20 Aug 1904 in Waldo, Coryell Co., TX. Died 12 Sep 1990 in Webster, TX. Buried 15 Sep 1990 in Chapel Hill Memorial Park, Waco, McLennan Co., TX.

She married **Harley Abijah Warren**, son of James Garfield Warren & Mattie Marrs, 29 May 1920 in Texas. Born 24 May 1901. Died 1979 in Buchanan Dam, Llano Co., TX. Buried in Chapel Hill Meml Park, Waco, McLennan Co., TX.

They had the following children:

  39 i. Doris Warren (Corbett)

  ii. Helen Louise Warren, 1925-2002

  iii. Harley Eugene Warren, 1928-1997

31. William Umberson McIlhaney. Son of John Richardson McIlhaney & Ollie Delilah Umberson. Born 25 Jun 1898 in Oglesby, Coryell Co., TX. Died 20 Jan 1976 in Hico, Hamilton Co., TX. Buried in Hico Cemetery, Hamilton Co., TX.

He first married **Deema Boyd Bradley**, May 1923. Born c. 1908 in Missouri.

They had the following children:

  i. Billy Jean McIlhaney

  40 ii. Jo Katherine McIlhaney

He second married **Cladye Loraine Massengale**. Born 17 Sep 1908 in Bosque Co., TX. Died 11 Oct 1983 in Hico, Hamilton Co., TX. Buried in Hico Cemetery, Hamilton, Co., TX.

32. Johnye Mae McIlhaney. Daughter of John Richardson McIlhaney & Ollie Delilah Umberson. Born 26 Dec 1900 in Waldo, Coryell Co., TX. Died 3 Aug 1993 in Los Lunas, Valencis Co., NM. Buried 7 Aug 1993 in Sunset Memorial Park, Albuquerque, NM.

She first married **Rev. William Marion Green**, 8 May 1920 in Las Vegas, San Miguel Co., NM. Born c. 1880. Died 14 Jan 1938 in Albuquerque, NM.

They had the following children:

  41 i. Johnye Marion Green (Phillips), 1922-1911

She second married **Clarence T. Gholson**, 18 Nov 1938 in Albuquerque, Bernalillo Co., NM. Born c. 1886 in Illinois. Died 14 Apr 1959 in Albuquerque, NM. Buried in Sunset Memorial Park, Albuquerque, NM.

33. Joe Singleton McIlhaney Sr. Son of John Richardson McIlhaney & Ollie Delilah Umberson. Born 18 Oct 1902 in Gholson, McLennan Co, TX. Died 27 Nov 1999 in Lubbock, Lubbock Co., TX. Buried 30 Nov 1999 in Resthaven, Lubbock, Lubbock Co., TX.

He first married **Lillian Opal Goodrich**, daughter of Fulton Miller Goodrich & Callie Kuykendall, 17 Dec 1927 in Lubbock, Lubbock Co., TX. Born 11 Jan 1910 in Red Oak, Latimer Co., OK. Died Aug 1991. They were divorced 18 Sep 1932 in Lubbock, Lubbock Co., TX.

They had the following children:

  42 i. JoAnne McIlhaney (Conely), 1928-1992

43	ii.		Nancy Jane McIlhaney (Rainwater), 1930-2010

He second married **Io Halbert**, daughter of Levi Thompson Halbert Sr. & Mary Ann Armstrong, 1 Sep 1934 in Lubbock, Lubbock Co., TX. Born 23 Sep 1906 in Milam, Sabine Co.,TX. Died 3 May 2004 in Lubbock, Lubbock Co., TX. Buried 7 May 2004 in Memorial Park, Lubbock, Lubbock Co., TX. They were divorced 30 Mar 1979.

They had the following children:

44	i.	Joe Singleton McIlhaney Jr.
45	ii.	Richard Gale McIlhaney
46	iii.	David Lee McIlhaney

34. George Truett McIlhaney. Son of John Richardson McIlhaney & Ollie Delilah Umberson. Born 21 Sep 1904 in Waldo, Coryell Co., TX. Died 15 Nov 1972 in Albuquerque, Bernalillo Co., NM. Buried 18 Nov 1972 in Sandia Memorial Cemetery, Albuquerque, Bernalillo Co., NM.

He married **Mary Elizabeth Walker (Rich)**, 22 Jun 1928 in Farmington, San Juan Co., NM. Born 17 Feb 1910 in New Mexico. Died 2 Sep 1987 in Albuquerque, Bernalillo Co., NM. Buried in Sandia Memorial Cemetery, Albuquerque, Bernalillo Co., NM.

They had the following children:

47	i.	Barbara Juanice McIlhaney
48	ii.	William Edward McIlhaney
49	iii.	Sam Carl McIlhaney
50	iv.	Wanda Celene McIlhaney
	v.	Ethyl Elizabeth McIlhaney
	vi.	Bonny Kay McIlhaney

35. Jesse Roland McIlhaney Sr. Son of John Richardson McIlhaney & Ollie Delilah Umberson. Born 12 Apr 1907 in Tolbert, Wilbarger Co., TX. Died 4 Mar 1998 in University Medical Center, Lubbock, TX. Buried 7 Mar 1998 in Resthaven Memorial Park, Lubbock, TX.

He first married **Mildred Davis**, 14 Sep 1930. Born 8 Aug 1912. Died 1 May 1932. Buried in Lubbock City Cemetery, Lubbock Co., TX.

He second married **Grace Patterson**, 24 Jun 1936. Born 22 May 1912. Died Oct 1978. Buried in South Beard Street Cemetery, Shawnee, OK. They were divorced.

They had the following children:

51	i.	John Randall McIlhaney Sr.
52	ii.	Jesse Roland McIlhaney Jr.
53	iii.	George Robert McIlhaney M.D.
54	iv.	Patty Jeanne McIlhaney

36. Jack McIlhaney. Son of John Richardson McIlhaney & Ollie Delilah Umberson. Born 6 May 1910 in San Angelo, Tom Green Co., TX. Died 19 Sep 1984 in Alamogordo, Otero Co., NM. Buried 21 Sep 1984 in Monte Vista Cemetery, Alamogordo, Otero Co., NM.

He married **Lucille Chamness**, 29 Dec 1940. Born 12 Oct 1914. Died 5 Jul 2000 in Kalispell, Flathead Co., MT.

They had the following children:

    55   i.   Jack Wesley McIlhaney

    56   ii.   Sharon Neal McIlhaney

37. Ollie Louise McIlhaney. Daughter of John Richardson McIlhaney & Ollie Delilah Umberson. Born 26 Jun 1913 in Lubbock, Lubbock Co., TX. Died 20 Jan 2009 in San Antonio, Bexar Co., TX. Buried 24 Jan 2009 in Resthaven Memorial Park, Lubbock, Lubbock Co., TX.

She married **Gordon Morris Deering Sr.**, 30 Jun 1935 in Lubbock, Lubbock Co., TX. Born 1 Nov 1911 in Winchester, Fayette Co., TX. Died 8 Feb 1992 in Lubbock, Lubbock Co., TX. Buried in Resthaven Memorial Park, Lubbock, TX.

They had the following children:

    57   i.   Gordon Morris Deering Jr.

    58   ii.   Beverly Gayle Deering

           iii.   Gary Kirk Deering

38. Samuel Frank McIlhaney Sr. Son of John Richardson McIlhaney & Ollie Delilah Umberson. Born 13 Jul 1916 in Lubbock, Lubbock Co., TX. Died 27 Sep 1998 in Georgia. Buried 29 Sep 1998 in Crown Hill Cemetery, Albany, Albany Co., GA.

He first married **Marian Grady**, Nov 1940. Born 12 Apr 1919. Died 9 Jan 2002 in Loveland, Larimer Co., CO. They were divorced before 1961.

They had the following children:

    59   i.   Janice Marian McIlhaney

           ii.   Sam Frank McIlhaney Jr.

    60   iii.   Patricia Annette McIlhaney

He second married **Flora Stickland**, 16 May 1961. Born 1 Jan 1924. Died 4 May 2000 in Gulf Shores, Baldwin Co., AL.

About the Authors

Robert Steven Rainwater
Son of Clois Miles Rainwater and Nancy Jane McIlhaney
Born 1962, Tyler, Smith Co., Texas
Married: 11 May 1991, Northwest Bible Church, Dallas, Dallas Co., Texas

Susan Chance
Daughter of T. Elbert Chance and Janet Ellen Bardo
Born 1956, Wilmington, New Castle Co., Delaware

R. Steven Rainwater

Steve Rainwater was born in Tyler, Texas. He attended elementary schools in Irving, Texas, before enrolling in First Baptist Academy in downtown Dallas for his middle and high school years. He attended the University of Texas Arlington as a computer science major.

Steve's early career was as a programmer for the Professional Information Library and Kimball Audio/Video. Having experienced both businesses going bankrupt, he decided he would be better running his own business. In 1992, Steve launched Network Cybernetics Corporation. Initially the company focused on selling an annual CD-ROM containing a curated collection of Artificial Intelligence and robotics software and documentation. As the CD-ROM business model became obsolete, and NCC shifted to contract software development and, experimentally to website hosting. Over time, website hosting and development became the primary focus of the business, and the company changed its name to NCC Internet Services.

Steve has been a member of the Dallas Personal Robotics Group since 1993. In 2010, he helped found Dallas Makerspace, the first hackerspace in Dallas. He was invited to speak at the 2010 Dallas Petcha Kutcha about the Makerspace project.

Steve writes monthly columns for SERVO Magazine. He writes occasional feature stories for SERVO and Robot Magazine, as well as providing photography of robot events. In 2000, with friends Roger Arrick and Jim Brown, Steve founded the well-known robot news website, Robots.net, and acted as senior editor for more than a decade. Since 2010, he has participated in Art Conspiracy, a local non-profit organization that raises money for arts-related charities in Dallas. His ArtCon participation includes creating a variety of artwork for the group's charity auctions and volunteering at the events. In 2013 Steve was appointed to the City of Irving Green Advisory Board.

Susan Rainwater

Susan Chance Rainwater was born in Wilmington, Delaware, and moved with her family to Newark, Delaware, at the age of seven. She attended Newark High School, where she became active in the school's cable television channel. Determined to pursue a career in television, she attended Ohio University in Athens, Ohio, where she earned a BSC in Radio-Television/Advertising. She worked for three years at WOUB-TV as a duty director, one of the station's rare paid positions.

After college, Susan worked short term jobs at WTAP-TV, Parkersburg, West Virginia, and at the Maryland Center for Public Broadcasting. College friends encouraged her to apply to WTCG-TV, and she was hired over the phone, on their recommendation. Abandoning everything that would not fit in her car, Susan drove ahead of a blinding snowstorm to reach Atlanta overnight.

WTCG soon became WTBS, the flagship of Turner Broadcasting. Susan worked in the production department for 5½ years in a variety of positions. She was the first female videotape editor ever employed by the WTBS production department, and remained so for the duration of her employment. She also freelanced for the major networks and ESPN, working sports remotes as a graphics and slo-mo operator. Offered a job in Dallas, she moved again, this time with a moving van. In Dallas, she worked as an editor for two commercial post-production facilities, before being named Senior Editor of Showcase Productions. In 1999, Susan left the video world to join Steve working in the emerging field of the Internet. She is both office manager and website technical specialist for NCC Internet Services.

Susan and Steve met through one of her video clients. They dated for three years, marrying in 1991, over the objections of his family.

Susan is politically independent, is an avid reader, listens to classical music and jazz, enjoys travel, day hiking, and cooking, is a fanatic genealogist, loves a good tramp through a graveyard, and adores her three cats. She is an active contributor to Findagrave, Yelp, Wikipedia, USGenWeb, Ancestry.com, Upper Shore Genealogical Society of Maryland, and the Dallas Genealogical Society. She maintains the genealogical website, *The Rainwater Collection* (therainwatercollection.com) as an archive of raw data for serious Rainwater researchers.

Susan credits the work of historians George Holbert Tucker and Alison Weir as influences upon her genealogical research.

Colophon

Our original research was collected and organized in Reunion for Windows v4.06, a now extinct genealogical program. We used Ancestry.com's family tree builder to timeline the data for each individual as part of our analysis process. These family trees still exist and can be viewed if you are an Ancestry.com subscriber.

- Nancy J. McIlhaney family tree:
  http://trees.ancestry.com/tree/42453847/family
- Clois Miles Rainwater family tree:
  http://trees.ancestry.com/tree/42448685/family

Software used to generate this book includes LibreOffice Writer v4, GIMP v2.8, Adobe Photoshop CS6, Adobe Illustrator CS3, Adobe Acrobat v9 Standard, and Superchart Family Tree. The final manuscript was printed by Lulu.com.

The typefaces used are Adobe Caslon Pro for body copy and footnotes, Trajan Pro Open Type for headlines, and Times New Roman for register reports.

Acknowledgments

The number of individuals who have contributed to this work over the last twenty years is probably in the hundreds.

We could not have undertaken this project without the spectacular resources of the Dallas Public Library Genealogy and Texas History Sections. We are also indebted to the Lubbock Public Library, at whose microfilm readers we discovered Dr. DeZita, and the Taylor Public Library, whose file of genealogical newspaper clippings added richness to our Williamson County work.

The Pulaski County Historical Society's many printed books of marriage, census, will and cemetery records formed the basis of our Kentucky work, allowing me to chart not just Steve's family, but the entire region of the county in which the Rainwaters and their kin lived for nearly a century.

The genealogical research of Roscoe Rainwater and the biographical writings of Annie Presnall Wood and C. V. Compton were invaluable. Likewise the memoir of Minnie Humberson Guyton, WPA interview of John Logan Tarter, and research of A. E. and Marion Phillips and T. Hugh McIlhaney. We also greatly appreciate the contributions made by two genealogical newsletters, now out of print, *The Rainwater Researcher*, edited by Robert O. Albert, Jr., and *Country Ties*, edited by Carol Ellis.

And then there are the individuals whom we met or corresponded with, who went above and beyond in assisting our research. Glidie Rainwater Mobley, the Rainwater family's extraordinary expert, never failed to answer my questions or provide insight with a healthy dose of wit. James D. Garner corresponded with me regularly for over five years on the subject of everything Weddle and Tarter, and took time out from his own research to get copies for me of two critical Rainwater marriage records in Adair County. His work on Jacob Tarter's divorce papers saved me months of transcription work. The late Betty Rainwater Floyd opened her home to us, fed us lunch, and told us everything she remembered about Josiah and Elizabeth Rainwater. The portrait of Josiah and Elizabeth Jane that now freely circulates on the Internet came from a photo that hung on Betty's family room wall. Don Raney, working on a Caughron project, traded for my Rainwater information, providing me with C. V. Compton's autobiography and several sets of pension papers. Historian Brandon Slone took an hour out of his day to enlighten me on the subject of the Kentucky post-Civil War militia and the Grand Army of the Republic. Joyce Beardon shared with me her many years of Humberson/Umberson research, and Virginia Humberson Owen, researching the same family, sent me the newspaper articles detailing the strange fate of Caleb W. Presnall. My mother-in-law, Nancy Rainwater, and her aunt, Louise McIlhaney Deering, provided detailed information on the McIlhaney side of the family. Linda Rainwater Davis undertook the thankless job of proofing the final manuscript before it was committed to print.

And there are so many others with whom I corresponded and exchanged information over the years:

Aderholt family: Frances Aderholt Smith, Polly Thorne Flory. **Atichison-Goodrich family:** Kay Atchison. **Fussell family:** Lynn E. Fussell. **Caughron family:** Betty Basket. **Carter family:** Sharon Hitt. **Compton family:** Zelva Compton Laird (dec.), Beth Walker. **Duck family:** Terri and Pat Chesney, Peter Morris. **Gibson family:** Michael Mason, Elreeta Weathers, Ruth Ann Godwin. **Gossett family:** Frank Gossett. **Halbert family:** Mary Sims. **Hodges family:** Diana Flynn. **Humberson/Umberson family:** Brian Humberson, Bill Umberson, Patricia Morrow, Ernest Humberson. **Kellum family:** Kay Tucker, Cynthia Simms Kirkland, Joe Neal Garrett, Gerald Irion. **McIlhaney family:** John R. McIlhaney, Jr., Joe Singleton McIlhaney, Jr., John Riley Conely (dec.). **Rainwater family:** Betty Rainwater Craig, Hal Irving, J. C. Halbrooks, Joanna Eads, Ross Cameron, Marjorie Thomas, Mark Sanborn, Darren Waters and Scott Burton, Terry E. Davis, John D. Roberts, Betty Light Eastham, Lisa Alexander, Helen Edlin, Joice Buis, Georgia and Gene Rainwater, Ray Rainwater (dec.), Lucky and Mike Baker. **Rexroat family:** Kim Knapp. **Singleton family:** Jim Hahn, John Ellis, Frances Gomillion Phillips. **Tarter family:** Carole Frederick Marcum. **Weddle family:** Thomas Kintigh, Christy Campell, Francis Corbett Weddle, Victoria Day-Cook, Jack Weddle.

Creative Commons License

This work is licensed under a Creative Commons Attribution-NonCommercial-ShareAlike 3.0 Unported License (http://creativecommons.org/licenses/by-nc-sa/3.0/) that says:

You are free:
- to Share – to copy, distribute and transmit the work
- to Remix – to adapt the work

Under the following conditions:
- Attribution – You must attribute the work in the manner specified by the author or licensor (but not in any way that suggests that they endorse you or your use of the work), as follows:

  Susan and R. Steven Rainwater, "The Family Tree of Clois Miles Rainwater & Nancy Jane McIlhaney: One Texas Family's Origins, 1706-2012," published 2013, Irving, Texas

- Noncommercial — You may not use this work for commercial purposes.
- Share Alike – If you alter, transform, or build upon this work, you may distribute the resulting work only under the same or similar license to this one.

With the understanding that:
- Waiver – Any of the above conditions can be waived if you get permission from the copyright holder.
- Public Domain – Where the work or any of its elements is in the public domain under applicable law, that status is in no way affected by the license.
- Other Rights – In no way are any of the following rights affected by the license:
    - Your fair dealing or fair use rights, or other applicable copyright exceptions and limitations;
    - The author's moral rights;
    - Rights other persons may have either in the work itself or in how the work is used, such as publicity or privacy rights.
- Notice – For any reuse or distribution, you must make clear to others the license terms of this work.